DATA COMMUNICATIONS

DATA COMMUNICATIONS

FACILITIES, NETWORKS, AND SYSTEMS DESIGN

Dixon R. Doll

President
DMW Telecommunications Corporation
Ann Arbor, Michigan
and
Adjunct Faculty Member
IBM Systems Research Institute
New York, New York

A Wiley-Interscience Publication
JOHN WILEY & SONS
New York . Chichester . Brisbane . Toronto

Library of Congress Cataloging in Publication Data:

Doll, Dixon R.
    Data communications.

    "A Wiley-Interscience publication."
    Includes bibliographical references and index.
    1. Data transmission systems.   2.   Computer networks.
I.   Title.

TK5105.D64   384   77-12508
ISBN 0-471-21768-9

Printed in the United States of America

10 9 8 7 6 5 4 3 2 1

PREFACE

Many people have directly and indirectly contributed to making this book possible. Technical suggestions from the dedicated employees and clients of DMW Telecommunications Corporation have materially influenced the book's organization and content. So have critical evaluations and review of the various manuscript stages by the long-suffering students of the IBM Systems Research Institute in New York and countless public seminar attendees.

The idea first originated more than five years ago when Dr. E. S. Kopley gave me the opportunity to join the small group of regular outsiders on the adjunct faculty at the IBM Systems Research Institute (SRI) in New York. Since Dr. Kopley's death, the present SRI director, Bob DeSio, has continued to foster a challenging and stimulating environment, which contributed greatly to my finishing the work. My friend and SRI colleague Jim Martin has been a vast source of motivation through his constant personal encouragement and the direct example set by his own prolific authorship. Executives at the International Communications Corporation in Miami also helped by originally agreeing to fund a nonprofit entity, the ICC Institute, which was dedicated to providing professional education in the public marketplace.

Over the years the topical outline has crystallized to closely follow a course entitled "Basics of Data Communications" which is taught each term at SRI. As a result, there have been numerous revisions, enhancements, and alterations to the original manuscript drafts. The book is written at a level enabling it to be used as a college text for basic or intermediate level courses as well as a valuable professional reference book for information systems and telecommunications personnel with widely varying professional training, experience, and responsibilities. To facilitate its use as a course textbook, questions and problems for each major topical area are collected at the rear of the book.

The book's primary objective is to provide a comprehensive, pragmatic source of knowledge about one of the information industry's most vital, yet least-well-understood areas—data communications. It commences with two introductory chapters presenting basic terminology, network structures, design tradeoffs, and the functions of typically used network building blocks.

Next, Chapters 3 and 4 involve a detailed consideration of important telecommunication services and facilities, from both economic and technical perspectives. Signal conversion devices for analog and digital network applications are also discussed.

Moving systematically out to the ends of data communication lines, Chapter 5 examines the different present and future teleprocessing terminals, including their physical interfaces to signal converters. This chapter also contains considerable discussion of distributed intelligence and distributed processing and how these important concepts will be reshaping the entire teleprocessing approaches of countless organizations around the world.

Chapter 6 presents the available error control strategies for data communication links and develops the formal definitions of transfer rate of information bits using example calculations. Methodologies for comparing and contrasting half and full duplex data link control are introduced, along with the historical rationale for the various error control approaches.

In Chapter 7, the important methods of sharing communications lines—multiplexing and concentration—are presented. The chapter also contains numerous examples of how these sharing strategies and devices are used to develop cost-effective and reliable networks for a broad spectrum of different application requirements.

Then in Chapter 8 the previous material is drawn together by a discussion of the network neural centers, which implement protocols and overall network control strategies. Both *data link* and *higher level protocols* are examined, as well as the significance of the public vs. private data network architecture controversy. Major data networking philosophies of the public carriers, computer vendors, and independent suppliers are contrasted in order to give an objective portrayal of their relative advantages and disadvantages.

The final chapter introduces a design methodology that systematically enables various centralized and distributed network architectures to be quantitatively evaluated, leading to the preferred overall network approach for collectively accommodating response time and throughput requirements at the lowest cost. Readers concerned with detailed network design calculations and overall network design and analysis should find the final chapter especially meaningful, although it can be omitted by those who need not become familiar with the specific *details* of teleprocessing network design and analysis.

In conclusion, I must express special appreciation for the unwavering motivation provided by my mother and father, Dr. and Mrs. Raymond J. Doll, and by my wife Carol's parents, Dr. and Mrs. Dominic L. Pucci. A major setback in my personal life and in the manuscript preparation occurred with Dr. Pucci's untimely death in April 1977. His perfectionist attitude and unusual perception of truly significant values were instrumental in my completing the final stages of the book.

The direct personal sacrifices and continuing encouragement of my wife, Carol, and sons, D. R., Alexander, and Andrew are, however, in the final analysis, the main reasons this book became reality.

DIXON R. DOLL

Ann Arbor, Michigan
August 1977

CONTENTS

CONTENTS

DATA COMMUNICATIONS

ONE

INTRODUCTION TO DESIGN ISSUES, TERMINOLOGY, AND METHODOLOGY

In the last decade, a voluminous amount of paper has been generated by various people and organizations involved in myriad aspects of designing, using, operating, and managing data communications-based computer systems. Much of the practically oriented material has necessarily been tutorial and qualitatively oriented, whereas the good quantitatively oriented work has often been so theoretical as to be of limited practical consequence for those involved in planning and configuring the operational networks of the mid-1970s and beyond. This book intentionally deemphasizes qualitative aspects of the various sytems design tradeoffs that have been considered at length in numerous other books, papers, and journal articles, many of which are cited as references throughout this book. Instead, its primary thrust is the formulation of a quasi-formal methodology that will provide a quantitative, yet practical, basis for the systematic resolution of the numerous design and analysis problems that must be considered by planners and systems designers.

1.1. A PERSPECTIVE OF CHANGING ALTERNATIVES

It is difficult to find anyone today who disputes the significant impact of data communications on business, government, and the educational profession over the last decade. It is also agreed that data (as contrasted with voice) communications continues to be the most rapidly growing segment of the common carrier business, in spite of a typical corporate voice communications budget nearly 10 times that for data. As evidence, some recent projections of the American Telephone and Telegraph Company (AT&T) indicated that it expects annual data-related revenues to increase from \$500–600 million in 1971 to \$5 or 6 billion by 1980. Total annual AT&T revenues, on the other hand, are expected to rise from approximately \$18 billion back in 1971 to more than \$40 billion by 1980. This abnormal data growth is being fueled by the burgeoning communications demands of the data processing departments within business, educational, and governmental organizations of all types. In many of these so-called teleprocessing systems, the hardware devices, software procedures, and communication lines used to interconnect the various terminals, computers, and data bases frequently accounts for more than half the total monthly operational costs of the entire computer–communications complex.[1] Unfortunately for many organizations, the problems associated with configuring and maintaining a cost-effective network are complicated by rapidly changing hardware and software technologies, difficult-to-anticipate traffic growth patterns, and an increasingly permissive regulatory climate. Equally significant to users are the myriad new service alternatives to conventional voice-grade telephone lines, including all-digital networks, packet switching systems, satellite services, and the initial domestic offerings of the specialized common carriers.

Before discussing any specific design or analysis techniques, it is important to establish that the operational objectives of a particular teleprocessing system depend strongly on the application environment and one's point of view. For example, in many situations the user of a system and the system designer will have conflicting objectives. The individual user may be concerned only about his individual terminal's 90th percentile response time level and availability levels. The system designer who has responsibility for allocating the entire system's hardware and software resources can ill afford not to use statistics and averages to his benefit. Often this implies that terminals sharing more heavily loaded lines may experience poorer response times than those that coincidentally happen to share more lightly loaded links. Whether the user and the designer of a system receive their paychecks from the same organization or whether they bear a client–vendor type of relationship also has a significant impact

---

[1] A concise definition of the term *teleprocessing* is found in Section 1.3. Both the original and current interpretations are cited and contrasted.

on the design objectives of a network. The objective of most communications-based computer systems is to enable terminals and processors in different physical locations to exchange programs, business data, messages, and so on in the least costly fashion that satisfies certain performance or throughput, reliability, availability, and expandability requirements. As will be seen throughout the book, there can be no universally applicable quantitative definitions for the constrained measures of interest. Specific examples will be cited in subsequent chapters, to illustrate, for example, frequently used response time and throughput interpretations for leased line and switched networks.

The search for the "best" overall configuration in any application situation can begin only after quantitative formulation of user requirements and system objectives has taken place. Then and only then should the numerous interacting decisions about terminals, modems, multiplexers and concentrators, network control, software, communication links, front-end processors, error control procedures, and the basic organization of the network begin to be evaluated.

1.2. PRELIMINARY DATA NEEDED—THE DESIGN CONSTANTS

Before any of the numerous possible network arrangements are considered, the constants of the application(s) must be properly gauged.[2] This initial step requires obtaining estimates of the following business application parameters:

- Number and locations of the processing sites.[3]
- Number and locations of the remote terminals.
- Information flow patterns between the terminals and the processing sites.
- Types of transactions to be processed.
- Traffic volumes for the transaction types, which may depend on the type of network configuration employed.
- Urgency of the information to be transmitted (when must a response be supplied to the remote station, or how soon is the data file required at the destination?).
- Capacity reserved for traffic growth.

[2]See References [1] through [5].
[3]In some situations the locations of the processing sites may actually be a variable, but these contingencies can be met by performing a design for each different set of possible locations under consideration.

- Acceptable undetected information error rates (bit or block).
- Reliability and availability requirements.
- Available financial resources.

These factors define the geography and performance requirements of the network. They must be thoroughly assessed before any major equipment decisions are made. There will inevitably be some interplay between the above parameters and the equipment choices in a network, but most factors should be treated as implementation independent in the first phase of design. Note that geographic separation of *sources* and *sinks* and urgency requirements of the messages are the primary justification for using a data communication network.[4] For example, nonurgent business data can always be transmitted for a few pennies using the U.S. mails, regardless of the geography involved. Several typical applications serve to illustrate the importance of having the parameters listed above fairly well defined before any equipment decisions are made.

In a typical automated brokerage environment, the network connects remote offices to a central computer; it processes customer orders, quotations, and administrative messages for intracompany correspondence. Typical performance requirements could involve the stipulation that low priority administrative messages be replied to within 2 hours, whereas customer orders must be processed and confirmed within 2 minutes. In an airline reservation system, requests from an agent stationed at a console ordinarily require some type of response within seconds. Conversational users of commercial time sharing systems will not usually tolerate any significant communication-network-induced delays in their dialog with the CPU. In general, when a company's network is being used by customers anxiously awaiting a response, the preferred communications layout will usually be significantly different and probably more costly than when data are being gathered or distributed on a low priority basis.

Until recently, most organizations justified each new network application (data collection, sales order processing, inventory control, remote batch, etc.) individually, leading to the use of separate computer facilities and data communication networks for each application. In many such instances, subsequent investigation of network traffic levels revealed *gross underutilization* of these expensive facilities. This motivated cost-conscious managements to seek improvements to these situations by evaluating the consolidation of multiple applications into a single mul-

---

[4]We use the terms *source* and *sink* to describe generalized terminal devices, programs, or data files that serve as the ultimate points of message *origination* and *destination*, respectively, for particular types.

tipurpose corporate data network. Whatever the choice of network organization, the planning efforts of the next few years are reflecting this trend toward increasing integration of broadly varying traffic types. The complexity of the planning process is thereby increased, but the potential payoffs are significant. Contemporary architectures for fully shared network facilities are discussed at length in Chapter 8.

1.3. TYPES OF COMMUNICATIONS-BASED COMPUTER SYSTEMS, CONTRASTS WITH GENERAL PURPOSE COMMUNICATION NETWORKS

Communication networks of all sizes, shapes, and types are commonly used to connect remote data terminals and computers to other terminals and processing complexes.[5] Regardless of the specific application, these communication networks have the primary objective of providing timely access to important business data, remote computing power (including special software and applications packages), and the contents of information files in various data bases. The diversity of possible applications for communications-based computer systems has spawned several rather well-defined types or categories of networks, each having its own unique functional objectives. For explanatory purposes, consider the following three categories of communications-based computer systems:

1. The special purpose (single-application) network interconnecting processing complexes operated and used by a single organizational entity.
2. The general purpose (multiapplication) network interconnecting processing complexes operated by a single organization, but possibly used by several organizational entities.
3. The resource sharing networks interconnecting processing complexes operated and used by numerous organizational entities.

The special purpose networks were historically the first to appear, examples being the early airline reservations systems such as the American Airlines SABRE system (see Reference [6]), the early defense networks such as the SAGE and BMEWS systems [7], and the prototype in-house time sharing nets such as MIT's well-known Project MAC system [8]. More general purpose systems such as the first commercial time

---

[5]The term *processing complex* is used to collectively describe all computational hardware, storage, software and applications programs, and data base resources available at a particular physical computer center.

sharing networks of the mid-1960s then followed [9, 10]. These systems represented virtually the first instances of using telecommunications to interconnect suppliers of computer services (processing power, software and applications packages, and data base storage) with their customers at remote locations. Then, with the pioneering Advanced Research Projects Agency (ARPA) network developed by the U.S. Department of Defense, the notion of interconnecting highly complex, often incompatible processing complexes became a reality in the late 1960s [11, 12]. A resource sharing network provides an enhanced computational and communication capability to the users within an individual organizational entity. The concept is that of a supernetwork in which any individual user or autonomous organizational entity is permitted to share part or all of the computational resources at any of the interconnected processing complexes. Individual processing complexes are economically justified on their own merits, with the communications network providing a value-added capability by enabling an individual to access a more diverse spectrum of computational and information resources than could ever be economically justified at the level of the individual processing complexes of a single organization.

The term *teleprocessing system* originally referred to "a digital computer with unscheduled inputs from a number of remote points connected over telecommunication lines of various types."[6] In this context, teleprocessing does not include the use of data communications to merely move information in a scheduled manner, as is common in data collection applications. In fact, by far the most popular usage of data communications in the last 10 years has been in applications where the workload submitted to the CPU is still at least partially scheduled or controlled, even though the information is moved into position by data communications.

Over the years, the term *teleprocessing* has come to be used in an all-encompassing context to include computer–communications applications such as remote job entry and data collection, where transactions arrive in a scheduled or unscheduled manner (including those where little or no actual processing is performed). This book makes no attempt to alter the current broad context of the term *teleprocessing system*. The only distinction to be made here is to cite the fundamental differences between teleprocessing systems and general purpose communication networks such as the public switched telephone networks operated by the world's telephone companies or the switched record (data message)

[6]W. P. Margopoulos and R. J. Williams, "On Teleprocessing System Design—Part I. Characteristic Problems," *IBM Systems Journal,* Vol. 5, No. 3, 1966.

transmission networks like Telex and the U.S.-based TWX service operated by the Western Union Telegraph Company.[7,8]

The primary objective of a general purpose communication network is to enable terminals or subscribers connected to the network to communicate with each other. In general communication nets such as the previously mentioned telephone and telegraph networks of the common carriers, a pronounced degree of homogeneity exists in the properties that characterize both source and sink terminals, for example, reaction time and total assimilation capacity. Furthermore, subscribers seek to access the terminals of any other subscribers for the purpose of transmitting and/or receiving information.

By contrast, the objective of teleprocessing networks is to provide geographically dispersed terminal users with connections to remotely located data bases and/or computing power. As a consequence, there exist two clearly different types of nodes in the network, those that represent entry/exit points to the system and those that denote processing and data base sites. In traditional systems, a relatively small fraction of the user terminals that originate and receive message traffic are equipped with processing facilities, because the cost advantages of teleprocessing begin to disappear as the processing and/or data base functions become duplicated at too many remote locations. In addition, a significant speed differential usually exists between the rates at which remote input/output stations and equipment at the processing sites are designed to operate. Thus there exists a definite case for the use of concentration and distributed communications control schemes in these specialized types of networks.

Recently, there has been a substantial trend toward increasing decentralization of many traditionally centralized functions in teleprocessing systems. For example, CRT screen formatting, transaction editing, verification, and the maintenance of smaller local data bases are usually possible directly at the user location in teleprocessing systems employing contemporary intelligent terminals.

These distributed intelligence attributes of teleprocessing systems are in marked contrast with traditional voice communications networks.

---

[7]The Telex network provides international message transfer service between its teletypewritter subscribers by using the circuits of the public telegraph networks. Telex transmits digital information in a five-bit code known as the Baudot code and at the single speed of 50 bits/sec between compatible teletypewriter terminals.

[8]The TWX (Teletypewriter Exchange) service was originally developed by AT&T but was sold to Western Union in 1971. The TWX network provides dial-up service between compatible teletypewriters but uses analog transmission over circuits of the public telephone network. It generally enables arbitrary codes or transmission rates under 150 bits/sec to be employed in the teletypewriters.

Even though computers are used extensively in such nets, they serve mainly for network control (to assign customer talking paths dynamically, perform billing, report failures, etc.). At this point in time, very few general purpose voice communications networks pass transmitted information directly through processing routines in the mainline flow between sender and receiver.

The efficient management of generalized communication nets also often requires the use of traffic concentration procedures. In traditional voice networks this is accomplished by using computer-driven or mechanically switchable trunk lines between telephone exchanges which are directly connected to the network's subscribers. With such concentration procedures, the statistically fluctuating needs of the subscribers may be exploited to provide a relatively economical approach to this *many-points-to-many-points* communication problem. By contrast, the typical teleprocessing system tends most frequently to provide a solution for a *many-points-to-few-points* communication problem.

Another important distinction involves tariffs and regulatory differences, which must be considered in designing these two types of networks. The user costs of communication lines, restrictions governing sharing, and limitations on interconnecting to the common carrier network facilities are stipulated by the carriers, subject to approval by the appropriate telecommunication regulatory agencies whenever the carriers are not directly controlled by governmental agencies. For example, the traditionally sacrosanct concept of a single nationwide average rate for telephone service means that costs to an individual voice telephone user may often bear little if any direct relationship to the carrier's cost of providing this particular service. Although some users are much more costly for the carrier to serve, its tariffs must be nondiscriminatory. This is the basis for the idea that prices for services can hardly ever be directly indicative of the carrier's costs across a diverse spectrum of users.

Because of the regulated nature of the entire communications common carrier industry throughout the world, the carriers tend to be the primary parties or organizations involved in designing generalized communication networks.[9] But in carrier–operated nets the cost functions and configuration options are completely different. Consequently, it is not too surprising that little of the systems design theory developed over the years by the carriers has been of direct practical significance to teleprocessing systems designers and end users. The carriers also have obvious incentives for wanting their teleprocessing customers to spend ever-increasing amounts on communications facilities. Hence it would be somewhat naive and

---

[9]See Reference [13], entitled *The Communications Act of 1934, as Amended.*

unrealistic to expect the carriers to be leading innovators in the development of techniques that reduce end-user communications costs. Fortunately for U.S. users, however, the landmark 1971 decision by the Federal Communications Commission creating the possibility of alternative suppliers for various types of communications facilities may ultimately lead to a healthier situation for all communications users [14]. Evidence of this prospect is the flourishing Canadian communications industry, which has, in many ways, led its U.S. counterparts. Canada has historically fostered competitive regulatory policies of alternative suppliers for virtually all offerings other than local telephone service.

Thus there are substantial differences between the design problems associated with configuring general purpose common carrier communication networks for voice telephone conversations and those confronting the teleprocessing system designer. The unique requirements of contemporary data networks have spawned the need for a completely new design methodology. It must comprise techniques for configuring cost-effective, reliable user systems that frequently employ existing common carrier facilities widely held to be inefficient for computer systems applications [15,16].

1.4. TYPICAL APPLICATIONS AND USES OF TELEPROCESSING NETWORKS

Data communications techniques are used in a multitude of different applications throughout education, government, and industry. As noted previously, the specific application of a network has a major effect on the performance goals, allowable configuration options, and ultimate cost of the network. Examination of the most popular current applications reveals the contrasting performance requirements, transaction frequencies, and traffic volumes in such systems. It must be emphasized, however, that the price/performance characteristics of existing communications facilities have exerted a pronounced influence on the evolution of contemporary teleprocessing applications. The relative popularity of these various usage modes may (and probably will) be dramatically different in 10 years as new services, facilities, and related price structures evolve. Many new usage modes will also appear as the availability of these new communications offerings makes new teleprocessing applications cost competitive with present-day manual methods of performing the same function.

Table 1.1 illustrates the most frequently used modes for teleprocessing systems, along with specific application examples and a discussion of the

Table 1.1 Typical Uses of Data Communications

Common Teleprocessing Usage Modes	Specific Application Examples	Distinguishing Characteristics of Typical Transactions
Source data entry data collection	Sales-status data; inventory control; payroll data gathering	Transactions collected several times per day or week, direct response message not issued for every transaction
	Point-of-sale system; airline reservations	Transactions arrive frequently (every few seconds) and demand response within a few seconds
Remote batch processing remote job entry	remote-city high speed card reading and printing; inexpensive local access to expensive distant computer power	Transactions usually are bunched and require processing times ranging from minutes to hours; input and output for each transaction individually may take seconds or minutes
Information-retrieval	Credit checking; bank account status; insurance policy status; law enforcement; state government social services; hospital information systems	Relatively low character volume per input transaction, response required within seconds; output message lengths usually very short for status inquiries, vary widely for other types of applications
Conversational time sharing	General problem solving; engineering design calculations; text editing	Conversational response required, usually within a few seconds
Message switching	Intracompany electronic mail; delivery and memo distribution	Delivery time requirements range from minutes to hours
Real-time data acquisition and process control	Numerical control of machine tools; remote meter and gauge reading	Remote sensors are continuously sampled and monitored at widely varying time intervals
Interprocessor data exchange	Processor, program, and file sharing applications of all types involving communications between computers; interorganizational networks	Infrequent, bursty arrivals consisting of large data blocks requiring transmission to another CPU, usually within milliseconds

characteristics of typical transactions; these usage modes have been listed in order of generally decreasing current popularity. It can be seen that the more popular modes generally involve less urgent transactions or ones less expensive to process than do the less popular modes of usage. This simply emphasizes the fact that user organizations can configure less costly systems when transaction urgencies and unit processing costs are lower, enabling more organizations to afford networks for these types of applications. Interprocessor data exchange has been slow to grow for several reasons, including the lack of a national or international broadband switched data network, the high cost of private broadband lines, software and operating system complexities, and several other factors that are discussed in subsequent sections.

1.5. TYPES OF NETWORK ORGANIZATION

The geographic separation of remote terminals and their communications partners (other remote terminals or CPUs) is the very essence of the network design problem. When all terminals are clustered within a few miles of a CPU, the economic justification for remote concentration and related money saving techniques often vanishes.

In these cases, elaborate efforts to minimize line mileage are usually not justified since line costs represent only a small fraction of total system expenditures. It still may be possible to optimize the network design using various distributed-intelligence schemes and/or line sharing techniques, such as multipoint lines that reduce the total complexity and cost of the central processor and/or communications controller. Other options such as the possible use of stand-alone communications processors to further reduce the required power of a central processor remain as important considerations.

Two basic network organizations are possible, a distributed network and a centralized network. In the distributed type of implementation shown in Figure 1.1, there are multiple processing centers which are usually controlled by different operating systems. The centers may be similar or differ widely in functional capability. In such nets, two basic types of traffic exist, terminal-to-computer and computer-to-computer. The statistical properties of these two types of traffic differ substantially. The purely centralized type of network shown in Figure 1.2 has only a single processing complex, and essentially all network traffic is between remote terminals and the central computer. Of course, there can be intermediate nodes such as concentrators, but these devices still process terminal–CPU traffic.

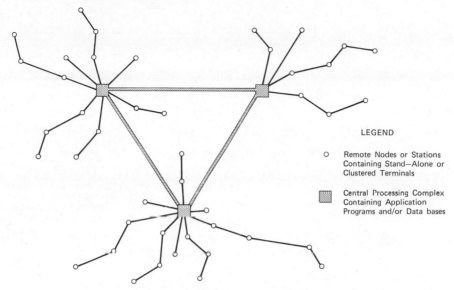

Figure 1.1. A distributed network.

In either type of network, many types or kinds of communications lines can connect the various nodes. Any line that operates between the nodes of a fixed source–sink pair is called a point-to-point line. The lines connecting nodes A, F, G, H, and I, respectively, to the processor in Figure 1.2 are examples of point-to-point lines. All the heavily shaded lines of Figure 1.1 are also point-to-point lines. Point-to-point lines may be either switched (dial-up) or leased (dedicated).[10] With a switched line, a common carrier facility like the dial-up telephone network establishes the connection, which is maintained only for the duration of a single call. Dedicated point-to-point lines provide a permanent communication path between nodes whether or not they are active.

Another type of leased or dedicated line is widely used in teleprocessing networks—the multidrop or multipoint line.[11] The line connecting nodes B, C, D, and E to the processor in Figure 1.2 is an example of a

[10]The term *private* line is often used (by communications regulatory agencies in particular) synonymously with *dedicated* line or *leased* line. Other organizations, notably those in the data processing industry, use "private line" to denote any type of nonpublic line (e.g., a line owned by a private individual or corporation). There is unfortunately no standard parlance throughout the industry.

[11]We make no distinction between the terms *multidrop* and *multipoint* line. Historically, "multidrop line" has connotations of analog transmission facilities. Recently, functionally equivalent services are using mixtures of digital and analog technology, giving rise to the more general term *multipoint* line. We will use "multipoint line" throughout the book.

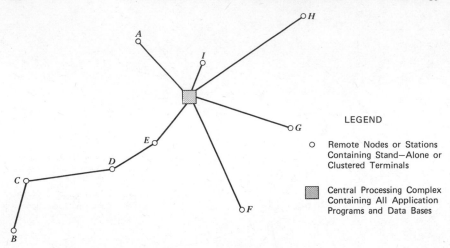

Figure 1.2. A centralized network.

multipoint line. A multipoint line is shared in real time by two or more remote nodes. At any instant, only one remote node or station on the line can communicate with the central node or station. The remote stations take turns on the line, typically sharing it under the control of a central software module that sequentially issues invitations to the remote stations. More will be said about multipoint lines in subsequent chapters.

1.5.1. Centralized or Distributed?

One of the most important issues in designing a network is the question of whether the network should be centralized or distributed. A variety of factors affect this tradeoff, but one key reason for considering a partially distributed network is the possibility of a cost curve shaped like the one shown in Figure 1.3. This illustration suggests that, although total processing complex costs usually increase with a rise in the number of computer centers, the total cost of required communications may in certain instances decrease even more rapidly as the number of regional processing complexes increases. It should be noted that the total system cost curve of Figure 1.3 will frequently have a minimum when only a single processing complex is used, so that the illustration applies only to examples for which some type of decentralization should be considered.

Up until now, far more centralized than distributed teleprocessing networks have been implemented. Whether or not careful comparative analysis led to this predomination of centralized systems is conjectural,

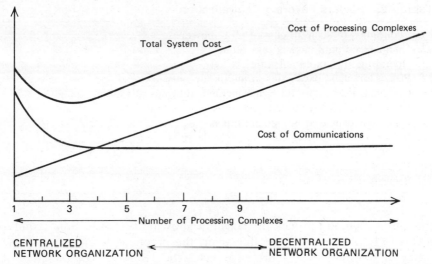

Figure 1.3. Cost variations between centralized and decentralized network organizations.

but probably some or all of the factors itemized in Table 1.2 affected many of these past decisions.[12] Of these factors, the first one constitutes the essence of the tradeoff. If the transactions emanating from remote terminals in a particular geographic region are more likely to access some well-defined subset of the data base, intuition suggests that long-distance communications costs can be reduced by positioning this portion of the data base in a regional center proximate to the terminal group in question. This potential advantage of decentralization, however, is much less attractive in applications where each portion of the data base is just as likely to be accessed by one group of terminals as by any other.

Other justifications for distributed data base networks deal with possible data access limitations in a single, large, centralized inquiry/response application. Data base sizes are generally growing rapidly, and complex software is required to manage the file update/access activity. When response time requirements approximate several seconds for each transaction, it may be impossible to satisfy them with a polled network feeding into a single large data base. An alternative structure that may perform satisfactorily is a multicenter network in which the total data base is distributed over several centers, thereby providing parallel access paths to portions of the data base or to all of it. This can reduce the queuing delays inherent in the serial process of accessing every file

[12]Some of these factors were discussed originally by Dennis [17] and later by Doll [18].

Table 1.2. Factors Favoring Centralization

1. Economies of scale in cost of CPU power.
2. Unclustered data base access requests.
3. Operating system complexities.
4. Processor incompatibilities in multinode networks.
5. Complexities of data base management routines at multiple sites.
6. Lack of switchable, broadband links.
7. High cost of leased broadband links.
8. Personnel and staffing costs at multiple sites.
9. Unbundling.
10. Politics of large organizations.
11. Security considerations.

through a common processor, possibly allowing response time require-ments to be met. To be sure, however, the practical deterrents to these types of distributed systems have been the technical complexities of coordinating data base management routines and operating systems in multicomplex networks. These limitations are aggravated still further if the individual processing complexes involve functionally incompatible computer systems.

Note that distributed networks contain requirements for two kinds of communications links—those connecting terminals to regional centers and those interconnecting the regional centers themselves. The backbone network tends to require much faster communication links than does the regional network because data transmission over the backbone takes place in a bursty fashion between two extremely fast devices, each capable of internal speeds in the megabit/second range. References [14], [15], and [16] all note the relatively high cost of transmitting data at kilobit and megabit/second rates, since such speeds cannot generally be attained over the so-called voice-grade links of the public telephone network.[13] (As an example, with today's U.S. tariffs an interstate private voice-grade line of several hundred miles might lease for an average of $1.50/mile/month. A leased line capable of transmitting data at 50,000 bits/sec between the same two points would lease for slightly more than $4/mile/month.) It is apparent that current costs for above-voice-grade transmission are so high as to make the backbone network portions of decentralized networks excessively costly. To this point in time, there has not been any nation-

[13]With today's technology, speeds from 3600 to 4800 bits/sec are attainable over the dial-up network. With special line conditioning equipment and compensating circuitry in the modems, speeds from 7200 to 9600 bits/sec can be achieved with private (leased) voice-grade lines.

wide carrier service for transmitting data at speeds faster than 4800 bits/sec over any type of switched network.[14] However, the *value-added* networking concept discussed in subsequent chapters may well alleviate this problem.

Most of the remaining factors in Table 1.2 relate to the direct and indirect costs of operating multiple, regional processing centers. Even though the actual hardware costs of computer system components are declining because of developments such as large-scale integration (LSI) of the circuitry, software costs have generally increased as a result of unbundling. In addition, the ratio of nonequipment cost to computer hardware cost has also been increasing considerably. In the early 1960s this ratio was estimated to be approximately 1:1, but by 1968 it was estimated that companies spent $187 on related staff for every $100 spent on hardware.[15] Numerous recent estimates have placed the typical hardware-related costs at less than one third of the operating costs of a total processing complex (including software, hardware, staff, maintenance, rent, taxes, etc.).

Nontechnical factors such as emphasis on increased administrative control in a single processing complex also tend to foster the continuing development of centralized systems. Data processing and systems executives often consider their corporate empires less vulnerable during intracompany power struggles if all the resources they manage are kept in a single central location.

Individuals planning future network organizations must factor all these items into the tradeoff analysis, remembering that computer processing equipment and long distance communications costs are generally declining. Processing equipment costs have declined with great rapidity over the past few years;[16] however, increases in non-hardware-related processing costs tend to offset some of the potential cost savings associated with decentralization.

Minicomputers and intelligent terminals make it economically possible to perform a greater number of mundane communications control functions such as code conversion, display control, error control, and

[14]Things are gradually changing, as indicated by the present offerings of MCI Communications Corporation and Southern Pacific Communications, as well as the new Bell System Dataphone Digital Service (DDS) network, which are discussed in greater detail in subsequent chapters.

[15]See pp. 91–92 in Reference [19] by David H. Li, as well as the report of McKinsey and Company, entitled *Unlocking the Computer's Profit Potential: A Research Report to Management* (New York: McKinsey & Company, Inc., 1968).

[16]With domestic satellite communications now available, the price of certain types of long distance links has been declining dramatically, since satellite channel costs are generally not closely related to the physical length or distance between source and sink.

polling at remote sites. There has certainly been a pronounced trend toward decentralization of control functions in recent years. On the other hand, the *applications processing* activities have for the most part remained centralized in the majority of existing teleprocessing systems. In the future, however, as applications arise involving user requirements for extremely large data bases and a broad spectrum of highly sophisticated programs, it is likely that more and more functions that can be cost-justified in local terminals will be positioned there. Increased accessibility to data, faster response times, lower transmission costs, and so on—all are attractive motivations for using intelligent terminals that perform transaction-preparation functions and substantial local preprocessing. This could accelerate the recent interest in distributed networks.

It has been this author's experience that these and other factors typically beyond the control of the network planner dictate answers to the "where and how many processors" issue. Consequently, in many applications the geographic location of the data base and computational resources is effectively a constant in the design problem. In situations where the processor locations are not fixed a priori (in advance), a parametric approach is often used. An optimum network layout is obtained for each of several alternative locations, and the best one is selected on the basis of suitable economic, performance, and reliability criteria. Specific techniques for designing both centralized and distributed nets are addressed in more detail in subsequent chapters.

1.6. TERMINOLOGY, GENERALIZED DESCRIPTIVE PROCEDURE

An important basis for all subsequent discussion of teleprocessing systems is the precise definition of key terms and the establishment of a systematic procedure for describing systems. The need for a general descriptive language and a system classification procedure arises because most networks are composed of widely varying types and makes of components such as terminals, modems, lines, multiplexers, interfaces, preprocessors, and central processing units.

The terminology and descriptive procedures presented here follow closely the proposals of the American Standards Association (Sectional Committee X3, Computers and Information Processing), which are discussed at greater length in Reference [20].

A teleprocessing network, taken in its entirety and including all terminal equipment and processing complexes, constitutes a *system*. In turn, each system consists of at least one *system segment,* which is either a *point-to-point segment* or a *multipoint segment*. Within a multipoint seg-

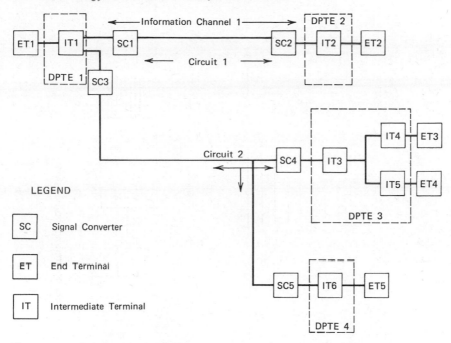

Figure 1.4. System configuration example with one point-to-point and one multipoint segment.

ment there exist multiple possible *information paths* involving one or more data sources and sinks. For example, Figure 1.4 illustrates a system composed of one point-to-point segment and one multipoint segment. Within the multipoint segment, several possible information paths exist, such as the one between DPTE 1 and DPTE 3 and one between DPTE 1 and DPTE 4. The acronym *DPTE* refers to *data processing terminal equipment*; it denotes all the equipment at the end points of a system segment between the signal conversion interface and the ultimate information source or sink, as shown in Figure 1.5.

Throughout this book (as is common in other works) the term *DPTE* will be used interchangeably with *data terminal equipment* or simply *DTE*. In all uses of the term, the ultimate source and sink devices are generally not included in the DPTE configuration.

In Figure 1.4, note that no information path is defined between DPTE 3 and DPTE 4 on the multipoint segment. One of the DPTEs on a multipoint segment is usually designated as the primary or central point; information paths must always include the central point. Hence two

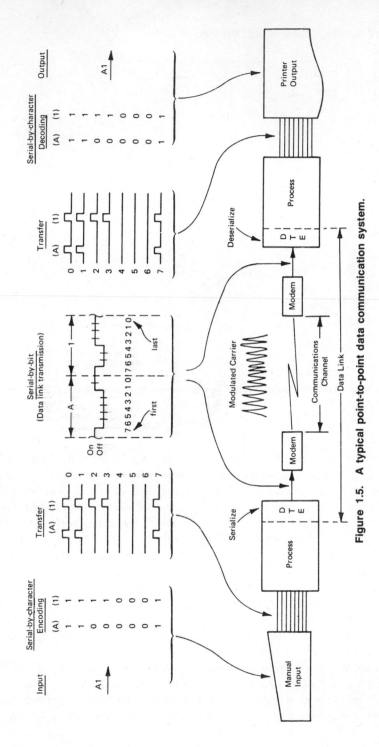

Figure 1.5. A typical point-to-point data communication system.

20

remote (noncentral) points are obliged to exchange information indirectly through the central point.

A DPTE describes all equipment that connects directly to the ends of an *information channel*.[17] This term refers to all the transmission media and intervening equipment involved in transferring information in a given direction between two DPTEs. Note that the information channel includes communication line facilities and signal converters *but not* the DPTEs.

Thus an information channel is composed of *channels* and signal converters; the channel includes the required communications or transmission facilities.

The signal converter is the equipment that converts the data signal of the DPTE into a form suitable for the transmission facility. Signal converters traditionally have converted from digital to analog forms at the sending DPTE and from analog back to digital at the receiving DPTE. These are the familiar analog modems or data sets.

The recent advent of all-digital transmission services has spawned a new type of signal converter which converts from the internal digital format of the DPTE to the different digital format of the communication line at the sending station. The complementary digital-to-digital conversion is performed at the receiver DPTE. For this reason the reader is advised to use the more generally inclusive term *signal converter*, instead of *modem*, whenever appropriate. Many people automatically associate a special type of conversion (digital/analog) with the generic term *modem*.

The distinction between a channel and a circuit is a subtle one. Circuits are the physical entities procured by users from the common carriers, whereas channels are logical components of circuits. At the most basic level, a channel is a means (or medium) for the one-way transmission of information. Thus a circuit capable of simultaneous transmission in both send and receive directions would contain two channels, a *send channel* and a *receive channel*.[18] For example, switched connections generally provide one channel when being used with conventional analog modems. This channel may alternatively be used in either the send or the receive direction but not in both directions simultaneously. By contrast, leased or dedicated lines generally contain two independent, equal-capacity channels, one for the send direction and one for the receive direction. Special

[17]Table 1.3 summarizes the standard definitions of these terms as recommended by the various international standards organizations.
[18]Whenever the receive channel is only capable of sending control information or data bits at significantly slower speeds than the send channel, it is known as a *reverse channel*. Here the primary data flow over the circuit is in one direction at a time.

Table 1.3. Glossary of Terms

END TERMINAL. An equipment comprising the ultimate source or sink, or both, in a digital data transmission system. It may include features designed to initiate or react to various end-to-end control procedures such as carriage return or line feed on a keyboard printer, but does not include features for the execution or control of communications procedures.

CHANNEL. A means (or medium) of one-way transmission (in either direction).

INFORMATION PATH. A discrete route by which information may be transferred between any two DPTEs within a multipoint segment. This term is not used in describing a point-to-point segment.

INTERMEDIATE TERMINAL. A device functioning as a part of the data path within a DPTE and including features for the execution or control of communications procedures. Its functions may also include code conversion, error control, multiplexing, or temporary buffering or storage of data. It may be a discrete item of equipment or an integral part of an end terminal.

SIGNAL CONVERTER. This term refers to the equipment which changes the data signal into a form suitable for the transmission medium, or the reverse. The signal converter comprises a modulator and/or a demodulator.

FORWARD CHANNEL. A data transmission channel in which the direction of transmission coincides with that in which information is being transferred, for example, from source to sink.

TERMINAL CONFIGURATION. The functional interconnection of an end terminal and one or more intermediate terminals within a DPTE for a specified mode of operation at a given time.

DPTE (DATA PROCESSING TERMINAL EQUIPMENT). The configuration of equipment at the end points of a system segment contained between the signal converter interface defined by EIA Standard RS-232 and the information source or sink utilized in a given application. It always includes at least one intermediate terminal and may include combinations of intermediate terminals and end terminals.

SYSTEM SEGMENT. A conceptual subset of a data transmission system containing the DPTEs connected to a common channel. A system segment may be either point-to-point or multipoint.

POINT-TO-POINT SEGMENT. A class of system segment that permits communications between only two DPTEs at a given time.

---

types of signal converters may be used to obtain variations of these basic circuit features; these will be discussed in the next chapter.

The terms *circuit* and *link* are used interchangeably in referring to a point-to-point segment. However, in a multipoint segment such as the one shown in Figure 1.4, the multipoint circuit consists of the complete communication connection between DPTE 1, DPTE 3, and DPTE 4, excluding signal converters. The portion of the complete circuit that interconnects DPTE 1 and DPTE 3 (or DPTE 3 and DPTE 4) is sometimes

MULTIPOINT SEGMENT. A class of system segment in which more than two DPTEs are connected to a common channel.

BACKWARD (REVERSE) CHANNEL. A data transmission channel used for supervisory and/or error control signals and associated with the forward channel, but having a direction of transmission opposite to that in which information is being transferred.

INFORMATION CHANNEL. The transmission media and intervening equipment involved in the transfer of information in a given direction between two terminals. An information channel includes the signal converters, as well as the backward (reverse) channel when provided.

CIRCUIT. A means of communication between two points, comprising associated send and receive channels. The two associated channels may be symmetrical (i.e., may offer the user the same possibility in either direction of transmission) or asymmetrical.

TRIB (TRANSFER RATE OF INFORMATION BITS). A basic unit of measurement that expresses numerically the ratio between two factors, number of information bits accepted by the sink, and the total time needed to accomplish transport of all bits required to get those information bits accepted. The units of the ratio are bits per unit time.

RESIDUAL ERROR RATE. The ratio of the number of bits, unit elements, characters, or blocks incorrectly received but undetected or uncorrected by the error control equipment, to the total number of bits, unit elements, characters, or blocks transmitted.

TRANSFER DELAY. A characteristic of system performance that expresses the time delay in processing information through a data transmission system.

STATION. One of the physical input or output points of a communication system, including all intermediate terminals and the associated end terminals to which they are connected. Examples are stand-alone terminals, clustered CRT terminals and their control unit, and computer ports.

DCE (DATA COMMUNICATIONS EQUIPMENT). Any equipment that connects to a DPTE using an RS-232 or CCITT V.24 standard interface.

DATA LINK. The configuration of equipment enabling end terminals in two different stations to communicate directly. The data link includes the paired DPTEs, signal converters, and interconnecting communications facilities.

referred to as a link or circuit segment. Thus the complete multipoint circuit consists of the several links or circuit segments that interconnect the various points of the circuit.

The term *link* should not be confused with *data link,* the configuration of equipment that enables two end terminals to communicate directly. As shown in Figure 1.5, the data link includes the sending and receiving DPTEs and all interconnecting signal converters and communication facilities. Note that it is possible for certain intermediate terminals such as basic time-division multiplexers to tie two or more physically cascaded circuits together, forming a single data link. As long as the intermediate terminal does not execute data link control procedures such as block error checking and buffering, it performs no DPTE functions and merely acts to regenerate/reformat the serial bit stream.

The hardware configuration connected to the end points of an information channel was referred to previously as a *data processing terminal equipment* (DPTE or DTE). The boundaries of a particular DPTE are the ultimate information source or sink on one side and the signal converter interface on the other. Standard conventions and rules for connecting DPTEs and signal converters are defined domestically by the EIA RS232-C[19] interface specification and internationally by the CCITT V24 specification.[20] The DPTE may be simple, consisting of a teletypewriter or line printer, or it may be a complex array of equipment encompassing a wide variety of interconnected peripherals and processors. Every DPTE always consists of at least one *intermediate terminal* (IT) and may include combinations of other modules called *end terminals* (ETs). The terms *ET* and *IT* are precisely defined in Table 1.3, but are now explained in further detail and finally illustrated by means of an example.

An ET is the ultimate source or sink (inanimate) of the information transmitted in a data communications system. It may include functions designed to initiate various end-to-end control procedures, such as carriage return in a teletypewriter, or react to them. An IT is a device interconnecting signal converters and one or more ETs. Its function may include code conversion, error control, or the execution of line control procedures. It may contain multiple data busses, as well as line buffers for the temporary storage of data bits and/or characters. Finally, the functional interconnection of ETs and ITs within a DPTE for a specified mode of operation, at a given time, is called a *terminal configuration*. Throughout this book, unless noted otherwise, the DPTEs considered will be described by a fixed or static internal interconnection of ETs and ITs. Sometimes ETs outside the DPTE boundaries are also integrated into a physical device like a clustered CRT controller. Here the external ETs and the basic terminal configuration will be collectively referred to merely as a station. To summarize, the term *station* is used to describe a complete terminal configuration of end terminals, intermediate terminals, and

---

[19]See Reference [21].
[20]The acronym CCITT refers to the Consultative Committee on International Telegraphy and Telephony, an international telecommunications standards group composed of representatives from most nations of the world.

their appropriate interconnections. A station may be either a stand-alone terminal, a cluster-controlled group of CRT tubes, a minicomputer, or a remote job entry (RJE) station, for example.

It should be noted that ETs are generally excluded from the DPTE whenever they perform only functions that have nothing to do with communications. On the other hand, if the device architecture of a terminal is such that control of the ultimate source and sink for a transmission is inexorably intertwined with the communications control, separation of the ETs from the DPTE may not be meaningful.

As the industry matures, vendors are designing systems with an ever-increasing concern for establishing rigid logical and functional boundaries between device control and data link control responsibilities. This suggests that it is ultimately desirable for the user to be able to alter ETs without modifying data link control procedures (and, of course, vice versa). Such flexibility is finally beginning to appear in the marketplace. This will make it easier for users to modify applications without having to frequently modify network control approaches.

The descriptive procedures thus outlined make it possible to describe any system completely in terms of point-to-point and multipoint segments. Each constituent segment is then further characterized by its DPTEs, information paths, information channels, and circuits. Finally DPTEs are described in terms of their constituent ITs, ETs, and appropriate interconnections. Figure 1.6 illustrates how this hierarchical descriptive procedure is used to characterize the system of Figure 1.4. It also shows the generality of the descriptive procedure and its suitability for describing vastly more complex systems.

A hierarchy of basic structural modules that comprise a teleprocessing system has been presented. To complete the establishment of terminology, several measures of performance are introduced:[21]

1. Transfer rate of information bits (TRIB).
2. Residual error rate (RER).
3. Reliability.
4. Availability.
5. Channel transfer delay (propagation delay).
6. Turnaround time.
7. Channel establishment time.

[21]See also Reference [22].

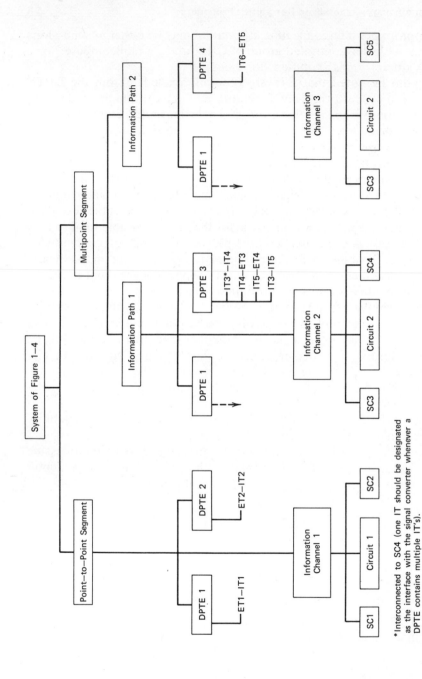

Figure 1.6. Hierarchical description of system in Figure 1.4.

*Interconnected to SC4 (one IT should be designated as the interface with the signal converter whenever a DPTE contains multiple IT's).

Note that there is no information path between DPTE3 and DPTE4.

1.6.1. Transfer Rate of Information Bits (TRIB)

The transfer rate of information bits corresponds to the net rate at which information bits are accepted by the sink [23,24].[22] It is an important unit of measurement that deducts various overhead components, such as time spent for retransmissions or for control signaling purposes, from the raw clocking rate at which bits are transmitted over a channel. The TRIB is most frequently applied to measure data transfer rates between the ultimate source and sink in an application and consequently involves a measurement between ETs. It is not merely an information channel characteristic, since the buffering techniques, control procedures, and operating terminal characteristics all directly affect TRIB, as will be seen in more detail in subsequent chapters. The units of TRIB are bits/second.

1.6.2. Residual Error Rate (RER)

The residual error rate is a quantitative measure of the accuracy of an information transfer between ETs. It is the ratio of bits, characters, or blocks incorrectly received but undetected or uncorrected by the error control equipment, to the total number of bits, characters, or blocks transmitted [23,24]. It should not be confused with the bit error rate of the information channel, which is a measurement of the bit error rate between a pair of terminal configuration boundaries. In the special case where the terminal configurations contain no error detection or correction provisions, the RER measured in terms of bits would correspond to the bit error rate of the corresponding information channel.

1.6.3. Reliability

Reliability is generally defined as the probability that a device will perform without failure for a specified time period or amount of usage. It is important to data communication system users because it formally describes a user's chances of successfully completing a given task, using networking facilities. If telecommunication facilities are inoperable when the user requires them, the costs may range from nothing (in the case of minor inconvenience) to substantial (in the case of highly time-critical applications). Reliability characteristics are also important because the expected maintenance and repair costs of a data communication system

---

[22]Information bits are generally defined as bits to be moved from the source that do not cause any device or data link control functions to be performed at intermediate points between the source and the sink.

depend jointly on the frequency of failures and the cost of service restoral once a failure has occurred.

1.6.4.   Availability

Availability is defined in Reference [23] as "the portion of a selected time interval during which the information path is capable of performing its assigned data communication function." Certain users measure availability as the fraction of operational terminal hours of a network in a regular business time interval like a month. The time reference for 100% availability includes all hours of normal system operation. Hence failures that do not affect normal system operation do not contribute to unavailability.

Alternatively, availability can be defined in terms of the ratio MTBF/ (MTBF + MTTR), where MTBF is the mean time between failures and MTTR is the mean time to repair a device. The general strategies for improving availability in a data communication system include the judicious use of redundant lines (e.g., dial-up backup techniques), terminals, signal converters, multiplexers, concentrators, and communications controllers or front-end processors. These approaches, coupled with the use of comprehensive diagnostic features for fault isolation and troubleshooting, jointly improve availability by increasing MTBF and decreasing MTTR.

One common problem in a data communication system is distinguishing between very short term "failures" of a system such as those that cause a burst of bit errors and longer term outages that render a system unavailable. To be sure, the threshold of distinction is arbitrary and is left to the user to define in the most meaningful terms. Generally, events that cause errors on communication lines are not defined as failures unless the facility is unusable for more than several seconds or minutes. "Unusable" may mean totally unavailable or having such a high error rate that the effective transfer rate (TRIB) is degraded below some minimum acceptable value. More will be said about these issues later.

1.6.5.   Propagation Delay

Channel transfer or propagation delay is the amount of time taken by a signal in passing through the telecommunications channel to the receiving station. Alternative interpretations are possible, but the most common is the time for a one-bit signal to move from the input of the information channel to the output. As will be seen in subsequent chapters, typical values of propagation delay on terrestrial circuits are in the milliseconds range, with actual values depending on physical circuit distances. On satellite channels, the delays typically increase to several hundred milliseconds. Since propagation delay usually appears directly in the TRIB equation (as will be seen in Chapter 6 on error control), understanding its precise effect is crucial to sound system design.

1.6.6. Turnaround Time

As noted in References [23] and [24], channel turnaround time is the delay required by circuits (which are not capable of simultaneous bidirectional transfer) to reverse their direction of transmission. This parameter generally depends primarily on the type of signal conversion devices and line facilities used. It can range from negligibly small values up to several hundred milliseconds. Generally this parameter is not of concern on most leased lines, since they are capable of simultaneous transmission in both directions. On most dial-up lines with conventional modems, or on the few leased lines provided with only one channel, however, the turnaround delay parameter is important because it will directly affect the efficiency with which the line may be used.

1.6.7. Channel Establishment Time

In Reference [22], channel establishment time is defined as the time required for a switched telecommunications facility to provide a circuit connection between a calling terminal and a called terminal. In dial-up applications, this delay may be regarded as an overhead delay which adds to the total time for each terminal session involving a new connection to the switched network. Conventional usage of the public telephone network for data transmission will involve dialing delays and connection establishment times as large as 15 to 30 sec in the worst case.

On the other hand, some of the newer switched digital data networks such as those discussed in the subsequent chapters on transmission services are designed for establishment delays of not more than several hundred milliseconds. The shorter the duration time for the use of the switched network, the more important a fast channel establishment becomes.

In networks employing transmission techniques such as packet switching (where messages and segments of messages are moved using intermediate buffers for storing and forwarding purposes), the conventional interpretation of channel establishment delay does not apply. One view of such nets is that there is no establishment delay, since the network can almost always accept the next input message from the sending user with no delay. The other view is that this delay is imposed on every data exchange between sender and receiver, since logical channels (as opposed to physical ones) must still be established. Even in the latter interpretation, channel establishment delays will generally be noticeably shorter than in conventional circuit switching systems.

1.7. SYNOPSIS OF THE REGULATORY ENVIRONMENT

It is important for anyone even remotely interested in problems related to the systems design of teleprocessing networks to realize the existence of constraints imposed by the regulated nature of the communications common carrier industry. This holds true both in the United States and in most foreign countries, although the precise nature of the constraints varies widely from one country to the next.

As noted previously, Congress acted to create the Federal Communications Commission (FCC) by its passage of the Communications Act of 1934. The scope and objectives of the Act are stated in its opening paragraph:

> For the purpose of regulating interstate and foreign commerce in communication by wire and radio so as to make available, so far as possible, to all the people of the United States a rapid, efficient, nationwide, and worldwide wire and radio communication service with adequate facilities at reasonable charges . . .[23]

In creating the FCC, Congress gave it full license and power to compel the common carriers to comply with the broad provisions and scope of the Act. Mathison and Walker have succinctly summarized several of the more important aspects of the Act:

> The provisions of the Act require that communications common carriers subject thereto furnish services at reasonable charges upon reasonable request. Carriers may not construct interstate lines or curtail service without FCC approval. Common carriers must file nondiscriminatory tariff schedules with the FCC (or concur in the tariffs filed by other carriers) showing all charges, practices, classifications, and regulations for interstate communication services offered to the public. A tariff, when filed, automatically becomes effective unless suspended or explicitly disapproved by the FCC.[24]

[23]*The Communications Act of 1934, as Amended,* Title 1, Section 1 (Washington, D.C.: U.S. Government Printing Office, 1971).
[24]See p. 3 of Mathison and Walker [25].

The discussion of this section makes no attempt to delve into the details of the key regulatory issues that affect teleprocessing. This section is concerned merely with calling to the reader's attention some of the more relevant current topics. From such discussions, it is hoped that the reader will gain an overview of these issues and the ways in which they can influence the systems design process. The serious student of regulatory affairs and their relationships to the computer and communications industries is urged to pursue in detail the numerous references cited throughout this section. One, in particular, is noteworthy for its thorough and insightful, yet compact, consideration of the important regulatory issues, namely, the previously cited book by Mathison and Walker [25]. Their work is recommended as the starting point for anyone interested in exploring any of the myriad policy-related issues in greater depth:

> . . . the primary contribution of this book [by Mathison and Walker] may be the fact that it brings together and interrelates these communications policy issues for the first time in one volume. The authors present the reader with the first cohesive consideration of communications policy in a computer-oriented framework. . . . The book deserves to be must reading for every person who wishes to consider himself well-informed in the field of computers and communications.[25]

Because of the monumental changes in the communications industry over the last 5 years, there have been numerous additional regulatory developments of major consequence that are not considered in Reference [25]. Excellent updating is available in more recent works by Mathison and Walker, noted as References [26], [27], and [28].

Table 1.4 summarizes the major policy-related questions to be discussed briefly in this section. These issues are generally quite provocative and controversial, in addition to being interrelated. Every attempt is made in subsequent discussion to present an objective overview in the elaboration of these points.

1.7.1. Regulation of the Computer Industry

Traditionally, the computer industry per se has not been subject to regulation. However, as this industry continues to grow at a far more rapid pace than the gross national product, and an increasingly broad spectrum of private and public sector applications becomes dependent on the computer, the question arises as to whether the public interest would best be

---

[25]Excerpted from *ACM Computing Reviews,* Vol. 2, No. 7, July 1970, pp. 374–375.

Table 1.4.   Key Regulatory Issues

Regulation of computer industry.
Hybrid data processing/communications services.
Cross subsidization.
Jurisdictional aspects.
Line sharing provisions, resale of service.
Competition among carriers, specialized common carriers.

served by some type of regulation. In the past 5 years, the question of whether commercial data processing services should be regulated by the FCC has been discussed as part of the FCC's continuing inquiry into the interdependence of computers and communications. There has been virtually unanimous concurrence by suppliers of data processing services, the communications common carriers, the government itself, and the general public that data processing services do *not* fall under the jurisdiction of the Communications Act of 1934, and hence are not under the jurisdiction of the FCC.[26]

A more important question is whether a continuation of the free enterprise status of the data processing industry will continue to best serve the public interest. The U.S. government has not yet taken any major steps in the direction of formal regulation. However, some recent evidence is indicative of growing public sentiment favoring some type of regulation.[27,28] No doubt this attitude is based to some degree on a sense of personal frustration experienced by the general public in one or more direct dealings with computers. In the final analysis, large-scale regulation of the computer industry will probably not occur unless the participants in this industry use their free market privileges to the detriment of the general public, or unless the individual's rights to privacy and security are unduly threatened by the misuse and improper control of large computerized data bases.[29]

1.7.2.   Hybrid Data Processing/Communications Services

Most of the currently *unregulated* data processing services provided in this country involve the use of communication lines or services obtained

[26]See Mathison and Walker [25], pp. 16–19.
[27]In a recent survey of the general public conducted by *Time* magazine and the American Federation of Information Processing Societies (AFIPS), as summarized in *Computerworld*, Vol. V, No. 47, Nov. 24, 1972, 84% of persons interviewed said the government should be concerned about regulating computer usage.
[28]Also see References [29] and [30].
[29]For a penetrating analysis of the privacy and security issues, see Miller [31].

from *regulated* common carriers. A hybrid data processing service is an offering that combines remote-access data processing and message switching in a manner wherein the message switching capability is incidental to the data processing function or purpose. The communications function (message switching) is thus incidental to and an integral part of the hybrid data processing service. To this point in time, the general attitude of the Federal Communications Commission has been that the operation of hybrid data processing systems does *not* constitute an activity that should be regulated under the scope of the 1934 Act. Almost every teleprocessing system in operation today technically involves a hybrid data processing service.

A hybrid communications service, on the other hand, involves a system where the data processing function is incidental to and an integral part of the message switching function or purpose of the type intended to be covered by the 1934 Act. (Message switching is an example of this type of communications activity, where a computer system stores and forwards recorded messages over communication lines connected to it.) Generally, hybrid communications services have been considered by the FCC to be within its regulatory jurisdiction as granted by the 1934 Act. Currently, the FCC evaluates specific hybrid computer–communications services on a case-by-case basis to determine whether a particular one is primarily a hybrid computer/data processing service (not regulated) or a hybrid communications service falling under the Communications Act.

The knowledgeable reader will immediately recognize the nebulous nature of the distinction between these two types of services. In fact, anyone who has ever used a time sharing system knows that messages can be stored in a file by one remote user and subsequently copied by or transmitted to another remote user. With regard to the entire subject of hybrid services several important issues need to be resolved. Among these are the following:

1. What constitutes a hybrid data processing service?
2. What constitutes a hybrid communications service?
3. Should either or both of these types of services be regulated?
4. What kinds of business organizations should be permitted to offer these types of services, and under what conditions?

Since hybrid communications services will presumably continue to be regulated, it is particularly important that the FCC address the second and fourth issues above. Many large corporations today operate their own internal message switching networks for intracompany record communications. These systems do not involve publicly available services and are hence not regulated. However, if several small companies, each individually unable to afford its own internal system, wished to operate a common message switching network, a multiorganization hybrid communications service would be involved. A similar situation would exist if an entrepreneur wished to operate a large message switching network service subscribed to by organizations and users not capable of economically justifying their own individual systems. The general need for services of this type is hard to dispute; however, the policy issues are extremely complex and replete with political and other nontechnical ramifications.[30]

Several years ago, the FCC initiated Docket 20097, a broad inquiry into the resale issues of hybrid computer–communications service offerings and the past practices of U.S. common carriers in these matters.

In mid-1976 a major policy development took place; the FCC issued a key ruling in Docket 20097 that eliminates previous restrictions on the resale or shared use of all leased line services. This ruling directs all leased line carriers to permit their customers to fully share and/or resell unused portions of the leased line transmission capacity. A precursor of this ruling occurred in 1974, when AT&T changed its policies to permit composite data service vendors (CDSVs) to use AT&T leased lines in providing communications services to their customers. The term *CDSV* is used by AT&T for companies that offer hybrid communications services to the public; at this time CDSVs must obtain FCC authorization to operate as common carriers before leasing lines to be used for resale to third parties.

This complex issue will probably take several years to be completely resolved, and the outcome will affect virtually every organization involved in the provision of these kinds of services. It is possible in the future that the current regulations requiring CDSVs to file tariffs with the FCC may be relaxed or eliminated, facilitating entry to this market by existing computer services firms and other large shared-user organizations that have avoided the lucrative communications market because of its regulated nature. Such possibilities would create numerous new options for users, stimulate competition, and complicate the design process still further.

1.7.3. Cross Subsidization

The issue of cross subsidization potentially applies to organizations involved in a variety of different business activities, some of which are inherently monopolistic and others competitive in nature.

---

[30]For additional background, see Reference [27].

Cross subsidy involves the establishment of predatory or unfairly low prices for goods or services sold in a competitive market activity, with prices in the monopolistic activities being set at higher than necessary levels to assure some aggregate level of profitability. Since certain companies supplying communications equipment and facilities to the public are involved in both types of business activities, the FCC has generally required each distinct business activity to be separated into an independent subsidiary to minimize the possibility of cross subsidization. Unfortunately, however, the FCC is not adequately staffed or funded to monitor properly the voluminous accounting reports filed periodically by the larger common carriers.

Another important aspect of the cross-subsidization issue involves whether carrier organizations like AT&T use the philosophy of fully allocated cost (FAC) or long run incremental costing (LRIC). With FAC approaches, the carrier allocates some proportion of the cost of common equipment to each competitive service. As a costing philosophy FAC tends to raise the assumed costs of AT&T's competitive services, allowing competition more leeway in its pricing structures. On the other hand, in rate development for the incremental service LRIC includes only the costs directly associated with its provision.

The conventional, established carriers tend to favor LRIC approaches, whereas their competitors generally prefer FCC policies that reflect realistic degrees of FAC accounting. At the time of this writing, the FCC has issued a policy directive favoring the FAC approach, following many years of debate and hearings, in Docket 18128, a proceeding concerned with developing acceptable costing practices for the industry. Until the general FCC policy in this matter has been finally established and approved, it will remain virtually impossible to test individual service pricing structures objectively and accurately for reasonableness and fairness.

1.7.4. Jurisdictional Considerations

The main idea here centers around the fact that the FCC approves rates and tariffs for interstate services, with various state or local regulatory agencies performing a similar function for intrastate communications services. Intrastate rates generally apply to services with all access points inside a state boundary. System designers often have a strong incentive to design networks that involve interstate services, since rates for comparable intrastate services are frequently more costly.[31] However, this relation-

---

[31]Numerous trade organizations and user groups have even gone so far as to suggest that all interstate and intrastate data communications common carriers be subject to FCC jurisdiction, thereby eliminating geographic variations in rate structures for computer users of communications services.

ship between interstate and intrastate prices does not hold true everywhere. An extremely knotty aspect of this situation is the question of precisely what constitutes an interstate communication service. With the complexity of today's tariffs, there are generally no pat answers to such questions. The spirit of the law has generally intended that services involved in the transmission of interstate communications traffic bear interstate tariffs. However, the vagaries of numerous dynamic application situations make the consistent application of this definition a difficult if not impossible task. An additional complication to the planner is that some intrastate rates are higher and some are lower than interstate rates. Moreover, intrastate prices are generally different from one state to the next.

1.7.5. Interconnection, Foreign Attachments

One of the most controversial regulatory issues of all arises because communications common carriers have traditionally imposed severe restrictions on the type of equipment that may be directly connected to their networks. Before 1969, AT&T strictly prohibited hardware interconnection to the dial-up telephone network, with exceptions allowed for certain government, military, and transportation organizations. For example, the pre-1969 tariff for the public switched network read:

> No equipment, apparatus, circuit, or device not furnished by the Telephone Company shall be attached to or connected with the facilities furnished by the Telephone Company, whether physically, by induction or otherwise . . .[32]

The common carriers' public statements justifying the need for such provisions have always been and will continue to be based on the valid premise that the technical integrity of their networks must be preserved. Hazardous voltages, signals with certain special energy characteristics, and other nonconforming features could harm the public switched network, or at least increase the carrier's cost of maintaining the network, a cost that presumably must be passed along to the users in the form of higher rates. A more obvious reason for the carriers' opposition to interconnection is centered on the threat to their revenue sources when competition is permitted in the supply of interconnection equipment.[33]

However, the proponents of a relaxed attitude toward interconnection

---

[32]Excerpted from AT&T Tariff 263 for interstate and foreign message toll telephone service.
[33]For an enlightening discussion of the entire interconnection situation, see *The Telephone Interconnect Market,* published by Frost and Sullivan, Inc. (New York: January 1972).

contended that the restrictions in the tariffs were excessively severe and unnecessary. The matter was finally brought to a climax in July 1968, when the FCC, in its landmark Carterfone decision, ruled that the above tariff "has been unreasonable, discriminatory, and unlawful in the past, and that the provisions prohibiting the use of customer-provided inter-connecting devices should accordingly be stricken."[34]

On January 1, 1969, AT&T revised its tariffs to permit the attachment of customer-provided devices such as modems to the public switched network, subject to three important conditions:

1. The customer-provided equipment is restricted to certain output power and energy levels, so as not to interfere with or harm the telephone network in any way.
2. The interconnection to the public switched network must be made through a telephone company-provided protective device, sometimes referred to as a data access arrangement or DAA.[35]
3. All network control signaling such as dialing, busy signals, and so on must be performed with telephone company equipment at the inter-connection point.

These restrictions of the 1969 Bell System tariff were strongly opposed by users and independent suppliers, who took issue mainly with the second and third conditions. The so-called DAAs add extra costs to a communications system that uses independently supplied modems and multiplexors, since DAAs are not required if comparable equipment is obtained from the carriers. The third restriction was opposed mainly by independent suppliers of private telephone exchange and handset equip-ment, since it curtailed the usefulness of their products.

All these objections led the FCC to establish an informal advisory committee composed of representatives from all interested organizations to either modify the terms of the existing tariff in a mutually acceptable way or to recommend that it be accepted as is. During 1976, preliminary

---

[34]Excerpted from the Carterfone decision, released by the FCC on June 28, 1968.

[35]In the summer of 1971, AT&T moved to require similar protective arrangements on connections to its leased lines. However, the move was violently opposed by users and independent suppliers of data communications equipment who had been operating private line systems quite satisfactorily without such devices for several years. In November 1971, AT&T agreed to a 1 year postponement of this requirement. The final arguments on this issue are not yet in, and it will probably remain unresolved for some time. However, it appears unlikely that leased line protective devices will ever be universally required, especially in light of 1976 developments relaxing the requirements for DAAs on switched network connections.

conclusions were reached that are likely to revolutionize the industry by phasing out requirements for DAAs altogether.

The FCC has recommended a plan whereby current protective devices would be phased out in favor of a so-called registration plan. Registration would permit direct switched network electrical connection of equipment that had been inspected and registered by an independent agency such as the FCC as technically safe for use on the switched network. These plans are similar to those currently used for controlling interconnection in many foreign countries.

The reason for discussing interconnection in this book is merely to illustrate the numerous ways in which this issue affects the systems designer and his spectrum of choices. In addition to the points cited above (which define his latitude and the costs of using independently supplied equipment), the long term outcome of interconnection will affect the rates for using both the public switched network and leased lines. The idea here is that the existing common carriers have generally adhered to a nationwide averaging of their costs and revenues to produce a uniform rate structure for interstate services. Obviously, if their revenues in supplying terminal equipment are adversely affected, they may contend that higher prices for other services are required. The advent of competition in other areas such as the supplying of private line services by the specialized common carriers poses similar difficulties for the traditional concept of a nationwide average pricing scheme.[36]

In the summer of 1974, the Bell System's initial route-priced tariff became effective, even though at that time the FCC had not completed its final investigation into the fairness and public interest issues posed by the new high density/low density (HiLo) tariff. Then, in early 1976, the FCC concluded that the HiLo tariff was unlawful for numerous reasons, most of which related to AT&T's failure to justify the cost assumptions used to derive the HiLo rate elements. Interestingly, even though the tariff was ruled unlawful, it was in effect for more than 2 years, and no refunds were ever given to users whose prices increased when HiLo became effective! This illustrates one of the major deficiencies of the so-called regulatory time lag inherent in the current regulatory process. As of this writing in mid-1976, AT&T has filed another route-priced tariff known as the multischedule private line (MPL) tariff to replace HiLo. Many organizations, including both AT&T users and competitors, will be even worse off with MPL than with HiLo. However, it is likely to again take many months for

[36]A very significant first step in the direction away from nationwide average pricing occurred on February 26, 1973, when AT&T filed for permission to introduce a two-tiered pricing schedule for the private line tariff known as the high density/low density tariff. Details of this now-defunct tariff and its successor tariffs may be found in subsequent chapters.

the FCC to decide on the validity of this new tariff alternative. Should it also be ruled unlawful, everyone will go back to the drawing board and wait for still another tariff to be filed, become effective, and ultimately be judged after many months of additional delay. It seems likely that some type of route-priced tariff structures will ultimately go into effect; however, one cannot be sure what the specific numbers will be until the FCC completes its most recent investigations into the MPL tariff and whatever successors may follow.

1.7.6. Line Sharing Provisions, Resale of Service

A key feature of most existing tariffs for communication lines is that the total cost of transmission capacity increases with increased capacity, but at a less than linear rate. Organizations that use communications facilities obtained from the carriers generally have an incentive to subdivide one large bandwidth (high capacity) channel instead of using multiple smaller bandwidth (lower capacity) channels, whenever possible and economically justifiable.[37] However, the user's ability to exploit this potential approach to reduced communications costs is closely geared to the regulatory restrictions regarding how and by whom a communication line may be shared.

Time-division multiplexers, frequency-division multiplexers, and concentrators, discussed at greater length in Chapter 7 on line sharing devices, may be used to subdivide one large channel into several smaller ones and thus exploit whatever economies of scale exist in today's tariffs. Specific examples of actual network configurations and savings produced by line sharing devices are presented throughout the following chapters to illustrate how these ideas can be implemented.

Generally speaking, the regulatory provisions regarding the technology restrictions on line sharing are much less severe than those governing who is permitted to share lines. Currently, an individual subscriber for leased line service is permitted to fractionate or subdivide the bandwidth of leased voice-grade and broadband communication lines with his own multiplexing equipment.[38] There is generally no regulatory restriction concerning the sharing of lines interconnecting terminals that are used by a single common carrier customer to transmit information related to his

---

[37]As noted in the publications by Mathison and Walker, private line communications users have traditionally been forced to pay more than necessary for service—first, because they must obtain full period (24 hour/day) service, and, second, because they cannot always obtain exactly the bandwidth or capacity their applications require. Sometimes users are forced to use one grade of line very inefficiently because no intermediate service is available.

[38]Broadband multiplexing by individual customers was not permitted before 1971.

business. In fact, the tariffs even permit a customer to connect his multiplexed or shared lines into the locations of "authorized users," such as suppliers, customers, and organizations with whom the customer needs to transmit information relating to his business. Moreover, several "authorized users" are permitted to share the same circuit in communicating with the customer. However, before mid-1976, they were not permitted to communicate with each other using the shared line, since the carrier's customer would then be involved in reselling services, an activity strictly forbidden by the 1934 Act.

As a result of its lengthy hearing into resale and shared use in Docket 20097, the FCC handed down a major ruling in mid-1976 directing all common carriers to remove all tariff bans and restrictions on shared use and resale of leased lines by the fall of 1976. Importantly, only leased lines were included in this directive, so that resale and/or shared use of switched services continues to be forbidden.

One obvious possibility for small private line users to exploit the economies of scale in the tariffs would be to pool their individual requirements for lower speed data channels and individual voice-grade lines via the formation of user consortiums or "shell" companies (whose sole purpose for existence would be the reduction of communications costs). The consortium or shared-user group would then lease voice-grade and wideband or bulk channels, provide its own multiplex equipment wherever required, and enable lower capacity channels to be provided to all the individual participants in the consortium. Before 1969, these sharing arrangements were not permitted, with few exceptions. Then AT&T revised its private line tariff to permit shared usage of most private lines of voice-grade or smaller capacity under certain conditions. (Importantly, broadband lines having capacities higher than 9600 bits/sec were excluded from joint usage.) The joint-usage provision, as it is known, basically permits several telephone company customers to pool their bona fide requirements for low speed leased line services, to share multiplex equipment, and to obtain lower costs by deriving the required channels from shared voice-grade lines.[39] Although the detailed provisions of the joint-user tariff are beyond the scope of the current discussion, several aspects of joint usage gained from this author's tangential involvements in the formation of one such group are worthy of note:

1. Joint users of an individual private line must have a bona fide requirement for communicating over the line. This provision was intended to prevent "brokers" from making a profit via the formation of such

[39]See January 1976 AT&T Private Line Tariff FCC 260: Section 3.1.5, entitled "Joint Use Arrangement."

groups. Such activities were considered to involve the resale of services, which was strictly prohibited under the original 1934 Act. (Of course this ban was slated for elimination as a result of the previously mentioned FCC ruling on Docket 20097 in mid-1976.)

2. One of the joint users may be designated as the network manager. The network manager performs all administrative duties relating to the operation of the network, and may charge a reasonable "network management fee" to the other users. This fee is separate and distinct from the prorated costs of the carrier-provided communications facilities. Attempts by an organization to artifically inflate a network management fee would probably raise questions of resale of services, although the joint-usage tariff did not explicitly quantify fee levels that would be regarded as excessive.

Several joint-usage groups have operated quite successfully through the early and mid-1970s. The specific cost savings resulting from the formation of such groups obviously depend on the geography and actual circuit requirements of the participating organizations; however, they are estimated to be in the range of 20 to 30% on the average.[40] The primary reason for the relative paucity of further literature on joint-user groups has been the regulatory controversy surrounding the concept. However, it can safely be assumed that such concepts will be applied with increasing frequency in the future, since the cost-reduction possibilities are real and recent regulatory policy has further stimulated such shared-usage networks.

One of the largest applications of the joint-usage provision of the tariffs was originally made by Tymshare Corporation in its nationwide computer services network. This intelligent communications network consists of minicomputers that dynamically share the capacity of Tymshare's communication lines. When the joint usage was in effect, the Tymshare communication network in effect performed two purposes:

1. It connected Tymshare Corporation's computer service customers into Tymshare computers and data bases.
2. The joint-user service offered by Tymshare enabled any organization (regardless of its requirements for computer services) to obtain certain types of communications capacity at whatever economy-of-scale price was made possible by the sharing.

[40]For a specific illustration of the cost calculations involved in the formation of one of the original joint-user groups, see H. C. Granger's paper entitled "User's Requirements for Low Cost Date Transmission Facilities," *NEREM Record,* Vol. 13 (1971), published by the Boston, Massachusetts, section of the IEEE.

In mid-1976, Tymshare created a subsidiary company, Tymnet Communications, which filed with the FCC to become a value-added carrier, bringing to an end the joint-user network concept, though of course the network continues to operate with the same economic benefits.

Tymshare and the other joint users thus effectively lowered their communications costs by the formation of the joint-user group. Reference [32] discusses this network and its technical properties in additional detail. Other discussions of the joint-user tariff and the line sharing/resale of services issue are found in the previously cited works by Mathison and Walker.

1.7.7. Competition among Carriers

The final regulatory issue considered involves the significant aspect of competition in the supply of communications services. Literally thousands of pages have been written on the pros and cons of allowing open competition in the supply of common carrier communications services, but one act taken by the FCC has most certainly changed the course of domestic communications history as few others have done in recent times. In August 1969, by a narrow 4-3 vote in favor, the FCC granted Microwave Communications, Inc. (MCI), permission to construct and operate a common carrier microwave system between Chicago and St. Louis.[41] Since then, several other construction permits have been issued to companies affiliated with the MCI organization; to the Data Transmission Company (Datran), then a subsidiary of University Computing Corporation; to Southern Pacific Communications Corporation; and to a host of other organizations interested in becoming specialized carriers.[42]

Adjectives such as *specialized* and *customized* have been used in describing the services now being offered by MCI and SPCC. In their FCC petitions, these organizations stated their intent to provide more flexible options for existing types of services, as well as previously unavailable types. They anticipated concentrating on a rather well-defined segment of the market for common carrier services. For example, MCI has concentrated exclusively on the private line market for both voice and data transmission. Prior to going out of business, Datran, on the other hand, serviced only the data transmission market, but offered both leased and switched services.

[41]In *Re Applications of Microwave Communications, Inc.*, FCC Docket 16509 to 19519, Decisions of the Commission, issued August 13, 1969.
[42]For a more penetrating look at specialized and conventional carriers, see References [33] to [37].

In addition to the specialized carriers noted above, the FCC also approved another class of carrier competition by authorizing domestic satellite carriers to begin offering services using satellite channels. Over time, the distinction between specialized and satellite carriers will become increasingly nebulous. Today's specialized carriers, whose networks are constructed mainly of microwave facilities, will utilize satellite transmission capacity to supplement existing transmission resources, either out of competitive necessity, ability to realize genuine cost savings, or both. Satellite carriers, on the other hand, will naturally use existing terrestrial facilities, such as those of the specialized carriers, to expand their geographic coverage.

Needless to say, the existing common carriers vehemently opposed the idea that specialized and satellite common carriers be allowed to compete in a previously closed marketplace. (In fact, it took 6 years for MCI to obtain its first construction permit.) Nonetheless, after conducting lengthy hearings on the issue the FCC stated:

> There is abundant support for the staff's conclusion that the specialized communications market, particularly for data communications, is growing at a rapid rate, and that there is a very large potential market yet to be developed.[43]

The advantages claimed for the service proposed by the specialized and satellite carriers are numerous, but essentially translate into benefits such as reduced costs, greater flexibility, and improved performance for communications users. (No attempt is made here to list the numerous claims and counterclaims presented to the FCC in the lengthy debate that preceded its favorable decision.)

The most significant functional and economic characteristics of these new common carriers and their proposed services are noted throughout the subsequent chapters in relevant discussions of specific technical topics such as error control, line sharing, and network design. Here the main concern is to highlight the important general trends that are likely to evolve because of the existence of multiple suppliers of communication services.

The primary effects of these new offerings on the data user and his systems analysis efforts will be threefold:

1. Hitherto unavailable digital data channels or channels into which a binary data stream may be submitted directly are becoming plentiful.

---

[43]Excerpted from *First Report and Order on Docket 18920,* by the Federal Communications Commission, Washington, D.C., adopted May 25, 1971.

Since such channels are designed for the primary purpose of data transmission, they will not require the relatively expensive modems that must be used with contemporary 4 kHz voice channels at speeds of 2000 bits/sec and above. It is also reasonable to expect a fairly wide range of speeds and substantially improved error performance on these new digital data channels. Satellite channels will afford similar speed and error rate improvements.

2. The transmission costs of using these facilities will, in most instances, be substantially lower than those for the best available alternative methods using predecessor carrier facilities.

3. The new specialized and satellite carriers will motivate existing carriers to offer competitive services. Users may expect overall improvements in transmission quality, as well as price reductions, along routes where direct competition becomes a reality.[44]

No attempt is made to consider all the details of these new offerings at this point. Some of the proposed rates are applied to certain network configurations for comparative purposes in subsequent chapters. There the most significant features of the proposed new services are summarized so that the reader may gain an appreciation of the types and costs of carrier facilities most likely to be widely available in the future.

It should be emphasized that large nationwide networks such as those being ultimately planned by MCI and SPCC do not get built overnight. Even though MCI, ITT, and Southern Pacific Communications are currently operational in numerous major U. S. cities, the full scale availability of nationwide service to several hundred major metropolitan areas is still at least several years away.

During 1976, a significant threat to all forms of common carrier competition began to develop in the U. S. Congress. Backed by the Bell System and independent telephone companies, legislation was drafted that would modify the original provisions of the 1934 Communications Act and effectively undo the previously noted specialized carrier decisions of the FCC. This legislation, known as the "Consumer Communications Reform Act," was essentially designed to enlist public support for the elimination of all specialized and satellite carriers and non-Bell communications equipment suppliers on the argument that such competition will ultimately result in higher costs for basic telephone service to the customer.

Bitter and heated debate has already begun. Only time will tell how politically influential and powerful the Bell System can be in influencing

---

[44]For example, the Bell System is currently expanding a new network for data transmission, known as the Dataphone Digital Service (DDS) network. Initial service commenced in 1974. More information about DDS may be found in Reference [37] and in subsequent chapters.

the outcome of this highly controversial legislation. It is safe to say, however, that its passage would turn back the hands of time at least 10 or 15 years. All competitive user choices and options that have become available would ultimately disappear unless the Bell System unilaterally decided to offer such services.

The reader interested in analyzing more fully the regulatory and public policy implications of the specialized common carriers and other competitors of the Bell System is urged to consult References [38] and [39].

1.8.   SYSTEMS DESIGN VARIABLES AND METHODOLOGY

The rest of the book is concerned with the development of systematic procedures whereby efficient, reliable, and cost-effective communications-based computer systems may be designed. A key concept followed throughout the book is that, if the user's requirements and previously cited design constants can be sufficiently quantified at the very first planning step, the design techniques and algorithms presented in subsequent chapters can be used to configure the minimum-cost network that will meet the stipulated performance criteria. Important variables that affect the design procedure are summarized here for the purpose of prefacing their detailed discussion in subsequent chapters. The approach taken in the first part of the book is to examine the important functional characteristics of the key subsystems within a teleprocessing network. After these have been considered, the subject of selecting and interconnecting the basic building blocks is then addressed.

In general, the system designer is free to work with any of the following parameters in configuring a network:

- Type of network organization (centralized or distributed).
- Types of communication services (switched, leased, or combination thereof).
- Line routings.
- Types of terminal equipment used at remote sites.
- Locations and types of communications control procedures.
- Error control procedures and software.

The total design process must recognize the interacting natures of these parameters and all the resulting tradeoffs. The material presented in the rest of the book is sequenced to first define the typical ranges and options of the individual variables listed above, and then address the subject of multivariable design techniques.

Frequently, there will be design situations in which one or more of the above parameters cannot be treated as a variable, for one reason or another. In general, the greater the latitude available to the system designer, the more cost effective will be the eventual implementation. One must usually pay a price for not giving full consideration to all the variables that affect the cost and performance of teleprocessing systems.

REFERENCES

1. D. R. Doll, "Planning Effective Data Communication Systems," *Data Processing Magazine,* Vol. 12, No. 11, November 1970.
2. D. R. Doll, "Data Communications Systems: Basics of Network Design," *Data Communications Systems, Electronics Deskbook,* Vol. 1, No. 1, 1972, McGraw-Hill, New York.
3. J. T. Martin, *Systems Analysis for Data Transmission,* Prentice-Hall, Englewood Cliffs, N. J., 1972.
4. J. T. Martin, *Teleprocessing Network Organization,* Prentice-Hall, Englewood Cliffs, N. J., 1970.
5. P. E. Green, Jr., and R. W. Lucky (Eds.), *Computer Communications,* IEEE Press, New York, 1975.
6. M. N. Perry and W. R. Plugge, "American Airlines SABRE Electronic Reservation System," *AFIPS Conference Proceedings,* Western Joint Computer Conference, No. 19, May 1961.
7. R. R. Everett, C. A. Zraket, and H. D. Benington, "SAGE: A Data Processing System for Air Defense," *Proceedings of Eastern Joint Computer Conference,* 1957.
8. R. M. Fano, "MAC System: The Computer Utility Approach," *IEEE Spectrum,* January 1965.
9. J. H. Morrisey, "The QUICKTRAN System," *Datamation,* February 1965.
10. S. D. Popell et al., *Computer Time Sharing,* Prentice-Hall, Englewood Cliffs, N.J., 1966.
11. L. G. Roberts and B. D. Wessler, "Computer Network Development to Achieve Resource Sharing," *Proceedings of 1970 Spring Joint Computer Conference,* AFIPS Press, 1970.
12. R. Rustin (Ed.), *Computer Networks,* Courant Computer Science Symposium, Prentice-Hall, Englewood Cliffs, N.J., 1970.
13. *The Communications Act of 1934, as Amended*, Title 1, Section 1, U.S. Government Printing Office, Washington, D.C., 1971.
14. *First Report and Order on Docket No. 18920*, Federal Communications Commission, Washington, D.C., adopted May 25, 1971.
15. S. J. Kaplan, "The Advancing Communications Technology and Computer Communications Systems," *AFIPS Conference Proceedings,* Spring Joint Computer Conference, 1969.
16. "Crisis in Data Communications," *Computer Decisions*, November, 1970.
17. J. B. Dennis, "A Position Paper on Computing and Communications," *Communications of the ACM,* Vol. 11, No. 5, May 1968.
18. D. R. Doll, "Topology and Transmission Rate Considerations in the Design of Cen-

tralized Computer–Communication Networks," *IEEE Transactions on Communication Technology*, Vol. COM-19, No. 3, June 1971.

19. D. H. Li, *Design and Management of Information Systems*, Science Research Associates, Palo Alto, Calif., 1972.

20. Description of Systems Used for Data Transmission, *Communications of the ACM*, October 1966, pp. 764–770.

21. "Interface between Data Terminal Equipment and Data Communication Equipment Employing Serial Binary Data Interchange," EIA Standard RS-232-C, Engineering Department, Electronic Industries Association, Washington, D.C., August 1969.

22. D. S. Grubb and I. W. Cotton, "Information Processing System Requirements for Supporting Telecommunications Services," Draft of Working Paper, National Bureau of Standards, Washington, D.C., December 1974.

23. "Determination of Performance of Data Communications Systems," American National Standard X3.44-1974.

24. "Procedures for the Use of Communication Control Characters of the American National Standard Code for Information Interchange in Specified Data Communication Links," American National Standard X3.28-1971.

25. S. L. Mathison and P. M. Walker, *Computers and Telecommunications Issues in Public Policy*, Prentice-Hall, Englewood Cliffs, N.J., 1970.

26. S. L. Mathison and P. M. Walker, "Regulatory and Economic Issues in Computer Communications," *Proceedings of the IEEE*, Vol. 60, November 1972, pp. 1254–1272.

27. S. L. Mathison and P. M. Walker, "Regulatory Policy and Future Data Transmission Services," Chapter 10 in *Computer Communication Networks*, edited by N. Abramson and F. Kuo, Prentice-Hall, Englewood Cliffs, N.J., 1974.

28. S. L. Mathison and P. M. Walker, "Specialized Common Carriers," *Telephone Engineer and Management*, Oct. 15, 1971.

29. B. Gilchrist and M. R. Wessel, *Government Regulation of the Computer Industry*, AFIPS Press, 1972.

30. P. M. Walker, "Regulatory Developments in Data Communications—The Past Five Years," *Proceedings of 1972 Spring Joint Computer Conference*, AFIPS Press, 1972.

31. Arthur Miller, *The Assault on Privacy*, University of Michigan Press, Ann Arbor, 1971.

32. M. Schwartz, R. Boorstyn, and R. Pickholtz, "Terminal-Oriented Computer Communication Networks," *Proceedings of the IEEE*, Vol. 60, November 1972, pp. 1408–1423.

33. F. Kuo and N. Abramson (Eds.), *Computer–Communication Networks*, Prentice-Hall, Englewood Cliffs, N.J., 1974.

34. J. T. Martin, *Future Developments in Telecommunications*, Prentice-Hall, Englewood Cliffs, N.J., 1973.

35. Stanford Research Institute, *Report to the FCC in Docket No. 16979*, February, 1969.

36. A. R. Worley, "The Datran System," *Proceedings of IEEE—Special Issue on Computer Communications*, November, 1972.

37. R. T. James and P. E. Muench, "AT&T Facilities and Services," *Proceedings of IEEE—Special Issue on Computer Communications*, November, 1972.

38. C. R. Cutter, "Beyond the Computer Inquiry," *Proceedings of 1972 International Conference on Computer Communications*, Washington, D. C., October, 1972.

39. U. S. Court of Appeals, Second Circuit, Final Decision on Docket Numbers 71-1300, 71-1484, 72-1486, 72-1566, 72-1578, decided February 1, 1973, New York.

TWO

A MORE DETAILED LOOK AT TYPICAL BUILDING BLOCKS AND NETWORK CONFIGURATIONS

This chapter considers the terminology, economic aspects, and functional characteristics of important data communications devices, techniques, and systems in more detail. It sets the stage for the rest of the book, in which the building blocks are treated first individually and then collectively. The objectives of this chapter are to thoroughly introduce the most prevalent building blocks, outline their purposes and typical application environments, and note their associated performance characteristics.

In subsequent chapters, emphasis shifts to the system level, where practical techniques for planning and configuring networks using these building blocks are considered. These discussions begin with the vital carrier-provided communication links and signal converters required to accomplish data transmission. Approaches to locating network faults and providing backup network facilities are also introduced. Terminals are considered next, followed by a discussion of how line transmission errors can be effectively controlled. Techniques for sharing and accessing lines to reduce costs are presented in the chapters on multiplexing and software. Finally, material from previous topics is combined in a discussion of important network organization alternatives and system design tradeoffs.

2.1. TERMINOLOGY, TYPES OF LINES, AND NETWORK CONFIGURATIONS

The simplest type of data communications application involves an exchange of information between a *source* and *sink* business machine, as shown in Figure 2.1. Business machines (also referred to as *stations*) may generally be either terminal devices of some type (e.g., teletypewriter, CRT, remote batch station, or front-end processor) or computers with appropriate communications interface units. In analog transmission, the *sending modem* or *data set* converts digital information from the source business machine into an electrical form suitable for transmission over the *communication line*. The *receiving modem* converts the signal from the communication line back into the digital format required for assimilation by the sink business machine. As will be seen in Chapter 4 on carrier facilities, the line signal changes continuously on conventional telephone lines designed for voice conversations—hence the term *analog* transmission. *Digital* transmission services, where the line signals are represented as digital pulses, are another alternative becoming more readily available to data transmission users.

Different kinds of communication lines can be used to connect terminals and computers. As shown in Chapter 1, any line that connects a fixed source–sink combination is called a *point-to-point* line. Figure 2.1 shows an example of a point-to-point line. A point-to-point line may be either *switched* (dial-up) or *leased* (dedicated). With a switched line, a common carrier facility like a public telephone network establishes a connection that is maintained only for the duration of a single call. Dedicated or leased lines, on the other hand, provide a permanent communication path

Figure 2.1. Point-to-point data communications configuration.

between business machines, whether active or not. A popular combination arrangement that provides protection from leased line failures is the *leased line with dial backup,* shown in Figure 2.2.

In cases where modems operated over the U. S. public switched network are *not* obtained from a Bell System-affiliated company, a protective device known as the data access arrangement (DAA) has historically been required.[1] Figure 2.2 illustrates the need for two DAAs at each modem–line interface point. This configuration is required because most leased voice-grade lines provided by the common carriers are four-wire circuits, whereas a dial-up connection provides only a two-wire path through the carrier's network. To provide a functionally equivalent backup for this four-wire circuit, two dial-up calls must be made, necessitating a pair of DAAs at each modem site. In some systems, a single dial-up line is used to back up four-wire leased lines. Whenever a single dial-up line is used, the stations will generally not be able to simultaneously send and receive data.[2] Here only one DAA is needed at each end, and the direction of the dial-up line must be reversed whenever the direction of transmission is changed (unless, of course, the special modems noted in footnote 2 are used).

In summary, communication lines are generally provided as either two-wire or four-wire terminations. Most leased lines involve four-wire connections, whereas an individual dial-up connection provides a two-wire path through the carrier's network. The terms *two-wire* and *four-wire* are frequently used interchangeably with the terms *half-duplex* and *full-duplex* carrier facilities, respectively. As shown later in this section, however, the terms are not always equivalent. Although four-wire facilities are always full-duplex facilities, two-wire connections can provide either full- or half-duplex line capability, depending on the type of modem used.

Another type of leased or dedicated line widely used in teleprocessing networks is the *multipoint* line, shown in Figure 2.3. A multipoint line is shared in real time by two or more remote stations. At any instant only one remote station can transmit to the central station; the exact order is prescribed by a *polling list* of stations which are to be queried for pending

---

[1]It was noted in Chapter 1 that this requirement began to be phased out during 1976, when the FCC and various state agencies instituted alternative registration plans to enable non-Bell modem vendors to integrate the necessary protective features directly into the basic modem circuitry.

[2]Special modems can enable one two-wire circuit to provide functionally independent, equal-capacity channels in the send and receive directions. These modems are discussed in more detail in Section 2.3.

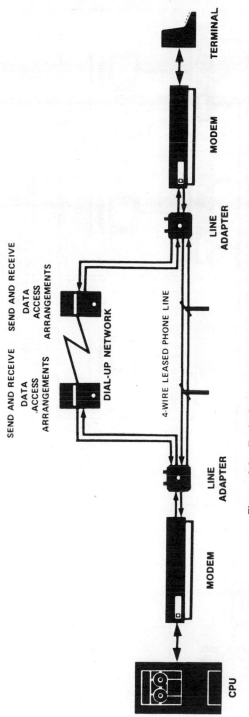

Figure 2.2. Typical point-to-point line with dial-up backup.

SEND AND RECEIVE
DATA
ACCESS
ARRANGEMENTS

SEND AND RECEIVE
DATA
ACCESS
ARRANGEMENTS

DIAL-UP NETWORK

4-WIRE LEASED PHONE LINE

TERMINAL

MODEM

LINE ADAPTER

LINE ADAPTER

MODEM

CPU

53

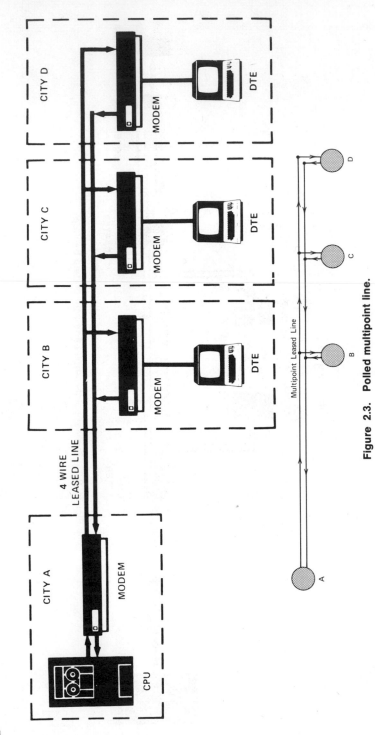

Figure 2.3. Polled multipoint line.

CITY A

CPU

MODEM

4 WIRE
LEASED LINE

CITY B

MODEM

DTE

CITY C

MODEM

DTE

CITY D

MODEM

DTE

Multipoint Leased Line

A   B   C   D

messages. Signals transmitted away from the modem at city A are electrically received at all remote stations; however, only one remote station will be addressed by each message and will actually accept the data. Thus the remote stations take turns on the line, sharing it in much the same fashion as a party-line telephone is used. Other control procedures for accessing multipoint lines are considered in References [1] to [3] and also in Chapter 8. The common carrier generally constructs an analog multipoint line using *analog bridges* located in its central offices to electrically connect intercity facilities with legs out to the customer premises. These bridges tie input and output wire pairs together electrically to provide the flow paths indicated in Figure 2.3.

Additional network configurations are illustrated in Figures 2.4 through 2.6; dial-up backup configurations are not shown, even though they could be employed to increase network availability. Switched-network structures enable multiple locations with modest amounts of traffic to communicate with the central site. A given number of *ports* into the CPU can usually service a larger number of remote dial-up stations, since all remote stations do not need to communicate with the CPU at the same time.[3] Dedicated networks, on the other hand, are used for interactive, fast-response applications where switched-network connection delays, transmission speed restrictions, and higher cost are unacceptable. Dedicated point-to-point lines are used whenever traffic volumes, user response times, or control software will not permit the sharing that multipoint lines can provide. Note that multipoint lines reduce the number of modems required, the number of ports, and usually the line charges in comparison to point-to-point structures. Multipoint networks, however, require more software to control access to these lines.

A configuration involving the use of DAA's and an analog bridging device on the user's premises for dial-up backup of a multipoint line is shown in Figure 2.7. The key feature of this configuration is that no software changes are required, even when the dial-up backup configuration is activated. Whenever a multipoint line failure is sensed, two dial-up connections are established to each remote site beyond the break. Then polling is reestablished, and the stations are again able to communicate. This arrangement necessitates dial-up line costs when activated. This extra expense must be weighed against the cost of not being able to use the affected stations.

Still another type of network configuration becoming popular in con-

---

[3] A *port* is the interface hardware, software, and control logic associated with each independent path or connection into the CPU.

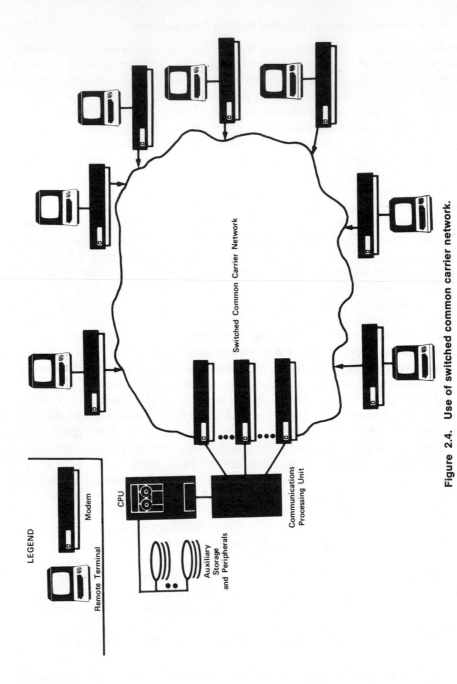

Figure 2.4. Use of switched common carrier network.

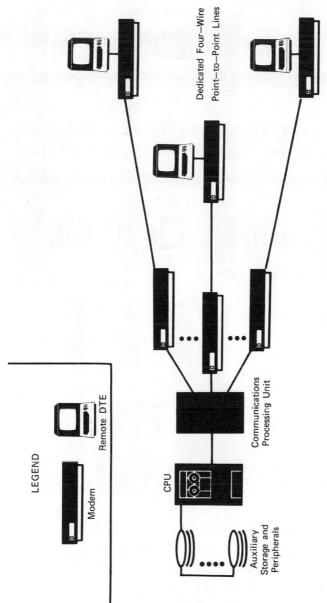

Figure 2.5. A completely point-to-point network.

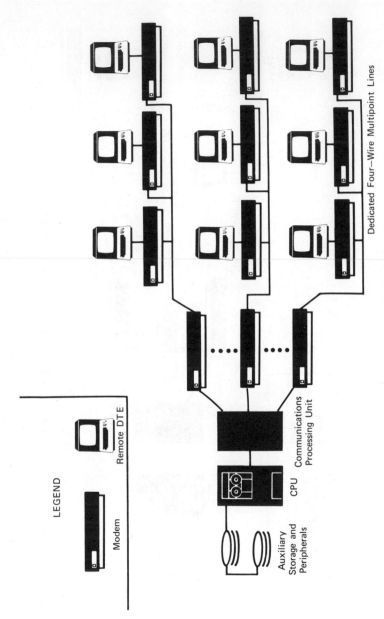

LEGEND

Modem

Remote DTE

Dedicated Four—Wire Multipoint Lines

Communications
Processing Unit

CPU

Auxiliary
Storage and
Peripherals

Figure 2.6. A multipoint network layout.

58

temporary systems is the *loop* arrangement shown in Figure 2.8. The loop network is composed of one-directional links that interconnect the remote stations in circular fashion. Any station may transmit or receive data by accessing the loop, which may be conceptually treated as a continuously circulating "train" of time slots or packets. Access to the loop is controlled in numerous ways discussed in Chapter 8.[4] However, the main characteristic of loops is that the signal must physically pass through the signal converter of each station between the input station and the controller for input traffic. For output traffic, the information must pass through all signal converters at stations between the loop controller and the output station. If one line or node in the serial configuration breaks, the loop is rendered nonfunctional, though bypass lines can be activated, as shown by the dotted lines in Figure 2.8. Another possible reliability enhancement approach is to run the loop back through the same physical location as the loop controller at several intermediate points on the logical loop, as shown in Figure 2.9. If one connection breaks, a new functional loop can be reconstructed at the central point to bypass the facilities deactivated by the failure. Still another possibility is shown in Figure 2.10, where four wires are physically strung between each location on the loop. Only two wires are normally activated for the primary path. However, if any element in the loop configuration becomes nonfunctional, the extra wire pair may be used to temporarily create two smaller loops and restore service.

Loops are useful in limited-distance applications where many individual terminal locations must be connected in a relatively small geographic area (such as a grocery store, a bank, a department store, or an industrial park). Here it might be prohibitively costly to run separate point-to-point or multipoint lines to each remote terminal site. Furthermore, adding new stations or moving existing ones might be very expensive and cumbersome, since it could involve the rewiring of buildings. The flexibility of loops can be highly advantageous in these circumstances. Major disadvantages of loops are their relatively inferior reliability and response time properties when connecting large numbers of terminals at traditional common carrier speeds up to 10,000 bits/sec. Common carrier lines operating at several hundred kilobits/second are prohibitively expensive. For this reason, loops are likely to remain popular, primarily in geographically closed environments not involving a common carrier service. In such applications limited-distance facilities may be used to provide sufficient line capacity at reasonable costs.

[4]For a detailed discussion of loops, see References [4] and [5].

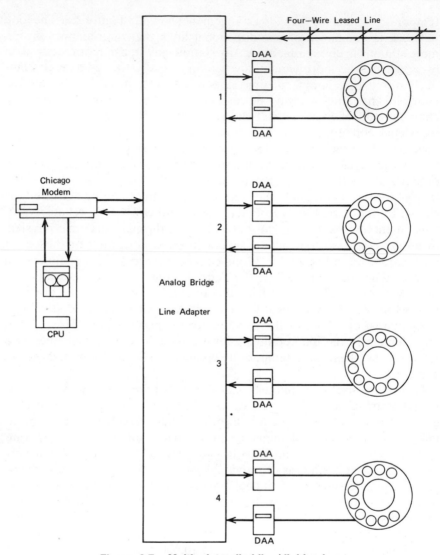

Figure 2.7. Multipoint polled line/dial backup.

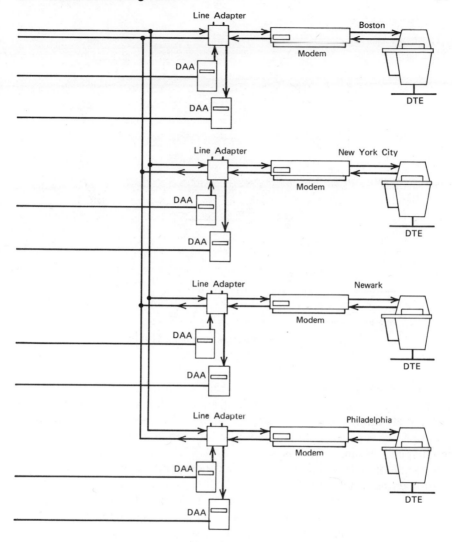

2.2. ADDITIONAL BUILDING BLOCKS

Figures 2.11 through 2.15 illustrate some additional networking concepts and devices known as *split streaming, channel remoting,* and *modem sharing.*

Split-stream modems make it possible to derive multiple, independent paths through a single common carrier line. The advantages are cost

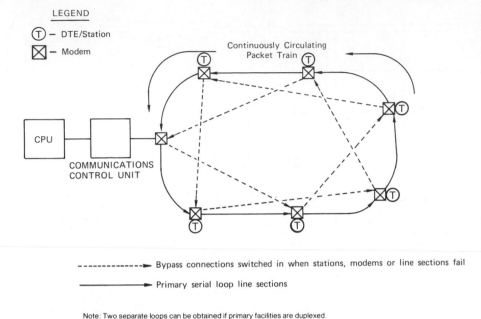

LEGEND

$\bigcirc$ — DTE/Station

$\boxtimes$ — Modem

Continuously Circulating Packet Train

CPU

COMMUNICATIONS CONTROL UNIT

- - - - - - - - - - ▶ Bypass connections switched in when stations, modems or line sections fail

────────────▶ Primary serial loop line sections

Note: Two separate loops can be obtained if primary facilities are duplexed.

Figure 2.8. Making serial loop circuits reliable.

related in that several communication lines can often be replaced with a single higher speed line and split-stream modems. Split streaming is effectively nothing more than using a modem with a built-in time-division multiplexer subsystem to combine the independent streams into a single high speed stream, which is sent over the line. At the receiving end, the independent data streams are reconstructed. More will be said about multiplexing in Chapter 7.

Channel remoting, as shown in Figure 2.13, makes it possible to terminate multipoint or point-to-point lines at remote sites to minimize line costs, yet they can still be controlled from a centrally located polling program (or other appropriate control software). In the configuration of Figure 2.13, costs were reduced by more than 15% from those for the network in which stations were connected into the central CPU site using point-to-point lines for remote batch traffic and multipoint lines for CRT traffic.

A *modem sharing device,* as shown in Figure 2.12, makes it possible to service a group of remote stations using a single modem and a point-to-point line, with the communications controller polling the terminals as

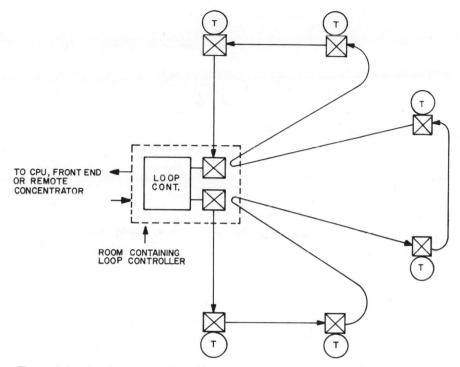

Figure 2.9. Another approach to enhancing loop reliability: passing the links back through the controller periodically.

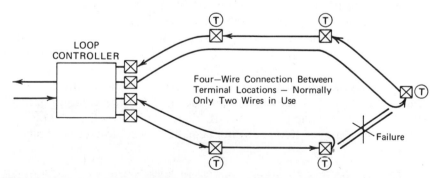

Figure 2.10. Using extra wire pair in four-wire circuit to create two smaller loops if one element in large loop fails.

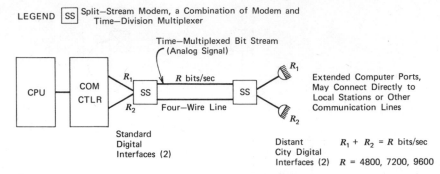

Figure 2.11.   Some additional useful building blocks: split-stream modems.

though they were on a single multipoint line.[5] Also known as a *fan-out feature* on certain modems, the device may be regarded as a *digital bridging mechanism* that enables only one of the remote stations to send data to the CPU at a time; it distributes the data from the central CPU to all remote stations in a broadcast type of operation. Sharing devices may also be used at the central site to minimize the number of ports needed, by treating several point-to-point lines as though they were a single multipoint line. This configuration is shown in Figure 2.15. When used at the central site, the digital bridging device is often referred to as a *port sharing device*. This digital bridging device enables additional stations to be added to a network without expanding the number of ports on the communications controller, assuming that the sharing group can accommoderate new traffic (i.e., no unacceptably large increases in response time will occur because of the new station additions).

The inverse multiplexer configuration of Figure 2.14 is a recent innovation that makes it possible to obtain a four-wire circuit of R bits/sec between two points. A pair of individual four-wire circuits of $R/2$ bits/sec are connected in parallel. This arrangement is useful whenever the communication service directly providing R bits/sec is either too costly, not available at all, or unavailable in a timely fashion. It also has the advantage of built-in redundancy in that the system can be slowed down to $R/2$ bits/sec

[5]Modem-sharing devices are offered by some modem vendors as options. Costs are generally quite modest, typically not exceeding $25 to $50/month for even the most elaborate kinds.

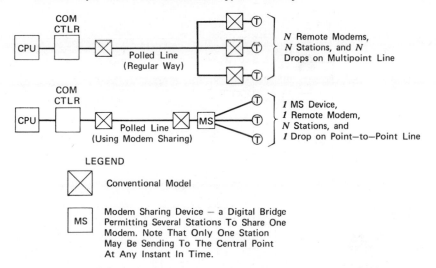

Figure 2.12.   Use of modem sharing device, *N* remote clustered stations.

and still operate if one of the leased circuits fails. Individual dial-up (two-wire) lines may also be used in pairs as an alternative to each four-wire leased line.

2.3.   MODES OF OPERATION CONTRASTED WITH TYPE OF FACILITY

The terms *simplex, half-duplex,* and *full-duplex* may be used to describe (*a*) the mode of station operation over a data link or (*b*) an intrinsic property of a communication line. The terms *two-wire* and *four-wire* refer solely to an intrinsic line property. As shown in Figure 2.16, simplex transmission is a one-way-only mode of using a line. The *simplex mode* of line usage is seldom used in data communication applications because of the almost universal need to exchange data and/or control signals in both directions at one time or another. The *half-duplex mode* of station operation uses a data link in one direction at a time. With this half-duplex data link operation, transmission may be in either direction but not in both directions simultaneously. Note that stations operating in the half-duplex mode may, of course, use either two-wire or four-wire facilities. Also, the common carriers frequently use the term *half-duplex* to describe two-wire facilities and *full-duplex* to describe four-wire facilities. As noted in Fig-

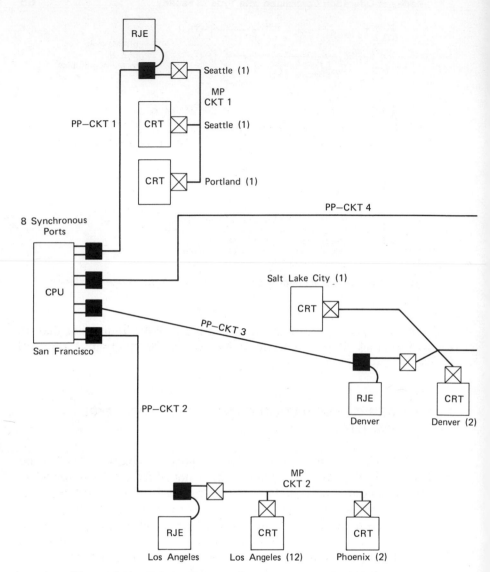

Figure 2.13. Using split-stream modems to reduce line costs.

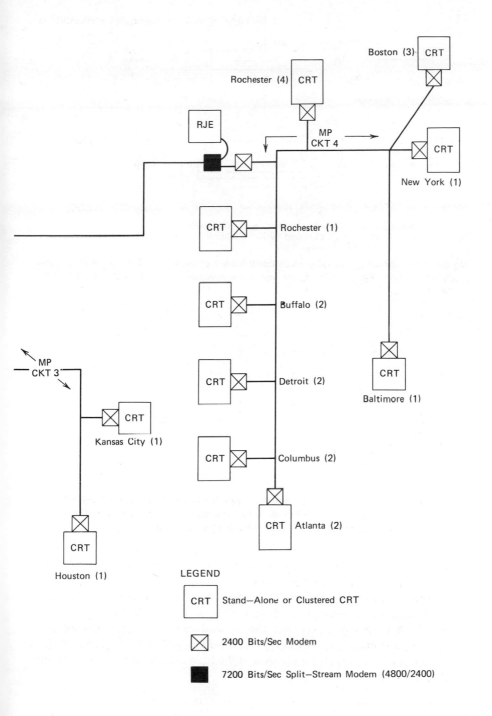

Boston (3)

Rochester (4)

RJE

MP
CKT 4

New York (1)

Rochester (1)

Buffalo (2)

Detroit (2)

Baltimore (1)

MP
CKT 3

Columbus (2)

Kansas City (1)

CRT Atlanta (2)

Houston (1)

LEGEND

CRT   Stand—Alone or Clustered CRT

2400 Bits/Sec Modem

7200 Bits/Sec Split—Stream Modem (4800/2400)

67

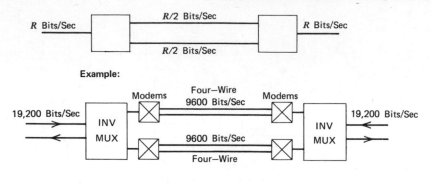

Application: Lower cost way of obtaining 19,200 bits/sec
service than obtaining 19,200 bits/sec lines per
sec in certain situations

**Figure 2.14.   Another recently developed building block: the inverse multiplexer.
Biplexer = Codex Corporation trade name; Lineplexer = Timeplex/ICC Corporation
trade name.**

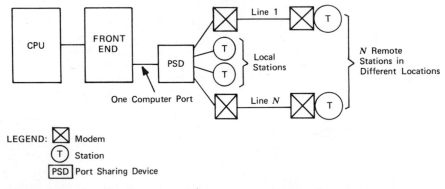

LEGEND: ⊠ Modem
Ⓣ Station
PSD Port Sharing Device

**Figure 2.15.   Using port sharing device at central location. Even though all stations
are connected over separate lines or locally they use a single computer/front-end port
and are polled as though connected to a single multipoint line.**

ure 2.17, it thus becomes possible to operate stations in the half-duplex
mode, using full-duplex communications facilities.

The *full-duplex mode* of station operation involves usage of a data link
for simultaneous transmission in both directions. On the time profiles of
Figure 2.18 it can be seen that the shaded areas for the forward and
reverse directions never overlap with half-duplex usage. With full-duplex
usage, on the contrary, transmission in the forward and reverse directions
definitely occurs simultaneously.[6]

[6]See Reference [7] for further discussions of these terms and concepts.

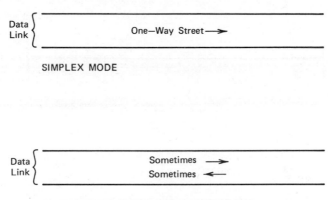

SIMPLEX MODE

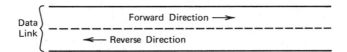

HALF—DUPLEX MODE (NEVER BOTH WAYS
SIMULTANEOUSLY)

Data Link {
Forward Direction ——➤
Reverse Direction ◄——

FULL—DUPLEX MODE (UTILIZED IN BOTH DIRECTIONS
SIMULTANEOUSLY)

Figure 2.16. Modes of data link operation.

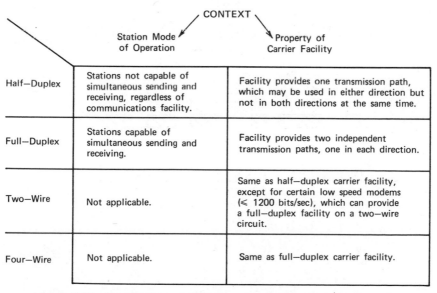

| | CONTEXT | |
	Station Mode of Operation	Property of Carrier Facility
Half—Duplex	Stations not capable of simultaneous sending and receiving, regardless of communications facility.	Facility provides one transmission path, which may be used in either direction but not in both directions at the same time.
Full—Duplex	Stations capable of simultaneous sending and receiving.	Facility provides two independent transmission paths, one in each direction.
Two—Wire	Not applicable.	Same as half—duplex carrier facility, except for certain low speed modems ($\leq$ 1200 bits/sec), which can provide a full—duplex facility on a two—wire circuit.
Four—Wire	Not applicable.	Same as full—duplex carrier facility.

Figure 2.17. Terminology: half-duplex, full-duplex, two-wire, four-wire.

69

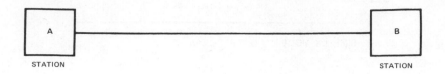

STATION   STATION

SIMPLEX AB

• DATA NEVER TRANSMITTED
FROM B TO A

SIMPLEX BA

• DATA NEVER TRANSMITTED
FROM A TO B

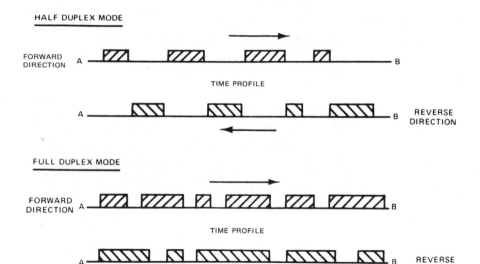

Figure 2.18. Different modes of using point-to-point line.

Until recently, most stations in the marketplace operated only in the half-duplex mode, using both half-duplex and full-duplex types of facilities. With the advent of advanced line control procedures such as Synchronous Data Link Control (SDLC), discussed in Chapter 8, an extensive switch to the use of full-duplex line operation may be expected. As noted in Reference [7], send and receive tasks for the communications line do not have to be serialized. Full-duplex data link usage enables parallel processing of send and receive tasks on the data link, thereby increasing the amount of work that can be done in a given period of time. This feature is regarded by many as the single most important advantage of the new full-duplex protocols.

It should also be noted that many of the newer line control procedures enable *half-duplex* stations to use multipoint lines in a *restricted full-duplex* mode where simultaneous sending and receiving are permitted, but only if different remote stations are involved in the concurrent activity. In Reference 7, for example, IBM refers to this operation as *multimultipoint* mode of line usage.

The distinction between mode of usage and type of facility is now complete. To have a true full-duplex data link usage, two *independent transmission* paths must be provided by a communication line. Since a pair of electrical conductors (two wires) is required for each voice-grade transmission path through the carrier network, only four-wire circuits are capable of operating in both directions simultaneously, unless special modems are used. Thus leased lines (which are usually four-wire) are uniquely *capable* of supporting the true full-duplex mode, although they can equally well be operated in a half-duplex mode (and often are). To obtain full-duplex data link usage capability at voice-grade speeds over a dial-up network generally requires that a pair of connections be established, as was shown in Figure 2.2. Dial-up connections are usually made over two-wire circuits, and each one is capable of supporting only the simplex or half-duplex mode at speeds exceeding 2000 bits/sec. Leased voice-grade lines are usually four-wire and hence may be operated in either the simplex, half-duplex, or full-duplex mode. It should be noted in passing that, at slower transmission rates of 1200 bits/sec and less, modems can easily be designed to support true full-duplex transmission over a two-wire or dial-up connection; however, this has not been a very common application situation until recently.[7] This technique is discussed in more detail in Chapter 4.

[7]The Vadic Corporation of Mountain View, California, pioneered this application by developing a modem that provides a full-duplex carrier facility at 1200 bits/sec over a single dial-up connection.

2.4. SYNCHRONOUS AND ASYNCHRONOUS TRANSMISSION, SIGNALING RATES

Data are usually transmitted between modems in bit-serial fashion; however, in some slower speed situations, the individual bits of a data character are transmitted in parallel, using independent subchannels created by the sending modem. Bit-serial transmission may be either start/stop (asynchronous) or synchronous (clocked). Most applications up through 1200 bits/sec use the asynchronous method, in which the data bits of each character are preceded and followed by special start and stop bit sequences. As shown in Figures 2.19 and 2.20, these special patterns separate characters and assure that the receiving terminal is properly synchronized with the sending terminal. Since transmission may take place at any instant in time, this type of transmission is not governed by a clock. Synchronous transmission, on the other hand, is usually employed for applications involving speeds of 2000 bits/sec and higher. Here a constant rate clock (usually in the modem) determines the exact time instant at which bits are sent and received, eliminating the need for the special start and stop bit sequences associated with asynchronous transmission. Synchronous transmission is thus more efficient in utilizing a given amount of available line capacity than is asynchronous or parallel transmission. Figure 2.21 illustrates the differences between line signaling rate (baud

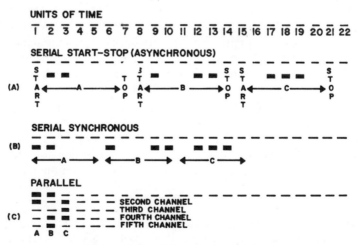

Figure 2.19.   Transmission modes.

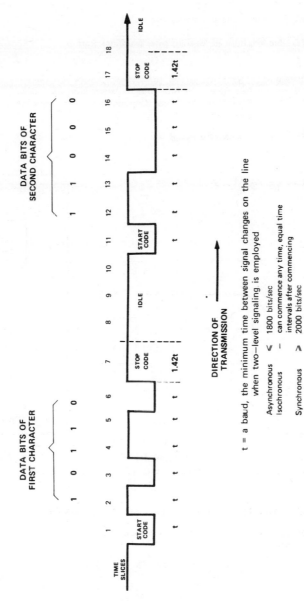

Figure 2.20. Asynchronous transmission of Baudot coded characters (five bits).

BAUD RATE = Rate of Signal Transitions on Line

BIT RATE = Modem/Business Machine Interface Clock Rate

Transfer Rate
of Information
Bits (TRIB)   =   Net Rate Info Bits Are Transferred Between Data
                      Source and Data Sink, Considering Control Signaling
                      Overhead

BIT RATE = Baud Rate X No Bits/Baud

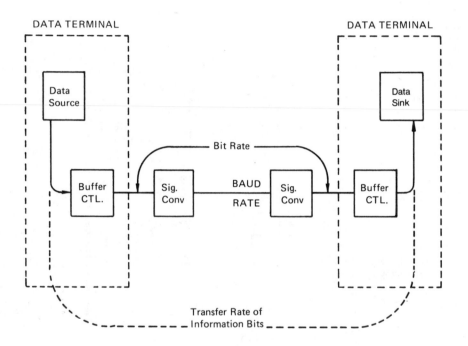

No. Bits Per Baud = $\log_2$ (No. Discrete Signal Levels Which Can Be Sent)

Example: Assume 1200 Bauds/Sec and 4 Phase Modem
           Bit Rate = 1200 $\log_2$ (4) = 2400 Bits/Sec

Figure 2.21.   Bits, bauds, and TRIB.

rate), modem clocking rate to business machines (bit rate), and net data transfer rate (Transfer Rate of Information Bits). More is said about these points in Chapter 6 and in Reference [6].

2.5. RECAPITULATION

The introductory discussions having been completed, the focus has now shifted to the individual subsystems. The checklist below provides a perspective for remaining chapters by summarizing the key building blocks available to the user in configuring efficient, reliable networks:

- Carrier-provided links.
- Modems.
- Terminals.
- Multiplexers, concentrators.
- Communications preprocessors.
- Teleprocessing software.
- Error control devices, techniques.
- Network management, diagnostic aids.

Subsequent discussions consider each of these topics, as well as the higher level issues of how to select and interconnect the subsystems in a manner that guarantees a smoothly operating, cost-effective data communications network.

REFERENCES

1. J. Martin, *Introduction to Teleprocessing*, Prentice-Hall, Englewood Cliffs, N. J., 1972.
2. J. P. Gray, "Line Control Procedures," *Proceedings of the IEEE*, November 1972.
3. W. P. Davenport, *Modern Data Communications*, Hayden Book Co., New York, 1971.
4. L. P. West, "Loop Transmission Control Structures," *IEEE Transactions on Communications*, Vol. COM-20, June 1972, Part II.
5. J. R. Pierce, "How Far Can Data Loops Go?" *IEEE Transactions on Communications*, Vol. COM-20, June 1972, Part II.
6. J. Martin, *Telecommunications and the Computer*, 2nd ed., Prentice-Hall, Englewood Cliffs, N. J., 1976.
7. *IBM Synchronous Data Link Control: General Information*, IBM Publication GA27-3093, IBM Corp., March 1974.

THREE

COMMON CARRIER
SERVICES, TARIFFS

The communications services offered by the common carriers have recently been going through a period of unprecedented change. These developments have upturned the pricing structures for virtually every major offering available 5 years ago and simultaneously spawned numerous additional offerings to be discussed in this chapter. It should be recognized that the material presented herein is illustrative of the options available at publication time. Since pricing structures and other aspects of the tariffs that govern these services are continually being revised by the common carriers, the reader is urged to verify that the numbers are current before using them in any design or pricing calculations.

Some may even question why this material is included in such detail, given the likelihood of continuing change in the foreseeable future. This author felt that a comprehensive discussion of the major options would be a useful contribution for the practicing professional as well as the individual seeking a broad overview of the available alternatives. This discussion also serves to highlight the major voids of the mid-1970s marketplace—for example, nationwide switched digital services and all types of services in the speed ranges above 230,400 bits/sec.

The chapter highlights the features of conventional offerings and the recently established specialized common carrier services, satellite services, and value-added services based on packet switching technology. Although most of the services currently available employ analog transmission (see Chapter 4 on transmission facilities), a few new offerings such as the Bell System's Dataphone Digital Service and the one formerly offered by Datran employ digital transmission techniques. It is obvious that digital transmission-based services are becoming a major new category of alternative for users, even though their availability is still relatively limited.

3.1. OVERVIEW OF SERVICES

From a practical point of view, the most critical components in typical networks are the communication links and attached signal converters. On analog lines the operating speed (transmission rate) is governed jointly by the type of link chosen and the particular modems used with that link. Data transmission over voice-grade telephone lines more than a few hundred feet in length usually requires modems, as is discussed at length in the next two chapters. The *links* used in most networks are provided by the *common carriers,* but *modems* may be obtained from either the *carriers* or a variety of *independent companies.* The features and costs of modems depend on the desired operating speed and other application-oriented requirements. Carrier-provided links are generally classified as being *switched* (dial-up) or *leased* (dedicated). Within these two major classifications, different *grades of service* are available. Each grade of analog service generally is associated with a *bandwidth* that permits certain ranges of transmission speed to be accomplished. Usually the network designer will choose one of *three categories of analog channels* provided by the carriers—either *sub-voice-grade, voice-grade,* or *wideband* (broadband). The actual operating speed of a communication link

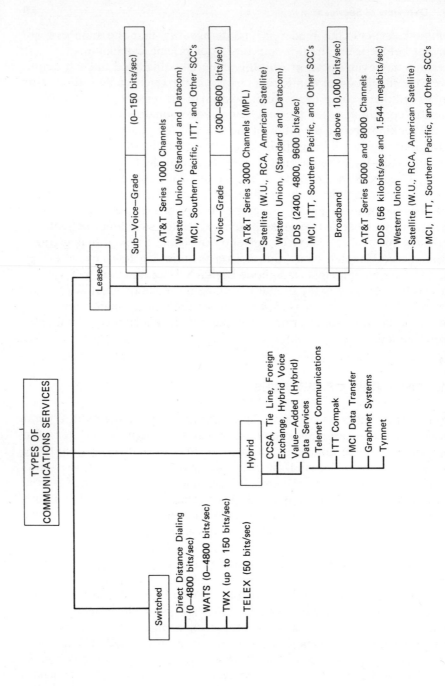

Figure 3.1. Types of communications services.

will depend ultimately on the type of modem used, once the basic grade of line has been selected. With digital transmission services, however, the user will not deal with bandwidth categories and analog modems; rather he will select a transmission rate for the digital service directly. Figure 3.1 illustrates the major classifications of services generally available in the United States today. The subsequent tables, charts, and discussion of this chapter consider the specific details of the services noted in Figure 3.1.

Throughout the book a distinction between services and facilities is emphasized. Since the constituency of the common carrier plant is extremely complex, there is never any way to know precisely what the physical and electrical properties of specific facilities (transmission channels) will be from one geographic area to another or, for that matter, from one point in time to another on the same facility. The main characteristics of services are *cost, gross transmission properties* (e.g., bandwidth or bit rate), *availability,* and *rules for usage* thereof. A service is thus a logical concept, whereas a facility is more nearly a physical entity. Chapter 3 emphasizes services, whereas Chapter 4 considers the physical properties of facilities that affect data transmission. It is never possible to completely separate the two notions. However, it is important to realize the above-mentioned major distinctions between a service and a facility.

3.2. SWITCHED OR DIAL-UP SERVICES, DDD AND WATS

Here we discuss the domestic services offered by AT&T for the use of its public switched network. Two basic rate plans are available: pay-as-you-go (direct distance dialing or DDD) usage or the blanket types of tariffs such as Wide Area Telecommunication Service (WATS). Both services are available on an intrastate or interstate basis and virtually always involve point-to-point, two-wire connections. With current technology, the maximum transmission properties of the DDD network are highly variable from one connection to the next. Finally, a dial-up call may take anywhere from 15 to 30 sec to establish. The important technical and application characteristics of switched network connections are summarized in Table 3.1.

3.2.1. Rates for Interstate Direct Distance Dial Network Usage

Table 3.2 summarizes the charges for using the U. S. public switched network on an interstate pay-as-you-go basis. The data are abstracted from AT&T's FCC Tariff 263, which covers long distance Message

Table 3.1.   Technical Aspects of Using the Dial-Up Network for Data Transmission

Less stable transmission parameters than private (leased) lines.
Different calls usually experience different transmission conditions.
Line conditioning unavailable.
Maximum rate of 4800 bits/sec.
Two-wire connections only.
Point-to-point connections only.
Up to 15 to 30 sec delay to establish connection.
Network signaling generally present.

Telecommunications Service. (These rates do not include any required telephone sets, modems, protective couplers, or end-terminal equipment.)

Rate mileages are computed using the airline distances between billing rate centers published by the common carriers. Rate centers are spelled out in FCC Tariff 255, where every entry has an associated four-digit V and H coordinate value [1]. Currently there are approximately 30,000 rate centers in the United States.

A common problem in system planning is obtaining the correct V and H coordinate values to use in pricing estimates. Coordinates may be obtained from the carrier or from FCC Tariff 255.

Example Problem: DDD Costs

Estimate the monthly transmission cost of using the DDD network for 1 hour/day to transmit batched data between a remote terminal in Chicago and a central computer in New York City.

Solution. The distance between the locations is slightly more than 700 miles. From Table 3.2 transmission costs for dial-up station-to-station calls are $0.50 for the first minute and $0.34/min thereafter. To simplify the computation, use only the cost per additional minute. (This is reasonable as long as the call holding times are several minutes or more.) Also, assume 22 business days per month.

Estimated monthly cost (daytime rate)   = (0.34)(60)(22)   = $448.80
Estimated monthly cost (evening rate)   = (0.221)(60)(22) = $291.72
Estimated monthly cost (nighttime rate) = (0.136)(60)(22) = $179.52

	Daytime rate	Evening rate	Nighttime rate
Cost/hour	$20.40	$13.26	$8.16

3.2.2. WATS Service—Interstate

Wide Area Telecommunications Service (WATS) is a bulk rate plan that allows customers to make multiple calls into or out of (but not both) a particular location for established monthly rates. Full business day WATS provides for up to 240 hours of monthly usage (or 14,400 calls, whichever comes first) at a fixed rate. Additional usage beyond 14,400 calls or 240 hours/month involves charges at approximately two thirds of the equivalent hourly rate for the initial period. The mid-1976 tariff provisions stipulate that each call automatically utilizes 1 minute of connect time against the monthly 240 hour quota; thus the maximum number of calls that can ever be placed in 240 hours without incurring the surcharge is 60 calls/hour $\times$ 240 = 14,440.

Measured time WATS establishes a minimum 10 hour usage period for a fixed price, with each additional hour being charged on a per hour basis. Interstate WATS is restricted to calls made between points in different states; intrastate WATS must be used between calling points in the same state. Intrastate WATS is available in most parts of the United States. However, prices for such offerings vary widely and are not considered here.

The interstate WATS tariff (Figure 3.2.) partitions the country into five progressively larger bands or territories, which can be described crudely as concentric circles with their common center at the location of the WATS line. The Band 1 region generally includes all adjacent states, and the Band 5 region encompasses the 48 contiguous states in the United States. Bands are organized so that the region associated with a particular WATS band includes all territory associated with lower numbered bands. For example, Band 3 territory includes all territory associated with Bands 1 and 2. Similarly Band 5 territory includes all territory associated with Bands 1 to 4. The numbers from 1 to 5 within a row in Figure 3.3 indicate the WATS band required to service the state at the top of the column. Once the required band is determined, monthly rates for full business day and measured time service can be obtained from Table 3.3. For example, to reach Wyoming from an Arizona WATS line, a Band 2 line is required. During mid-1976, full business day service cost $1630/month, whereas the first 10 hours of measured time service cost $236/month, for this example.

It can be seen from the rate information given above that, when monthly measured time usage approaches 70 to 80 hours, the breakeven point for fulltime WATS service is approached. The carriers have no obligation to inform a measured time customer that full-time service might be more economical or to suggest that he convert. These planning and control activities are strictly up to the user. It should also be noted that

Table 3.2. Interstate Dial-Up Rates (Tariff 263), September 1976

	Sat.	Sun.	Mon.	Tues.	Wed.	Thurs.	Fri.
8:00 A.M. TO 5:00 P.M.				Day rate			
5:00 P.M. TO 11:00 P.M.		Evening rate					
11:00 P.M. TO 8:00 A.M.	Weekend and night rate						

Operator-Assisted Calls
Interstate (Except Hawaii and Alaska)

	Initial 3 Min		Additional Min		
Rate Mileage	Station to Station	Person to Person	Day Rate	Evening Rate [a]	Night and Weekend [b]
1–10	$0.45	$1.45	$0.08	$0.052	$0.032
11–16	0.60	1.60	0.11	0.0712	0.044
17–22	0.80	1.80	0.13	0.0845	0.052
23–30	1.00	2.00	0.17	0.1105	0.068
31–40	1.10	2.10	0.20	0.13	0.08
41–55	1.35	2.35	0.24	0.156	0.096
56–70	1.60	2.60	0.26	0.169	0.104
71–124	1.75	2.75	0.28	0.182	0.112
125–196	1.85	2.85	0.29	0.1885	0.116
197–292	1.95	2.95	0.31	0.2015	0.124
293–430	2.00	3.05	0.33	0.2145	0.132
431–925	2.05	3.15	0.34	0.221	0.136
926–1910	2.15	3.30	0.36	0.234	0.144
1911–3000	2.25	3.55	0.38	0.247	0.152

Table 3.2. *(Continued)*

Dial Station to Station
Interstate (Except Hawaii and Alaska)

Rate Milage	Day Initial 1 Min	Day Additional 1 Min	Evening[a] Initial 1 Min	Evening[a] Additional 1 Min	Night and Weekend[b] Initial 1 Min	Night and Weekend[b] Additional 1 Min
1–10	$0.19	$0.08	$0.1235	$0.052	$0.076	$0.032
11–16	0.23	0.11	0.1495	0.0712	0.092	0.044
17–22	0.27	0.13	0.1755	0.0845	0.108	0.052
23–30	0.31	0.17	0.2015	0.1105	0.124	0.068
31–40	0.35	0.20	0.2275	0.13	0.14	0.08
41–55	0.39	0.24	0.2535	0.156	0.156	0.096
56–70	0.41	0.26	0.2665	0.169	0.164	0.104
71–124	0.43	0.28	0.2795	0.182	0.172	0.112
125–196	0.44	0.29	0.286	0.1885	0.176	0.116
197–292	0.46	0.31	0.299	0.2015	0.184	0.124
293–430	0.48	0.33	0.312	0.2145	0.192	0.132
431–925	0.50	0.34	0.325	0.221	0.20	0.136
926–1910	0.52	0.36	0.338	0.234	0.208	0.144
1911–3000	0.54	0.38	0.351	0.247	0.216	0.152

[a]Evening rates are calculated as 65% of the day rate.
[b]Weekend and night rates are calculated as 40% of the day rate.

WATS service provides only one line out of a service location, and if undesirable busy signals cannot be controlled or tolerated, multiple lines may be required.

From a technical standpoint, WATS service is identical to that obtained by using the DDD network on a pay-as-you-go basis. Any allegation that WATS service has data transmission properties *different* from those of plain long distance service is *technically erroneous* because WATS lines use the switched facilities of the DDD network—the only ostensible difference between the services lies in the rate structures for this usage of the public telephone network. Occasionally, the user may notice slight differences between DDD and WATS because WATS lines may utilize different telephone company central offices.

Example Problem: WATS Costs

Assume that a business in New York City employs a WATS line to connect multiple remote locations, all in the Band 3 service area, to its

Table 3.3 Interstate WATS Rates in Effect, 1976 and 1977

RATES:

The monthly charge for Interstate WATS is a combination of the initial period rate and applicable overtime rate. Calls are metered and time accumulated in 6 sec (0.1 min) increments, with any fraction counting as a full increment. Overtime is billed in 0.1 hour (6 min) units. Charges below are per access line, inward or outward.

SERVICE AREA (BAND)

STATE	1	2	3	4	5	STATE	1	2	3	4	5
Alabama	D	G	I	K	P	Nevada	D	H	L	P	R
Arizona	F	I	K	O	R	New Hampshire	B	F	J	N	R
Arkansas	D	G	I	K	N	New Jersey	A	C	I	M	R
California No.	G	J	N	P	R	New Mexico	F	H	J	M	P
California So.	H	K	N	P	R	New York N.E.	C	G	I	M	R
Colorado	G	H	I	K	P	New York S.E.	A	F	I	M	R
Connecticut	A	D	J	N	R	New York West	C	E	I	M	R
Delaware	A	D	H	L	R	North Carolina	D	F	H	K	R
Dist. of Columbia	A	D	G	K	R	North Dakota	E	I	K	M	O
Florida	G	J	K	M	R	Ohio No.	C	E	G	I	P
Georgia	D	G	I	K	P	Ohio So.	C	E	G	I	P
Idaho	E	H	K	O	R	Oklahoma	E	G	I	K	N
Illinois No.	C	E	H	J	N	Oregon	E	I	N	P	R
Illinois So.	C	F	H	J	N	Pennsylvania E.	A	D	H	K	R
Indiana	C	E	G	I	P	Pennsylvania W.	C	D	H	K	R
Iowa	D	G	H	K	N	Rhode Island	A	E	J	N	R
Kansas	E	G	H	K	N	South Carolina	D	G	I	K	P
Kentucky	C	E	G	I	P	South Dakota	E	H	I	L	N
Louisiana	E	H	J	L	O	Tennessee	E	F	H	J	P
Maine	E	H	L	O	R	Texas E.	F	I	K	M	P
Maryland	A	D	H	L	R	Texas So.	H	J	K	M	P
Massachusetts	A	E	J	N	R	Texas W.	G	I	K	M	P
Michigan No.	E	H	I	J	P	Utah	F	G	J	N	P
Michigan So.	D	G	H	J	P	Vermont	B	F	J	N	R
Minnesota	D	G	J	L	N	Virginia	C	D	G	K	R
Mississippi	E	G	I	K	O	Washington	H	K	N	P	R
Missouri	E	F	H	J	N	West Virginia	B	D	G	J	P
Montana	G	I	K	N	P	Wisconsin	C	G	I	K	O
Nebraska	E	G	I	K	N	Wyoming	E	H	J	L	P

Table 3.3. *(Continued)*

RATE TABLE

	Measured Time		Approximate	Full Business Day	
	Initial 10 Hours	Over- Time	Hours for Breakeven	Initial 240 Hours	Over- Time
A	$196.00	$14.70	58	$ 900.00	$2.50
B	207.00	15.53	66	1075.00	2.98
C	214.00	16.05	68	1150.00	3.19
D	219.00	16.43	77	1315.00	3.65
E	224.00	16.80	80	1400.00	3.89
F	226.00	16.95	85	1500.00	4.16
G	230.00	17.25	88	1570.00	4.36
H	234.00	17.55	88	1610.00	4.47
I	236.00	17.70	89	1630.00	4.52
J	238.00	17.85	89	1640.00	4.55
K	239.00	17.93	88	1645.00	4.56
L	240.00	18.00	88	1650.00	4.58
M	241.00	18.08	88	1655.00	4.59
N	242.00	18.15	88	1660.00	4.61
O	243.00	18.23	88	1665.00	4.62
P	244.00	18.31	88	1670.00	4.63
R	245.00	18.38	88	1675.00	4.65

central computer. Transmission volumes are such that between 2 and 4 hours of daily usage are anticipated. Compute estimated line charges, using measured time and full business day service. Again assume 22 days per month.

Measured time cost for 2 hours/day = 236.00 + (44 − 10)(17.70) − 837.80

	2 Hours/ Day	3 Hours/ Day	4 Hours/ Day
Measured time total cost	$ 837.80	$1227.20	$1616.60
Measured time cost/hour	19.04	18.59	18.37
Full business day service total cost	1630.00	1630.00	1630.00
Full business day service cost/hour	37.04	24.70	18.52

3.3. OTHER SWITCHED SERVICES

The other two switched services to be summarized are provided by the Western Union Telegraph Company for the transmission of record com-

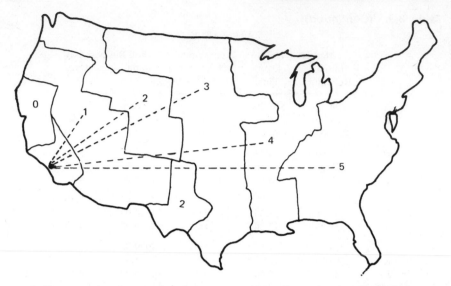

1. Charges are based on the size of the area to which calls are placed, or from which calls are received.

2. Subscribers are billed according to the zones to be called on a full business day or measured-time basis, or from which calls are received on a full business day or measured-time basis.

3. Available on Interstate and Intrastate basis. Need both types for complete nationwide coverage.

Figure 3.2. Major features of interstate WATS.

munications between special types of terminals at certain speed rates (in characters/second). Whereas TWX service is available on a straight interstate basis, TELEX service is billed according to rate areas; each rate area generally includes several states.

TWX service permits a subscriber with a certain type of teletypewriter to dial up or to be dialed by other TWX stations and to transmit data at speeds up to 150 bits/sec. Customers may either obtain terminals from Western Union or provide their own, subject to certain compatibility restrictions. Since the carrier does not always provide the terminals, all TWX stations cannot communicate directly. Charges for using the TWX network are based on time and distance factors. Representative TWX usage rates are shown in Figure 3.4.

TELEX is a switched data service that operates at 66 words/min (50 bits/sec), using a five-bit Baudot code. Terminals are provided only by the carrier (Western Union in the United States) and may all communicate

INTERSTATE SERVICE AREA (BANDS) *— ALABAMA — NEBRASKA

LOCATION OF ACCESS LINE	ALA	ARIZ	ARK	CALIF(N)	CALIF(S)	COLO	CONN	DEL	D.C.	FLA	GA	IDAHO	ILL(N)	ILL(S)	IND	IOWA	KAN	KY	LA	ME	MD	MASS	MICH(N)	MICH(S)	MINN	MISS	MO	MONT	NEBR
ALA	#	5	2	5	5	5	5	4	3	1	1	5	3	2	2	3	4	1	1	5	3	5	4	4	5	1	2	5	5
ARIZ	4	#	4	2	1	1	5	5	5	5	5	3	4	4	5	4	3	5	4	5	5	5	5	5	4	4	4	3	3
ARK	2	5	#	5	5	4	5	5	4	3	3	5	2	2	3	3	2	2	1	5	5	5	4	4	4	1	1	5	3
CALIF(N)	5	2	4	#	#	2	5	5	5	5	5	1	4	4	4	3	3	5	4	5	5	5	4	4	4	4	4	2	3
CALIF(S)	5	1	4	#	#	2	5	5	5	5	5	2	4	4	4	3	3	5	4	5	5	5	4	4	4	4	4	3	3
COLO	5	1	3	4	4	#	5	5	5	5	5	3	4	4	4	3	1	5	4	5	5	5	5	5	3	4	3	2	1
CONN	4	5	4	5	5	5	#	2	2	4	3	5	3	3	3	4	4	3	4	2	2	1	3	3	4	4	5	5	4
DEL	4	5	4	5	5	5	2	#	1	4	3	5	3	3	3	4	4	3	4	3	1	2	3	3	4	4	4	5	5
D.C.	4	5	4	5	5	5	2	1	#	4	3	5	3	3	3	4	4	3	4	3	1	3	3	3	4	4	4	5	5
FLA	1	5	2	5	5	5	4	2	2	#	1	5	3	3	2	4	5	2	1	5	2	4	4	4	5	1	3	5	5
GA	1	5	2	5	5	5	4	3	3	1	#	5	3	2	2	4	5	1	2	5	3	4	3	3	5	1	3	5	5
IDAHO	5	3	4	2	3	2	5	5	5	5	5	#	4	4	5	3	3	5	5	5	5	5	4	4	3	5	4	1	3
ILL(N)	3	5	3	5	5	5	5	4	4	5	3	5	#	#	1	1	3	2	4	5	4	5	2	1	2	3	2	5	3
ILL(S)	3	5	2	5	5	5	5	4	4	5	3	5	#	#	1	1	3	1	4	5	4	5	3	2	3	2	1	5	3
IND	3	5	3	5	5	5	4	3	3	5	3	5	1	1	#	3	4	1	4	5	3	4	3	1	4	3	2	5	4
IOWA	3	5	3	5	5	3	5	5	5	5	4	5	1	1	2	#	2	3	4	5	5	5	2	2	1	3	1	4	1
KAN	4	4	2	5	5	1	5	5	5	5	4	4	3	3	3	1	#	4	3	5	5	5	4	4	3	3	1	4	1
KY	2	5	3	5	5	5	4	3	3	4	2	5	2	1	1	3	4	#	3	5	3	4	3	3	4	3	1	5	4
LA	1	5	1	5	5	4	5	5	4	3	2	5	3	2	3	3	3	2	#	5	4	5	4	4	4	1	2	5	3
ME	4	5	4	5	5	5	1	2	2	4	4	5	3	3	3	4	5	3	5	#	2	1	3	3	4	4	4	5	4
MD	4	5	4	5	5	5	2	1	1	4	3	5	3	3	3	4	4	3	4	3	#	3	3	3	4	4	4	5	5
MASS	4	5	4	5	5	5	1	2	2	4	3	5	3	3	3	4	4	3	4	2	2	#	3	3	4	4	4	5	5
MICH(N)	4	5	4	5	5	5	3	3	3	5	4	5	1	2	2	1	4	3	5	4	3	3	#	#	1	4	2	5	4
MICH(S)	4	5	4	5	5	5	3	3	3	5	4	5	1	2	1	2	4	2	5	4	3	4	#	#	3	4	3	5	4
MINN	4	5	3	5	5	3	5	5	4	5	5	4	2	2	3	1	2	3	5	5	5	5	1	2	#	4	2	3	1
MISS	1	5	1	5	5	5	5	4	4	2	1	5	3	2	3	3	3	2	1	5	4	5	4	4	4	#	2	5	4
MO	3	5	1	5	5	1	5	5	5	5	4	5	1	1	2	1	1	1	3	5	4	5	3	3	3	2	#	5	1
MONT	5	3	4	3	3	2	5	5	5	5	5	1	4	4	5	3	3	5	5	5	5	5	4	4	2	5	4	#	2
NEB	4	4	3	5	5	1	5	5	5	5	5	4	3	3	3	1	1	4	4	5	5	5	4	4	2	4	1	3	#
NEV	5	1	4	1	1	3	5	5	5	5	5	1	4	4	4	5	3	5	4	5	5	5	5	5	4	4	4	3	3
N.H.	4	5	4	5	5	5	1	2	2	4	4	5	3	3	3	4	5	3	4	1	2	1	3	3	4	4	4	5	5
N.J.	4	5	4	5	5	5	1	1	1	4	3	5	3	3	3	4	4	3	4	3	1	2	3	3	4	4	4	5	5
N.M.	4	1	3	3	3	1	5	5	5	5	5	3	4	4	5	3	2	5	3	5	5	5	5	5	4	4	3	4	2
N.Y.(NE)	4	5	4	5	5	5	1	2	2	4	3	5	3	3	3	4	4	3	4	2	2	1	3	3	4	4	4	5	4
N.Y.(SE)	4	5	4	5	5	5	1	1	2	4	3	5	3	3	3	4	4	3	4	2	2	1	3	3	4	4	4	5	4
N.Y.(W)	4	5	4	5	5	5	2	2	1	4	3	5	3	3	3	4	4	3	4	3	2	2	3	2	4	4	4	5	4
N.C.	3	5	4	5	5	5	3	1	1	3	1	5	3	3	3	4	4	2	4	4	1	3	4	4	4	3	4	5	5
N.D.	5	4	3	5	5	2	5	5	5	5	5	3	2	3	3	2	2	4	5	5	5	5	2	3	1	5	3	1	1
OHIO(N)	4	5	4	5	5	5	3	3	2	4	3	5	2	2	1	4	4	1	4	4	2	4	3	1	4	4	3	5	5
OHIO(S)	4	5	4	5	5	5	3	3	2	4	3	5	3	2	1	4	4	1	4	4	2	4	3	1	4	4	3	5	5
OKLA	3	4	1	5	5	1	5	5	5	5	4	5	3	3	3	3	1	3	2	5	5	5	4	4	3	3	1	5	2
ORE	5	3	4	1	2	3	5	5	5	5	5	1	4	4	5	3	3	5	5	5	5	5	4	4	3	5	4	2	3
PA(E)	4	5	4	5	5	5	2	1	2	4	3	5	3	3	3	4	4	3	4	3	1	2	3	3	4	4	4	5	5
PA(W)	4	5	4	5	5	5	2	1	1	4	3	5	3	3	3	4	4	3	4	3	1	2	3	3	4	4	4	5	5
R.I.	4	5	4	5	5	5	1	2	2	4	3	5	3	3	3	4	4	3	4	2	2	1	3	3	4	4	4	5	4
S.C.	1	5	3	5	5	5	4	2	2	2	1	5	3	3	3	4	4	1	3	4	2	4	4	4	5	3	4	5	5
S.D.	5	4	3	5	5	2	5	5	5	5	5	3	3	3	3	1	2	4	5	5	5	5	3	3	1	4	2	1	1
TENN	1	5	1	5	5	5	5	4	3	3	1	5	2	2	2	3	4	1	3	5	3	5	3	3	5	1	1	5	5
TEX(E)	2	3	1	5	5	3	5	5	5	4	3	5	3	2	3	3	1	3	1	5	5	5	4	4	4	1	1	5	2
TEX(S)	2	2	1	5	5	2	5	5	5	4	3	5	3	3	3	3	1	3	1	5	5	5	4	4	4	1	2	5	3
TEX(W)	3	2	1	5	5	1	5	5	5	4	3	5	3	3	3	3	1	3	2	5	5	5	4	4	4	2	2	5	2
UTAH	5	1	4	2	2	1	5	5	5	5	5	1	4	4	4	4	3	5	4	5	5	5	5	5	4	4	4	3	3
VT	4	5	4	5	5	5	1	2	2	4	4	5	3	3	3	4	5	3	5	1	2	1	3	3	4	4	4	5	4
VA	3	5	4	5	5	5	3	1	1	4	3	5	3	3	3	4	4	1	4	4	1	3	3	3	4	4	4	5	5
WASH	5	3	4	1	2	3	5	5	5	5	5	1	4	4	5	3	3	5	5	5	5	5	4	4	3	5	4	1	3
W.VA	4	5	4	5	5	5	3	2	1	4	3	5	3	3	2	4	4	1	4	4	1	3	3	3	4	4	4	5	5
WIS	4	5	3	5	5	4	5	4	4	5	4	5	1	2	2	1	3	3	5	5	4	5	1	1	1	4	2	5	3
WYO	5	3	4	3	3	1	5	5	5	5	5	1	4	4	5	3	2	5	5	5	5	5	4	4	3	5	4	1	1

* Service To Any Number Service Area (BAND) Includes Service To All Lower Numbered Service Areas (BANDS)

Figure 3.3. Band numbers required for WATS service between states.

INTERSTATE SERVICE AREA (BANDS)'— NEVADA — WYOMING

LOCATION OF ACCESS LINE	NEV	N.H.	N.J.	N.M.	N.Y.(NE)	N.Y.(SE)	N.Y.(W)	N.C.	N.D.	OHIO(N)	OHIO(S)	OKLA	ORE	PA(E)	PA(W)	R.I.	S.C.	S.D.	TENN	TEX(E)	TEX(S)	TEX(W)	UTAH	VT	VA	WASH	W.VA.	WIS	WYO
ALA	5	5	4	5	4	4	4	2	5	3	2	3	5	4	4	5	1	5	1	3	3	3	5	5	3	5	3	4	5
ARIZ	1	5	5	1	5	5	5	5	4	5	5	3	3	5	5	5	5	3	5	3	3	2	1	5	5	3	5	4	2
ARK	5	5	5	4	5	5	5	4	5	3	3	1	5	4	4	5	3	4	1	1	3	3	5	5	4	5	3	3	5
CALIF(N)	1	5	5	3	5	5	5	5	3	5	5	3	1	5	5	5	5	3	5	3	3	3	1	5	5	1	5	4	2
CALIF(S)	1	5	5	1	5	5	5	5	3	5	5	3	1	5	5	5	5	3	5	3	3	2	1	5	5	2	5	4	2
COLO	3	5	5	1	5	5	5	5	3	5	5	1	4	5	5	5	5	2	5	3	4	2	1	5	5	4	5	4	1
CONN	5	1	1	5	1	1	2	3	5	3	3	5	5	2	2	1	3	5	3	5	5	5	5	2	2	5	3	4	5
DEL	5	3	1	5	2	1	2	3	5	3	3	4	5	1	2	2	3	5	3	5	5	5	5	3	2	5	2	5	4
D.C.	5	3	1	5	3	2	2	2	5	3	2	4	5	1	1	3	3	5	3	5	5	5	5	3	1	5	1	4	5
FLA	5	5	3	5	4	4	4	1	5	3	2	3	5	3	3	4	1	5	1	4	4	4	5	5	2	5	2	5	5
GA	5	5	3	5	4	4	4	1	5	3	2	4	5	3	3	4	1	5	1	4	4	4	5	5	2	5	2	4	5
IDAHO	1	5	5	3	5	5	5	5	3	5	5	3	1	5	5	5	5	3	5	4	4	4	1	5	5	1	5	4	1
ILL(N)	5	5	4	5	4	4	4	3	4	2	2	3	5	3	3	5	4	4	2	5	5	5	5	5	3	5	3	1	5
ILL(S)	5	5	4	5	4	4	4	3	4	2	1	3	5	3	3	5	4	4	1	5	5	5	5	5	3	5	3	2	5
IND	5	5	4	5	4	4	4	3	5	1	1	4	5	3	2	4	3	4	2	5	5	5	5	4	3	5	2	2	5
IOWA	5	5	5	4	5	5	5	5	3	3	3	3	5	4	4	5	5	1	3	4	4	4	5	5	4	5	3	1	3
KAN	5	5	5	2	5	5	5	5	3	4	4	1	5	5	5	5	5	2	3	2	3	2	4	5	5	5	4	3	3
KY	5	5	3	5	4	4	4	3	5	2	1	4	5	3	3	4	2	5	1	5	5	5	5	4	1	5	1	3	5
LA	5	5	5	4	5	5	5	3	5	3	3	1	5	4	4	5	3	4	2	1	1	2	5	5	4	5	3	4	5
ME	5	1	2	5	1	1	2	3	4	2	3	5	5	2	2	1	3	4	4	5	5	5	5	1	3	5	3	3	5
MD	5	3	1	5	2	2	2	2	5	3	3	4	5	1	1	2	3	5	3	5	5	5	5	3	1	5	1	4	5
MASS	5	1	1	5	1	1	2	3	5	3	3	5	5	2	2	1	3	4	3	5	5	5	5	1	2	5	2	4	5
MICH(N)	5	3	3	5	3	4	2	3	4	2	2	4	5	3	2	3	4	4	3	5	5	5	5	3	3	5	3	1	5
MICH(S)	5	4	3	5	3	3	2	4	4	1	1	4	5	2	2	4	4	4	3	5	5	5	5	3	3	5	2	1	5
MINN	5	5	5	4	4	4	4	5	1	3	3	3	5	4	4	5	5	1	3	5	5	5	4	5	4	5	3	1	3
MISS	5	5	4	4	5	5	5	3	5	3	3	2	5	4	4	5	2	5	1	1	3	3	5	5	3	5	3	4	5
MO	5	5	5	4	5	5	5	4	4	3	3	1	5	4	4	5	4	3	1	3	3	3	5	5	4	5	4	2	5
MONT	2	5	5	3	5	5	5	5	1	5	5	4	2	5	5	5	5	1	5	4	4	4	1	5	5	1	5	3	1
NEBR	4	5	5	3	5	5	5	5	2	4	4	2	5	5	5	5	5	1	4	3	3	3	5	5	5	5	4	2	1
NEV	#	5	5	3	5	5	5	5	3	5	5	3	1	5	5	5	5	3	5	3	3	3	1	5	5	2	5	4	2
N.H.	5	#	2	5	1	1	2	3	4	3	3	5	5	2	2	1	3	4	4	5	5	5	5	1	2	5	3	3	5
N.J.	5	2	#	4	1	1	2	3	5	3	3	4	5	1	2	2	3	5	3	5	5	5	5	2	2	5	2	4	5
N.M.	3	5	5	#	5	5	5	5	4	5	5	1	4	5	5	5	5	3	4	2	2	1	1	5	5	5	5	4	2
N.Y.(NE)	5	1	1	5	#	#	#	3	5	2	2	5	5	1	1	1	3	4	3	5	5	5	5	1	2	5	2	3	5
N.Y.(SE)	5	1	1	5	#	#	#	3	5	2	2	5	5	1	2	1	3	4	3	5	5	5	5	1	2	5	2	3	5
N.Y.(W)	5	3	1	5	#	#	#	3	5	1	2	5	5	1	1	3	3	4	3	5	5	5	5	2	3	5	2	3	5
N.C.	5	4	2	5	3	3	3	#	5	2	1	4	5	2	2	3	1	5	1	5	5	5	5	4	1	5	1	4	5
N.D.	4	5	5	3	5	5	5	5	#	4	4	3	4	5	5	5	5	1	4	4	4	4	3	5	5	3	5	2	1
OHIO(N)	5	4	3	5	3	3	1	3	5	#	4	#	5	2	1	4	3	5	3	5	5	5	5	4	2	5	1	3	5
OHIO(S)	5	4	3	5	3	3	2	2	5	#	4	#	5	2	1	4	3	5	2	5	5	5	5	4	1	5	1	3	5
OKLA	5	5	5	1	5	5	5	5	4	4	4	#	5	5	5	5	4	3	3	1	2	1	4	5	5	5	4	3	4
ORE	1	5	5	3	5	5	5	5	3	5	5	3	#	5	5	5	5	3	5	4	4	4	1	5	5	1	5	4	2
PA(E)	5	2	1	5	1	1	2	3	5	2	3	4	5	#	#	2	3	5	3	5	5	5	5	2	2	5	2	4	5
PA(W)	5	3	2	5	1	2	1	3	5	1	1	4	5	#	#	3	3	5	3	5	5	5	5	3	1	5	1	4	5
R.I.	5	1	1	5	2	1	2	3	5	3	3	5	5	2	2	#	3	5	3	5	5	5	5	1	2	5	3	4	5
S.C.	5	4	3	5	3	3	3	1	5	1	2	4	5	3	2	4	#	5	1	5	5	5	5	4	1	5	1	4	5
S.D.	4	5	5	3	5	5	5	5	1	4	4	3	4	5	5	5	5	#	4	4	4	4	3	5	5	4	5	2	1
TENN	5	4	5	4	4	4	4	1	5	2	2	4	5	3	3	5	2	5	#	4	4	4	5	5	1	5	2	3	5
TEX(E)	4	5	5	2	5	5	5	4	4	4	4	1	5	5	5	5	4	3	2	#	#	#	3	5	5	5	4	4	3
TEX(S)	4	5	5	1	5	5	5	4	4	4	4	1	5	5	5	5	4	3	3	#	#	#	3	5	5	5	4	4	3
TEX(W)	4	5	5	1	5	5	5	4	4	4	4	1	5	5	5	5	4	3	3	#	#	#	3	5	5	5	4	4	3
UTAH	1	5	5	1	5	5	5	5	3	5	5	3	3	5	5	5	5	3	5	3	3	3	4	5	5	3	5	4	1
VT	5	1	2	5	1	1	2	3	4	2	3	5	5	2	2	1	3	4	4	5	5	5	5	#	3	6	3	3	5
VA	5	3	2	5	3	3	2	1	5	2	1	4	5	2	1	3	2	5	1	5	5	5	5	3	#	5	1	4	5
WASH	2	5	5	3	5	5	5	5	3	5	5	3	1	5	5	5	5	3	5	4	4	4	2	5	5	#	5	4	2
W.Va.	5	4	2	5	3	3	2	2	5	1	1	4	5	2	1	3	2	5	3	5	5	5	5	4	1	5	#	4	5
WIS	5	5	4	5	3	3	3	4	3	2	2	4	5	3	3	5	4	3	3	5	5	5	5	4	4	5	3	#	4
WYO	2	5	5	2	5	5	5	5	2	5	5	3	3	5	5	5	5	1	5	4	4	4	1	5	5	3	5	4	#

Service To Any Numbered Service Area (BAND) Includes Service To All Lower Numbered Service Areas (BANDS)

MILEAGE BETWEEN STATIONS	CHARGE PER MINUTE
0-50	.20
51-110	.25
111-185	.30
186-280	.35
281-400	.40
401-550	.45
551-750	.50
751-1030	.55
1031-1430	.60
1431-2000	.65
2001-UP	.70

NOTE: ALL RATES ARE APPROXIMATE AND DO NOT INCLUDE
FEDERAL TAX OR STATION EQUIPMENT CHARGES.

Figure 3.4.   Usage charges for TWX service between points in the United States.

directly with other TELEX terminals within the United States, Canada, or Mexico. TELEX may also be used to send or receive messages to terminals in a large number of other foreign countries, although not on a direct dial basis. TELEX calls are billed according to a time and distance relationship whose details are beyond the scope of this discussion. Specific charges may be obtained from Western Union, or from the agency sponsoring TELEX service in foreign countries.

During the early 1970s Datran Corporation began providing an ultrafast connect digital dial-up service for data transmission in the United States. Known as Datadial Service, it charged users a speed-sensitive rate for either 2400, 4800, or 9600 bits/sec dial-up connections. Typical Datran rates in effect on September 1, 1975, are summarized in Figure 3.5. These costs were highly attractive for the data transmission user who could

DESCRIPTION: DATADIAL I IS A METERED USE EXCHANGE SERVICE FOR DATA COMMUNICA-
TIONS. CUSTOMER ACCESS IS VIA SEVEN DIGIT DIAL FOR 2400 BPS,
4800 BPS or 9600 BPS TERMINALS. AS OF MID 1976 SERVICE WAS
AVAILABLE IN APPROXIMATELY 25 MAJOR U.S. METROPOLITAN AREAS.

RATES: THE TOTAL MONTHLY CHARGE IS THE SUM OF THREE COMPONENTS:
1. METERED USE CHARGE,
2. ACCESS CHANNEL CHARGE, AND
3. NETWORK INTERFACE EQUIPMENT CHARGE.

I. METERED USE CHARGE (PER MINUTE)

		Hours Of Use				
Speed		0-40	41-100	101-240	241-1440	Over 1440
2400	bps	.25	A+.167	B+.0457	E+.098	.10
4800	bps	.30	A+.217	C+.02714	E+.108	.11
9600	bps	.35	A+.267	D+.18	F+.158	.17

A = $3.32 divided by hours of use
B = $15.42 divided by hours of use
C = $22.28 divided by hours of use
D = $12.00 divided by hours of use
E = $2.867 divided by hours of use
F = $17.27 divided by hours of use

II. MONTHLY ACCESS CHANNEL CHARGE

Type of Service	Up to 5 Miles	Each Additional Mile
2400 or 4800 bps	$35	$2.00
9600 bps	$60	$2.00

III. NETWORK INTERFACE EQUIPMENT PER MONTH

Speed	Charge
2400 bps	$ 50
4800 bps	100
9600 bps	150

Figure 3.5. Datran Datadial rates, September 1975. Service was discontinued several months later.

obtain significant geographic coverage from Datran. Datadial Service was also the first commercial circuit switched service offering speeds faster than 4800 bits/sec. The only major problem associated with Datadial was the limited number of locations and/or subscribers reachable. Unfortunately for users, Datran was financially unable to continue operations and went into backruptcy during August 1976. The service details have been included here primarily for historical purposes.

3.4. LEASED LINE SERVICES—INTERSTATE

Leased line services are available in major U.S. cities from AT&T, IT&T, Western Union, MCI, and Southern Pacific, and from other specialized common carriers in a limited number of cities, as of this writing. These services are generally classified as either interstate or intrastate. Since intrastate services and rates vary widely, the discussion here involves exclusively the interstate types of services where two or more of the access points lie in different states. Leased lines are offered in sub-voice-grade, voice-grade, and wideband denominations. By far the most widely used source of leased lines in the United States is AT&T, whose rates for all such services are contained in FCC Tariff 260. Until recently, most Western Union rates were similar or identical to AT&T's for comparable service. However, with the advent of route-priced tariffs such as Bell's controversial high density/low density tariff and its successor, known as the multischedule private line tariff (MPL), this similarity of pricing structures has come to an end.

The primary objective here is to present an overview of AT&T Series 1000, 2000, 3000, 5000, and 8000 interstate leased (private) line tariffs and to indicate how HiLo, MPL, and related developments have affected these price structures.

No attempt is made to duplicate the voluminous material in the tariffs; the objective here is merely to survey the typical costs and service features associated with the more widely used types of leased line offerings. Figure 3.6 illustrates the composition of a typical interstate line (circuit) ordered from a Bell System affiliate; it illustrates the various billing components of private line service and defines some popular terminology used in the industry. An IXC is an *interexchange channel* or the portion of a private line service between common carrier central offices. *Local loops* are the facilities that connect subscriber premises to central offices. *Service terminals* are a logical concept (rather than a physical one), since there is no physical entity known as a service terminal. Recent tariff

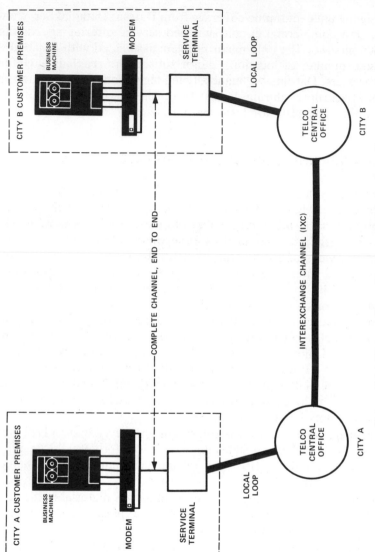

Figure 3.6. Composition of carrier-provided private line

changes have also introduced the concept of a *station terminal;* this is simply a new, equivalent name for a service terminal.

Costs for most leased lines are based on charges for (*a*) IXC channels, (*b*) station or service terminals, and (*c*) in some cases additional equipment and maintenance service. Costs of IXC channels are usually mileage dependent and may include a fixed component. As noted in subsequent figures and examples, a *channel terminal* is a fixed charge component of an IXC channel. Whenever IXC channel costs contain both fixed and mileage-dependent rate components, a charge for one or two channel terminals (one at each end of the IXC) is usually included.

Service or station terminal charges are associated with the costs of local loops which connect customer premises to the common carrier central offices. In most private line services the billing mileage is calculated on the basis of the airline mileage between rate centers serving the end-terminal locations. Customers thus pay for IXCs and for one service or station terminal for each separate local loop or drop on a circuit.

The formula given below may be used to calculate billing mileage distances between two stations, *A* and *B*, whose associated rate center coordinates are V_A, H_A and V_B, H_B, respectively. Distance *D* is in miles and always is rounded upward to the next highest integer whenever the square root value contains any fractional parts.

$$D_{A,B} = \sqrt{\frac{(V_A - V_B)^2 + (H_A - H_B)^2}{10}}$$

Example

Calculate the distance between Chicago ($V = 5986, H = 3426$) and New York ($V = 4997, H = 1406$).
Solution. **Distance** = 712 miles.

It should be emphasized that the coordinates associated with any terminal location are for that site's associated rate center or central office, and not for the terminal location. Rate centers are small geographic regions containing one or more central offices or exchanges. An imaginary point within the region, labeled with a unique *V, H* coordinate, is used for computing distances to all other rate centers.

3.4.1. Sub-Voice-Grade Services—Series 1000 Channels

Series 1000 channels are generally capable of transmitting data at speeds up to and including *150 bits/sec* when equipped with proper modems and/or signaling equipment. The three most widely used types of Series 1000 channels are Type 1002 for rates up to 55 bits/sec, Type 1005 for rates up to 75 bits/sec, and Type 1006 for rates up to 150 bits/sec. Service charges consist of a one-time fee for installation, plus a monthly recurring charge for service terminals, channel terminals, and the mileage-dependent portion of the channel. Table 3.4 summarizes the charges for

Table 3.4. Monthly Rates for AT&T Series 1000 Service, June 1976[a]

Mileage[c]	0–55 bits/sec (Type 1002)		0–75 bits/sec (Type 1005)		0–150 bits/sec (Type 1006)	
	HDX	FDX	HDX	FDX	HDX	FDX
First 100 miles	$1.25		$1.25		$1.55	
Next 150 (101–250)	1.00		1.00		1.25	
Next 250 (251–500)	0.60		0.60		0.80	
Next 500 (501–1000)	0.40		0.40		0.50	
Each additional mile	0.25		0.25		0.30	
Main service terminals[b]	$40	$44	$40	$44	$60	$66
Extension service terminals[b]	$25	$27.50	$25	$27.50	$40	$44
Installation (one time only)[b]	$52.55	$52.55	$52.55	$52.55	$52.55	$52.55

[a] A monthly charge for two channel terminals applies for each two-point IXC section on a circuit. Charge per channel terminal is $30/month.
[b] Charge is per service terminal.
[c] Mileage rates are per mile per month.

Type 1002, 1005, and 1006 channels. FDX service implies that a channel has the ability to support true full-duplex communication and also implies actual full-duplex usage by the customer.[1] Multipoint service is generally available with possible restrictions; its costs are calculated by considering the individual legs separately for the mileage-dependent component of a channel. The sample cost calculations of Figure 3.7 illustrate how Type 1005 multipoint service charges would be determined in a typical situation.

Whenever two or more drops or separate accesses on the same mul-

[1] This is a recent policy change by AT&T, which no longer requires customers to pay an extra 10% for a full-duplex facility unless that facility is actually being used in both directions simultaneously. Administering or policing this restriction is virtually impossible, so the carrier depends on the honesty of the customer to know which rate (FDX or HDX) to charge.

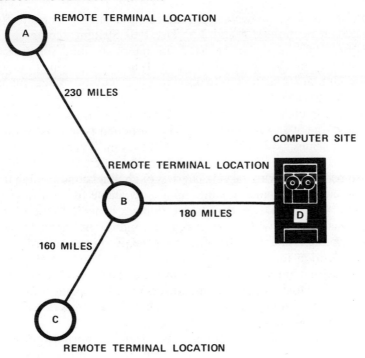

Channel Component	Monthly Charge
Leg *AB* (230 Miles)	$315
Leg *CB* (160 Miles)	$245
Leg *BD* (180 Miles)	$265
Service terminal at *A*	$ 44
Service terminal at *B*	$ 44
Service Terminal at *C*	$ 44
Service terminal at *D*	$ 44
Total	$1001

Figure 3.7. Example line cost calculation—Type 1005 FDX multipoint service, June 1976.

tipoint circuit have the same *V* and *H* billing coordinates, the first location is priced using main service terminal charges; all additional drops with the same coordinates are priced as *extension service terminals*.

3.4.2. Conventional Analog Voice-Grade Services

In this section, the voice-grade service alternatives provided by the Bell System and Western Union are discussed. Digital offerings in the comparable speed range, as well as specialized and satellite carrier offerings, are noted in Sections 3.4 and 3.5. The Bell System denotes all leased voice-grade lines that can be used for interstate data transmission as Series 3000 channels, unless such channels are priced using certain quantity discount tariffs such as Telpak (which is discussed in Section 3.4.4 on broadband services).

Voice-grade channels are generally required for data transmission applications from 300 to 9600 bits/sec. The particular type most widely used for data transmission or alternate voice/data is the Type 3002 voice-grade channel, which has an approximate bandwidth of from 300 to 3300 Hz. It can also be ordered with varying degrees of channel conditioning from the common carrier. Channel conditioning is available in the following services: C1, C2, C4, D1, and D2 conditioning. (The full technical specifications associated with these types of conditioning are considered in detail in the next chapter.) It suffices for the present to regard conditioning as an option for widening the usable bandwidth and effectively increasing the maximum rate at which data may be transmitted over a Type 3002 channel. Most modem manufacturers publish specifications as to the type of line conditioning required for operation at prescribed data rates with their various models.

From a transmission standpoint, the electrical parameters of leased lines are relatively stable, since a fixed physical circuit is set aside in the carrier's plant. Although there may be occasional switches or rerouting of dedicated circuits through the carrier's long haul transmission facilities, the electrical environment is relatively fixed in comparison to the dial-up network. Speeds from 7200 to 9600 bits/sec are attainable over private, conditioned lines, whereas the upper speed limit over the dial-up network is from 3600 to 4800 bits/sec. Private voice-grade lines are available in point-to-point and multipoint configurations; virtually all domestic leased voice-grade lines involve four-wire terminations at the customer premises, but in some foreign countries two-wire leased lines are still common. As a final point, it should be noted that synchronous (or clocked) transmission is used on virtually all voice-grade line applications with data rates of 2000 bits/sec or faster.

Prices for leased voice-grade lines were changed dramatically during 1974, when the Bell System introduced its controversial high density/low density (HiLo) tariff for Series 2000 and 3000 leased lines.[2] It profoundly affected network layout and pricing in organizations of all sizes. However, certain provisions of the tariff gave the user new options in deter-

---

[2]Series 2000 channels are leased voice-grade lines used solely for voice transmission purposes. Whenever the same facilities are used for data transmission or alternate voice/data transmission, AT&T denotes them as Series 3000 channels.

mining the least-cost layout for networks. Western Union followed with a similar, though less complicated, version of HiLo. During 1976 the FCC rejected the HiLo tariff as being unlawful and instructed AT&T to replace it with a tariff in which all rate elements were fully supported by justifiable costs. The successor tariff, known as multischedule private line (MPL), was still being evaluated by the FCC as of this writing.

Interestingly enough, the HiLo tariff was used for actual customer invoices for more than 2 years even though it was subsequently ruled unlawful! Under current regulatory policies, there was no basis for any rebates or adjustments for customers who were adversely affected by the illegal rates.

We now highlight the major features of HiLo and its MPL successor.

3.4.2.1. AT&T High Density/Low Density and Multischedule Private Line (MPL) Interstate Tariffs

In November 1973, AT&T filed a tariff with the FCC to drastically alter the methods used to price interstate leased lines. During 1976, the FCC rejected the HiLo tariff and AT&T proposed a similarly controversial tariff known as MPL. As of early 1977, this new MPL pricing structure was still being evaluated by the FCC, but had officially taken effect.

Voice-grade channels passing partially through bulk bandwidth offerings like Telpak were not affected by HiLo. Since many of the largest communication users made substantial use of these bulk bandwidth offerings, the cost impact of HiLo tended to be relatively minimal on such customers. However, in networks where users were employing individual circuit pricing schemes, the impact was substantial, necessitating reevaluation of cost justification decisions in many cases.

The essence of HiLo was a partitioning of all 30,000-odd billing rate centers in the United States into two categories, high density and low density, based on certain criteria for levels of equipment and numbers of customers. In the subsequently filed MPL tariff, the two classes of rate centers were maintained. However, the criteria for classification was modified, and new names—Class A and Class B—were introduced for the high and low density rate centers, respectively. Table 3.5 lists the originally filed Class A rate centers.

Under both HiLo and MPL, route-sensitive pricing became a reality as nationwide averaging of costs and prices was abandoned. For example, under the originally filed MPL tariff shown in Table 3.6, three different pricing structures applied, depending on the mileage and the classification of the service point rate centers (those where user terminals are located). As though previous nomenclature were not sufficiently confusing, new terminology was also introduced with HiLo and MPL to describe termina-

Table 3.5. Originally Filed Category A Rate Centers for MPL Tariff

(a) Category A Rate Centers for All Customers

Alabama

Anniston
Birmingham
Decatur
Huntsville
Mobile
Montgomery
Troy

Arizona

Flagstaff
Phoenix
Prescott
Tucson
Yuma

Arkansas

Fayetteville
Forrest City
Hot Springs
Little Rock
Pine Bluff
Searcy

California

Anaheim
Bakersfield
Chico
Eureka
Fresno
Hayward
Los Angeles
Oakland
Redwood City
Sacramento
Salinas
San Bernardino
San Diego
San Francisco
San Jose

San Luis Obispo
Santa Rosa
Stockton
Sunnyvale
Ukiah
Van Nuys

Colorado

Colorado Springs
Denver
Fort Collins
Fort Morgan
Glenwood Springs
Grand Junction
Greeley

Connecticut

Bridgeport
Hartford
New Haven
New London
Stamford

Delaware

Wilmington

District of Columbia

Washington Zone 1

Florida

Chipley
Clearwater
Cocoa
Crestview
Daytona Beach
Fort Lauderdale
Fort Myers
Fort Pierce
Fort Walton Beach

Gainesville
Jacksonville
Key West
Lake City
Miami
Ocala
Orlando
Panama City
Pensacola
St. Petersburg
Sarasota
Tallahassee
Tampa
West Palm Beach
Winter Garden
Winter Haven

Georgia

Albany
Atlanta
Augusta
Columbus
Conyers
Fitzgerald
Macon
Thomasville
Waycross

Idaho

Boise
Twin Falls

Illinois

Centralia
Champaign-Urbana
Chicago
Collinsville
De Kalb
Hinsdale
Marion

Newark
Peoria
Rockford
Rock Island
Springfield

Indiana

Bloomington
Evansville
Fort Wayne
Indianapolis
Muncie
South Bend
Terre Haute

Iowa

Boone
Burlington
Cedar Rapids
Davenport
Des Moines
Iowa City
Sioux City
Waterloo

Kansas

Dodge City
Kansas City
Manhattan
Salina
Topeka
Wichita

Kentucky

Danville
Louisville
Madisonville
Winchester

100

Table 3.5. *(Continued)*

Louisiana

Alexandria
Baton Rouge
Lafayette
Lake Charles
Monroe
New Orleans
Shreveport

Maine

*Calais Int. Bdry
Portland

Maryland

Baltimore
Washington Zone 3

Massachusetts

Boston
Brockton
Cambridge
Fall River
Framingham
Lawrence
Springfield
Worcester

Michigan

Detroit
Flint
Grand Rapids
Houghton
Iron Mountain
Jackson
Kalamazoo
Lansing
Petoskey
Plymouth
Pontiac

*Port Huron
   Int. Bdry
Saginaw
Traverse City

Minnesota

Duluth
Minneapolis
St. Paul
Wadena

Mississippi

Biloxi
Columbus
Greenville
Greenwood
Gulfport
Hattiesburg
Jackson
Laurel
McComb
Meridian

Missouri

Cape Giradeau
Joplin
Kansas City
St. Joseph
St. Louis
Sikeston
Springfield

Montana

Billings
Helena
*West Sweetgrass-
   Int. Bdry

Nebraska

Grand Island
Omaha
Sidney

Nevada

Carson City
Las Vegas
Reno

New Hampshire

Concord
Dover
Littleton
Manchester
Nashua

New Jersey

Atlantic City
Camden
Hackensack
Morristown
Newark
New Brunswick
Trenton

New Mexico

Albuquerque
Las Cruces
Roswell
Santa Fe

New York

Albany
Binghamton
Buffalo
*Buffalo Peace-
   bridge Int.
   Bdry

Huntington
*Mooers Forks
   Int. Bdry.
Nassau Zone 5
New York City
Poughkeepsie
Rochester
Syracuse
Westchester
   Zone 8

North Carolina

Asheville
Charlotte
Fayetteville
Greensboro
Greenville
Laurinburg
New Bern
Raleigh
Rocky Mount
Wilmington
Winston-Salem

North Dakota

Bismarck
Casselton
*Crosby Inter-
   national-
   Crossing
   Int. Bdry
Dickinson
Fargo
Grand Forks
*Neche Int.
   Bdry

Ohio

Akron
Canton

Table 3.5. *(Continued)*

Cincinnati
Cleveland
Columbus
Dayton
Toledo
Youngstown

Oklahoma

Muskogee
Oklahoma City
Tulsa

Oregon

Haymaker
Medford
Pendelton
Portland

Pennsylvania

Allentown
  (Lehigh Co.)
Altoona
Harrisburg
Philadelphia
Philadelphia-
  Suburban
  Zone 26
Philadelphia-
  Suburban
  Zone 33
Pittsburgh
Reading
Scranton
Williamsport

Rhode Island

Providence

South Carolina

Charleston
Columbia
Florence
Greenville
Orangeburg
Spartanburg

South Dakota

Huron
Sioux Falls

Tennessee

Chattanooga
Clarksville
Jackson
Johnson City
Knoxville
Memphis
Nashville

Texas

Abilene
Amarillo
Austin
Beaumont
Corpus Christi
Dallas
El Paso
Fort Worth
Harlingen
Houston
Laredo

*Laredo
  Int. Bdry
Longview
Lubbock
Midland
San Angelo
San Antonio
Sweetwater
Waco

Utah

Logan
Ogden
Provo
Salt Lake
  City

Vermont

Burlington
White River
  Junction

Virginia

Blacksburg
Leesburg
Lynchburg
Newport News
  Zone 1
Norfolk Zone 2
Petersburg
Richmond
Roanoke
Washington
  Zone 8

Washington

Kennewick
North Bend
*Port Angeles
  Int. Bdry
Seattle
Spokane
Yakima

West Virginia

Beckley
Charleston
  Zone 1
Clarksburg
Fairmont
Huntington
  Zone 1
Morgantown
Parkersburg
Wheeling
  Zone 1

Wisconsin

Appleton
Dodgeville
Eau Claire
Green Bay
La Crosse
Madison
Milwaukee
Racine
Stevens Point

Wyoming

Casper
Cheyenne

*These rate centers, only defined as Category A when used as gateway locations for international leased lines, are referred to as *International Boundary* rate centers.

Table 3.5. *(Continued)*

(b) Additional Category A Rate Centers for U.S. Government Services Only

Alabama
Drewton
Jasper

Arizona
Superstitition-Apache
   Junction

California
Baker
Julian
Lodi
Mojave

Colorado
Lamar

Connecticut
Cheshire

Florida
Polk City

Illinois
Plano

Iowa
Red Oak

Kansas
Fairview

Kentucky
Williamstown

Maryland
La Plata
New Market
Waldorf

Massachusetts
Chesterfield
Littleton

Michigan
Parma

Minnesota
Wyoming Switch

Mississippi
Pickens

Missouri
Antonia

Montana
West Glendive

Nebraska
Lyons
North Bend

New Jersey
Berlin
Succasunna

New Mexico
Socorro

New York
Rosendale
Tully

North Carolina
Locust

Ohio
Benton Ridge

Oklahoma
Bristow

Pennsylvania
Blue Ridge Summit
Pottstown

Texas
Apollo
Ennis
Seguin
Spring

Utah
Delta

Virginia
Bethia
Herndon
Warrenton

Table 3.6. Summary of MPL Tariff, April 1977, Illustrative Monthly Rates[a]

Circuit Section (miles)	INTEREXCHANGE CHANNEL		
	Schedule I	Schedule II	Schedule III
1	$ 51.00	$ 52.00	$ 53.00
2–14	51.00 + $1.80/mile	52.00 + $3.30/mile	53.00 + $4.40/mile
15	76.20	98.20	114.60
16–24	76.20 + 1.50/mile	98.20 + 3.10/mile	114.60 + 3.80/mile
25	91.20	129.20	152.60
26–39	91.20 + 1.12/mile	129.20 + 2.00/mile	152.60 + 2.80/mile
40	108.00	159.20	194.60
41–59	108.00 + 1.12/mile	159.20 + 1.35/mile	194.60 + 2.10/mile
60	130.40	186.20	236.60
61–79	130.40 + 1.12/mile	186.20 + 1.35/mile	236.60 + 1.60/mile
80	152.80	213.20	268.60
81–99	152.80 + 1.12/mile	213.20 + 1.35/mile	268.60 + 1.35/mile
100	175.20	240.20	295.60
101–999	175.20 + 0.66/mile	240.20 + 0.66/mile	295.60 + 0.68/mile
1000	769.20	834.20	907.60
over 1000	769.20 + 0.40/mile	834.20 + 0.40 mile	907.60 + 0.40/mile

STATION TERMINALS

Main voice and additionals for separate local facilities—$25 each
Main data—$25 each
Data transfer arrangements—$5 each
Additional voice bridged—$5 each

Schedule I: For service between cateory A cites.
Schedule II: For service between category A and B cities.
Schedule III: For service between category B cities.

[a]All table entries containing a fixed cost plus a per mile monthly cost should be interpreted as follows—the per mile monthly cost only applies to mileage in excess of that covered by the fixed cost.

tion charges. *Station terminals* are generally identical to the *service terminals* used for billing purposes through the end of 1973. *Channel terminals* represented a new type of termination charge introduced under HiLo. They applied to each link in the billing network for a leased line, as shown in Figure 3.8. Under MPL, channel terminal charges were eliminated as a specific tariff element. However, large fixed charges for each IXC were introduced, so the same basic price elements were carried over from HiLo into MPL.

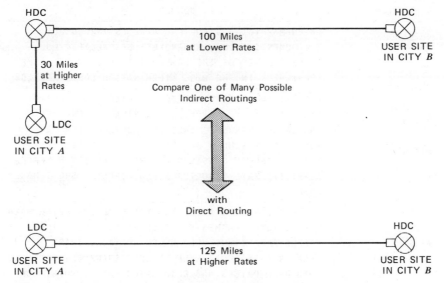

Before HILO: Only the direct routing was possible.
With HILO: Either alternative could be considered. Lowest cost route was used for
    pricing.
With HILO successor, the MPL tariff: Only the direct route is possible unless user
    actually terminates the line at the intermediate location.

Figure 3.8. Comparison of two routing procedures between an LDC and a HDC. LDC
= low density center, category B; HDC = high density center, category A.

One of the major characteristics of HiLo was that a billing network for
even a single leased line could be routed through certain nearby high
density rate centers to take possible advantage of lower long haul
charges, even though no customer terminals or computers were located at
these so-called *high density homing point* rate centers. (See Table 3.7 and
Figure 3.9.) The net impact was that numerous billing alternatives had to
be evaluated, even for a simple point-to-point leased line.

Under the MPL replacement of HiLo, indirect routing alternatives

Table 3.7. Summary of AT&T Alternative Pricing Arrangements Available
            for Two-Point Circuit under the HiLo Tariff

Direct or indirect routing under HiLo.
Direct routing as a Telpak Extension.
Indirect routing as a Telpak Extension.
Other wideband bulk services such as Series 8000 even if no data transmission is
involved.

TIME FRAME	COMMENTS
PRE-1974	UNIFORM PRICING STRUCTURE APPLIES THROUGHOUT THE DOMESTIC U.S., REGARDLESS OF SPECIFIC LOCATIONS. LINES OF THE SAME DISTANCE COST THE SAME EVERYWHERE IN THE U.S. TERMINATION COSTS ARE LOW.
MID-1974 TO MID-1976	COMPETITION FORCES ATT TO A CHANGE. HIDENSITY-LODENSITY TARIFF APPLIES, TERMINATION CHARGES INCREASED SHARPLY. INDIRECT ROUTINGS THROUGH HOMING POINTS MUST BE EVALUATED TO OBTAIN BEST PRICE. TARIFF CONSISTS OF TWO DIFFERENT MILEAGE-SENSITIVE RATE STRUCTURES PLUS SPECIAL SHORT-HAUL RATES.
AFTER MID-1976	FCC REJECTS HILO AFTER TWO YEARS OF ITS BEING USED FOR CUSTOMER PAYMENTS. BELL FILES MPL, A THREE-TIERED RATE STRUCTURE, WHICH CONTAINS SHARP INCREASES IN SHORT HAUL PRICES, SHARP DECREASES IN LONG HAUL PRICES AND ELIMINATES HOMING POINT CONCEPT. ONLY ONE PRICE APPLIES BETWEEN ANY TWO POINTS AND THERE ARE NO MORE SPECIAL SHORT-HAUL RATES.

Figure 3.9. History of shifting tariff computation alternatives for AT&T leased lines of voice-grade type.

were effectively eliminated by the elimination of the homing point concept. Nonlinear mileage-sensitive rates for each of the three rate categories enabled AT&T to accomplish the same pricing and revenue goals as with HiLo, even though homing points were eliminated. This modification simplified network optimization somewhat, although computerized procedures are still highly advisable. This is so because costs under MPL do not depend directly on distance, and locations generally have to be placed in Class A or B categories via table lookup procedures of some type.

These new types of route-priced tariffs generally have numerous immediate consequences for users. First, the termination-related charges as a percentage of the entire service charge have generally increased dramatically. Second, it is no longer possible to compare prices of competitive carriers (or different routes for the same carrier) without considering the specific geography of the points involved. Third, many older tools for network design have been rendered obsolete, along with the designs they produced. Finally, the importance of using computer-based techniques for pricing, evaluating, and controlling networks of all types has assumed a new degree of significance. It will no longer be possible to effectively administer a medium or larger sized network that changes frequently unless all the ramifications of route-priced tariffs are thoroughly understood. These points and others related to the history of changing leased line prices are illustrated in Figures 3.10 to 3.12.

3.4.2.2. Western Union High Density/Low Density Interstate Tariff

During 1974 the Western Union Corporation introduced a similar route-priced tariff for leased voice-grade lines. Most of the high density cities designated by Western Union's HiLo tariff are also found in AT&T's list in Table 3.5. Figure 3.13 summarizes the major elements of Western Union's first HiLo tariff. The provisions, restrictions, and so on are similar to those for AT&T's HiLo tariff, with a slightly different interpretation for channel terminals.

Another important difference between the two tariffs is that Western Union has not employed the concept of high density homing points. Any low density point can be connected to any of Western Union's designated high density points to obtain the lowest cost layout. With AT&T's tariff, a low density point could be directly connected only to other service points

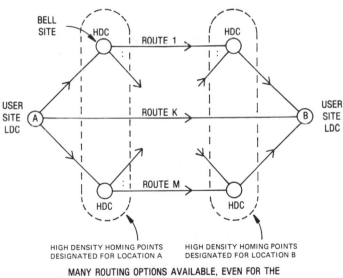

HIGH DENSITY HOMING POINTS
DESIGNATED FOR LOCATION A

HIGH DENSITY HOMING POINTS
DESIGNATED FOR LOCATION B

MANY ROUTING OPTIONS AVAILABLE, EVEN FOR THE
SIMPLE TWO POINT SITUATION SHOWN ABOVE

USER COMPLETELY RESPONSIBLE FOR CHOOSING
BEST ROUTING OF BILLING MILEAGE NETWORK

Figure 3.10. Homing point concept originally introduced with HiLo and subsequently eliminated under MPL.

Date	Tariff in Effect	Tariff Price
January, 1974	Nationwide Averaged Cost Tariff	$262.50
January, 1975	Original HiLo	$205.00
June, 1975	HiLo with First Rate Increase	$215.20
June, 1976	HiLo with Another Rate Increase	$222.00
September, 1976	Multischedule Private Line- MPL	$225.20

NOTE: HILO RULED UNLAWFUL AND REPLACED DURING AUGUST, 1976 AFTER BEING IN EFFECT FOR MORE THAN 2 YEARS!

Figure 3.11. Example price comparison for 100 mile link between AT&T High density locations: a turbulent history of change during the mid-1970's.

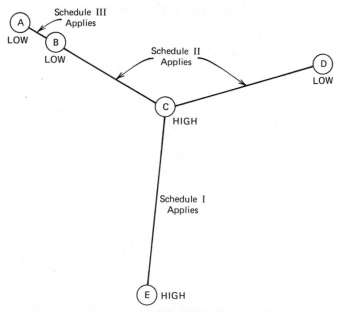

Figure 3.12. Multipoint optimization under the MPL Tariff. User locations A, B, C, D, E (no homing points anymore). Locations A, B, D are low density (Class B); locations C, E are high density (Class A). Note that the minimum-cost network for this individual circuit is not always the minimum-distance network.

108

PRICE OF A LINE DEPENDS ON THREE FACTORS

I. MILEAGE

II. CHANNEL TERMINALS

III. STATION TERMINALS

I. MILEAGE CHARGES PER MONTH

Lo Density: $1.00/Mile (Between Lo's or Lo's and Hi's)

Hi Density: $ .75/Mile (Between Hi's)

II. CHANNEL TERMINALS PER MONTH

Charge of $50/Month Applies for Each Service Point on a Two Point or Multipoint Circuit. A Service Point is a Municipality Where A Customer Station is Located or A Rate Center Through Which a Channel is Routed at the Customer's Desire.

III. STATION TERMINALS, COST PER MONTH

First Termination Per Customer Premises $25.00

Each Additional Termination on Same Premises $5.00

Figure 3.13. Western Union's HiLo tariff, effective in early 1976.

on the same circuit or to a designated high density homing point for one of the service points.

3.4.2.3. Intrastate Leased Voice-Grade Lines

Leased lines are also available on an intrastate basis from the Bell System and independent telephone companies. Price structures usually include charges for service terminals and mileage-sensitive IXC costs. Specific prices for these offerings vary widely. Generally mileage charges are higher than those for comparable interstate offerings. Termination charges, however, are frequently less costly than their interstate counterparts. In some statewide applications, use of the interstate tariff produces a more expensive network than does the appropriate intrastate tariff.[3] This may be true, for example, when a network involves a relatively large number of low density locations (which are the most costly to serve under

[3]Interstate rates apply if at least one point outside the state is connected to the circuit. Users sometimes treat such a point as a variable that enables them to employ whichever tariff is cheaper (interstate or intrastate).

MPL). Judicious evaluation of alternative combinations of interstate and intrastate circuits is essential to obtaining the lowest total cost network.

3.4.3. Dataphone Digital Service (DDS)

In the past few years, the Bell System has been developing a digital transmission network to service computer and data transmission users that cannot tolerate error rates and other shortcomings of conventional analog transmission facilities. Initially, Dataphone Digital Service (DDS) provides synchronous data channels at 2400, 4800, 9600, and 56,000 bits/sec, as shown in Figures 3.14 and 3.15 and Table 3.8. Prices have been in a constant state of flux since the initial offering in late 1974; for illustrative purposes, mid-1976 rates are illustrated in Table 3.8.

The DDS network employs bipolar pulse code modulation techniques over an integrated combination of local distribution facilities, intermediate length regional lines (T1 and T2 carrier), and long haul microwave facilities. (See Figures 3.16 and 3.17.) As shown in Figure 3.18,

- ## PRIVATE LINE, FULL DUPLEX, SYNCHRONOUS CHANNELS

- ## SPEEDS: 2.4, 4.8, 9.6 AND 56 KB/s

- ## POINT-TO-POINT SERVICE EARLY IN 1975
    24 CITIES OPERATIONAL IN MID-1976
    ULTIMATELY TO SERVE TOP 100 MARKETS
    ALTHOUGH REGULATORY CONTROVERSY IMPEDES EXPANSION

- ## MULTIPOINT SERVICE LATER IN 1975
- SWITCHED 56 KBPS INTRODUCED IN 1976
- ANALOG EXTENSION SERVICE TO OFF-NET LOCATIONS

- USES THREE TYPES OF TRANSMISSION FACILITIES

    - Unloaded Twisted Pairs (Customer To Central Office)
    - T Carrier (Central Office To Hub Office)
    - Long Haul Microwave (Between Hub Offices), Data
      Under Voice, DUV, To Start With

- EXTENSIVE NETWORK DIAGNOSTICS, TEST, AND FAULT
  ISOLATION FEATURES

- RATES HAVE BEEN SUBJECT TO MUCH CONTROVERSY AND
  FLUCTUATION. MID-1976 TARIFF SHOWN IN SUBSEQUENT
  FIGURE FOR ILLUSTRATIVE PURPOSES.

Figure 3.14.   AT&T Dataphone Digital Service (DDS) (Formerly Digital Data System).

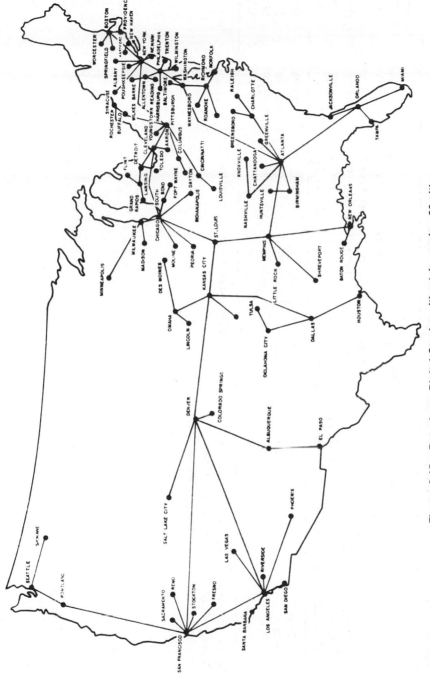

Figure 3.15.   Dataphone Digital Service ultimately serving 96 cities.

111

Table 3.8. Summary of Bell's Dataphone Digital Service (DDS) Tariffs, June 1976

Data Speed (bits/sec)	Monthly Fixed Charge for Intercity DDS Channel	Monthly Rate per Airline Mile	Monthly Rate per Type 1 Digital Access Line[a]	Monthly Rate per Type 2 Digital Access Line[b] Fixed-Rate Price	per Airline Mile	One-Time Installation Charge per Digital Access Line[c]	Monthly Rate per Digital Signal Converter (Data Service Unit)[c]
2400	$20.60	$0.41	$66.95	$92.70	$0.62	$103.00	$15.45
4800	$41.20	$0.62	$87.55	$113.00	$0.93	$103.00	$15.45
9600	$64.50	$0.93	$113.00	$134.00	$1.34	$103.00	$15.45
56000	$129.00	$4.12	$206.00	$258.00	$6.18	$103.00	$20.60

[a]Each point-to-point DDS service requires two access lines and two digital signal converters.
[b]Airline mileage rates used for accessive cost.
[c]Installation charge for each Data Service Unit: $25.75.

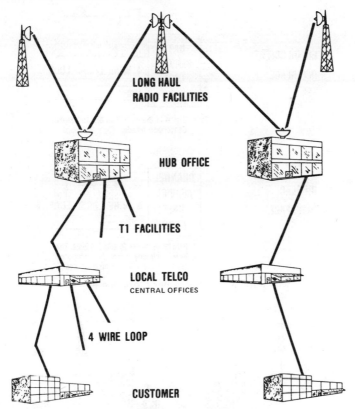

LONG HAUL
RADIO FACILITIES

HUB OFFICE

T1 FACILITIES

LOCAL TELCO
CENTRAL OFFICES

4 WIRE LOOP

CUSTOMER

Figure 3.16. Point-to-point DDS channel.

the network contains extensive diagnostic features for fault isolation and troubleshooting from carrier offices. Initially the DDS microwave facilities are piggy-backed onto existing plant, using the famous data under voice technique shown in Figure 3.19. Local loops will be obtained by removing loading coils from existing local plant, enabling data rates of 56 kilobits/sec and faster to be obtained out to the customer premises. Regenerative repeaters will be employed every few thousand feet in the local loops to refresh the digital pulse train. This will also eliminate the need for expensive analog modems along DDS routes. It is expected that the average bit error rates afforded by the DDS network will be as low as 1 error/10^7 bits transmitted. Moreover, AT&T claims that over 99.5% of the 1 sec time intervals will, on the average, be error free. Furthermore, the DDS system is designed for 99.96% availability, corresponding to not more than 4 hours of outage in every 10,000.

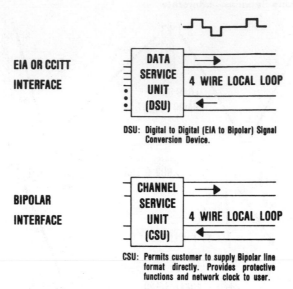

EIA OR CCITT INTERFACE

DSU: Digital to Digital (EIA to Bipolar) Signal Conversion Device.

BIPOLAR INTERFACE

CSU: Permits customer to supply Bipolar line format directly. Provides protective functions and network clock to user.

Figure 3.17. Customer's premises.

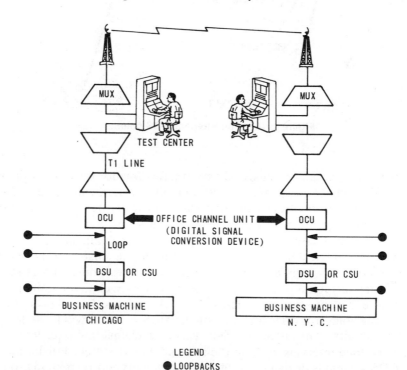

LEGEND
● LOOPBACKS

Figure 3.18. Fault isolation and diagnostics in point-to-point DDS channel.

114

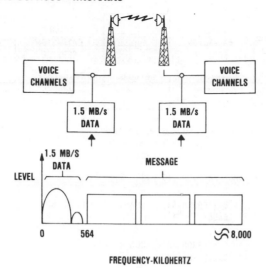

Figure 3.19. Data under voice (DUV).

Several points of caution are appropriate, however, with respect to DDS. First, it will be available only in the several hundred largest metropolitan areas of the United States (see Figure 3.15). Also, there may be many regions of the country, even those around major population centers, where basic telephone service is supplied not by the Bell System but by an independent telephone company; DDS service may not be available in these areas either. To accommodate user locations not reachable by DDS, it will be necessary to employ analog facilities (with conventional modems at each end) between such locations and the nearest DDS network entry point. For example, a user of DDS between two locations not in the DDS service area would have to obtain analog extension service at each end of the DDS portion of the connection. This would necessitate charges for four conventional modems (as opposed to the regular analog way) and expensive mileage charges along two low density links to get connected into DDS. Finally, the error characteristics of the service on an end-to-end basis would be worse than those of existing analog lines because bit errors could arise from either of the three links shown in Figure 3.20. In this case the bit error rate of the end-to-end service would be the sum of the bit error rates on the two analog extension links and on the DDS link. Another important restriction is that regular DDS users will not be able to use dial-backup schemes without analog modems. Nor will they be able to use DDS lines for alternate voice and data transmission until such time as voice digitizers become available at reasonable prices.

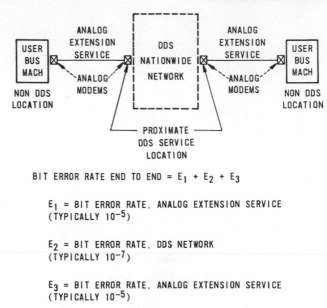

$$\text{BIT ERROR RATE END TO END} = E_1 + E_2 + E_3$$

E_1 = BIT ERROR RATE, ANALOG EXTENSION SERVICE
(TYPICALLY 10^{-5})

E_2 = BIT ERROR RATE, DDS NETWORK
(TYPICALLY 10^{-7})

E_3 = BIT ERROR RATE, ANALOG EXTENSION SERVICE
(TYPICALLY 10^{-5})

Figure 3.20.   Accommodating off-net locations in DDS.

Although most user networks will overlay extensively with DDS locations and high density rate centers, the existence of even a few noncon-
formist points will complicate the network administration process and the
logistics of troubleshooting, and will distort the economic arguments in
favor of these new price structures and service facilities. Only by a
systematic, objective evaluation of all the advantages and disadvantages
of these various networking alternatives will it be possible to determine
the best network configuration.

3.4.4.   Wideband or Broadband Private Line Services—Series 5000 Channels

Interstate private line services for data transmission at speeds in excess of
10,000 bits/sec are available in the form of Bell System Series 5000 and
8000 channels. In both services analog transmission is used. Digital
transmission, on the other hand, is utilized to provide 56,000 bits/sec
leased channels to users of the Bell System's new DDS network in
locations where the service is available.

There are two types of Series 5000 (also known as Telpak) channels:
Series 5700 and 5800 offerings. Telpak channels are bundles of transmission capacity including arbitrary mixtures of the following:

- Sub-voice-grade (teletypewriter) channels.
- Voice-grade channels.
- Wideband data channels.

In both Telpak services, a sub-voice-grade channel equates arbitrarily to one-half a voice channel. Data channels at 19.2 kilobits/sec equate to 6 voice channels, whereas 40.8 and 50 kilobits/sec channels equate to 12. Subject to the above capacity equivalences, the Series 5700 (Telpak C) user may mix and match any combination of the services totaling not more than 60 voice channel equivalents for a fixed mileage-dependent price. On the other hand, the Series 5800 (Telpak D) user may combine individual channels totaling not more than 240 voice channels for a fixed mileage-dependent price. Table 3.9 displays recently effective prices for these offerings.

Termination charges in Telpak depend on the constituent services that comprise the bundle. For example, each point-to-point teletypewriter or voice channel in the bundle has individual termination charges for each drop where the channel connects to a customer primise. Modem charges are separate and additional to these so-called Telpak service terminal charges, except in the case of wideband data channels. Wideband data termination charges include the local drops and wideband modems.

Individual voice-grade lines may also be connected through Telpak channels, even if one or more of the end points does not coincide with the Telpak end point. As shown in Figure 3.21, the individual voice circuit from location A to location C passes through Telpak to location B. It is then connected from B to C as a Telpak extension channel. Mileage-dependent prices for Telpak extension channels (see Figure 3.22) are currently similar to those in effect for individual voice channels before the advent of the HiLo tariff discussed previously. These unique pricing structures for Telpak extension channels have recently been ruled discriminatory by the Federal Communications Commission, and it appears likely that in the near future such structures may be eliminated. It is anyone's guess what price structure will replace the Telpak extension tariff. However, something similar if not exactly equivalent to MPL prices may be anticipated.

The example of Figure 3.23 illustrates different individual channel types passing through a Telpak C bulk channel from location A to location B. In the Telpak are:

- Eight point-to-point teletype channels from A to B.
- Ten point-to-point voice-grade channels from A to B.
- Fourteen point-to-point voice-grade channels from A to C routed through B.

Table 3.9. Wideband Private Line Services, AT&T Typical 1976 Rates[a]

Type of Channel	Data Rate (bits/sec)	One-Time Installation Charge, per Service Terminal	Monthly Charge, First Service Terminal (Includes Modem)	Monthly Charge, Additional Service Terminals in Same Exchange	Channel Mileage Charges, Monthly Rate per Airline Mile
5701	40,800 or 50,000	$216	$460	$324	$32.50
5703	19,200	$216	$460	$406	$32.50
5751	230,400	$216	$704	n.a.	$32.50
8801	40,800 or 50,000	$216	$460	$324	First 250 miles: $16.20
					Next 250 miles: $11.40
8803	19,200	$216	$460	$406	Each additional mile $8.15

[a]Series 5700 offerings provide 60 voice channels worth of bandwidth. Each 50,000 bits/sec data stream uses 12 of these. Other voice channels are available for voice or additional data applications. A 19,200 bits/sec data stream utilizes only 6 voice channels of the allotment.
Above service terminal charges are for wideband service only. See Figure 3.21 for voice channel termination charges in Telpak.

CIRCUIT REQUIREMENTS

A to *C*	1 Circuit
A to *B*	29 Circuits

SERVICE TERMINALS

A: 30 Telpak Service Terminals
B: 29 Telpak Service Terminals
C: 1 Voice Service Terminal for Telpak
Extension Channel

PLUS TELPAK CONNECTING ARRANGEMENT AT *B* (for circuit from *A* to *C*)

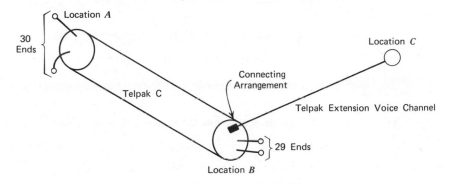

Recent Telpak service terminal charges for voice circuits: $43.30/month
Recent Telpak connecting arrangement charges: $43.30/month

Figure 3.21. Pricing components of Telpak layout.

IXC MILEAGE	PER MILE $ COST PER MONTH
FIRST 25	$3.24
NEXT 75	2.28
NEXT 150	1.63
NEXT 250	1.13
EACH ADDITIONAL	.81

ABOVE RATES PROVIDED CLEVER USERS WITH A LOOPHOLE. WHENEVER HILO
RATES ON A CIRCUIT WERE MORE EXPENSIVE THAN THOSE ABOVE, USERS
WOULD EMPLOY A SHORT TELPAK STUB OF ONLY SEVERAL MILES, ROUTING
THE VOICE CHANNEL AS A TELPAK EXTENSION TO SAVE CONSIDERABLE COST.
AGAIN THE LOOPHOLE PROVOKED ANOTHER REGULATORY CONTROVERSY WHICH
WAS UNRESOLVED AT END OF 1976.

Figure 3.22. Series 5200 and 5300 Telpak extension rates applied to IXC portions of an individual voice channel outside Telpak whenever a portion of entire channel is in Telpak.

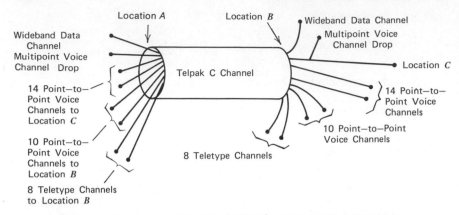

Figure 3.23. An example of a Telpak C channel with extensions.

- One multipoint voice-grade circuit with drops in locations *A, B,* and *C.*
- A wideband 50 kilobits/sec circuit from *A* to *B.*

The total bandwidth equivalent of this Telpak mixture is 41 voice-grade equivalents (8 halves for the teletypes and 12 for the wideband channel).

The total cost for the above network (assuming that the bulk Telpak services shown in Figure 3.23 costs less than individually provided offerings) would be the sum of the costs for the following:

- Telpak mileage from *A* to *B.*
- Eight teletype terminations in Telpak at location *A.*
- Eight teletype terminations in Telpak at location *B.*
- Twenty-five (10 + 14 + 1) regular voice-grade channel terminations in Telpak at location *A.*
- Eleven (10 + 1) regular voice-grade channel terminations in Telpak at location *B.*
- Fourteen voice-grade channel Telpak connecting arrangements at *B* for the circuits routed to location *C.*
- Individual voice-grade channel mileage charges for fifteen (14 + 1) channels from *B* to *.C.*
- Fifteen (14 + 1) individual voice-grade channel termination charges at location *C.*
- Two wideband data service terminals, one at *A* and one at *B.*

No modem or conditioning charges are included in this tally, except for the wideband data channel. Whenever channels pass through several

Telpaks in cascade, there are no termination charges at Telpak junction points except for circuits that terminate or depart from Telpak at such points.

An interesting aspect of Telpak is that it will often be the least expensive way of obtaining bundled service, even if the full capacity of the Telpak channel is not used. For instance, in the above example an additional 19 voice channels could be added between A and B for an incremental cost of terminations alone. This aspect of Telpak, coupled with the frequently changing circuit requirements of typical large communications users, creates an awesome nightmare for the manager faced with the need to continually keep total costs at a minimum.

In summary, Telpak service is an accounting structure. The least cost Telpak configuration can and often does change, without any electrical routing changes of the circuits in the common carrier network. Such complicated pricing structures have frustrated communications managers for years, but have been a source of great satisfaction (and income) for consulting organizations specializing in network optimization. Things are changing, however, as the pricing structures of the specialized carriers (noted in the next section) indicate. On one hand, the problem of cost-optimizing facilities obtained from an individual carrier may be getting easier. On the other hand, however, the problem of determining the best mixture of offerings from several carriers remains just as difficult.

3.4.5. Series 8000 Wideband Channels for Data Transmission

Series 8000 channels correspond to the equivalent of a bundle of 12 voice-grade channels and may be arranged to provide 19,200, 40,800, or 50,000 bits/sec data transmission capacity. When 19.2 kilobits/sec is used, 6 voice-grade channels are available for another 19.2 kilobits/sec channel or individual voice usage. Series 8000 channels may also be employed solely for voice usage, enabling customers to obtain an alternative to multiple voice lines whenever a Telpak C cannot be justified.

Table 3.9 summarizes the basic channel and service terminal charges associated with Series 5000 and 8000 channels. It should be emphasized that service terminal charges here include the wideband modem necessary to obtain data transmission capability over the analog channel bundles. In the future it is likely that these price structures will be modified in much the same fashion as those for Series 5000 channels, but details are not known at the time of this writing.

There are three main differences between Series 5000 and 8000 channels:

1. The amount of aggregate analog bandwidth available for conversion into voice and data channels of lower capacity.
2. The price for the service.
3. The fact that Series 8000 channels are available only between two end points; therefore individual voice channels cannot be picked up or dropped off at intermediate sites along the way.

3.5. SPECIALIZED CARRIER AND SATELLITE LEASED SERVICES

Several additional services have recently become domestically available, both from new organizations and from established ones. In this section, offerings of the major specialized common carriers, including MCI Telecommunications, Southern Pacific Communications Company, and the satellite carriers, are overviewed. The main objective here is to highlight the components of the pricing structures. The exact details of carrier tariffs and the specific locations of service availability have been changing frequently over the past few years, and it is reasonable to expect that such changes will continue. The cost-conscious user should recognize that these offerings exist, understand their advantages and limitations, and know how to estimate their possible cost impacts on his networking requirements. In this section these objectives are addressed.

3.5.1. Specialized Carrier Offerings from MCI and Southern Pacific

Both organizations offer service on a coast-to-coast basis in many major cities. Their pricing structures are similar, as are their transmission technology (analog voice-grade lines with modems used for data channels). However, the exact details of the pricing structures differ slightly, as shown in Figures 3.24 and 3.25.

For MCI offerings, the users' charges are the sum of two rate elements: (1) IXC mileage and (2) channel termination charges. Mileage structures are noticeably different from the previously noted Bell System offerings. The MCI user is offered a sliding scale discount on individual voice-grade IXC mileage costs, the discount increasing as the total number of channels increases. Interestingly, this discount structure depends only on the number of channels involved and *not* on the geography of the locations being connected. The MCI user of 240 channels qualifies for the maximum discount, even if all 240 channels have no geographic route commonality. Once the cost per mile is determined (from the total number of channels), the IXC charge for each circuit is obtained by applying this rate to the point-to-point distance between circuit end points. The Bell System Telpak D user of 240 channels, on the other hand, obtains the maximum discount only if all 240 channels are provided along a common route.

Channel termination charges for MCI customers cover the local distribution facilities required to connect MCI long haul offices with customer premises and reflect costs for maintenance and miscellaneous expenses of the carrier. As noted in Figure 3.24, the computation depends on the average channel mileage and number of channel ends in the total customer network.

Southern Pacific Communications prices are similar in structure and level to MCI charges; however, the rate elements are different. The major elements of Southern Pacific rate structures in effect during 1976 are as follows:

1. IXC mileage charges.
2. Channel termination charges.
3. Local access channel charges.

Southern Pacific also provides special voice-grade and digital service prices not shown in Figure 3.25 between certain pairs of locations, in contrast to MCI. This is generally a competitive response to the satellite carriers' service between these pairs of locations.

3.5.2. Satellite Carrier Services

Domestic satellite services commenced during July 1974, offering reductions of 40 to 50% for coast-to-coast voice-grade lines and proportionately smaller reductions for shorter distances. Key organizations involved in providing satellite services at the beginning of 1976 were Western Union, RCA, and American Satellite. Comsat, Aetna Life, and IBM have also announced plans to jointly enter the domestic satellite business via a partnership known as Satellite Business Systems. However, numerous regulatory and organizational details must be resolved before this joint effort makes its initial service offerings.

For the user, satellite services afford many interesting and unique possibilities. However, not all of these potentialities have as yet been introduced as commercial offerings. Wideband services much faster than any currently available become possible. With earth stations located at customer premises, all dependence on existing carrier facilities for local distribution connections can be eliminated. Multiaccess, time-shared channels are also readily possible, even though none has been tariffed by the satellite carriers as of this writing. More will be said about these technological developments in the next chapter on carrier facilities.

PRIVATE LINE FACILITIES

MCI TELECOMMUNICATIONS CORPORATION

DESCRIPTION: Point-to-point communication channels for voice, data, facsimile and various wideband applications. Offered in increments of 1 to 240 voice-grade (VF) channels, each with a nominal bandwidth of 4 kHz.

RATES: The total monthly charge for an end-to-end facility is the composite of two rate elements: (1) IXC mileage and (2) channel termination charge.

I. MILEAGE: Monthly Cost per VF Channel Mile

TOTAL CHANNEL MILES (thousands)	TOTAL NUMBER OF CHANNELS									
	1–9	10–39	40–49	50–74	75–99	100–149	150–239	240–499	500–999	Over 1000
0–1	$0.87	0.87	0.87	0.87	0.87	0.87	0.87	0.87	0.87	0.87
1–5	0.87	0.87	0.74	0.73	0.72	0.70	0.70	0.70	0.70	0.70
5–10	0.87	0.86	0.72	0.70	0.69	0.68	0.67	0.67	0.67	0.67
10–25	0.87	0.79	0.70	0.67	0.66	0.63	0.61	0.59	0.58	0.58
25–50	0.87	0.75	0.68	0.66	0.65	0.62	0.59	0.56	0.56	0.55
50–75		0.72	0.67	0.65	0.64	0.61	0.55	0.51	0.51	0.50
75–100		0.72	0.65	0.63	0.62	0.59	0.51	0.44	0.44	0.44
100–125		0.72	0.63	0.60	0.59	0.57	0.49	0.44	0.44	0.44
125–150			0.62	0.59	0.58	0.56	0.48	0.43	0.43	0.43
150–175				0.58	0.57	0.54	0.47	0.42	0.42	0.42
175–200				0.57	0.56	0.51	0.46	0.41	0.41	0.41
200–250				0.56	0.55	0.49	0.45	0.41	0.41	0.41
250–300					0.54	0.48	0.44	0.41	0.41	0.40
300–350						0.47	0.44	0.41	0.41	0.40
350–400						0.46	0.43	0.41	0.40	0.39
400–450							0.42	0.40	0.39	0.38
450–500							0.42	0.40	0.39	0.38
500–550							0.41	0.39	0.38	0.37
550–600							0.39	0.39	0.38	0.37
600–700							0.39	0.38	0.37	0.37
700–1000							0.38	0.38	0.37	0.37
1000–3000								0.37	0.37	0.37
Over 3000										0.37

MILEAGE—Data Channels
        75 baud—50% of VF Channel Rate
        150 baud—75% of VF Channel Rate
        300–9600 bits/sec: Same as VF Channel Rate

Figure 3.24. Overview of MCI Telecommunications Corporation specialized carrier rate structure—September, 1976 illustrative rates.

II. CHANNEL TERMINATIONS—Monthly in Cumulative Channel Ends

VOICE

Channel Terminations		Channel Terminations	
Number	Monthly	Number	Monthly
1	$ 57.90	37	$1349.40
2–21	57.90ea.	38–60	25.20ea.
22	1224.30	61	1962.00
23–36	7.20ea.	Ea. Add'l	32.10

DATA AND TELEPRINTER

75 bits/sec TTY:	$ 27.90	7200 bits/sec Data:	$ 87.90
150 bits/sec TTY:	38.10	9600 bits/sec Data:	102.80
4800 bits/sec Data:	65.40		

ALTERNATE VOICE/DATA (AVD)

300–4800 bits/sec	$ 80.40
7200 bits/sec	102.90
9600 bits/sec	117.90

Figure 3.24. (Continued)

Currently, the substantial cost savings potentially afforded by the satellite carriers are frequently offset by the high costs of connecting customers to earth stations. As shown in Figure 3.26, at the end of 1975 even the largest domestic satellite carrier had fewer than 10 earth stations for public channel provision. Costs to a satellite carrier customer include charges for the following:

- The satellite channel itself.
- Any charges between customer premises and serving earth stations.

Charges for the connections into earth stations are quite significant unless intracity local distribution facilities can be employed by the satellite carriers. This requires an earth station in each city where service is available, a setup that is well beyond the current state of the industry, as noted in Figure 3.26. Even when an earth station is located in a city where service is available, the satellite carrier will have to charge for local distribution facilities comparable to those currently used by the specialized carriers.

These local distribution facility costs (and corresponding service limitations) can ultimately be eliminated—but only when each customer premise contains its own earth station! More will be said about this possibility in subsequent chapters. However, such events appear unlikely (on a widespread geographic basis) for many years to come.

PRIVATE LINE FACILITIES
SOUTHERN PACIFIC COMMUNICATIONS COMPANY (SPCC)

DESCRIPTION: Point-to-point communication channels for voice, data, facsimile, and various wideband applications. Offered in increments of 1 to 240 voice-grade (VF) channels, each with a nominal bandwidth of 4 kHz. Service is offered on both a "metered use" and full period (24 hour/day) basis.

FULL PERIOD SERVICE RATES Except for SPCC'S digital data service, the total monthly charge for a facility is the composite of three elements: (1) IXC mileage, (2) channel termination charge, and (3) local access channel charge.

1. IXC MILEAGE: HDX OR FDX MONTHLY
Channel Mileage, 100 or Over[b]

Facility	First 1000 Miles (per Mile)	Each Additional Mile
0–75 bits/sec	$0.22	$0.22
0–150 bits/sec	0.32	0.32
0–300 bits/sec	0.44	0.44
1–45 vf	0.60	0.39
48–59 vf	0.596–0.499[a]	0.392–0.45[a]
60–157 vf	0.494	0.494
158–172 vf	0.493–0.458[a]	0.453–0.458[a]
173–239 vf	0.456–0.351[a]	0.456–0.351[a]
Each additional channel	0.350	0.350

[a]Sliding scale rates: Carrier's Tariff 2 contains exact values.
[b]*Short Haul:* Under 100 miles, each VF is $0.745/mile/month.

II. CHANNEL TERMINATION (per Channel End)

	Installation	Monthly Charge
0–75 bits/sec	$ 25.00	$ 23.00
75–300 bits/sec	25.00	23.00
600–9600 bits/sec	40.00	25.00
Data with C-2 conditioning	120.00	53.00
4000 Hz (Two Point)		
1–9 terminals/city	40.00	25.00
20–30 terminals/city	40.00	23.00
31–40 terminals/city	40.00	22.00
41 or more terminals/city	40.00	21.00
4,000 Hz (multipoint)	32.00	37.00
Short haul surcharge		
(under 100 Miles) per VF	—	10.00
48,000 Hz	75.00	78.00
240,000 Hz	150.00	172.00

Figure 3.25. Typical rates charged by Southern Pacific specialized carrier unit September, 1976.

III.   LOCAL ACCESS CHANNELS (per voice-grade channel between carrier's operating center and a premise of the subscriber)

	Installation	Monthly Charge
Within local distribution area		
1–19 VF terminations/premises	$60.00	$32 + $1/mile
20–30 VF terminations/premises	60.00	$32.00
31–40 VF terminations/premises	60.00	30.00
41 or more VF termination/premises	60.00	24.00
Outside local distribution area	Actual cost plus 5%	Actual cost plus 5%
Additional station, same premises	30.00	2.00
Termination at CCSA switch	60.00	10.00

Figure 3.25.   (Continued)

3.6.   HYBRID SERVICES

Other services are available which have certain properties of both switched and leased services. These are known as *hybrid services*. We now discuss *foreign exchange, tandem tie line, CCSA, and value-added services*.

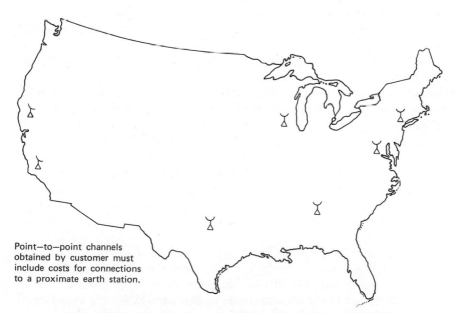

Point—to—point channels obtained by customer must include costs for connections to a proximate earth station.

Figure 3.26.   Western Union satellite earth stations, early 1976.

3.6.1. Foreign Exchange Service

A foreign exchange (FX) line is a dedicated (leased) line that connects two cities; one end terminates at a fixed location, while the other is connected to the direct distance dial network via a regular business telephone. Inward FX service enables any customer to dial a local seven-digit number in city *B*. The phone will ring at a fixed switchboard or telephone instrument in city *A*. The city *B* user thus needs only to dial a local call to be connected to the city *A* phone. Outward FX service enables the fixed location phone in city *A* to place calls to any direct dial location in city *B* merely by dialing seven digits, once the FX line has been obtained.

Thus FX service is a hybrid leased line/dial service with one open end and one closed (or fixed) end. Pricing for FX service is typically determined by the monthly rate for the leased line between the two cities plus the prices for the regular phone line in the open-ended city. Modems are also required if the FX connection is to be used for data transmission.

3.6.2. Tandem Tie Lie Services and CCSA

The Bell System provides several shared-user private line services with dedicated lines and switching machines to interconnect the diverse locations of a single corporate telecommunications user. The lowest level service is known as tandem tie line service. Here any extension phone connected to the tandem tie line network switchers may call any other phone by dialing a series of addressing digits, which are used to establish the route or path between the calling and the called parties.

The disadvantages of this service are that the user is forced to select his own route and must therefore know the makeup of the network. Alternative automatic rerouting in case of busy trunk lines between switchers is not possible. The calling sequence is generally not uniform and depends on which path the user selects. For example, it can be seen in Figure 3.27 that a user in Newark must dial 83 to talk with Dallas. To talk with Oklahoma City the user must dial 83 + 245. Another disadvantage is that tie line service as currently provided by the Bell System does not enable the user to obtain usage statistics for the trunk lines. Also, detailed identification of calling and called parties plus statistical information on holding times for individual calls is not available as part of the tie line service.

The main advantage of tie line service is that a network consisting of leased lines and switching machines is available at a fixed monthly price for connecting geographically diverse yet fixed user locations.

Since there are many disadvantages of this service for the very largest corporate users (no automatic routing; no uniform numbering plan for

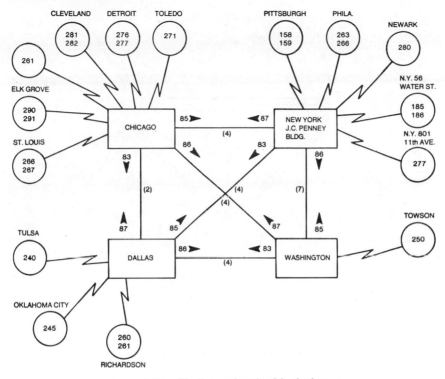

Figure 3.27. Tie line network of typical user.

addressing; no off-net capability, i.e., access to distant noncorporate locations; no traffic measuring features), the Bell System has developed a very elaborate service known as Common Control Switching Arrangement (CCSA).

As shown in Figure 3.28, CCSA service is in effect a miniature replica of the public telephone network, dedicated to users within one corporation. Portions of Bell System switching centers are reserved exclusively for access lines and trunks leased by the CCSA user. Each CCSA switch has a unique three-digit prefix and individual extensions reachable by the subsequent four digits in the seven-digit dialing sequence used to access locations hooked into the CCSA network. A user typically obtains access to the CCSA network by dialing a special code (say, the digit 8 followed by the seven digits of the uniform numbering plan).

Each CCSA customer receives a monthly traffic sample for nominally 20% of all calls placed over the network. This is useful for cost-accounting and traffic study purposes. A CCSA call will be automatically rerouted

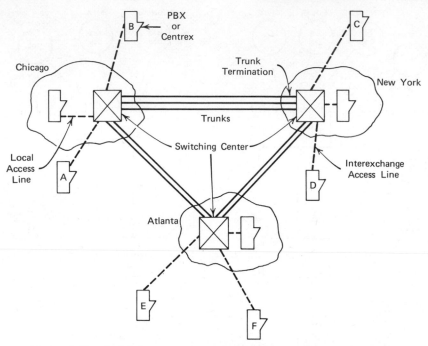

Figure 3.28. CCSA (common control switching arrangement) network.

along an alternative path if all trunks in the primary path are busy. Importantly, this rerouting takes place automatically, unbeknown to the calling party. In regular tie line service, the user must attempt to reroute the call by dialing along a different path whenever all trunks are busy between two switches.

Another useful optional feature of CCSA service as it is presently provided enables users to call a distant telephone not connected to the network automatically by using the CCSA network facilities and outbound FX and/or WATS lines. The user placing the call accesses the network in a similar way and dials 10 digits (instead of the 7 for on-network calls). Here the 10 digits consist of the standard 3-digit area code plus the 7-digit telephone number of the desired off-net location. The CCSA network automatically routes the call along the CCSA network's trunks to the most appropriate switch, where an FX or WATS line is automatically accessed to complete the call.

3.6.3. Other Types of Hybrid Services

In the next few years, the common carriers in the United States will be drastically revising their services such as tie line and CCSA to overcome many of the objections and limitations noted above. In fact, certain specialized carriers have already announced their competitive responses to the Bell System's tie line service and CCSA offerings. One can reasonably expect the differences between tie line and CCSA service to all but disappear in the not-too-distant future as uniform services with numerous options become available from the specialized and satellite carriers. The following are some possible new characteristics of such services:

- Miniature business-only direct dial services between major cities.
- Full traffic statistics on access line and trunk usage.
- Identification of calling and called parties on 100% of all calls.
- Automatic routing of calls over the best complement of facilities connected to switches (leased lines, WATS, FX, and direct distance dial).
- Authorization codes for improved control of network usage.

The possibilities for innovation here appear limitless. Only time will fully reveal the full spectrum of viable new services.

3.6.4. Value-Added Carrier Offerings

Still another new data transmission service alternative became available to users during the summer of 1975. The initial value-added offering of Telenet Communications Corporation involves the much publicized concept of a public, intelligent packet-switched network connecting subscriber terminals and computers (see Reference [7]). Then in 1976 Tymnet Communications Corporation commenced a similar service based on minicomputer switching. No attempt is made to discuss the technological features of such networks in detail. Other organizations offering similar services will doubtlessly emerge in the coming months. However, the user should be aware of the major service characteristics and pricing components of value-added carrier offerings. As before, the exact prices for such services will change frequently; hence the value-added carrier should be consulted for exact price quotations. Notwithstanding these dynamics of an embryonic offering, several major pricing elements that the user must deal with can be identified (with the assistance of Table 3.10 and Figures 3.29 and 3.30) as follows:

1. Cost of dedicated host-access lines, including any required software, modems, and dedicated portions of the value-added carrier's minicomputers consumed by host-access lines.
2. Cost of any other dedicated equipment in the carrier's minicomputers for terminal connections, including:
    (a) Dedicated line ports.

Table 3.10. Value-Added Carrier Networks

Carrier gets basic leased lines from existing carrier; adds value by sharing lines with packet switching minicomputers.

Services typically are line protocol dependent (not transparent like conventional offerings); X25 rapidly emerging as worldwide standard; see Chapter 8.

Regulatory status of value-added vendors still unresolved.

Possible value-added service features (enhancements):
- Speed changing.
- Code conversion.
- Security of data.
- Virtually error-free transmission.
- Alternate routing.
- Priority service levels, delayed delivery.
- Broadcast message transmission.
- Elastic port capacity—time-variable bandwidth.
- User eliminates maintenance operation of network.
- Possibly lower transmission charges.

Costs to user depend on mix of:

- Connect time.
- Volume.
- Priority.
- Local distribution arrangement.
- Software modifications required (if any).

Typical examples:

- Telenet Communications Corporation (U.S.A.).
- Tymnet Communications (U.S.A)
- Datapac (Canada).
- EPSS Experimental Packet Switching System (U.K.).

(*b*) Dedicated switched ports (those usable only by a particular customer).
3. Cost of any shared equipment in the carrier's minicomputers (e.g., for public dial ports).
4. Cost of any dedicated lines and/or dedicated equipment from customer premises into the value-added carrier's minicomputers (central offices).

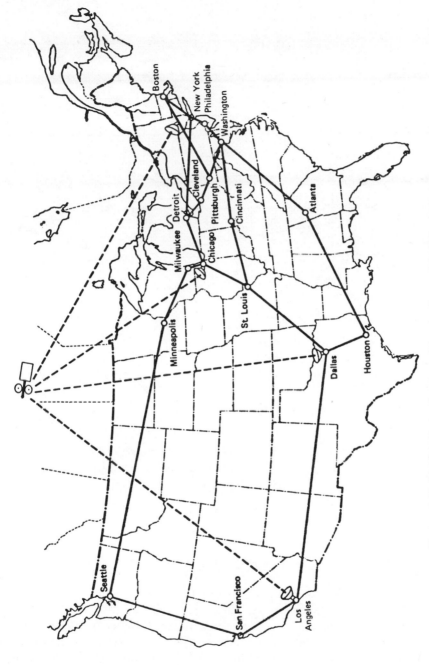

Figure 3.29. Initial 18-city line layout for the first public U.S. packet switching network, operated by the Telenet Communications Corporation.

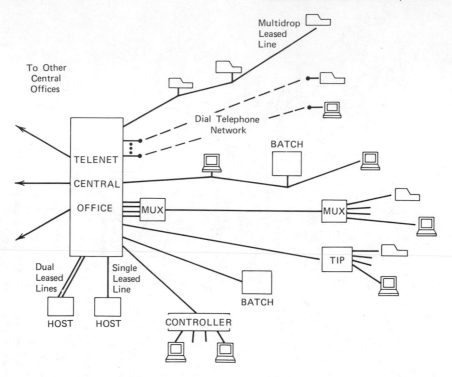

LEGEND

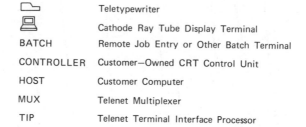

	Teletypewriter
	Cathode Ray Tube Display Terminal
BATCH	Remote Job Entry or Other Batch Terminal
CONTROLLER	Customer—Owned CRT Control Unit
HOST	Customer Computer
MUX	Telenet Multiplexer
TIP	Telenet Terminal Interface Processor

Figure 3.30.   Illustrative Telenet local distribution arrangements.

5. Transmission charges for dial-up local distribution (often treated as connect time charges).
6. Data-volume-dependent charges for actual transmission through the wideband lines of the value-added carriers (the packet or character charge). Usually this charge does not depend on distance between terminal and computer.

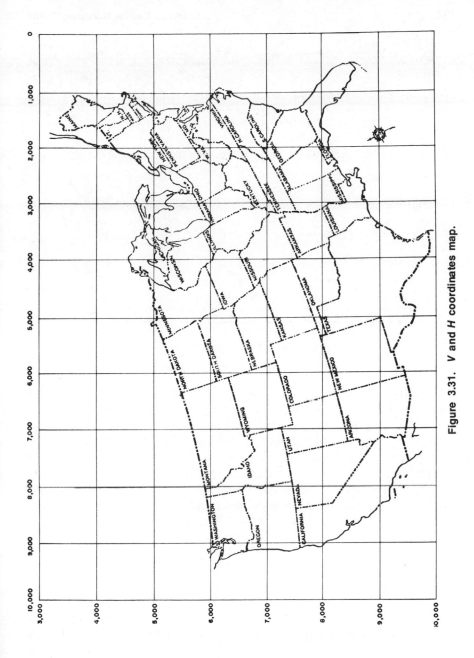

Figure 3.31. *V* and *H* coordinates map.

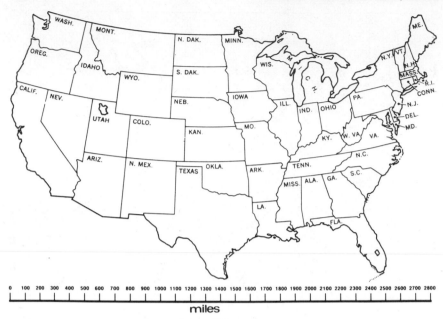

Figure 3.32. Mileage estimator.

Once all appropriate costs of using the value-added carrier service have been identified, the user can compare these estimates with costs of current networking approaches. The major potential advantages and characteristics of value-added services to the user are summarized in Table 3.10. After all these benefits have been quantified, the best approach can be selected.

In closing it should be noted that value-added carrier service can eliminate user concern about topological optimization, network maintenance, and network operational costs. Such administrative benefits cannot be overlooked in today's cost-conscious climates. They may, in fact, be the primary argument in favor of such services.

3.7. RECAPITULATION

The material in this chapter was intended to show the types of dial-up and leased line services available to data transmission users, the typical costs, and the cost calculation procedures associated with these services. Actual numbers cited in the figures and tables must be recognized as being subject to confirmation by the appropriate carrier, inasmuch as tariffs are continually being expanded, modified, and even withdrawn every month.

Furthermore, no attempt has been made to pass judgment on which types of services are most suitable for specific applications. Detailed comparisons and systems design calculations of this type are discussed in detail in subsequent portions of this book.

Figures 3.31 and 3.32 are useful mileage estimator maps.

REFERENCES

1. FCC Tariff 255, List of Rate Centers, filed by American Telephone & Telegraph Co. with the FCC.

2. FCC Tariff 260, Rates, Practices and Procedures Governing Use of Interstate Leased Lines, filed by American Telephone & Telegraph Co. with the FCC.

3. FCC Tariff 263, Rates, Practices, and Procedures Governing Interstate Use of Public Switched Network, filed by American Telephone & Telegraph Co. with the FCC.

4. *The Guide to Communication Services*, pocket summary of rates for all types of communication services and facilities, Center for Communications Management, Ramsey, N.J.

5. "Wide Area Telecommunications Service (WATS)," booklet describing prices and service areas for all types of interstate WATS, American Telephone and Telegraph Co., New York.

6. *Intercity Services Handbook*, American Telephone and Telegraph Co., Long Lines Marketing Department, New York.

7. D. R. Doll, "Telecommunications Turbulence and the Computer Network Revolution," *IEEE Computer*, February 1974.

FOUR

TELECOMMUNICATIONS TRANSMISSION FACILITIES AND SIGNAL CONVERSION DEVICES

In this chapter, the facilities that the carrier organizations use to provide their respective service offerings are discussed. The characteristics of the signal conversion devices that interface these facilities to the user's business machines are also considered. An understanding of these facilities is vital to the planning and/or implementation of any successful data network, since network cost and performance are inexorably linked to the quality of the transmission lines and the ability of the signal converters to function satisfactorily.

The primary focal points of this chapter are the facilities of the voice-grade telephone networks and the new all-digital networks being employed exclusively for data transmission. Examples of the voice networks are the U.S. public telephone network operated by the Bell System and similar networks operated in Canada and in England, France, Germany, and other European countries. The architectural characteristics of most of these networks are similar, although specific technical implementations vary from one country to the next. Examples of all the digital networks considered are the U.S. Bell System's Dataphone Digital Service (DDS) network and the Canadian Dataroute network. The Datran Company is another U.S. organization that was involved in providing data transmission services employing digital transmission facilities; because of major financial problems it ceased operations during 1976. However, this chapter does consider the Datran network, both for historical purposes and because of the real possibility that the same facilities will be used for comparable services offered by a different common carrier organization acquiring the Datran physical plant for operational purposes.[1]

The physical facilities and network organizations employed by the value-added carriers to provide intelligent network services are also rapidly becoming important for users and network planners to understand and evaluate. Facilities for these types of networks are discussed at length in Chapter 8.

In summary, the organizational architecture of conventional voice and data networks operated by various common carrier organizations is discussed in this chapter. Specific examples are cited, primarily involving Bell System facilities, although it should be recognized that other carrier networks in the United States and elsewhere are similar. The goal is to discuss standard networking facilities in a general context without getting tied down to specific details unique to one common carrier implementation.

4.1. ANALOG VERSUS DIGITAL TRANSMISSION

Throughout the industry, considerable ambiguity surrounds the usage of the term *data communications, data transmission, digital communications,* and so forth. This section attempts to distinguish the basic modes of usage of carrier facilities by the terms *voice* and *data* communications. Inside the carrier network, the end-user information (either voice or data) may be sent or propagated by means of either *analog* or *digital* transmission signals. As shown in Figure 4.1, "analog transmission" thus refers to

[1]This actually happened in late 1976 when Southern Pacific Communications Company (SPCC) acquired Datran assets and announced its intention to subsequently reintroduce Datran's original switched digital services.

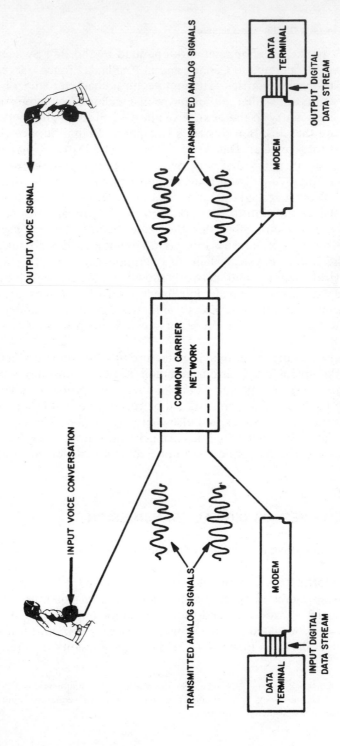

Figure 4.1. Analog transmission of voice or data signals.

the use of continuously varying signals in the carrier network. "Digital transmission," on the other hand, implies propagation of the user information (voice or data) by means of discrete signal levels, as shown in Figure 4.2. Whenever digital transmission is used to carry voice conversations, it is necessary for the carrier network to convert the continuously varying user voice signal into a pulse stream. The reverse conversion of a

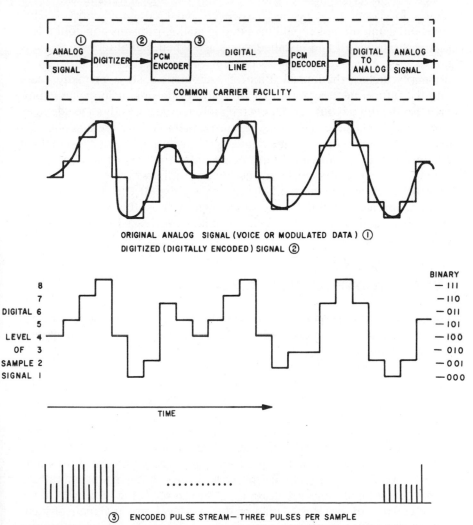

ORIGINAL ANALOG SIGNAL (VOICE OR MODULATED DATA) ①
DIGITIZED (DIGITALLY ENCODED) SIGNAL ②

③ ENCODED PULSE STREAM— THREE PULSES PER SAMPLE

Figure 4.2.   Digital transmission of voice or data signals using pulse code modulation (PCM).

pulse stream back into a continuously varying signal is required to reconstruct the user voice conversation at the output point.

Most carrier networks designed for handling voice conversations employ a mixture of analog and digital transmission techniques to propagate these conversations through the carrier network, using different transmission techniques along different portions of the electrical route or path. It is fair to conclude that a complete common carrier network being constructed from scratch today would probably use digital transmission techniques for economic reasons. However, most common carriers have substantial amounts of capital invested in analog transmission equipment that was purchased and installed years ago when digital technology was not as cost effective as it is at present. Utility accounting procedures ordinarily dictate the amortization of equipment costs over many years into the future, necessitating that the carrier continue using such equipment for the full payout period, even if more technically advanced devices later became available. The common carrier plant is therefore a continually evolving system, and one may find early twentieth century switching equipment and transmission lines intermixed with the most contemporary equipment. Generally speaking, the higher traffic portions of the carrier network facilities are most likely to employ digital transmission. Conversely, the least traffic-dense routes such as those between individual subscribers and their serving central offices are least likely to use the digital mode.

4.2. TELEPHONE NETWORK ORGANIZATION

Figure 4.3 shows the hierarchy of switching centers and transmission lines used to provide end-to-end switched connections for regular telephone conversations.

The U.S. telephone network interconnects approximately 140 million subscribers and is currently valued at approximately $75 billion. It is truly one of the most technologically complex systems man has ever built. Because of its mammoth size and universal accessibility, it is a natural vehicle for use in transmitting information other than voice conversations—for example, facsimile signals and computer data. However, because it was designed primarily for voice communications purposes, a number of its technical properties impose important limitations on data communications applications. An example is the requirement for signal conversion devices to change the two-level digital signals of business machines into continuously varying (analog) signals that effectively use the capacity of the voice network. It is important to understand the

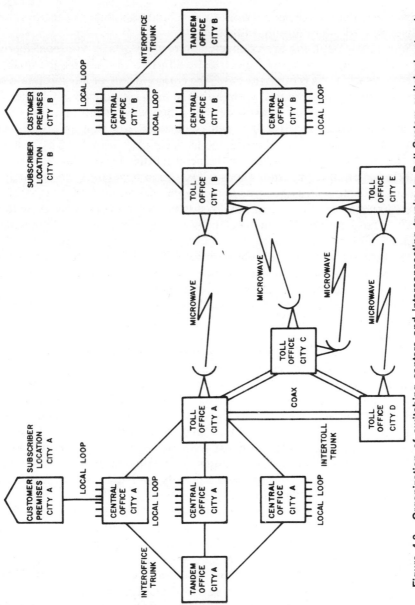

Figure 4.3. Organization of switching centers and interconnecting trunks in Bell System switched network.

organization of the carrier network to appreciate a number of factors that influence basic data terminal functions.

Subscriber locations are connected to *central offices* via *local loops,* which are copper cable pairs electrically adjusted to optimize the quality of conversation. As is often the case, the common carrier interpretation of loop should not be confused with the serial loop introduced in Chapter 2. The local loop typically provides either a two-wire or a four-wire point-to-point electrical facility. If a call is destined for another subscriber serviced by the same central office, the talking path is completed by switching the two local loops together in the central office for the duration of the call. In larger cities, central offices (COs) are in turn connected to higher order switching nodes known as *tandem offices,* since it would be prohibitively expensive for the carrier to directly interconnect all the COs within a city. These connections between COs and tandem offices are known as *trunks*.

The next switching node in the hierarchy is the *toll office* or *center*; it is involved in connecting two subscribers that cannot be directly interconnected by using lower level nodes in the hierarchy. As shown in Figure 4.4, *toll centers,* in turn, feed upward into *primary centers,* which feed *sectional centers*. The highest level of switching node is known as a *regional center*.

The carrier networks contain transmission facilities like multipair cable, coaxial cable, and microwave channels that directly connect the four types of nodes at the upper levels in the switched network hierarchy. The type of facility best suited for a particular connection depends on the number of connections or paths required between the nodes and on the distance between the nodes. With mid-1970s technology, microwave transmission is used on the highest traffic/longest distance routes. Multipair cable and other similar facilities are employed along medium and lower density paths. On the lowest density path (CO to subscriber) a single wire pair (the local loop) is adequate.

In the future this switching hierarchy will probably be altered to reflect the advantages of newer technologies like optical waveguides and satellites (see References [1] and [2]). Since a satellite enables any transmitting station to communicate directly with any receiving station, there would hardly be justification for four different levels of toll centers if the entire public network were being reconstructed from scratch today! In addition, the cost of employing a satellite-based connection between major metropolitan areas is virtually independent of distance. Here we see proof positive of how past decisions and technology commitments by carriers stand in the way of improvements to their physical networks that could dramatically enhance the spectrum of services available.

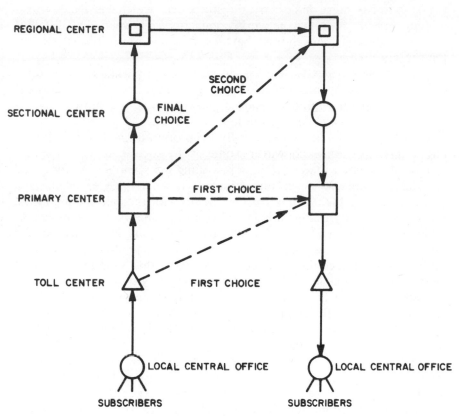

Figure 4.4. Hierarchy of switching centers in Bell System switched network.

In examining Figures 4.3 and 4.4, it is apparent that the switching plan gives rise to a wide variation in the transmission characteristics associated with different connections. The choices associated with each node indicate the preferred path for the switching machine at that node. However, since all intertoll trunks along the preferred route may be occupied, alternative choices must also exist. Generally, the priorities are established so that the user will experience a minimal amount of delay in establishing the connection. This implies a control structure that minimizes the number of switching points comprising the end-to-end path. In Section 4.9 delay statistics for establishing switched connections are presented.

Each added switching center in the connection will also degrade the transmission quality of the path, since the analog switching equipment is a major source of noise and electrical disturbances which cause data transmission errors. Switched network connections between two different cities will typically pass through between four and nine different switching centers.

The carrier provides leased lines to customers by establishing end-to-end paths through its network in which the facilities comprising a particular path are permanently set aside or reserved for one subscriber. No other customer shares any of the links along the end-to-end path.

Most leased lines have traditionally been offered only on a 24 hours/day, 7 days/week basis; however, some of the specialized common carriers in the United States are now providing *part-time leased lines* and statistically available leased connections. With a part-time leased line, the carrier dedicates the facilities for the line only for the daily period of the service contract (typically during regular business hours, for example). At other times, the carrier is technically free to employ these facilities for other purposes such as handling switched traffic, or to offer low prices for off-hours-only leased lines. In actual practice to this point in time, however, most part-time leased lines are constructed by the carrier in exactly the same fashion as full-time leased lines. Only when substantial business requirements exist for other uses of these facilities at off-hours will the carriers find it economically attractive to physically reconstruct the part-time leased lines every day.

A statistical leased line is effectively a geographically restricted type of switched connection as viewed by a single end-user customer. However, a collection or group of leased line customers between two cities may be electrically interconnected by intelligent switches so that the intercity portion of their leased line connection is available on a statistical basis. (Recall that with a conventional leased line the intercity portion is 100% available under normal opeating conditions.)

The main difference between a network configured for switched service and one configured for statistical leased line service is indeed subtle. With a switched network, any customer local loop connected to the switch may be connected to any customer local loop, either at the same end or the distant end. With a statistical private line, however, the switches are operated so that customer *A* local loops at one end may be connected only to customer *A* local loops at the other end. Similarly, customer *B* loops at one end may be connected only to customer *B* loops at the other end.

As a final point, the intercity facilities used for the statistical leased line service may be organized in two fundamentally different ways. The carrier may organize its network so that trunks can be reserved or partitioned into groups enabling customer A to use only intercity trunks in the A group, customer B to use only those in the B group, and so on. In this configuration there is a clear-cut relationship between customer identity and the facilities used by that customer. The offsetting disadvantage is that more trunks are required than when the second strategy involving trunk sharing organization is used. This alternative way of providing statistical leased line service involves all intercity trunks being thrown into a contention pool and allocated according to some control discipline like first-come/first served. Even though the intercity facilities are used more efficiently in this case, it is more difficult to provide well-defined grades of statistical availability to each customer. Note, however, that the key criterion for statistical private line service (namely, that customer X loops on one end may connect only to customer X loops on the other) can still be readily enforced and controlled.

4.3. COMPOSITION OF FACILITIES OBTAINED FROM SPECIALIZED AND SATELLITE CARRIERS

During the mid-1970s, many users began obtaining service from specialized and satellite carriers. These organizations operate intercity microwave and satellite networks but must generally rely on the local Bell System or independent telephone company for local distribution facilities.[2] Generally speaking, a specialized carrier operates a microwave terminal in a centrally located area in a major city. The specialized carrier obtains large numbers of local loops between his terminal and the serving telephone company's central office, as shown in Figure 4.5. In turn, the local operating telephone company, at the request of the specialized carrier, will interconnect the latter's customer location with another local loop to its serving central office. (Of course, the same central office may serve both the customer location and the specialized carrier microwave terminal.) Then the two central offices are interconnected to form the complete local distribution configuration. One of the big obstacles to the emergence of the specialized common carriers has been their need to obtain local distribution facilities from organizations affiliated with or controlled by companies they are trying to compete with! Much regulatory progress has been made in recent years, however, in establishing well-defined guidelines for the provision of such facilities on an equal-rights basis.

---

[2]Recent satellite service proposals have outlined nework organizations with rooftop earth stations that would communicate directly with the satellite, thereby eliminating dependence on local telephone companies in numerous situations.

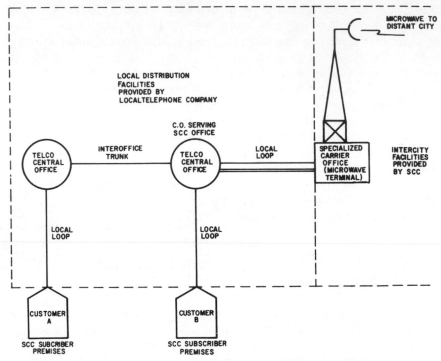

Figure 4.5. Specialized carrier local distribution arrangement.

Over the long term, as technology matures, it is realistic to expect that specialized carriers may begin providing their own local distribution facilities, using devices such as portable microwave radios, optical links, CATV links, and satellite transmission directly to the rooftops or parking lots of major buildings. In the cases of rooftop and parking lot transmission, the local distribution problem has been virtually eliminated.

Satellite-provided circuits will initially use a facilities arrangement like the one shown in Figure 4.6. The main difference between the configurations of Figures 4.5 and 4.6 is that the satellite carrier must connect customer locations into earth stations, whereas specialized carriers connect their customers into serving microwave terminals. In some cases where a satellite vendor desires to service a customer location in a city that does not have an earth station, it is necessary to utilize a microwave or coaxial channel between the customer location and the nearest earth station. This results in the hybrid arrangement shown in Figure 4.6, where the earth station and the customer premises are in different cities.

In the long term, it is reasonable to expect that satellite networks will be

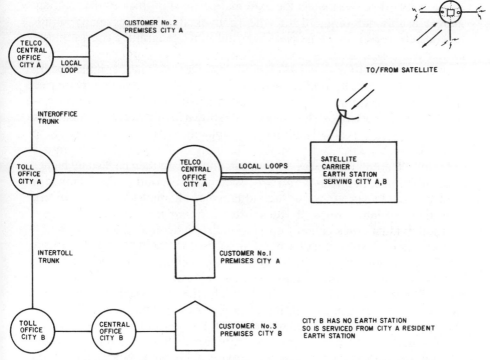

Figure 4.6. Single channel end interconnection of three circuits; earth station to customer premises for two channel ends in city A and one channel end in city B. Each customer premises is connected to a corresponding site in a distant city via the local distribution facilities, satellite, and similar local facilities at the other end.

able to bypass local distribution problems altogether by transmitting to small (possibly even portable), inexpensive earth stations located on customer rooftops or in parking lots.

4.4. FREQUENCY HIERARCHY OF THE TELEPHONE NETWORK

Regardless of whether switched or leased lines are involved, voice-grade telephone connections are intended to propagate human voice conversations which are converted into continuously varying (analog) signals at the input telephone instrument. In a broad sense, this can be successfully accomplished by passing only frequencies that lie in the voice band or below 4000 Hz. For protection and separation-in-packaging purposes, a full 4000 Hz slot is reserved for each voice channel passed through the carrier network, even though the extremal portions of this 4000 Hz slot are neither usable nor required for voice conversations. Since many simultaneous conversations must pass over the same geographic routes on the carrier networks, some type of bundling must be accomplished by these networks. In traditional voice-oriented networks, this is accomplished by the use of slots of different frequencies for different channels, giving rise to a hierarchical frequency-domain relationship along the various portions of the carrier network. This hierarchy, shown in Figure 4.7, illustrates how the lowest level of multiplex equipment in the overall switching hierarchy will neatly pack groups of 12 individual voice channels into 4 kHz slots. The 48 kHz *groups,* as they are known, are then packed by higher order multiplexers into *supergroups,* which correspond to the bandwidth equivalent of five groups or 60 individual voice channels. *Supergroups* are then bundled into groups of 10 each to form *master groups.*

An individual voice channel corresponds to a dedicated bandwidth of 0 to 4 kHz at each subscriber location, although only the portion between 500 and 3300 Hz is readily usable for data transmission. As this 4 kHz channel passes through the long haul transmission hierarchy to its destination subscriber location, it is shifted back and forth and possibly assigned to a different 4 kHz slot in each different group, supergroup, or master group through which it passes. Each of these shifting operations is performed by the frequency-division multiplexing equipment of the common carrier. The common carriers are able to provide wideband data transmission services by using special signal conversion devices and local loops that operate directly into a *group channel,* thereby bypassing the lowest level of packaging or bundling in the FDM hierarchy.

4.5. LOCAL LOOPS

One portion of the switched telephone network is effectively used by only a single subscriber and therefore is not multiplexed with any other signals. The *local loop,* or *subscriber loop* as it is sometimes known, is effectively nothing more than a suitably adjusted wire pair whose length seldom exceeds 4 to 5 miles; in fact, the average length of a local loop is less than 2 miles. Many different grades of wire are employed in local loops, and their transmission properties vary with distance and the gauge of wire being used.

To improve the quality of the local loop for analog signal transmission, devices known as *loading coils* are selectively employed. These inductive components offset the shunt capacitance, which builds up as the distance of the loop increases. These loading coils tend to enhance voice transmis-

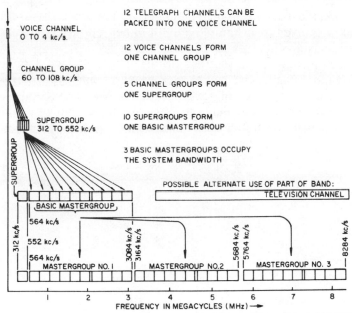

12 TELEGRAPH CHANNELS CAN BE
PACKED INTO ONE VOICE CHANNEL

VOICE CHANNEL
0 TO 4 kc/s.

12 VOICE CHANNELS FORM
ONE CHANNEL GROUP

CHANNEL GROUP
60 TO 108 kc/s.

5 CHANNEL GROUPS FORM
ONE SUPERGROUP

SUPERGROUP
312 TO 552 kc/s

10 SUPERGROUPS FORM
ONE BASIC MASTERGROUP

3 BASIC MASTERGROUPS OCCUPY
THE SYSTEM BANDWIDTH

POSSIBLE ALTERNATE USE OF PART OF BAND:
TELEVISION CHANNEL

BASIC MASTERGROUP

564 kc/s
552 kc/s
564 kc/s

312 kc/s

3084 kc/s
3164 kc/s

5684 kc/s
5764 kc/s

8284 kc/s

MASTERGROUP NO. I   MASTERGROUP NO.2   MASTERGROUP NO. 3

FREQUENCY IN MEGACYCLES (MHz) ⟶

A TYPICAL BREAKDOWN OF AN 8-MEGACYCLE BANDWIDTH TO CARRY 1860 VOICE CHANNELS, OR 600
VOICE CHANNELS AND A TELEVISION CHANNEL — THE BELL L3 SYSTEM.

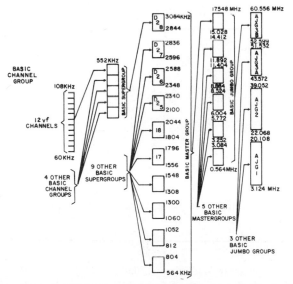

Figure 4.7. **Frequency hierarchy of telephone network. From James Martin, *Tele-communications and the Computer,* copyright 1969. Reprinted by permission of Prentice-Hall, Inc., Englewood Cliffs, New Jersey.**

153

sion quality within the 0 to 4 kHz voice band but are not especially useful if the local loop is ever to be employed for other purposes such as wideband data transmission.

As will be seen in subsequent sections of this chapter, a local loop *by itself* is nothing more than a wire pair that, if properly employed, can be used to transmit data at speeds of several hundred kilobits/second and faster. Figure 4.8 depicts the signaling rates that are theoretically possible over a pair of 22 gauge wire (after all loading coils have been removed),

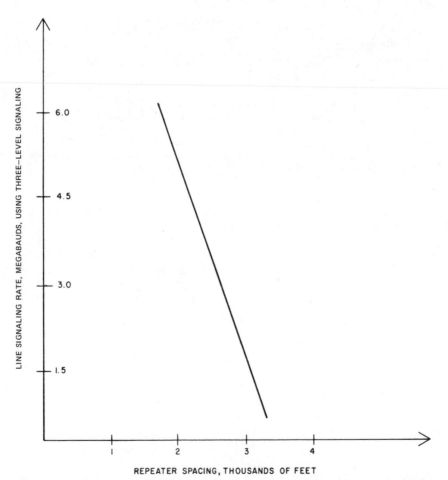

REPEATER SPACING, THOUSANDS OF FEET

Figure 4.8. Approximate signaling rates achievable over 22 gauge pulp cable to achieve acceptable error rates (a bit error per 10^7 bits transmitted) using ternary signaling.

assuming the major impediment to be impulse noise induced by central offices.

The data rates that can effectively be accomplished using digital transmission over local loops depend significantly on the distance and signaling technique being used. However, the use at specified intervals of *regenerative repeaters* (devices that clean up a distorted pulse stream and start it out again without distortion) can allow speeds in the megabits/second range to be achieved, if they are positioned sufficiently close to each other. For example, Reference [2] notes that speeds well into the megabits/second range can be accomplished with digital transmission over unloaded wire pairs if repeaters are placed every 2000 to 3000 feet.

4.6. DIGITAL TRANSMISSION TECHNIQUES

As noted previously, the telephone network employs a mixture of transmission media and signaling approaches, depending primarily on such factors as the length of the facility and the number of circuits that must be passed between the two locations in question. Digital transmission is today being used almost exclusively on higher density portions of the common carrier voice network for various economic and performance purposes. It also is being used exclusively as the transmission vehicle for new data service offerings such as the Bell System DDS network and the Canadian Dataroute network.

One of the main advantages of digital transmission is that distortion of the pulse stream along the path does not result in a loss of information unless the receiver makes an improper decoding decision about the pulse polarity or amplitude encoded at the transmitter.

A family of digital transmission systems known as the T-carrier systems has been evolving within the Bell System and other carrier networks over the past decade. In the T-carrier systems, voice-band analog signals are digitized and sent through the carrier network using pulse-coded modulation (PCM). Each analog signal sample is transmitted through the T-carrier system using a group of encoded binary digits. Two types of T-carrier systems are presently in widespread use by the common carriers, the T1 for distances up to 50 miles and the T2 for distances up to 500 miles. Other higher capacity T-carrier systems are also evolving, but are not yet found with as much regularity as the T1 and T2 systems.

A T1 system samples the incoming analog voice signal 8000 times/sec, quantizing it into one of 128 possible discrete levels. Since each sample requires $\log_2 128 = 7$ binary digits, the resulting digital stream bit rate for the voice channel is 8000 samples/sec $\times$ 7 bits/sample = 56,000 bits/sec.

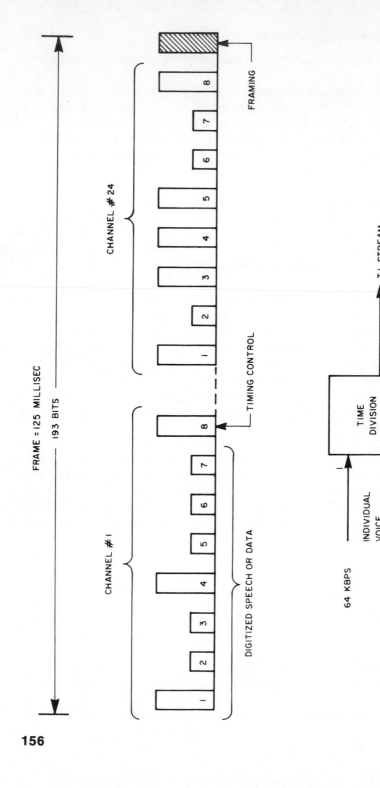

Figure 4.9. T1-carrier frame structure.

Twenty-four voice channels are then multiplexed together over a single T1 stream, using the format shown in Figure 4.9. An eighth bit is added to every 7-bit sample for timing and control functions. One frame bit is also added to each group of 8 bit samples from the 24 voice channels. Thus there are 192 + 1 bits to be sent in each frame; since 8000 frames/sec must be sent, the total bit rate of the T1 line is 193 × 8000 = 1.544 megabits/sec.

The T1 system employs a wire path with repeaters spaced about every mile to clean up the signal for transmission over the next leg of its path. Even though the Bell System has standardized on the use of 56,000 bits/sec for representing each voice channel in the T-carrier system, it is possible that in the future a reasonably high quality voice conversation may be passed through the carrier network by employing a slower digital bit rate, perhaps 19,200 or maybe even 9600 bits/sec.

As is the case with voice channels sent solely by analog transmission, these digitized voice channels must be bundled together in a so-called digital hierarchy, as shown in Figure 4.10. The T2 systems are used to transmit four time-division-multiplexed T1 data streams, producing an aggregate bit rate of 6.3 megabits/sec after control and timing pulses have been inserted.

One of the key challenges of the future to both users and carriers is to find ways to use digital transmission exclusively in data communications applications. At the current time, it is not unusual for data communications traffic on the regular telephone network to undergo at least four format conversions between the source and sink business machines, as shown in Figure 4.11. Even though digital transmission facilities are employed by the common carrier, conventional analog modems are required whenever the carrier network cannot be directly accessed using digital signals.

A significant economic breakthrough for data communications users will occur when they can exploit the fact that conventional leased voice-grade lines use 56,000 bits/sec of carrier digital capacity, whereas the use of 56,000 bits/sec of digital capacity for data applications currently costs customers anywhere from two to five times more than a leased voice line. It would certainly appear that competitive considerations are vastly more important factors than actual costs in determining the price structures governing data communications services in the current marketplace.

4.7. CHANNEL CAPACITY, BAUD RATE, AND BANDWIDTH

Back in 1928, Nyquist showed that the maximum *signaling rate* achievable over a communication line of W Hz bandwidth is $2W$ distinguishable

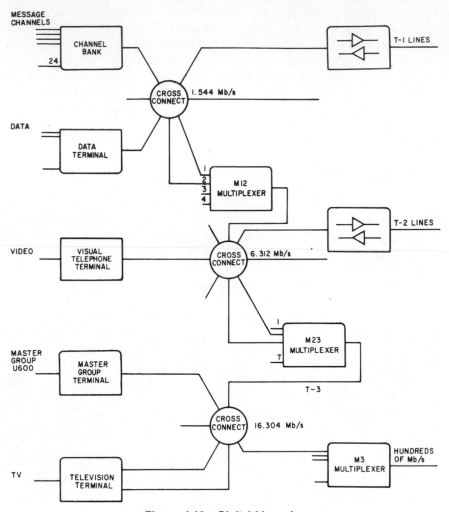

Figure 4.10. Digital hierarchy.

signal elements or symbols/second. Bandwidth is an electrical property of a transmission facility which indicates the range of frequencies that the facility can successfully pass. The bandwidth capacity of a facility is therefore measured in hertz, since frequency ranges are most readily described in this unit.

Earlier, we defined a baud as the minimum time interval that must elapse between successive symbols or signal elements on the line. Hence "baud rate" and "signaling rate" may be used synonymously. Coupling

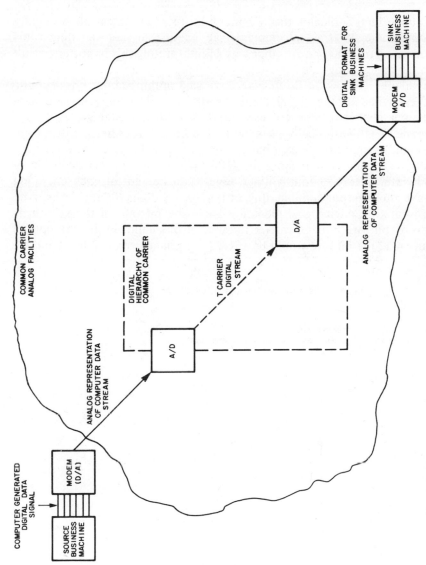

Figure 4.11. Conversions from digital → analog → digital → analog → digital in a data channel provided by using some T-carrier facilities inside carrier network.

159

the above facts indicates that a bandwidth of 2400 Hz can theoretically accommodate 4800 signal elements/sec or sustain line signaling rates (baud rates) of 4800/sec. Another way of interpreting this important result is that line signaling rates of 2 bauds/sec can be achieved for every hertz of available bandwidth. So far, we have said nothing about bits/second.

If each one of the signal elements or symbols being encoded at a particular instant of time corresponds to one of two voltage levels, for example, it is theoretically possible to send one bit (either a 1 or a 0) in each unit of time known as a baud. Thus a two-voltage-level system can theoretically signal at the rate of 4800 bits/sec, using only 2400 Hz of bandwidth. If any of four voltage levels can be sent at each encoding instant, then all four combinations of two binary digits (dibit pairs) can be represented in each signal element. Since the bit rate of the system is given by bit rate = baud rate × number of bits/baud, in the example of Figure 4.12 the bit rate would be $1/(t_{i+1} - t_i)$ bauds/sec × 2 bits/baud. In

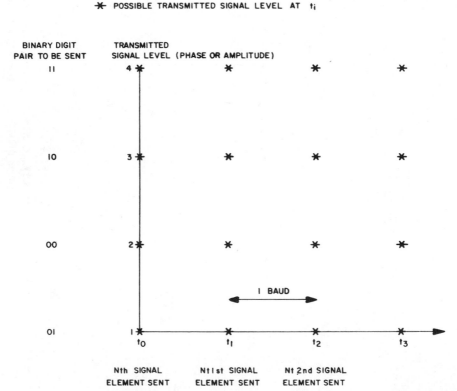

Figure 4.12. Relationships of transmitted signal level and baud time. In this system, baud rate = one-half rate.

the same example the minimum theoretical bandwidth requirements are one-half the baud rate or $\frac{1}{2} [1/(t_{i+1} - t_i)]$ Hz.

In a noisy environment where only two signal levels are being used for each signal element, Shannon has shown that the maximum bit rate is given by

$$C = W \log_2\left(1 + \frac{S}{N}\right)$$

where S/N is the signal-to-noise power ratio and W is the bandwidth in hertz.[3] Typical voice-grade channels exhibit a maximum usable bandwidth of $W = 2500$ Hz and are engineered for S/N ratios of 30 dB. Since 30 dB corresponds to a power ratio of approximately 1000 to 1, the theoretical limit of capacity is given by

$$C = 2500 \log_2\left(1 + \frac{1000}{1}\right) \cong 24,900 \text{ bits/sec.}$$

The effect of employing multilevel (> two signal levels) transmission schemes will not actually increase the theoretical capacity, since the S/N ratio will be decreased for an increased number of levels. Multilevel systems may, however, enable the theoretical limit to be more nearly achieved than is possible with two-level systems.

Care should be taken not to apply the Shannon capacity equation indiscriminately, since it is based on a number of assumptions that are not always satisfied in practice. For example, it assumes that Gaussian or white noise is the only disturbance phenomenon; many other phenomena actually exist in telephone channels that will make the Shannon-predicted goal difficult if not impossible to achieve. It appears that commercial data modem designers have reached the point of diminishing returns in achieving speeds of 9600 bits/sec over leased lines and 4800 bits/sec over the dial-up network. Not many efforts are currently being made to surpass these accomplishments, probably because of the uncertainty of success and the associated cost. Of course, in isolated cases with good quality dial-up lines, speeds faster than 4800 bits/sec may be selectively achieved.

In actual practice, the impediments previously discussed dictate modem designs that employ signaling rates (baud rates) between one fourth and one half of the Nyquist-stipulated theoretical limit. As will be seen later, most of the standard commercial voice-grade modems that operate at 9600 bits/sec signal at the rate of 2400 bauds/sec. By encoding four binary digits into each signal element, these speeds can be obtained in practice. Note that this combination of modem design parameters

[3]See Claude E. Shannon, "Mathematical Theory of Communications," *Bell System Technical Journal*, July–October 1948.

requires 16 discrete signal levels to be utilized in each baud time interval. Signaling occurs at approximately one half of the maximum theoretical rate possible, assuming 2400 Hz of usable bandwidth.

4.8. TRANSMISSION IMPAIRMENTS OF VOICE-GRADE CARRIER FACILITIES

Having discussed the organization of the carrier network, as well as analog and digital transmission, we now consider the electrical parameters commonly used to characterize voice-grade channels on an end-to-end basis. The approach used here is to explain the factors that are usually most important in data communications applications. Knowledge of these parameters and the ways in which they are measured is important because most modems require that the transmission lines meet certain specifications. Users must be aware of such parameters in order to perform network troubleshooting and diagnose system malfunctions involving line problems. Line transmission specifications are usually stipulated in terms of numerical values or ranges for the parameters to be discussed. Some of these parameters are also mentioned in the tariff filings of the common carriers.

Table 4.1 summarizes the major parameters that affect data communications over voice-grade lines. These parameters are also discussed at considerable length in References [2], [3], and [4]. The reader interested in additional detail should consult these references.

Before considering these parameters individually, it is necessary to quickly summarize the concept of relative power measurement so com-

Table 4.1. Analog Transmission Properties of Voice-Grade Lines

1. Attenuation distortion—frequency response.
2. Delay distortion—envelope delay.
3. 1000 Hz loss.
4. Phase jitter.
5. Impulse noise.
6. Background noise–message circuit noise.
7. Frequency shift.
8. Harmonic distortion.
9. Hits, dropouts.
10. C notch noise.
11. Nonlinearities.

monly encountered in telecommunications. In general, the unit of signal intensity or power known as a *decibel* or *dB* is defined as

$$\text{relative power (in dB)} = 10 \, \log_{10}\left(\frac{P_{\text{meas}}}{P_{\text{ref}}}\right)$$

where P_{meas} is power measured for some specific set of conditions and P_{ref} is the reference power level. It is quickly seen that, whenever $P_{\text{meas}} = P_{\text{ref}}$, relative power = 0 dB. Strictly speaking, the unit dB has meaning only in terms of power measurements, although as a practical matter, voltage and current ratios also are sometimes expressed in dB.[4]

Other similar, commonly encountered terms in telecommunications are *dBm* and *dBrn*. The dBm is a unit of relative power measurement in which the reference power is 1 milliwatt (mW). Hence

$$\text{dBm} = 10 \, \log_{10}\left(\frac{P_{\text{meas}}}{1 \text{ mW}}\right)$$

where P_{meas} is also expressed in milliwatts. For example, a P_{meas} value of 1 watt corresponds to 30 dBm.

In measuring noise, certain standard or reference noise power levels have customarily been used by the common carriers. One such level is 10^{-12} W or -90 dBm. In measuring the intensity of noise at a particular point in a telecommunications system under investigation, it is often meaningful to relate the measured noise power to this -90 dBm standard or reference point. Measurements made in relation to the -90 dBm standard are recorded in *decibels above reference noise* or *dBrn*. For example, a 1000 Hz tone measured at a power level of -90 dBm corresponds to a 0 dBrn reading. A different noise power of 10^{-9} W is 1000 times above the 10^{-12} W (-90 dBm) level and so would correspond to a level of 30 dBrn.

For the purpose of this discussion and for consistency with commonplace usage of the term *db* in telecommunications, we define the concept of *transmission level:*

At any point in a transmission system, the transmission level at that point is the ratio in db of the power of a signal at that point to the power of the same signal at the reference point.

The examples of the next section will serve to clarify this definition.

One final concept of the db measurement is important. When the

---

[4]The reader interested in a thorough discussion of this point should consult pp. 15–19 of Reference [3].

relative power gains or losses along several cascaded sections of an analog telecommunications line are known individually, the power gain or loss on an end-to-end basis is obtained by algebraic addition of the db values for the individual links. For example, note Figure 4.13, which shows an analog voice channel consisting of two local loops and the middle link between the central offices. The transmission level is 3 dB higher at station B than at station A. The first local loop contributes 4 dB of loss, the mid-link 10 dB of gain, and the last local loop 3 dB of loss. Thus, no matter what absolute signal is inputted at station A, the end-to-end connection will amplify the inputted signal power by 3 dB.

4.8.1. Attenuation Distortion—Frequency Response

The frequency response characteristics of a telephone line is defined as a dB measurement performed with the configuration of Figure 4.14. The P_{ref} is the power measured at the receiving end of the line for a 1000 Hz tone at the input end. Attenuation distortion describes the electrical phenomenon that occurs when the input signal generator frequency is varied across the voice-grade frequency range. A curve for a typical leased line with so-called C2 conditioning is shown in Figure 4.15. Conditioning will be discussed in complete detail later; for the time being it suffices to regard conditioning as a service provided by the carrier which assures that the frequency response (and other parameters) will fall within specified limits.

4.8.2. 1000 Hz Loss

This is an end-to-end measurement which relates the net loss that a 1000 Hz input signal will experience on an end-to-end connection. The P_{meas} is the power measured at the *receiving* end of the line for a 1000 Hz input tone; the P_{ref}, the power of the 1000 Hz tone at the input end of the line.

4.8.3. Envelope Delay Distortion

In a band-limited (limited bandwidth) analog system such as a voice-grade telephone line, not all frequency components of the input signal will propagate to the receiving end in exactly the same elapsed time. (Absolute propagation delay is not considered of importance here—only the relative differences in propagation delay across the voice band.) The zero delay reference point is defined as the nominal middle-of-the-band frequency or 1500 Hz. Envelope delay measures how much time difference exists in the propagation of a specified frequency, *relative to the delay* experienced at 1500 Hz.

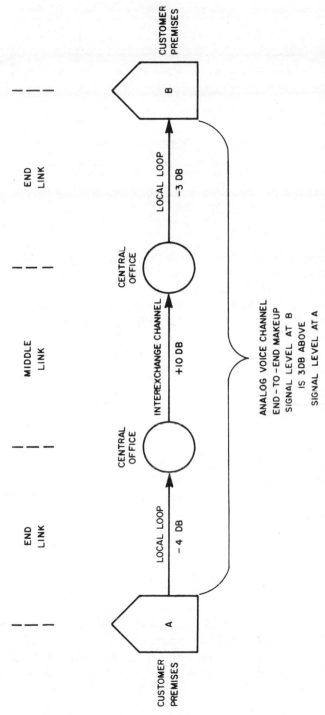

Figure 4.13. End-to-end signal gains/losses on analog channel are the sum of db gains/losses on the individual links.

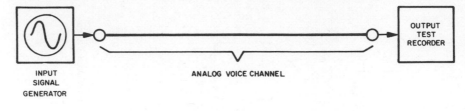

P ref ≜ POWER LEVEL RECORDED AT OUTPUT TEST RECORDER
FOR A 1000 hz INPUT SIGNAL.
P meas ≜ POWER LEVEL RECORDED AT OUTPUT TEST RECORDER
FOR ANY ARBITRARY INPUT SIGNAL FREQUENCY

Figure 4.14. Equipment configuration for measurement of attenuation distortion (frequency response) of an analog voice channel.

In higher speed data communications systems, this phenomenon causes energy from successively transmitted symbols to overlap in time, making it more difficult for the receiving modem to correctly detect the amplitude, frequency, and phase of the incoming signal. This so-called intersymbol interference phenomenon is another reason why conditioning is required for higher speed data modems. As shown in Figure 4.16, conditioning assures that the relative delay differences will fall within certain limits as the extremities of the voice band are approached from the center frequency of 1500 Hz.

One way in which the carrier networks provide the compensation for this distortion is by introducing devices known as *equalizers* into the transmission path. As shown in Figure 4.17, these equalizers generally have a mirror-image delay characteristic that causes frequency components in the middle of the voice band to be slowed more than those at the ends. The effect of an equalizer, then, is to flatten out the shape of the envelope delay curve. Equalizers are also found in modems; these are discussed in Section 4.16.

4.8.4. Incidental Phase Disturbances

Phase jitter, phase wobble, and phase hits are all carrier network-induced disturbances that cause the phase of the transmitted signal to experience acceleration, slowdown, or even sudden discontinuities. Figure 4.18 shows how phase jitter causes successive cycles of a sinusoidal input signal to cross the zero amplitude point at various time points, making it more difficult for the receiving modem to accurately sense the phase changes induced by the transmitting modem. Figure 4.19 shows how a phase hit causes a sudden shift in the phase of the received signal.

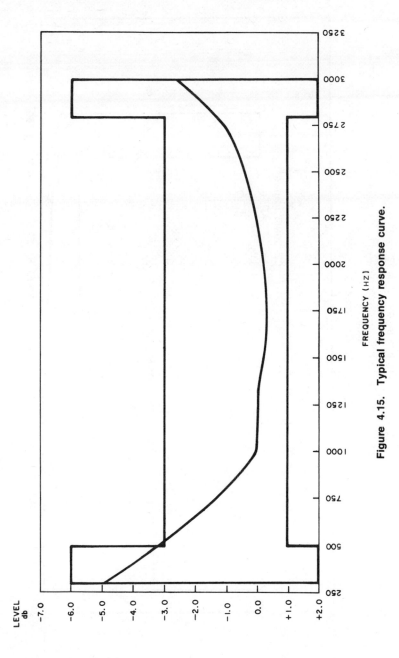

Figure 4.15. Typical frequency response curve.

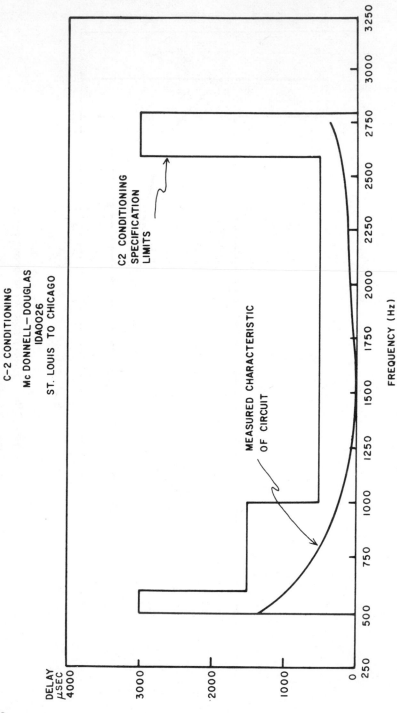

Figure 4.16. Typical envelope delay curve.

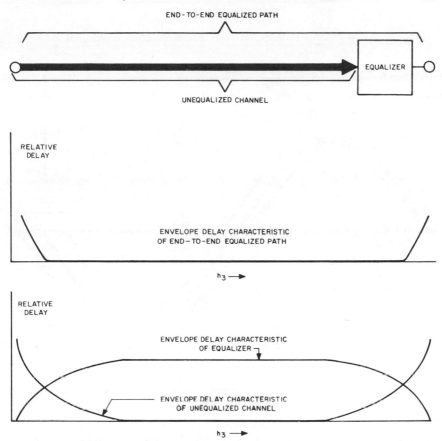

Figure 4.17.   Equalizers flatten out the end-to-end envelope delay curve by slowing down frequencies in middle of band.

The main problems caused by phase jitter and phase hits occur in applications where the modems systematically change the phase of a carrier signal to convey the 1's and 0's over the telephone line. Most modems specify the maximum amount of phase fluctuation that they can tolerate in consecutive cycles of the carrier signal whose phase is being shifted systematically by the sending modem. This value is known as the maximum *peak-to-peak phase jitter or fluctuation* that can be tolerated.

4.8.5.   Impulse Noise and Background Noise

The term *impulse noise* refers to any sudden excursion of the received signal beyond a certain amplitude level. It is usually measured in counts/

PHASE JITTER

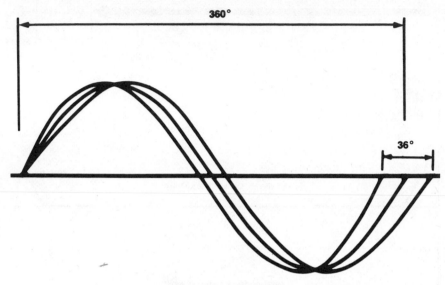

Figure 4.18. Phase Jitter.

unit of time. For example, one recent objective of the Bell System is that fewer than 20% of all connections experience more than 15 counts within 15 min, a count of impulse noise being defined as a noise transition within 6 dB of the received signal power level which would normally be observed with a modulated input signal. Impulse noise is measured by attaching a counter to the receiving end of an unmodulated circuit; the counter is incremented each time the threshold range is crossed (Figure 4.20). Obvi-

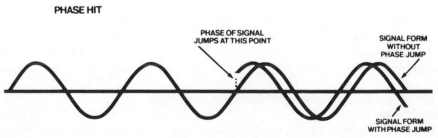

Figure 4.19. Phase hit.

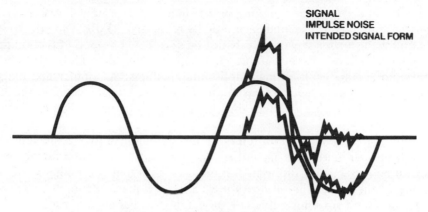

Figure 4.20. Impulse noise effects.

ously, threshold settings other than 6 dB are possible for use in impulse noise measurement. However, the 6 dB value is typically employed by most common carriers and users in determining whether or not a voice-grade circuit is in need of repair because of excessive impulse noise.

Background noise is effectively random and can be attributed to the random movement of free electrons in a telephone channel. It does not constitute a major source of difficulty to data transmission users, since the carriers have always attempted to keep it at minimal levels for voice conversations.

4.8.6. Other Types of Distortions

Frequency shift occurs whenever a single frequency signal at the input end of the transmission line is moved to a different frequency by the time it appears at the other end of the common carrier line. Most data communications applications employ modems capable of living with the small values of frequency shift likely to occur (typically less than 0.05 Hz).

Quantization noise results from digitization of a continuously varying analog signal somewhere inside the carrier network. If the carrier network's amplifiers cause the sampling network to assign a slightly incorrect level or to incorrectly decode an incoming digitized sample, quantization error results. Newer, high quality equipment systems such as the previously discussed T-carrier have been successful in minimizing the adverse effects of quantization noise.

Harmonic distortion results whenever an input signal is clipped or limited by the telephone channel. Most signals in the voice band have second harmonic component power levels more than 25 dB below the fundamental. Thus, for example, power in a 700 Hz tone will exceed the power in its 1400 Hz second harmonic by more than 25 dB. The effects of harmonic distortion will ordinarily not be severe in a properly functioning analog telephone channel, although it is not unusual to find noticeable harmonic components in malfunctioning channels. A popular line diagnostic activity is to measure harmonic power levels to see whether the 25 dB threshold is being violated, thus indicating some type of line malfunction.

Intermodulation distortion refers to the combining of two frequencies f_1 and f_2 or their harmonics nf_1 and mf_2 ($n, m = 0, 1, 2, \ldots$) to produce new signal components of different frequencies. In a malfunctioning system, some of these modulation cross-product frequencies, denoted as $nf_1 + mf_2$, may end up with sufficient power in the bandwidth used by the receiving modem to cause bit errors. Most modems are engineered so that the new frequency components generated by the modulation process do not have significant power in the band of interest at the receiver.

As shown in Figure 4.21, sets of compressing/expanding amplifiers known as *compandors* are usually employed in voice-grade channels to limit the dynamic range of signal strength that needs to be accommodated over the carrier facilities. These devices will produce *compandor distor-*

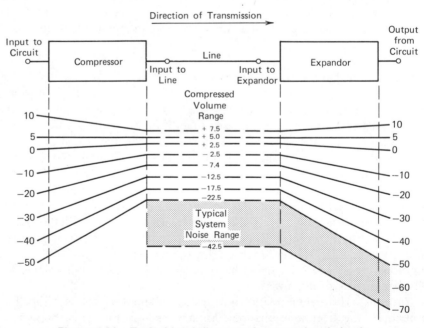

Figure 4.21. Typical level diagram of compandored circuit.

tion of analog signals unless they are perfectly matched and adjusted. Compandors can be completely disconnected from leased voice-grade lines for data communications applications without adverse effect, although the common carriers usually are reluctant to take these measures unless absolutely necessary.

4.9. OTHER VOICE-GRADE TRANSMISSION LINE PROPERTIES

Supervisory signaling exists on all connections established over the switched network, although it generally does not exist on leased lines. The control functions of the DDD network, such as the need to propagate ringing signals, busy signals, on hook/off hook indicators, and address digits, necessitate that the data communications modems must avoid putting energy into certain portions of the voice-grade line. Otherwise these signals could be mistakenly interpreted by the switched network as in-band control signals. An example of a restriction of this type is one that precludes the use of switched network modems which put power on the line at 2600 Hz when the rest of the bandwidth is not activated.

Signaling also is responsible in large part for the time delays required to complete calls over the switched network. Table 4.2 indicates typical values of these delays; they depend statistically on the distance involved, the type and speed of switching equipment being used, and the number of switches that comprise the path. Control signaling time in the switched network is also a major influence on these values. For example, in some calls within the same exchange serviced by an electronic switch, the user may hear ringing with virtually no delay following his dialing of the last digit. By contrast, on some long distance calls exceeding 1500 to 2000 miles these delays may begin to exceed 15 to 20 sec.

Table 4.2. Connect Times for Direct Distance Dial (DDD) Calls

Airline Distance (miles)	Connect Times (sec)	
	Mean	Standard Deviation
0–180	11.1	4.6
180–725	15.6	5.0
725–2900	17.6	6.6

Most common carrier switched networks employ a wire pair between the subscriber premises and the serving central office. Whereas this two-wire transmission facility is usually capable of energy transfer in only one direction at a time, the carrier facilities between serving central offices are usually bidirectional four-wire paths, as shown in Figure 4.22.

Because a small amount of the energy transmitted in one direction over the switched network is often reflected at the receiving end of the carrier network path, echo suppressors are selectively employed by the carrier networks. These devices prevent a person talking on the telephone from hearing reflections (echoes) of his own voice (which would be very annoying and would interfere with the conversation). Echo suppressors are used on intercity trunks to sense which talker is active and to block the return of any echoes to the active telephone instrument. After the active talker ceases talking, this blocking of the return path continues for a time period known as the *echo suppressor holdover time*. This value is about 100 msec in the Bell System network. In switched network data communications applications, it is usually desirable to propagate at least some energy in both directions simultaneously (with different frequencies). Thus it is necessary to deactivate the echo suppressors. A design provision of the public message network makes it possible to do this by the transmission of any signal that is within 18 dB of the input transmit level for at least 400 msec in the frequency range between 2010 and 2240 Hz. The echo suppressors will remain inactive as long as there is a continuous presence of energy in the voice channel bandwidth, provided that this energy is not interrupted for periods longer than 100 msec.

In switched network applications where the connection is used first in one direction and then in the other, the echo suppressor holdover time normally adds about 100 msec to the time required for reversing the direction of transmission. Clever modem designers have, however, figured out ways to reverse the direction of a switched network call so rapidly that this 100 msec limit is not exceeded. If the voice band in the other direction is reenergized within 100 msec, the echo suppressors will remain disabled throughout the line turnaround operation. This means that a subsequent 400 msec disabling time and the 100 msec holdover time can both be avoided, saving over 500 msec of time otherwise required for a switched line turnaround. As will be seen in Chapter 6, this saving will usually have a highly advantageous effect on the net data throughput that can be achieved over the switched network.

The *absolute propagation delay* characteristics of telephone network connections vary widely, both as a function of distance and even on successive calls between the same two points. Once a connection is established, however, the delay characteristics of switched and leased line connections will be similar. The propagation time is dependent on the

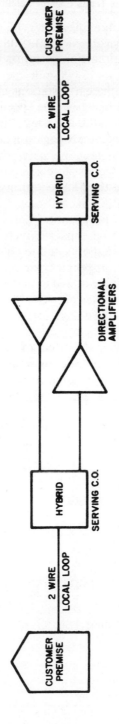

Figure 4.22. Two wire connections usually involve four wire paths between serving central offices.

media used by the common carrier to provide the connections. For example, signals propagate at about 100,000 miles/sec over unloaded cable and on long haul carrier systems. On loaded cable, propagation speeds may be as slow as 15,000 miles/sec. On satellite channels, propagation speed (between the earth stations and the orbiting transponder) is approximately 186,000 miles/sec (the speed of light), and the satellite itself is positioned about 22,400 miles above the earth in synchronous orbit.

Table 4.3 summarizes the propagation delays recorded in recent experiments over the U.S. telephone network. In all cases where satellite channels are not used, a coast-to-coast connection should not have propagation delays of more than 80 to 100 msec. Again the major limitation here would stem from the use of loaded wire pairs for the local loops.

On the average, the propagation delay over nonsatellite voice-grade telephone channels can be conservatively estimated at 1 msec/100 miles (including modems). One-hop satellite channels (those involving one trip up to and back from a transponder), on the other hand, typically involve a one-way propagation delay of 250 to 300 msec, the exact value depending on the length of the land lines between the user locations and their serving earth stations. Round trip delays for satellite channels will approximate 500 to 600 msec.

Another way of viewing the effect of satellite transmission on propagation delay is to consider the incremental delay effect of using a satellite channel instead of a conventional terrestrial line. In each direction, the satellite channel will add an extra 250 to 300 msec of delay beyond that for the regular terrestrial line.

These delay factors, as will become apparent in subsequent chapters, play a substantial role in limiting the net data throughput achievable over such links.

4.10. LINE CONDITIONING

In an attempt to establish minimum standards for analog line quality, most common carriers offer service features known as *conditioning* options.

Table 4.3. Propagation Delays Over DDD Network

Distance of Connection (miles)	Average Propagation Delay (msec)
0–180 (short calls)	7.5
180–725 (medium calls)	4.0
Above 725 (long calls)	15

Although conditioning defines certain ranges of acceptability for numerous analog transmission parameters discussed previously, one of the primary effects of conditioning is to compensate for envelope delay distortion. The common carrier, by the insertion of equalizing filters, causes the relative delay differences across the entire usable voice band to fall within the limits specified in Table 4.4. Therefore one effect of conditioning is a reduction in the energy interference between successive pulses due to nonuniform propagation times for the various frequency components of these pulses. This means that with increased conditioning levels faster line signaling rates can be employed. In turn, these faster baud rates make it possible to achieve faster bit rates over voice-grade lines.

Conditioning is not obtainable on switched connections since the physical facilities comprising the end-to-end path through the carrier network vary from one call to the next. This variance is so pronounced that conditioning types of enhancement cannot realistically or cost effectively be provided on the switched network.

Table 4.4 shows one series of current conditioning specifications. Known as the C-Type specifications, they address historically well-known and well-understood parameters. A recent Bell System offering is the high performance data channel conditioning known as D1 conditioning. This option is generally required only for data transmission at speeds of 9600 bits/sec with voice-grade modems. It is intended to provide the user with specific standards better than any otherwise available for nonlinear distortion and C-notched noise power. The provision of the special D1 conditioning was motivated by the need to constrain parameters such as C-notched noise, which were never even considered in older conditioning specifications like those displayed in Table 4.4. The common carriers should be consulted for complete technical details.

Individual signal conversion devices vary widely in their requirements for conditioning. Most devices specify what type of conditioning (if any) is required for successful operation. The main task of the user is to select lines that meet modem requirements (and vice versa) with respect to conditioning.

4.11. DIGITAL DATA TRANSMISSION NETWORK FACILITIES

The transmission facilities discussed to this point have been considered from the standpoint of their ability to send analog signals (either voice conversation or signals generated by conventional modems). By far the most promising transmission approach for data communications in the future is the use of digital techniques. Even though digital transmission has been increasingly used to send voice conversations during the past

Table 4.4. Specifications for Voice Bandwidth Data Channel and C-Type Conditioning

Interstate Tariff FCC No. 260	3002 Channel	C1 Conditioning	C2 Conditioning	C4 Conditioning
I. Circuit designation use[d,a]	Alternate voice/data or data only	Alternate voice/data or data only	Alternate voice/data or data only	Alternate voice/data or data only
II. General characteristics				
Type of service	2-point or multipoint	2 point or multipoint	2-point or multipoint	2-point or 3-point[f]
Mode of operation	Half- or full-duplex	Half- or full-duplex	Half- or full-duplex	Half- or full-duplex
Method of termination	2-wire or 4-wire	2-wire or 4-wire	2-wire or 4-wire	2-wire or 4-wire
Impedance source and load	600-ohm resistive bal.	600-ohm resistive bal.	600-ohm resistive bal.	600-ohm resistive bal.
Maximum signal power[h]	0 dBm for composite data signal, 0VU for voice	0 dBm for composite data signal, 0VU for voice	0 dBm for composite data signal, 0VU for voice	0 dBm for composite data signal, 0VU for voice
III. Attenuation characteristics				
Measured between 600 ohm independances (recommended)	16 dB ± 1 @ 1000 Hz	16 dB ± 1 @ 1000 Hz	16 dB ÷ 1 @ 1000 Hz	16 dB ± 1 @ 1000 Hz.
Expected maximum variation of $(L)^a$	Short term = 3 dB Long term = 4 dB	Short term = 3 dB Long term = 4 dB	Short term = 3 dB Long term = 4 dB	Short term = 3 dB Long term = 4 dB
Frequency response (Ref. 1000 Hz)[b]	Freq range, Var. dB 300–3000, −3 to +12 500–2500, −2 to +8	Freq range, Var. dB 300–2700, −2 to +6* 1000–2400, −1 to +3* 2700–3000, −3 to +12	Freq range, Var. dB 300–3000, −2 to +6* 500–2800, −1 to +3*	Freq range, Var. dB 300–3200, −2 to +6 500–3000, −2 to +3
Frequency error	±5 Hz	±5 Hz	±5 Hz	±5 Hz
IV. Delay characteristics				
Absolute delay[c]	Not specified	Not specified	Not specified	Not specified
Envelope delay distortion	Less than 1750 μsec over band from 800 to 2600 Hz	Less than 1000 μsec over band from 1000 to 2400 Hz*	Less than 500 μsec over band from 1000 to 2600 Hz*	Less than 300 μsec over band from 1000 to 2600 Hz*

	Less than 1750 μsec over band from 800 to 2600 Hz	Less than 1500 μsec over band from 600 to 2600 Hz*	Less than 500 μsec over band from 800 to 2800 Hz*
		Less than 3000 μsec over band from 500 to 2800 Hz*	Less than 1500 μsec over band from 600 to 3000 Hz*
			Less than 3000 μsec over band from 500 to 3000 Hz
V. Noise characteristics			
Message circuit noise	See Table III in Ref. [4]	See Table III in Ref. [4].	See Table III in Ref. [4].
Impulse noise[e,h]	15 counts in 15 min at 69 dBm VB (69 dBm C)	15 counts in 15 min at 69 dBm VB (69 dBm C)	15 counts in 15 min at 69 dBm VB (69 dBm C)

*These specifications are tariffed items. All others are the current administrative instructions of AT&T Co.

[a](L) is the net loss as measured at 1000 Hz. Short term variations are those likely to be observed during a measurement interval. They are caused by amplitude and phase hits, dropouts, and maintenance activities. Long term variations include seasonal changes and tube aging.

[b]DC continuity is not provided on any of these offerings.

[c]Absolute delay and propagation times are not specified. Where satellite channels are employed, the delay may be several tenths of a second and telemetry and retransmission schemes may be either unusable or limited.

[d]If alternate voice/data operation is desired and the data modulation does not allow the use of compandors (such as many AM systems where instantaneous power varies rapidly), the voice mode may be degraded by excessive noise. If signaling is required, the data modulation must not interfere with 2600 Hz SF signaling units, and response is not specified between 2450 and 2750 Hz.

[e]These impulse noise limits are primarily plant maintenance limits. In cases where they are exceeded, Engineering will evaluate the performance on impulse noise distribution, that is, how rapidly the counts (impulse) fall off as counting level (impulse noise peak voltage) is raised, and the effect on data system performance.

[f]Third-point operation describes the conditioning where point A (master) can transmit to B and C (slaves) simultaneously and both B and C can respond to A. Transmissions between B and C are possible, but the characteristics are not specified.

[g]C3 conditioning, not included in this table, describes conditioning of access lines and trunks in central office switching applications. An end-to-end connection consisting of four trunks and two access lines with C3 will approximate C2 conditioning overall.

[h]The "VB" in the objectives refers to the voice-band and filter in the measuring set. This approximates the "C" message, filter and the typical response of the voice-grade channel.

decade, only within the last few years have all-digital carrier networks designed solely for data communications users become a reality. In North America, several such networks are currently operational, although they are constantly expanding to serve additional geographic locations. The first of these networks to become operational was the Canadian Dataroute network, operated by a consortium of Canadian telephone companies known as the Trans-Canada Telephone System. The next all-digital network was the Datran network, which commenced operation in the southwestern United States in early 1974. Then, in mid-1974, AT&T Long Lines filed tariffs with the FCC to begin operating its Dataphone Digital Service (DDS) network in the United States. As of this writing, DDS is operational in several dozen major U.S. cities and is scheduled to accommodate close to 100 total service locations by the end of the 1970s.[5]

Some of the architectural and functional characteristics of the Dataroute and DDS networks are now discussed. The main objective is to note the service ramifications for users and to explain how digital network service improvements are linked to certain basic differences between the organizations of analog and digital networks. The reader interested in price information and additional details of these service offerings should refer to the illustrative tariffs noted in Chapter 3 and consult the respective common carrier organizations directly.

4.12. CANADA'S DATAROUTE SYSTEM

Dataroute service was commenced during 1973 and provides four-wire, full-duplex, private line serial transmission between designated Dataroute serving areas (DSAs) in a broad range of asynchronous and synchronous speeds from 110 bits/sec up to 50 kilobits/sec. Asynchronous channels are engineered for the specific codes shown in Table 4.5, whereas synchronous lines are code transparent. Even though service is leased line, it is possible to access the Dataroute system at speeds up through 1200 bits/sec using the dial-up network. Future plans call for the Dataroute system to provide switched connections as well, although such service was not yet available at the time of this writing.

On dial-up access to the Dataroute network the customer may supply his own analog modem, although it must be compatible with the carrier-provided modem at the Dataroute central office where the digital channel is accessed.

Figure 4.23 illustrates the network building blocks of the major

[5]See Reference [12] for a more detailed description of the DDS network.

Table 4.5. Codes and Speeds for Dataroute Asynchronous Channels

Baud Rate	Characters/ Sec	Start Bits	Data Bits	Stop Bits	Normal Code
110	10	1	8	2	DIC
134.5	14.8	1	7	1	BCD
150	15	1	8	1	ASCII
300	30	1	8	1	ASCII
600	60	1	8	1	ASCII
600	66	1	7	1	BCD
1200	120	1	8	1	ASCII

Dataroute subsystems. The *local loop* subsystem consists of the subscriber terminal equipment (STE); intermediate repeaters, known as loop regenerative repeaters (LRRs), located in carrier offices; and the terminating regenerator, known as the office loop regenerator (OLR). The intermediate repeaters are used only when the STE–OLR path has a loss exceeding 30 dB at 10 kHz. The initial engineering objectives of Dataroute local loops, as stated in References [6] and [7], stipulated that the error rate for the loop system not exceed one error incident (burst)/10^8 bits transmitted at 9600 bits/sec. Most of the digital service offerings, including Dataroute, do not stipulate goals for end-to-end bit error rates. As shown in Figure 4.23, the end-to-end customer channel is composed of the long haul microwave backbone system with the local loops at each end. The Dataroute network (as well as the Datran and DDS networks) obtains its synchronous clock from a single centralized point, meaning that customer business machines must derive their clock signals from the carrier network. Finally, the network is designed with a continuously operating alarm system so that personnel in the common carrier central office are immediately informed of outages. In most cases such an outage or malfunction is noticed in the carrier central office before it is realized at the customer premises.

If a customer wishes to obtain service in a geographic location not serviced by the digital network, this is possible using a conventional analog line with a pair of modems at each end of this extension link. In Canada, the common carrier is currently tariffed as the only organization permitted to supply modems for these analog extension links. If a customer requires an analog extension link at each end of his Dataroute channel, four conventional analog modems are needed. In these situations, the potential cost advantages of digital service may be severely diluted if not eliminated altogether.

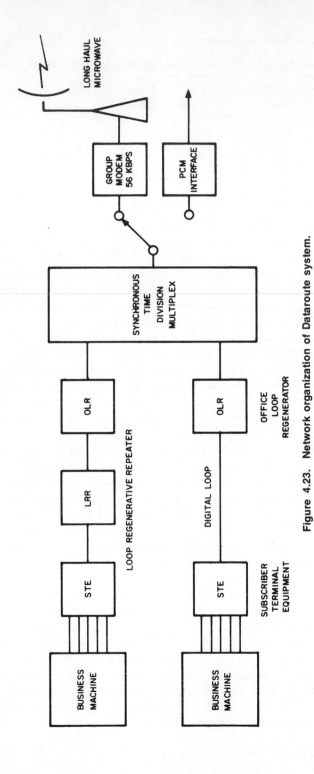

Figure 4.23. Network organization of Dataroute system.

182

In the Canadian Dataroute network a user may obtain a data channel from the common carrier and attach his own multiplexing equipment to derive a multiplicity of lower speed channels. The economic tradeoff that must be evaluated is whether a single high speed Dataroute line plus customer-provided multiplex equipment will result in a lower cost than obtaining the individual channels directly from the common carrier. One important distinction between the currently offered Dataroute and Bell's DDS involves the spectrum of speeds available from the common carrier. Dataroute enables a user to obtain speeds all the way down to 110 bits/sec directly from the carrier, whereas DDS is not presently offered at speeds below 2400 bits/sec. Users will probably find more situations where it is attractive to provide their own time-division multiplexing equipment in conjunction with DDS in the United States than with Dataroute service in Canada. It is a distinct possibility, however, that the U.S. Bell System may later introduce DDS options that will enable data channels at rates below 2400 bits/sec to be obtained directly. Only time will tell.

To the present time, Dataroute has been tariffed so that the digital signal conversion devices known as STEs can be only supplied by the common carrier. This is in contrast to the Bell System DDS network policy, where the customer's business machine can generate the PCM line signal format directly. The Bell System DDS network organization is now considered.

4.13. BELL SYSTEM DDS NETWORK

As originally filed, DDS offered the user with leased 2400, 4800, 9600, and 56,000 bits/sec channels between his business machines, using an integrated blend of facilities shown in Figures 4.24 and 4.25. In addition, a new leased service speed of 1.544 megabits/sec has recently been added to the DDS offerings, as well as switched 56,000 bits/sec service in selected locations. The switched service has been named Dataphone Switched Digital Service (DSDS) by the Bell System.

Starting at the customer premises, the data signals are transmitted over four-wire local loops using a bipolar (three-level) type of PCM encoding. At the serving DDS central office these data signals are packed into 1.544 megabits/sec T1 carrier streams for eventual passage over the long haul microwave facilities of the Bell System network. Initially, the famous data under voice (DUV) technique of utilizing existing microwave equipment provides the intercity portions of DDS channels, although other transmission alternatives will begin to be utilized at a later date. As shown in Figure 4.25, DUV enables a portion of the frequency spectrum on

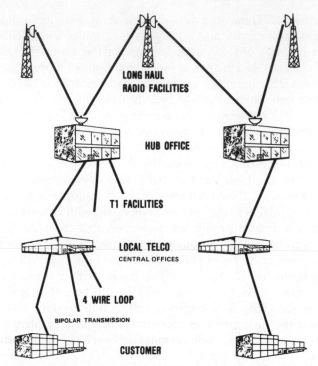

Figure 4.24. Elements in typical point-to-point DDS channel.

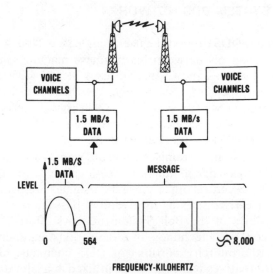

Figure 4.25. Data under voice (DUV).

184

microwave links that has traditionally been unusable for voice to be gainfully employed in sending digital data signals. The impact of DUV has been to enable the Bell System to quickly modify existing long haul microwave facilities to support the DDS offerings, avoiding extensive and expensive construction of new long haul facilities.

It is common to hear someone talk about DUV as a service offering per se. Obviously this is not so. Data under voice is merely a clever transmission technique that has enabled DDS service to become available at a more rapid rate and (it is hoped) at a lower cost than would otherwise have been possible.

Subscribers have two choices of interfaces to the network, as shown in Figure 4.26. *Channel service units* (CSUs) are furnished as an integral part of the digital access line (local loop) whenever the user wishes to furnish his own timing recovery and signal conversion equipment. The CSU provides a looparound testing capability and regeneration of received line signals and protects the carrier network. The subscriber's signal must be submitted in bipolar format which complies with DDS encoding rules whenever CSUs are employed.

If the DDS user elects not to provide his own signal conversion devices, the Bell System will install a *data service unit* (DSU) operating at the desired data rate. The DSU provides a loopback point and performs the conversion of the user two-level data signals into the standard bipolar line format. (See Figures 4.26 and 4.27.)

At the serving central office, a unit complementary to that on the customer's premises terminates the four-wire local loop, regenerates the bipolar signal, and prepares it for transmission through the next stage in the DDS digital hierarchy of Figure 4.24. This device is known as the

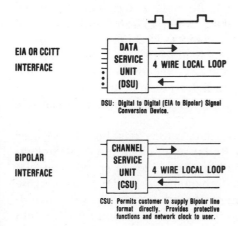

DSU: Digital to Digital (EIA to Bipolar) Signal Conversion Device.

CSU: Permits customer to supply Bipolar line format directly. Provides protective functions and network clock to user.

Figure 4.26. Customer premises.

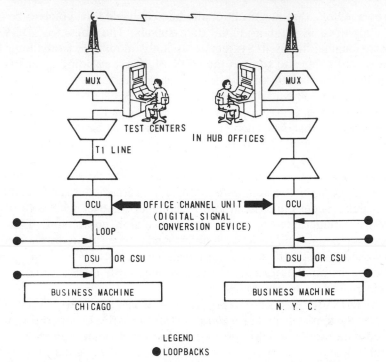

LEGEND
● LOOPBACKS

Figure 4.27. Fault isolation and diagnostics in point-to-point DDS channel.

office channel unit (OCU). Several OCUs feed into the first-stage time-division multiplexer, which outputs the T1-carrier stream. T1-carrier streams then are merged into higher level multiplexed stages at the hub offices shown in Figure 4.24. (It is also possible to terminate wideband customer loops directly in hub offices if necessary.) The hub offices contain the DDS test centers, as well as cross-connect (switching matrix) facilities to connect incoming T1 lines to the long haul trunks going in the desired direction. (Here switching merely implies a connection of input to output links.) It is from the hub office that the Bell System actually routes DDS customers through its long haul microwave network in the most sensible manner.

Note that the slowest available user data rate is 2400 bits/sec. A user may attach his own time-division multiplex equipment into a DDS channel and subdivide the high speed line into several lower speed channels. The economics of deriving low speed channels with DDS channels and customer-provided multiplex equipment depend on many factors, including the speeds and distances involved. One possible reason for DDS data rates not going below 2400 bits/sec is a desire by the Bell System to make its DDS network truly insensitive to particular character codes or code/speed groups. Such code and speed sensitivities generally characterize lower speed (asynchronous) transmission channels.

As shown in Figure 4.27, the DDS network has been equipped with data test centers in hub offices that allow an individual subscriber's data stream to be directly monitored. (This should be a boon to entrepreneurs in the encrypting business.) It is thus possible for common carrier maintenance personnel to send out known test patterns in either direction from the test center and perform fault isolation rapidly. By selectively employing loopbacks, a single test center operation can probe every portion of the end-to-end DDS channel in the sequence of steps shown in Figure 4.27.

On a malfunctioning circuit, activation of a loopback switch at a particular step may inhibit the correct return of the test signal, whereas all previous loopbacks produced satisfactory results. In such cases the fault can logically be attributed to the equipment added to the test path at the last step.

The main benefit of such diagnostic features is their ability to reduce repair times in case of circuit outages. It should be noted that the mere existence of such loopbacks and diagnostic features is by no means sufficient to guarantee reductions in circuit outage time. Only if the carrier personnel manning the data test center actually utilize these tools will the user see noticeable improvements in the overall availability of service as compared to that provided by existing analog facilities.

Other points of caution for DDS users involve the loss of any ability to utilize alternate voice/data service and to implement switched network backup of DDS connections unless regular analog modems are available. Unfortunately, however, the analog modem is one of the main cost components that a user generally looks forward to eliminating with DDS! In addition, auxiliary slow speed control channels, which can often be obtained with conventional analog modems, are not available when DDS channels are used. These channels are of vital importance for end-user-provided network diagnostic strategies.

In regard to transmission performance the Bell System has published specifications that suggest a goal of at least 99.5% of the 1 sec time intervals being free of error. Furthermore, circuit availability levels of at least 0.9996 are claimed for DDS. Recalling the basic definition of availability, A, as the fraction of the time a system is operational,

$$A_{DDS} = \frac{MTBF}{MTBF + MTTR} \geq 0.9996$$

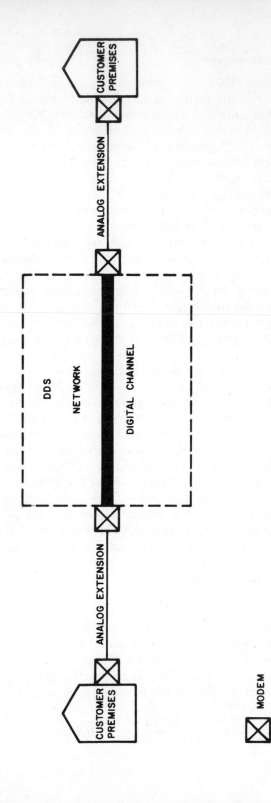

Figure 4.28. Use of analog extension lines to service customer locations not reachable with DDS network facilities.

188

where MTBF is mean time between failures and MTTR denotes mean time to repair. This DDS specification implies, for example, that if outages occur every 10,000 hours on the average, they must take less than 4 hours to fix. Or, if outages occur every 1000 hours on the average, they must be fixed in less than 24 min, approximately.

Whenever a user cannot obtain DDS service at his particular site, he can get connected by using regular analog extensions with a pair of modems for each such extension. The present plan is to permit users to employ their own modems, but only if they employ modulation procedures compatible to those of the Bell System central office units which terminate analog extension channels. Unfortunately, as shown in Figure 4.28, most of the performance advantages of DDS over analog private line service are lost because of the analog line's limiting effect. Since modems are required for extending DDS in these situations, many of the cost benefits may also be significantly diluted. It is up to the user to ascertain whether the residual benefits of DDS with one or two analog extension links and their corresponding modems are sufficient to dictate conversion from regular analog lines connected on a direct basis.

In summary, all-digital networks such as Dataroute and DDS will offer many potentially desirable features to data users in comparison to regular voice-grade lines. However, their geographic availability and accessability are limited. There is no universally available switched network to back up DDS lines without regular modems. For these reasons the user must carefully evaluate his requirements and then decide whether these digital data network services make good sense in his particular situation.

4.14. ANALOG SIGNAL CONVERSION REQUIREMENTS AND THE VOICE-GRADE TELEPHONE LINE

Voice-grade telephone lines are designed to propagate energy resulting from human voice conversations, which are usually represented as continuously varying analog signals at the input telephone instrument. Crudely speaking, the telephone line can be approximated by a band-limited analog system whose typical transfer characteristic is shown in Figure 4.29. Obviously, no two telephone lines will ever have exactly the same transfer characteristic, but the generally usable bandwidth of such a channel for data communications is ordinarily restricted to the range between 500 and 3300 Hz. Frequency components in the 0 to 4 kHz range but outside this usable interval will be so severely attenuated that they cannot be utilized by modems for data transmission.

Basic Fourier analysis says that any time varying signal such as the

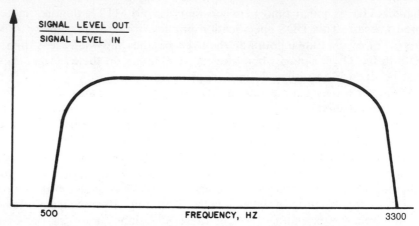

Figure 4.29.   Transfer characteristic, "typical" voice-grade line.

digital output of a business machine can be represented in the frequency domain by a sum of individual frequency components of varying magnitude. For example, a pure sine wave has the frequency-domain representation shown in Figure 4.30. Most data communications systems involve modems or signal conversion devices that will convert an incoming digital signal into a continuously varying one whose myriad frequency

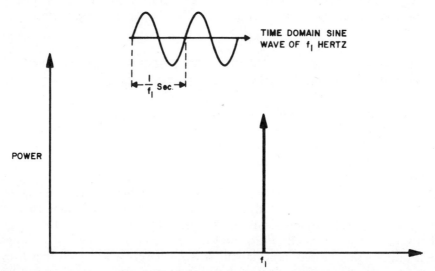

Figure 4.30.   Frequency-domain representation of pure f_1 Hz sine wave in time domain.

components all lie within the usable portion of the voice-grade line bandwidth.

Since a digital signal contains discontinuities that result in high frequency components in its frequency-domain representation, the passage of such a signal through a band-limited telephone line will result in the total loss of any frequency components outside the 0 to 4 kHz range. Figure 4.31 illustrates this effect schematically, showing the effects of passing a digital pulse stream over systems of varying, limited bandwidths.

The basic function, then, of the analog signal conversion device or modem is to *modulate* or *convert* the incoming digital stream by superimposing the 1's and 0's onto a continuously varying signal known as the *carrier signal.* The digital information can be encoded by systematically changing either the *amplitude,* the *frequency,* the *phase,* or some combination of these characteristics of the carrier signal. Figure 4.32 illustrates these basic concepts of *amplitude, frequency,* and *phase* modulation.

No attempt is made here to present a mathematical discussion of modulation techniques. The objective is merely to note the basic characteristics of modems and the types of modulation they use, and to relate these modulation approaches to the transmission properties of the telephone lines just discussed. The discussion is organized around the three types of modems and signal conversion devices commonly found in data communications applications, namely, *asynchronous modems, synchronous modems,* and *short haul modems or line drivers.* Technically speaking, short haul modems often do not involve either analog transmission or voice-grade lines. These distinctions will be noted and clarified more fully in the discussion of such devices.

In most countries of the world modems are usually supplied by the common carriers or independent companies. In many foreign countries it is typical for a governmental agency known as the PTT to have approval power to certify any modem attached to common carrier lines. In the United States, by contrast, tariffs have historically required the usage of a cumbersome protective device known as the data access arrangement (DAA) whenever independently supplied modems are used on the switched network.[6] Figure 4.33 shows a recent version of the DAA in all its spendor. Data access arrangements consist of the protective circuitry, housing, separate power transformer, connector block, telephone handset, and cord to the standard plug-in alternating current outlet. During 1976, prices for most DAAs ranged from $4 to $6/month. Re-

---

[6]Prior to 1969, independently-supplied modems could not be attached to the switched network. Since that time, connections have been permitted, but only with DAAs.

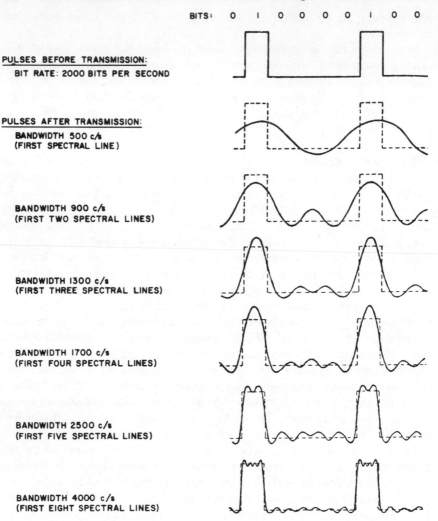

Figure 4.31. The effect of transmitting pulses over differing bandwidths. From James Martin, *Telecommunications and the Computer,* copyright 1969. Reprinted by permission of Prentice-Hall, Inc., Englewood Cliffs, New Jersey.

cently there has been increasing regulatory pressure for substantial lowering of these prices, the introduction of less complicated, more standardized units, and the development of consistent rules to which all modem vendors, including the common carriers, must adhere in interconnecting with the domestic switched network. As noted in Chapter 1, during 1976 legislation became effective that would completely eliminate

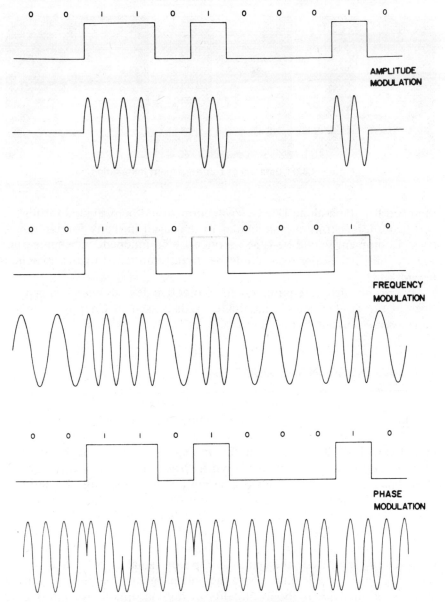

Figure 4.32. Modulation techniques.

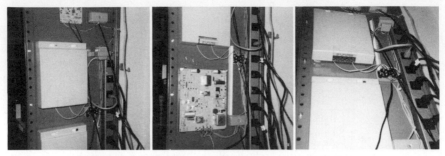

Figure 4.33. Data access arrangement installation.

the need for stand-alone DAAs. Protection would be provided through a certification/registration plan similar to that used in many foreign countries. Equipment would be type certified by an independent engineering agency and, once approved, could be directly attached to the switched network.

There is no current requirement for protective devices per se on private lines in the United States, although, as discussed in Chapter 1, much controversy surrounds this rule.

4.15. ASYNCHRONOUS MODEMS

Asynchronous modems are the least complex from a technology standpoint. Virtually all modems operating at speeds up to 1800 bits/sec are of the asynchronous or start/stop variety. The most popular type of modulation for data applications in this speed range is the binary frequency modulation technique known as *frequency shift keying* (FSK), shown in Figure 4.34. With FSK, a pair of tones f_1 and f_2 are alternatively sent over the line for the binary 1's and 0's of the asynchronous data stream. The receiving modem consists merely of two filters that sense the frequency (f_1) or f_2) having the greater power. Whenever f_1 is sensed, the receive modem puts out a binary 1 (mark) to the business machine; whenever f_2 is sensed, the binary 0 (space) signal is outputted to the receiving business machine. About the only aspect of complexity in these slow speed modems is the availability of myriad options for interfacing and control circuitry. Some of the important feature/option decisions a user must make in selecting an asynchronous modem for a specific application are summarized in Table 4.6.

Prices of low speed modems vary substantially, depending on speed and options. In the mid-1970's, stand-alone units typically leased for

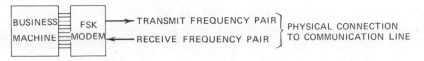

ONE MODEM'S ENCODING RULE		OTHER MODEM'S DECODING RULE	
Whenever Business Machine Transmit Data Lead Is in	Then Transmit	Whenever Modem Senses the Line Frequency to Be	Then Send Binary Level Below to the Business Machine
Binary 0 State	Frequency f_2 Hz	Frequency f_2 Hz	Binary 0
Binary 1 State	Frequency f_1 Hz	Frequency f_1 Hz	Binary 1

MOST FSK MODEMS USE DIFFERENT TRANSMIT AND RECEIVE FREQUENCY PAIRS, ENABLING SIMULTANEOUS BIDIRECTIONAL TRANSMISSION. FOR COMPATIBLE PAIRWISE OPERATION, ONE MODEM'S TRANSMIT FREQUENCY PAIR MUST BE IDENTICAL TO THE OTHER MODEM'S RECEIVE FREQUENCY PAIR.

Figure 4.34. Frequency shift keying modulation concept.

somewhere between $15 and $40/month in the United States. Rack-mount units or units integrated into the business machine can be purchased in quantity for not more than several hundred dollars, by contrast. These price ranges have been fairly stable and are likely to remain so for the foreseeable future. Costs for this category of modems are not likely to change significantly because of a relatively mature and stable low speed modem technology.

One interesting development of the last few years has been the intro-

Table 4.6. Some Low Speed Modem Options

Two-wire or four-wire interface.
Switched network or leased line interface.
Automatic calling/answering unit interface.
Send only, receive only, or alternate send/receive.
Simultaneous send/receive (full duplex).
Reverse channel for control signaling.
Other control signals employed.
Stand-alone or rack mount.

duction of an asynchronous modem that can operate in full-duplex mode over a two-wire (dial-up) facility at speeds up to 1200 bits/sec. This is presently accomplished by partitioning the voice-grade frequency spectrum into two halves, as shown in Figure 4.35. One of the halves is used for all energy going in one direction, whereas the other half serves for modulation in the opposite direction. This capability means that a dial-up line can be employed in alternating directions without line turnarounds or in both directions simultaneously. Either way, substantial reductions in overhead control signaling time result, leading to improved efficiency and increased throughput in many applications. More is said about throughput in Chapter 6. It should also be noted that the two-wire full-duplex mode of operation has historically been widely supported with Bell System Series 100 modems at speeds of approximately 110 bits/sec. The significance of Vadic Corporation's device, illustrated in Figure 4.35, is that it has made full-duplex two-wire operation feasible at speeds

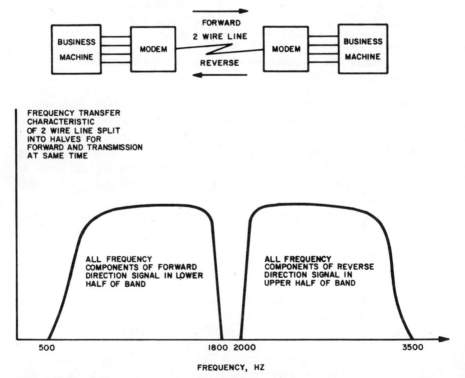

Figure 4.35. Full-duplex operation of a data link using two wire facilities.
Concept courtesy of Vadic Corporation, Mountain View, Calif.

significantly beyond those previously available with Bell System Series 100 modems.

During 1976, the Bell System formally announced a full-duplex dial-up modem for operation at speeds up to 1200 bits/sec. This action finally indicated broad-scale marketplace acceptance of the full-duplex dial-up modem at faster speeds and may perhaps pave the way for future versions that operate at speeds up through 2400 bits/sec.

4.16. SYNCHRONOUS VOICE-GRADE MODEMS (2000 TO 9600 BITS/SEC)

This category of modems is capable of operating at speeds up to 9600 bits/sec over conditioned private voice-grade lines. Similar performance can be expected on comparable voice-grade lines in other countries of the world where such lines and modems are available. Many different modulation techniques are employed, depending on speed and application factors. However, the most widely used approaches are *phase modulation* and *combined phase–amplitude* schemes. Phase modulation in the form of *differential phase shift keying* (DPSK) is commonly used in 2000 and 2400 bits/sec modems. The examples of Figures 4.36 and 4.37 illustrate how DPSK works.

The first example of Figure 4.37 shows a 2400 bits/sec modem using a signaling rate of 1200 bauds/sec; in each baud time the phase of the carrier signal is shifted by either 45, 135, 225, or 315° from its previous level. With four possible phase shifts all possible combinations of two-bit pairs (dibit pairs) can be represented (00, 01, 10, 11). As shown in the other example of Figure 4.37, another possibility is to use 0, 90, 180, and 270° phase changes for the same purpose. The former arrangement has the detection advantage that some measurable phase change will occur in every baud. Demodulation involves the receiving modem comparing the phases of two consecutive signal samples and inferring which pair of bits was sent over the line by the observed magnitude of this phase difference. Figure 4.38 shows the effect of a sending modem grouping pairs of bits in the incoming serial bit stream and forcing a particular phase shift to encode these dibit pairs. Note the difference in the bit rate and baud rate of this system. Bits arrive at the modem at the rate of 2400/sec. After being grouped into dibit pairs, only 1200 phase changes (bauds) must be systematically made every second, since each phase change contains two bits of information.

At speeds of 4800 bits/sec and faster it is common to find combination phase and amplitude modulation systems being employed. These may be

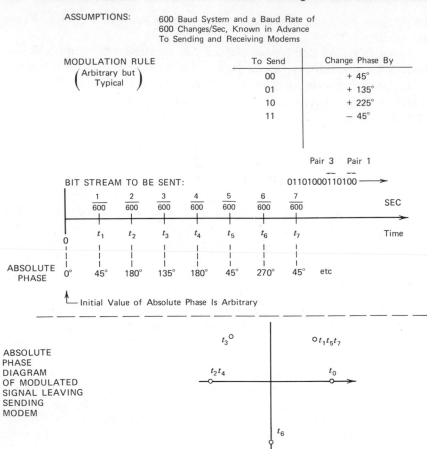

Figure 4.36. Example explaining how differential phase modulation works.

illustrated by vector diagrams such as those discussed in Reference [13] and illustrated in Figure 4.39. The carrier signal may be regarded as a vector rotating about the origin whose length at any instant corresponds to the maximum amplitude of the encoded signal and whose phase is the angular displacement from the x axis. Figure 4.39*a* denotes a four-phase, two-amplitude modem, giving rise to eight discrete signal elements (points) in phase-amplitude space. A modem using this type of encoding could therefore use these eight different signal elements (points) to send all possible combinations of three-bit groups (000, 001, 010, 011, 100, 101, 110, 111). For example, 4800 bits/sec operation could be achieved using a baud (line signaling) rate of 1600 signal elements/sec with three bits in

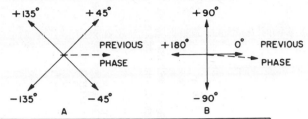

VECTOR DIAGRAM A	
BITS TO BE SENT	PHASE CHANGES TO BE GENERATED
00	$-135°$
01	$-45°$
11	$+45°$
10	$+135°$

VECTOR DIAGRAM B	
BITS TO BE SENT	PHASE CHANGES TO BE GENERATED
00	$-90°$
01	$0°$
11	$+90°$
10	$+180°$

Figure 4.37. Two different four-phase encoding schemes.

each baud. In Figure 4.39*a* a signaling rate of 1600 bauds would imply that the receiving modem samples the incoming carrier signal's amplitude and phase 1600 times/sec. Each sample produces one of the eight discernible points of amplitude and phase change from the prior sample, enabling the data bits to be reconstructed.

Figure 4.39*b* shows a similar two-amplitude system with the phase displacements positioned differently to obtain the same eight discrete points. The scheme of Figure 4.39*b* would be a preferable design choice in practice since it provides more tolerance to amplitude disturbances and can still tolerate acceptable amounts of phase error without making decoding errors. As can be seen from the diagram, a decoding error will not result as long as the amplitude and phase changes recorded at the receiving modem have values that cause the sample point to lie within the appropriate circle for the transmitted bit grouping.

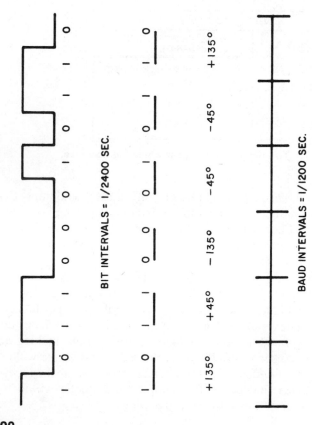

ORIGINAL 2400 BIT PER SEC. STREAM
PRESENTED TO SENDING MODEM.

DIBIT PAIRS

PHASE CHANGE IMPOSED ON CARRIER BY
SENDING MODEM DURING EACH BAUD.

SENDING MODEM FORCES ONE PHASE
CHANGE EVERY 1/1200 SEC.

BIT INTERVALS = 1/2400 SEC.

BAUD INTERVALS = 1/1200 SEC.

BIT RATE = BAUD RATE ✳ NOT BITS/BAUD = 1200 BAUDS/SEC. ✳ 2 BITS/BAUD = 2400 BIT/SEC. IN ABOVE EXAMPLE.

Figure 4.38.   Dibit encoding procedure for a 2400 bit/sec, 1200 baud, four-phase modem.

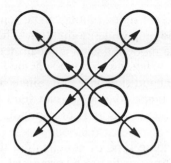

A) COMBINATION OF 4 PHASES AND TWO AMPLITUDES
    LEVELS TO PRODUCE 8 DIFFERENT SIGNAL LEVELS
    IN EACH BAUD. HERE 3 BITS MAY BE ENCODED IN
    EACH BAUD.

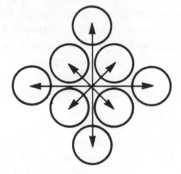

B) COMBINATION OF 8 PHASE AND TWO AMPLITUDE
    LEVELS TO PRODUCE 8 DIFFERENT SIGNAL LEVELS
    IN EACH BAUD. HERE THREE BITS MAY BE ENCODED
    IN EACH BAUD.

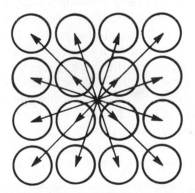

C) COMBINATIONS OF PHASE AND AMPLITUDE YIELDING
    16 DIFFERENT SIGNAL LEVELS IN EACH BAUD. HERE
    4 BITS MAY BE ENCODED IN EACH BAUD.

Figure 4.39. Example of combination phase-amplitude encodings used in multilevel synchronous modems.

Figure 4.39c shows a way whereby 16 discrete signal points can be sent in each baud time, using combined phase and amplitude modulation. The practical limit of achievability in voice-grade modem design is illustrated by this diagram; 9600 bits/sec is achieved by using the 16 point scheme in conjunction with a modem employing a 2400 baud signaling rate. Since 16 points can encode all combinations of four binary digits, we can send 4 bits/baud. With a line signaling rate of 2400 bauds/sec, the corresponding bit rate would be 9600 bits/sec.

Synchronous modems generally employ some type of equalization to minimize the effects of envelope delay distortion, as discussed previously. Equalizers, originally included as options, have lately become rather standardized and integral parts of a synchronous modem. *Fixed equalizers* (sometimes known as *statistical equalizers*) are designed to permanently compensate for an "average" envelope delay distortion curve. Their settings are permanent and do not change. Manual equalizers may be adjusted by an operator to tune their settings for optimum performance over a given line. Once set, manual equalizers will usually not adjust themselves automatically and so may need to be readjusted periodically as line conditions fluctuate.

Automatic equalizers adjust themselves without manual intervention to compensate for line conditions at the time when modem operation commences. This training period during which the modems equalizers set up is known as the request-to-send/clear-to-send delay time (RTS/CTS delay); RTS and CTS are two of the signals found on the multipin digital interface that interconnects modems and business machines. These and other control signals are described in detail in the next chapter.

It is desirable to have modems in which the equalizers can set up as rapidly as possible, to minimize the effect of this idle time on throughput. Although each brand of modem is usually different (and can be adjusted individually for different values of RTS/CTS delay at the time of installation), most 2400 bits/sec units have delays of less than 15 msec. Most 4800 bits/sec and faster units require at least 50 to 100 msec for establishing automatic equalizer settings. (Some clever designers, however, have designed units to operate with only 10 to 15 msec of RTS/CTS delay at 4800 bits/sec.)

Another recent innovation is the variable transmission speed modem introduced by the Codex Corporation of Newton, Massachusetts. Known as the "gear-shift" modem, it has been designed to combine the best features of fast RTS/CTS start-up inherent in 2400 bits/sec transmission with the higher transmission rate of 4800 bits/sec devices. As shown in Figure 4.40, the modem commences operation at 2400 bits/sec speed after a 10 msec RTS/CTS delay interval. Then, after 30 msec of transmission

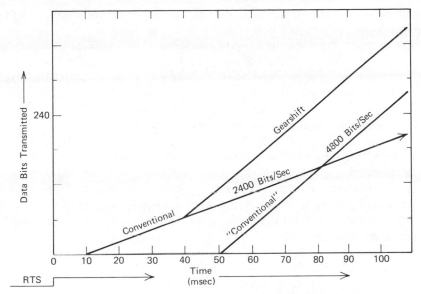

Figure 4.40. Gearshift training in Codex variable-speed modem.

at 2400 bits/sec, the transmission speed is automatically increased to 4800 bits/sec. It can be seen that for short data block lengths the dominant time factor is the RTS/CTS delay, whereas for long data block lengths the operating speed of the modem is more important in determining total block transfer time. The "gear-shift" modem clearly provides the best of both worlds.

In the late 1960s and early 1970s it was not uncommon to find RTS/CTS delay times of anywhere from 3 to 10 sec. However, such slow designs prevented the effective use of higher speeds on dial lines and on multipoint lines where RTS/CTS delays are an important factor in the net data throughput rates that can be achieved. These points are more fully illustrated by examples in Chapter 8.

Adaptive equalizers can dynamically sense changing line conditions and can change their equalizer adjustments on the fly. Most adaptive equalizers are also automatic equalizers. However, the converse is not generally true.

Equalizers in switched network modems must generally be more sophisticated than those for a leased line modem operating at the same speed, because the leased line has a wider usable bandwidth and can be obtained with carrier-provided equalization known as conditioning. In dial-up applications, the modems must perform all equalization, since no conditioning can be obtained from the carrier over switched network connections.

The primary types of options on modems of this type are diagnostic loopback switches, indicator lights, and possible features allowing several logically independent data and/or voice transfers to be accomplished over the same data channel. Loopback features allow troubleshooting, fault isolation, and diagnostic functions to be performed, as shown in Figure 4.41. Loopback features are sometimes also known as busback options and self-test features for reasons that should be apparent. Teleprocessing systems of the future will incorporate such features extensively to minimize network downtime arising from fingerpointing among vendors. Users employing such features extensively may expect to find a much greater degree of vendor and carrier cooperation in their performance of maintenance and repair duties whenever an initial checkout is performed using such equipment.

The concept of *split streaming* or *dual streaming* was introduced in an earlier chapter and so will not be discussed at length here. As noted previously, it is a time-division multiplexing system combined with a modem. The application value of such features is obvious since they can be used to eliminate the need for and the cost of multiple voice-grade lines between the same two locations. Generally, any mixed combination of 2400, 4800, and 7200 bits/sec synchronous speeds can be derived, as long as the aggregate speed of the incoming ports does not exceed the operating speed of the split-stream modem. Figure 4.42 shows how a split-stream modem can also be used to extend computer ports out to remote locations, eliminating the need to bring every polled multipoint line all the way back to the computer center. In the example shown in Figure 4.42 the use of split-stream modems made it possible to reduce total network costs by almost 15% from the costs for the situation in which separate lines were used for the CRT and remote job entry terminals. Additional examples of the benefits that can be obtained from multiplexing will be noted in subsequent chapters.

Another important modem option, especially in international applications, is the possible provision of functionally independent asynchronous side channels. Typical modems can provide one or two slow speed side channels for the simultaneous transfer of synchronous data and lower speed (50 to 150 bits/sec) administrative message traffic. Use of this option can eliminate the need to use separate, expensive leased lines for the message switching traffic. Coupled with an alternate voice capability, the modem can provide the user with numerous different operating modes such as high speed data plus slow speed side channels or voice plus slow

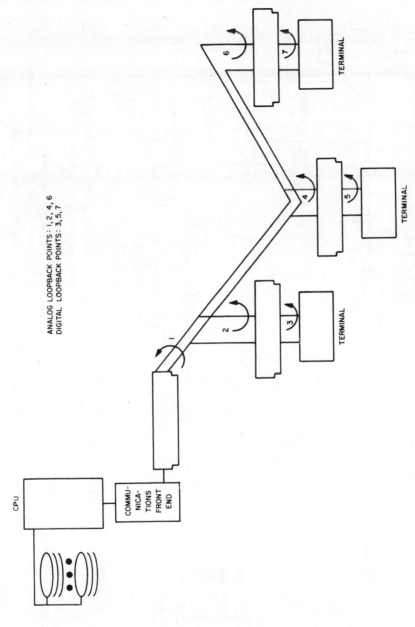

ANALOG LOOPBACK POINTS: 1, 2, 4, 6
DIGITAL LOOPBACK POINTS: 3, 5, 7

Figure 4.41. Use of loopback switches for fault isolation on multipoint circuit.

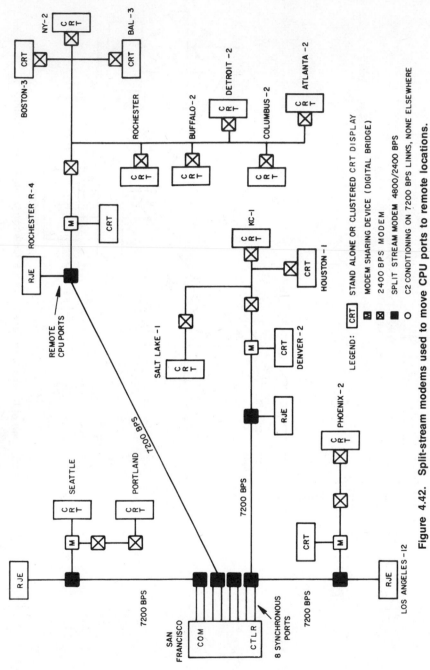

Figure 4.42. Split-stream modems used to move CPU ports to remote locations.

206

speed side channels. The advantages of such flexibility are significant indeed.

Prices for synchronous modems vary widely, depending on the application environment and the options selected. Furthermore, the prices for synchronous modems changed relatively often during the early 1970s because of advancing technology and very substantial competitive considerations. In the early 1970s, it was generally true that synchronous modems could be purchased for approximately $1/bit/sec (e.g., 9600 bits/sec modems sold for about $10,000).

In the mid-1970s, however, large scale integration (LSI) technology became a reality. Purchase prices have declined appreciably with the most notable reductions at the slower speed end of the range. Prices at the time of this writing range anywhere from 60 to 70% below the $1/bit/sec rule for certain 2400 bits/sec devices to 40% below the $1 rule at higher speeds of 9600 bits/sec. The prices most likely to continue declining in the future are those in areas where LSI technology has not yet been fully exploited. Generally speaking, LSI began to become a major factor in the 4800 bits/sec modem market during 1975 and 1976. In the next 2 years it began to appear with some regularity in the 7200 and 9600 bits/sec marketplaces.

Table 4.7 lists some major U.S. suppliers of synchronous modems of various speeds. It is difficult to compare prices among vendors because most common carrier-supplied modems cannot be purchased outright; they are available only on a lease basis. Larger noncarrier suppliers of modems, including many of the computer vendors and independent modem companies such as Codex Corporation and International Communications Corporation, offer leasing arrangements to meet a wide variety of user financing requirements.

4.17. OTHER TYPES OF SIGNAL CONVERSION DEVICES

4.17.1. Analog

In addition to the above types of analog modems, data transmission applications sometimes employ other analog signal conversion devices known as *wideband* or *group* modems for synchronous transmission at speeds of 19,200, 40,800, 50,000, and 56,000 bits/sec, and selected other speeds above 10,000 bits/sec. These analog modems require a wider bandwidth than is available from an individual voice-grade telephone line. The common carrier provides the required bandwidth by using an entire group channel consisting of 4 × 12 kHz total bandwidth. In carrier central

Table 4.7. Typical Suppliers of Synchronous Modems in the United States

Speed (bits/sec)	Vendor[a]
2400	Bell System
	Codex Corporation
	General Datacomm
	IBM
	ICC
	Intertel
	Paradyne
4800	Bell System
	Codex Corporation
	IBM
	ICC
	Intertel
	Paradyne
9600	Bell System
	Codex Corporation
	ICC
	Intertel
	Paradyne

[a]Certain vendors also offer units at 3600 and 7200 bits/sec, although these speeds are less common.

offices this type of facility is obtained by bypassing the last stage of the frequency-division multiplex hierarchy (recall that this last stage breaks a group channel down into individual voice channels).

Although most commercially available versions of group modems operate at 40,800 to 56,000 bits/sec, the technology of individual voice-grade modems suggests that speeds faster than 100,000 bits/sec should be practically obtainable for group modems. This conclusion is reached by noting that an individual 4 kHz voice channel can accomplish 9600 bits/sec data transmission. By extrapolation, a bandwidth 12 times greater should be able to accommodate a bit rate nominally 12 times greater. Certainly, there is no significant commercial availability of such devices at this time. However, the specialized common carriers in the United States have recently been working with the independent suppliers of modems to begin providing analog modems that efficiently utilize bandwidths greater than 4 kHz to offer faster speeds. Progress in extending the maximum data rate achievable in practice over a group channel may be expected in the market place over the next few years.

The primary causes for a historically stagnant technology in wideband modems include such factors as a relatively small demand for 50 kilobits/sec speeds in the marketplace and a resulting minimal market incentive for the equipment vendors and carriers to develop such devices. Another significant reason for the lack of activity in these areas is the difficulty and expense that the common carriers must incur in providing local distribution facilities for wideband transmission. Prospects for the increased availability of inexpensive short range microwave radio, CATV, and optical transmission facilities are likely to make wideband transmission using analog modems notably more widespread in the future. This is particularly true when one realizes that most of the specialized common carrier networks have been implemented using conventional analog long haul facilities.

The final type of analog signal converter to be discussed is the *short haul modem* (also often known as the *baseband modem* or *limited-distance adapter*). These devices are used in limited-distance environments where transmission facilities other than 4 kHz voice-grade channels are available. Their application benefits are similar to those of short haul digital signal converters which are discussed in the next subsection. The only difference between these analog and digital short haul signal converters is in the type of encoding employed. Baseband analog modems do not always involve modulation or signal conversion per se, since they merely convert a digital signal into a continuously varying one whose frequency components exceed the 4 kHz capacity of a regular voice-grade line. Virtually all these frequency components are sent directly over the facility without being converted or shifted—hence the term *baseband device*. Because of the previously noted benefits of digital transmission, the future of analog devices in this application area certainly appears to be limited.

4.17.2. Digital

Another very promising approach to solving the wideband local distribution problem involves the use of digital transmission. The main requirement here is for suitable local transmission facilities which can be employed in conjunction with various pulse code modulation (PCM) signal converters and other types of short haul devices.

Many data communications users have employed digital transmission techniques for years in limited-distance applications where the availability of unloaded wire pairs needed for PCM transmission has permitted such an approach. These digital signal conversion devices require that the end-to-end transmission facility not pass through any frequency-division multiplexing equipment (carrier systems) in the common carrier network.

They are known by various names, including *line drivers, short haul modems, baseband modems,* and *limited-distance adapters,* depending on the vendor. They employ many different types of PCM transmission such as those discussed in Reference [13]. Their popularity is due to their superior performance and cost characteristics in relation to analog modems operating over a voice-grade line, especially in the limited-distance environment. Unfortunately, however, the availability of unloaded wire pairs is generally restricted to lines where (*a*) both user end points are serviced out of the same carrier central office (Figure 4.43) or (*b*) the user provides his own transmission facilities within a closed geographic area such as an industrial park site or within a building (Figure 4.44).

Specific tariffs providing for the wire pairs required by such signal conversion devices are currently not available everywhere. When users are able to obtain such facilities, it is usually on a special assembly basis. However, AT&T has published some specifications for transmission over metallic pairs. Signal conversion devices meeting these specifications will be acceptable (will not cause harm to the public message network). Reference [11] should be consulted for specific details on these transmission specifications.

Specific price and performance characteristics for limited-distance devices vary widely and are strongly application dependent. Prices ranging from $500 to $1000 for digital signal conversion devices capable of operating at speeds of up to 50,000 bits/sec are typical. Transmission performance definitely depends on distance, type of wire or cable used, and modulation technique employed. As an example, transmission at 56,000 bits/sec over distances between 8 and 10 miles is practically achievable with broadly available unloaded cable pairs using devices that meet the metallic pair specifications noted in Reference [11].

As discussed previously in this chapter, regenerative repeaters that refresh the distorted digital pulse stream may be used at intermediate points between the two end locations to improve the bit error rate and extend the maximum distance over which this transmission technique can be applied. One practical problem with the regenerative repeater concept is that the organization employing these devices must have physical access to the entire facility. In most end-user applications of PCM signal

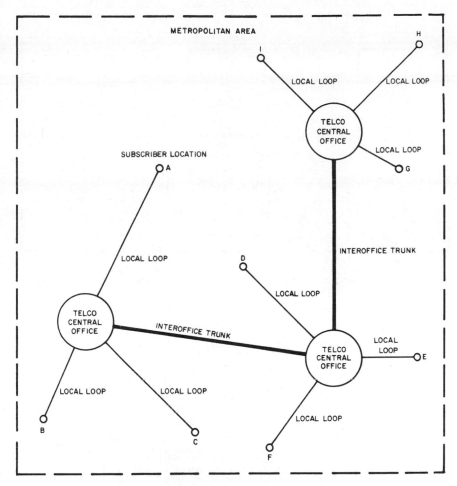

SUBSCRIBER LOCATIONS SERVICED BY SAME CENTRAL OFFICE COULD
BE PROVIDED WITH METALLIC PAIRS IF LOCAL TELEPHONE COMPANY
PERMITS SUCH CONNECTIONS.
PAIRS COULD BE OBTAINED BETWEEN ANY TWO SUBSCRIBER LOCATIONS
IN THE FOLLOWING GROUPS:

GROUP 1   A, B, C
GROUP 2   D, E, F
GROUP 3   G, H, I

Figure 4.43. Locations where wire pairs could be obtained.

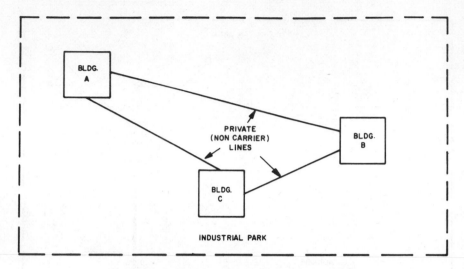

ANY LOCATIONS IN INDUSTRIAL PARK CONNECTED BY PRIVATE (NON CARRIER) LINES COULD BE CONFIGURED FOR DIGITAL TRANSMISSION ON A SHORT HAUL BASIS.

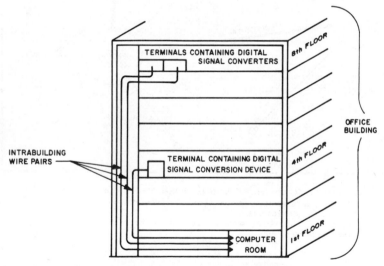

Figure 4.44.   Other situations where short haul signal converters could be employed.

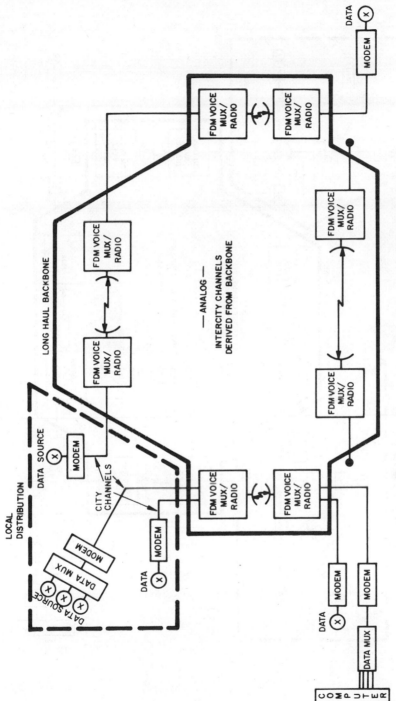

Figure 4.45. Data customers serviced using end-to-end analog transmission.

213

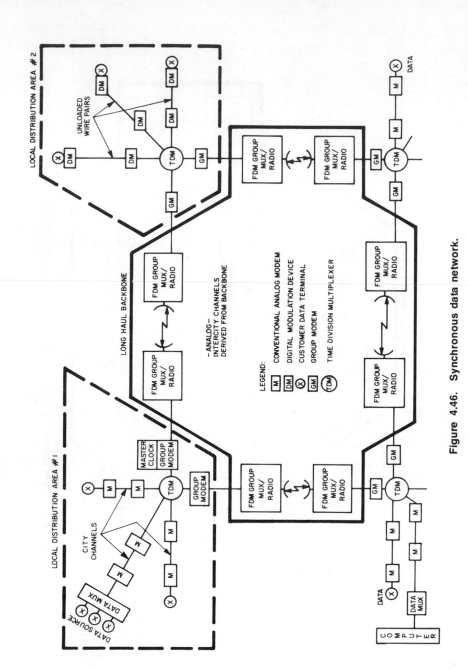

Figure 4.46. Synchronous data network.

LEGEND:

M	CONVENTIONAL ANALOG MODEM
DM	DIGITAL MODULATION DEVICE
X	CUSTOMER DATA TERMINAL
GM	GROUP MODEM
TDM	TIME DIVISION MULTIPLEXER

LOCAL DISTRIBUTION AREA #2

UNLOADED WIRE PAIRS

LONG HAUL BACKBONE

–ANALOG–
INTERCITY CHANNELS
DERIVED FROM BACKBONE

LOCAL DISTRIBUTION AREA #1

MASTER CLOCK GROUP MODEM

CITY CHANNELS

DATA MUX

DATA SOURCE

GROUP MODEM

FDM GROUP MUX/RADIO

DATA

DATA

DATA MUX

COMPUTER

converters using common carrier-provided wire pairs, the end user has no access to the unloaded wire pair except at the end points.

Probably the largest potential source of application for these signal conversion devices is the common carrier in providing digital local channels for the evolving data networks discussed previously. This trend is readily apparent when one notes the large number of such devices required in the Bell System DDS and Canadian Dataroute networks. These networks use digital signal conversion devices known, respectively, as Data Service Units, Office Channel Units, Subscriber Terminal Equipment, and Office Loop Regenerators. Though these networks are designed for computer traffic, it is apparent from the large scale trend to digital transmission in voice networks (e.g., T carrier) that digital signal converters will also be used extensively in local distribution systems involving digitized voice.

At the current time, even though there are many long haul common carriers, most of the local distribution facilities in the United States and Canada are owned by the various Bell System organizations or independent telephone companies in these two countries. It will be difficult if not impossible for competing carriers to economically build and operate data networks similar to DDS and Dataroute unless they can obtain the same access to unloaded wire pairs for local distribution that the Bell System has in constructing its networks. Proof of this difficulty is evident in the demise of the Datran Corporation during 1976.

Even though regulatory progress has been miniscule in this area up to the present time, it is likely that the FCC's stated policy will enable this equality of access to unloaded wire pairs to materialize eventually. Until then, the specialized and satellite carriers will of necessity employ conventional end-to-end analog transmission with two modems per data channel (Figure 4.45) or build their synchronous data networks using a pair of modems on each local loop to a customer's premises, as shown in Local Distribution Area 1 of Figure 4.46. Even though it is possible to design low cost special purpose modems for this limited-distance environment using LSI technology, the costs and transmission are not as good as they would be with digital signal conversion devices over unloaded wire pairs, as shown in Local Distribution Area 2 of Figure 4.46. The U.S. and Canadian Bell Systems have shown their preference for the latter approach by selecting it as the basis for their data networks. Since they control all the local facilities, they could technically and practically use either approach. Their selection of digital transmission using wire pairs unequivocally indicates the technological superiority of digital transmission over the use of paired analog modems for each local loop.

REFERENCES

1. J. T. Martin, *Future Developments in Telecommunications,* Prentice-Hall, Englewood Cliffs, N.J., 1971.
2. J. T. Martin, *Telecommunications and the Computer,* 2nd ed., Prentice-Hall, Englewood Cliffs, N.J., 1976.
3. *Transmission Systems for Communications,* 4th ed., Bell Telephone Laboratories, 1970.
4. Transmission Specifications for Voice Grade Private Line Data Channels, Engineering Director of Data Communications, American Telephone and Telegraph Co., 195 Broadway, New York, March 1969.
5. Data Communications Using the Switched Telecommunications Network, Engineering Director of Data Communications, American Telephone and Telegraph Co., 195 Broadway, New York, August 1970.
6. A. W. Meyer and A. J. Delorenzi, "Dataroute Digital Loop Equipment," *Proceedings of International Communications Conference,* 1974.
7. "The Dataroute," series of five papers presented at International Communications Conference, 1975.
   a. "An Overview of Dataroute: System and Performance."
   b. "Multiplexing."
   c. "The Dataroute Digital Loop Equipment."
   d. "Network Synchronization and Alarm Remoting in Dataroute."
   e. "Dataroute Transmission: System Growth and Expansion."
8. R. J. Blackburn and P. E. Muench, "The Bell System's Digital Data System—An Overview," *Conference Record,* 1972 IEEE International Communications Conference, June 1972.
9. R. T. James and P. E. Muench, "AT&T Facilities and Services," *Proceedings of IEEE,* November 1972.
10. Dataphone Digital Service Brochure, American Telephone and Telegraph Co., 195 Broadway, New York, 1974.
11. Preliminary Specification for Transmission over Metallic Pairs, Engineering Director of Data Communications, American Telephone and Telegraph Co., 195 Broadway, New York, 1971.
12. C. Moster and L. Pamm, "The Digital Data System Launches a New Era in Data Communications," *Bell Laboratories Record,* Vol. 53, No. 11, December 1975.
13. P. Bryant, F. W. Giesin, and R. M. Hayes, "Experiments in Line Quality Monitoring," *IBM Systems Journal,* Vol. 15, No. 2, 1976.

OTHER READINGS

Abramson, N., and F. F. Kuo, *Computer-Communication Networks,* Prentice-Hall, 1973.
Andrews, F. T. and R. W. Hatch, "National Telephone Network Transmission Planning in the American Telephone and Telegraph Company," *IEEE Transactions on Communication Technology,* Vol. COM-19, June 1971.

Bayless, J. W., S. J. Campanella, and A. J. Goldberg, "Voice Signals: Bit-by-Bit," *IEEE Spectrum,* October 1973.

Bennett, W. R., and J. R. Davey, *Data Transmission,* McGraw-Hill, New York, 1965.

Brooks, John, *Telephone,* Harper and Row, New York, 1976.

Brunn, R., "Dataroute—Pioneer in Data Communications," *Infosystems,* November 1973.

Chu, W. W., *Advances in Computer Communications,* Artech House, Reprint Volume, 1975.

Davenport, W. P., *Modern Data Communication,* Hayden Book Co., New York, 1971.

Davies, D. W., and D. L. A. Barber, *Communications Networks for Computers,* John Wiley and Sons, 1973.

Green, P. E., Jr., and Robert W. Lucky (Eds.), *Computer Communications,* IEEE Press, New York, 1975.

IEEE Transactions on Communications—Special Issue on Computer Communications, Vol. Com-20, No. 3, June 1972.

IEEE Transactions on Communications—Special Issue on Computer Communications, January 1977.

Lucky, R. W., J. Salz, and E. J. Weldon, *Principles of Data Communication,* McGraw-Hill, New York, 1968.

Maley, S. W., and W. J. Chiu, "An Introduction to PCM," *Business Communications Review,* May–June 1973.

Mathison, S. L., and P. M. Walker, "Specialized Common Carriers," *Telephone Engineer and Management,* Oct. 15, 1971.

McKenzie, A. A., "What's Up in Satellites?" *IEEE Spectrum,* May 1972.

Proceedings of IEEE—Special Issue on Computer Communications, November 1972. Refer especially to articles on modems and common carrier networking approaches.

Ristenbatt, M. P., "Alternatives in Digital Communications," *Proceedings of IEEE,* Vol. 61, No. 6, June 1973.

Rubin, M., and C. E. Haller, *Communication Switching Systems,* Reinhold, New York, 1966.

Vilips, Vess V., *Data Modem Selection and Evaluation Guide,* Artech House, 1972.

FIVE

DATA COMMUNICATIONS TERMINALS AND THEIR INTERFACE WITH SIGNAL CONVERTERS

In this chapter we overview the various types of popularly available terminal devices that are used to encode data at remote locations into a form suitable for transmission over the lines discussed in preceding chapters. In Chapter 1, the term *data processing terminal equipment* or DPTE (sometimes abbreviated as DTE for "data terminal equipment") was defined as the configuration of equipment at the end points of a system segment contained between the signal converter interface and the ultimate information source or sink utilized in any application. Throughout this chapter "terminal" represents a broad variety of different kinds of terminal devices; we consider both stand-alone terminals and the vastly popular clustered terminal systems centered around a control unit that connects multiple input/output consoles like CRT displays and keyboard/printer mechanisms to the signal converter. In this clustered system context, the individual peripherals connected to the cluster controller are often referred to as terminals and the entire configuration as a terminal system or station.

Terminals have traditionally been utilized in data communications applications to convert source data into machine-processable bit groupings by using a two-step procedure involving *(a)* a human being who converts the data from the source document into a key stroke and *(b)* a machine (the terminal) which converts the key stroke into the appropriate group of binary digits for internal representation and subsequent transmission to a computer or data base. Since the early days of teleprocessing, applications for terminals have broadened materially to include many situations where there is no requirement for the direct involvement of a human being for data entry. Examples of terminal devices for these applications, expected to play a major role in communications-based systems of the future, are the familiar remote batch processing stations, facsimile units, optical character readers, and magnetic ink character readers, to mention a few. Here the source data are originally available in some form suitable for direct recognition by the terminal, so a human being need not be involved.

The major items to be presented in this chapter include an overview of the different types of terminals, including low speed teleprinters, CRT displays, batch processing terminals, transaction terminals, and intelligent workstation terminals. Our objective is to discuss the various functional characteristics found in these different kinds of devices and to summarize the kinds of applications for which each type of device is best suited. Also covered are various selection criteria to be used in evaluating terminals for a specific application.

Considerable emphasis is placed on the terminal implications for distributed processing, including a discussion of the major reasons why users consider such approaches and the desirable terminal system features for distributed processing applications. The last major item in the chapter is a discussion and explanation of the interface by which business machines and common carrier data links are electrically interconnected in teleprocessing networks.

In the United States and North America in general this interface is known as the Electronic Industries Association (EIA) RS-232-C interface. In other countries of the world, CCITT Standards provide an interface functionally similar to the one used in North American applications. Interfaces are important because there are many different variations commonly employed in existing networks. A clear understanding of the functions and procedures whereby the terminals exchange information over the data link is vital to the planning, design, and day-to-day operation of an efficient network.

For data arriving from the computer over the communication link, traditional terminals perform the inverse procedure—namely, converting the arriving bit representations into a form suitable for presentation to and processing by a human being. Typically this means printing the characters in hard copy form at the user location or visually displaying them on cathode ray tube screens. The classic example of a familiar terminal is the teletypewriter device, a combination of a typewriter and data communications interface. The teletypewriter terminal, commonly known as a teletype or TTY, has been widely used in data applications for years and will continue to be popular in the future. However, in recent years a substantially new array of different terminal devices has become available in the marketplace. These types of devices go well beyond the traditional functions of a teletypewriter in networking applications. They provide certain types of intelligence, and hence the ability to execute programs and store data at the man/machine interface point distant from the computer. The trend toward increasingly intelligent terminals and the resultant distributed processing capabilities they afford is certain to accelerate in the years ahead, particularly as user data volumes grow to the point where traditionally centralized data processing approaches become excessively costly, unresponsive, unreliable, or generally unacceptable to the end user for whatever reason.

5.1. IMPORTANT TYPES OF TELEPROCESSING TERMINALS

Table 5.1 contains an overview of the five functional types of terminals to be considered in this chapter. Each category is individually discussed in detail, after some initial commentary on the reasons for using these types and resulting caveats.

Any attempt to categorize data communications terminals will inevitably produce legitimate questions about number of categories used, criteria for including specific device types in one category, and so on. Another difficulty intrinsic to the categorization procedure is a rapid technology trend toward the use of programmable intelligent control mechanisms in virtually all terminals being presently manufactured.

In the next decade, it is likely that the vast majority of terminal systems manufactured will be highly modular, clustered-controller-based configurations in which the user will select CRT displays, keyboards, printers, local storage mechanisms, and programs customized for special applications like data entry, inquiry, and batch job entry. The unique feature of such systems will be their reliance on common peripherals and controller hardware, with variable software and firmware installed to accommodate specific user requirements. The hardware distinctions between the five terminal categories listed in Table 5.1 will blur and give way to a proliferation of multiple-function, multiapplication devices based on the generalized workstation terminal architecture discussed later in the chapter. Such an evolution is harmoniously supported by the significant trends to distributed processing.

5.1.1. Low Speed Teleprinter Terminals

The low speed teleprinter is commonly employed at speeds up to 1200 bits/sec and is unquestionably the most widely used type of terminal. These devices typically operate using a variety of code formats and start/stop (asynchronous) transmission at speeds such as 50, 75, 110, 134.5, 150, 200, 300, 600, 1200, and, finally, 1800 bits/sec. Many teleprinters can operate at several of these speeds, the specific speed being determined by an operator-controlled switch. A key characteristic of low speed devices is their availability in either a buffered or an unbuffered configuration. Historically, most low speed terminals have been unbuffered, as illustrated by the teletypewriter models of the early and middle

Table 5.1. Major Categories of Teleprocessing Terminals

1. Low speed teleprinter
    Buffered or unbuffered
    Limited intelligence
    Used on dial or dedicated lines, but mostly dial
    Popular applications—time sharing, message switching
2. Low and medium speed visual display
    Alphanumeric or graphic (limited numbers)
    Mostly buffered with moderate intelligence
    Used on dial or dedicated lines
    Popular applications—fast response, data base inquiry systems
    Used in stand-alone or clustered configurations
3. Batch processing terminals
    Card reader, printer, operator console in minimal configuration
    CRT display, tape, cassette, diskette capability optional
    Mostly buffered, frequently programmable
    Either dial or dedicated lines (dial restricted to 4800 bits/sec or less)
    Popular applications—extend card reader, line printer, access to batch job
    queue to distant locations
4. Transaction terminals
    Low cost per workstation, driven by buffered, shared controllers
    Use mostly dedicated lines
    Mostly buffered and designed around particular industry application
    Popular applications—retail point-of-sale, banking, credit checking,
    supermarket checkout
5. Intelligent workstation terminal
    Usually involves a cluster controller to handle local peripherals and per-
    form other functions
    Buffered, highly modular, programmable (always by vendor, sometimes by
    user), often contains high-level language compiler(s).
    Substantial functional capability independent of host CPU (e.g., local data
    entry, transaction editing and verification, and data base inquiry indepen-
    dent of host CPU)
    Cluster controller can function as remote data entry station controller,
    remote display controller, communications concentrator for polling and
    code conversion, and applications processor
    Can control such devices as teleprinters, CRTs (both local and remote),
    transaction terminals, tapes, diskettes, cassettes, disks, and on-line storage
    as well as other communication lines
    Uses either dial or leased lines and can perform many functions without
    connection to host CPU

1960s. In these unbuffered configurations, the line transmission speed is dictated by the electromechanical speed with which the printing mechanism can generate characters in hard copy form on the paper. Furthermore, unbuffered systems cannot perform any automatic error control functions.

Recently, a number of vendors have begun to offer several-thousand-character add-on buffers which can be used in conjunction with low speed teleprinter terminals to perform such additional functions as (1) error checking between a terminal and its communication partner at the other end, (2) code conversion, (3) local display and editing of lines before transmission over the data link, (4) off-line data entry, and (5) operating the transmission line at a speed independent of the electromechanical speed of the teleprinter device. These add-on devices are significant because the important functions they perform cannot be accomplished in basic unbuffered terminals.

The primary applications for low speed teleprinter terminals are conversational time sharing and administrative message switching. In message switching, teleprinters are often equipped with paper tape readers to enable off-line message preparation and facilitate the storage and handling of in-transit messages. It is reasonable to expect the applications for low speed teleprinters to continue to be significant in the future, primarily at the faster speeds in the range given above and in devices employing buffers to enhance the traditional functions of the basic teleprinters.

The biggest growth in teleprinters will probably not occur at the lower end of the speed spectrum. Rather, a substantial number of teleprinter devices will continue to find widespread uses in dial-up applications where portability, flexibility, and economy are the major considerations of the user. As sophistication and added function become increasingly important, there will be a greater interest in utilizing other kinds of terminals.

Most low speed teleprinter terminals involved in conversational time sharing employ the dial-up network, which is readily available and quite inexpensive for connections over short distances to time-shared computers. It is also particularly attractive for applications where the specific locations of terminals are not known to the system designer. It is common and even customary in many organizations to utilize a teleprinter terminal for connections into several different computer facilities for different purposes. Recent dial-up tariff changes to usage-sensitive billing by domestic telephone companies, however, are making local dial-up time sharing dramatically more expensive. As a result, many users are switching to leased line networks even for local time sharing.

The relatively low costs for teleprinters are their biggest advantage, ranging from approximately \$50/month upward to \$100/month or more, although most of the currently popular 300 bits/sec devices cost \$100/month or more. Thus the day when teleprinter terminals can be afforded by persons in the home is not too far away. This will open up fantastic new possibilities for working in the office at home, electronic banking, shopping electronically in conjunction with CATV, and so on. However, one of the major limitations to substantial usage of teleprinter terminals in these and other new endeavors has been the reliability aspects of the lower speed devices. Being primarily electromechanical in design, they contain many moving parts that must continuously be maintained and frequently repaired. Devices introduced recently in the marketplace get away from the typewriter-like mechanisms traditionally found in the teletypewriters of 10 years ago. These new terminals employ different types of printing technology and generally represent a progressive step in the direction of improving device reliability. The reliability of these low speed devices will be substantially increased in the future as more and more of their components become electronic and smaller percentages of the mechanical variety remain. As a final point, many teleprinter terminals contain built-in modems, eliminating the need for a separate stand-alone signal converter.

5.1.2. Low and Medium Speed Visual Display Terminals

The second type of widely used teleprocessing terminal is the visual display unit for applications between 1200 and 4800 bits/sec, although some can operate even faster than 4800 bits/sec. Often this device is referred to as the cathode ray tube or CRT display. It is available in two main types: *(a)* the alphanumeric (displays only characters, letters, and text symbols) and *(b)* the graphic (handles lines and line drawings, and provides varying levels of geometric manipulation).

The concern here is with the alphanumeric type, primarily because it is much more prevalent. Although graphic CRT applications are growing, the considerable expense and relatively limited spectrum of applications for these devices have tended to restrict their acceptance.

Alphanumeric CRT displays enable an operator to enter data onto a screen, either directly from a keyboard or by pulling it up from local storage, for editing and verification before transmission into a computer. Information returned from the computer to the CRT display is displayed on the screen. Many of these devices are equipped with a feature known as scrolling, which is a visual emulation of the upward motion of paper being passed through a teleprinter station. Information displayed on the screen may be inspected by the terminal operator and can usually be converted into hard copy on a selective basis. In these cases the operator is equipped with a function key that enables the screen of data to be moved to an adjacent printing unit for conversion into hard copy. Most CRT displays are equipped with a buffer for input and output activity to perform the blocking and error checking of messages sent over the data link. These buffers also enable standard forms or ''masks'' of constant text to be stored and selectively retrieved by the CRT operators handling different types of transactions. Cathode ray tubes are presently being provided with substantial intelligence and in some cases employ completely self-contained microprocessors. These devices are usually employed either in stand-alone configurations or in clustered arrangements such as the one shown in Figure 5.1. When a clustered arrangement is used, individual CRTs share the common buffering and data link control mechanisms with all the tubes connected to the cluster. The cluster concept enables applications requiring substantial numbers of workstations in the same physical area to be economically serviced by the sharing of the control function.

Various input/output devices can be attached to the remote terminal controller, such as printers, magnetic tape cassettes, disks, and diskettes.

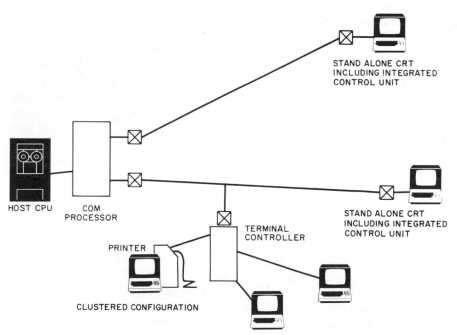

Figure 5.1. Stand-alone and clustered CRT configurations.

The more local intelligence provided with a CRT display, the more editing related to data entry functions can be done locally. The advantages of intelligence can be illustrated by noting what happens for the entry of input with a typical nonintelligent terminal. Here a user will typically request a preformatted screen of character information stored at the central computer. After this request of the central application, the preformatted display mask is transmitted out to the CRT. Next, the operator enters some variable text information and returns the entire message to the central computer. Clearly this is wasteful of line capacity and requires the movement of more data over the lines than are necessary. It also involves unnecessary activation and utilization of the central application program processor, since preformatted screens could be stored at the terminal location. With intelligent devices, screen formats can be called up and displayed locally. Then, after the message is composed via the insertion of the variable text, the entire screen of information can be sent back to the main computer.

Other areas of enhancement in the CRT display reflect the continuing desire of users for functions and features that minimize the time required for the entry, editing, and verification of data, thereby maximizing operator productivity. To illustrate one particularly useful function, certain intelligent terminals make it possible to enter often-used character strings with a single key stroke.

Cathode ray tube displays are also particularly useful in on-line data base access applications. The record (or records) being used for the data base query, known as the search key (s), is entered on the screen and sent to the central computer. After the data base has been searched, the associated information associated with that input record (key) is displayed back at the operator location. With the substantial growth of data base applications, CRT display stations for this purpose are becoming exceptionally popular and will multiply very rapidly in the future.

Since average response time requirements for inquiry/response types of applications are ordinarily in the range of 3 to 8 sec, leased lines are usually a necessity because the establishment of a dial-up connection will often require from 5 to 25 sec before any data transmission can take place! Most CRT terminals can be connected over either point-to-point or multipoint leased lines.

If queries or updates for a data base application do not demand such rapid response times, they can be batched at the remote site, enabling a multiplicity of transactions to be processed during a single dial-up connection time, and possibly enabling switched connections to be utilized. Here the dial-up time and connect times are a one-time overhead that will not be encountered for each data base access. Dial-up lines can, of course, be utilized for CRT applications where accesses are not as frequent or response time requirements as urgent as those noted above.

Prices for CRT terminals vary widely, depending on the sophistication and geographic clustering of the terminals. Generally it is possible to obtain minimally configured CRTs that emulate teleprinter stations for $75 to $100/month if no hard copy output capability is required. More sophisticated CRT devices with minimal intelligence, hard copy output features, local editing, and other capabilities will generally range upward from $125 to $150/month/workstation, based on mid 1976 prices. These ranges include the cost of the terminal itself and prorated costs of associated control units, but do not include any required signal conversion equipment.

5.1.3. Batch Processing Terminals

The next category of terminal device is known as the batch processing terminal. Here we include the broad range of systems used to extend batch card readers, tapes, printers, and so on to a distant location. We also include the enhanced terminal devices known as remote entry (RJE) systems which operate in conjunction with host CPU software to provide job status inquiry and job prioritization to the remote site. Batch terminals are typically employed at speeds of 2400 or 4800 bits/sec over dial-up lines and at speeds up to 9600 bits/sec on dedicated point-to-point lines. Multipoint leased lines have traditionally been used only in limited scope, primarily because communications software support for such configurations has not been widely available. In the future, however, it appears that line control software based on concepts like Synchronous Data Link Control (SDLC) (discussed in Chapter 8) will permit remote batch terminals and devices like CRTs to share multipoint lines, thereby reducing line costs and providing more efficient use of networking facilities.

The traditional purpose of the RJE terminal is to extend the functions of the input and output peripherals in the computer room out to remote locations using data communications. Batch job entry, printing, and card reading may all be accomplished at a remote location with a remote batch processing station, thereby eliminating the need for a stand-alone computer at many remote locations.[1] Remote batch processing terminals are becoming increasingly modular, enabling the user to specify at the time of purchase which input/output peripherals (including readers, printers,

---

[1]The terms *station* and *terminal* are used interchangeably here without ambiguity, since the batch processing terminal automatically implies a control unit and multiple peripherals attached to it.

CRTs, magnetic tape units, diskettes, and cassettes) are to be supplied in conjunction with the controller. Almost all remote batch processing stations are buffered for error checking purposes and for maximizing the efficiency of data link operation. Some programmable devices even allow different line control procedures to be emulated. Even though this trend has not become substantial, it will be more important in the future when a particular type of station needs to communicate with different computer facilities in different locations.

One can envisage the remote batch processing station of the future as containing many additional functions beyond those available today. For example, as shown in Figure 5.2, a remote batch station can be equipped with the ability to perform such functions as the following:

1. The polling of multipoint lines terminated in the batch station complex in question.
2. Concentration functions in which other nearby dial-up stations could connect into the batch station and have the messages sent over the dedicated line to the central location.
3. Data entry onto a cassette or diskette of some type, in which case the batch station would function as an intelligent data collection station.
4. Teleprinter terminal connection to the control unit, for communication over the data link to interactive applications running concurrently in the distant CPU.
5. Direct file inquiry to data bases at the distant CPU.
6. Off-line local processing, depending on available peripherals.
7. Connection to multiple CPUs over logical channels and/or multiple communication lines.

The device being described here is so flexible that the same physical equipment configuration is capable of performing virtually any kind of terminal function. This is the concept of a generalized workstation terminal. In the future, the distinctions between the remote batch processing terminal and the intelligent type of device to be discussed shortly will probably disappear. Users will identify the functions necessary for a given application and then construct a modular terminal configuration to meet these needs. It is certain that these devices will have to begin accommodating additional functions beyond those that are the traditional domain of the RJE terminal on today's market, because most users, for economic purposes, are demanding the ability to share lines, modems, and terminal equipment across a broad variety of applications.

Prices for RJE terminals currently vary over a wide range, usually

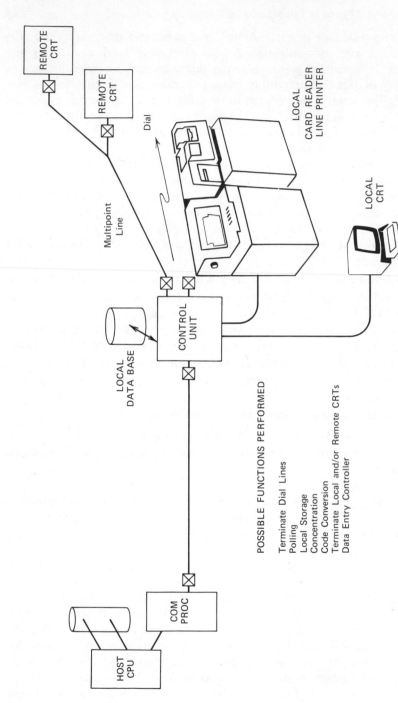

REMOTE CRT

REMOTE CRT

Dial

Multipoint Line

LOCAL CARD READER LINE PRINTER

LOCAL CRT

LOCAL DATA BASE

CONTROL UNIT

POSSIBLE FUNCTIONS PERFORMED

Terminate Dial Lines
Polling
Local Storage
Concentration
Code Conversion
Terminate Local and/or Remote CRTs
Data Entry Controller

COM PROC

HOST CPU

Figure 5.2. Remote batch processing system with numerous functional enhancements.

230

starting at a minimum of about \$200 to \$300/month. The \$200 to \$300/month remote batch stations are not very sophisticated. As one works his way upward to the \$700 to \$1000/month range, it is possible to obtain remote batch capabilities of reading and printing plus a buffered error control system and a few other related functions like remote operator console. The generalized workstation terminals of the future will tend to take advantage of cost reduction possibilities, using LSI and microprocessors to provide substantially larger numbers of functions than do today's devices at comparable prices.

Remote batch stations are operated either over dial-up lines or over leased lines. Host CPU-resident operating software used to control batch stations on leased lines typically consists of the automatic spooling programs offered by the larger computer vendors. Unfortunately, many of these software packages do not permit the operation of remote batch stations on a multipoint dedicated line. Certainly some vendors offer batch terminals that can be configured onto a multipoint line to reduce the costs of leased lines, and have done so for years. No technical difficulty is associated with developing software that will permit multipoint dedicated line usage of remote batch stations. The probable reason for limited multipoint line usage software is the relatively long, continuous transmissions typically associated with remote batch processing. Consequently, designers of such devices and their control software have thought that sharing a communication line across two or more batch users, each with continuous transmission requirements, would not be practicable because one station could prevent the line from being accessed by others for lengthy periods of time. This thinking has changed in recent years, however, with the advent of more sophisticated full-duplex data link control procedures and increasingly powerful telecommunications control software. These new control approaches make it possible to dynamically allocate the transmission capacity of a line to multiple remote stations (both batch and other types) so that virtually concurrent operation by several remote terminal users becomes feasible.

Also of major significance is the capability of these new data link control mechanisms to support terminals capable of simultaneous sending and receiving. Until recently, by far the greatest number of remote batch devices (and other terminals as well) could not simultaneously send and receive data over the same communication line. Primarily because of the half-duplex architecture of the widely used Binary Synchronous Communications (BSC) discipline discussed in Chapter 8, all send and receive tasks for the communication line had to be processed in single-thread, one-at-a-time fashion under this approach. In future systems equipped with full-duplex line control software, send and receive tasks can be performed in parallel, thereby enabling input from job $n + 1$ at a remote station to be accepted while output from job n is being transmitted. Numerous other advantages accrue from the ability of remote batch stations to operate in true full-duplex fashion. More will be said about these benefits in subsequent chapters.

Many batch stations in operation today use dial-up lines because user companies have facilities such as WATS lines which can be used for remote batch applications at off-hours. It is customary to find user organizations employing large groups of WATS lines for data transmission in the evening, although these lines are cost-justified and used primarily for voice communication purposes during normal business hours.

Usually the tradeoffs in the tariffs will lead to justification for dedicated lines in today's remote batch station whenever the total transmission time exceeds several hours per day of connect time, on the average. In the future if prices for dedicated lines decline and the cost for using the dial-up network continues to increase, it is reasonable to anticipate an even greater percentage of remote batch stations employing dedicated lines. The only possible disadvantage to using a dedicated line is that it connects the station to a single processor. Many companies like to use one remote batch station for alternate connection to a variety of CPUs at different times during the day. In these cases use of the dial-up network would be preferable. Of course there is nothing to prevent the same batch station from being connected to one CPU over a dedicated line and to others via dial lines (or other leased lines) on an alternating basis.

5.1.4. Transaction Terminals

Transaction terminals are special purpose industry-oriented terminals used for various applications, including banking, supermarket checkout, retail point-of-sale, credit authorization, and the like. These terminals tend to have a low cost per input/output device and are often (but not always) driven by shared controllers which are, in turn, connected to other computers. One unique aspect of the transaction terminal is its connection to the first layer of shared control, often using lines that are not provided by the common carriers. In these cases, limited-distance, intraplant, or intrabuilding communication facilities are threaded through the transaction terminal locations to connect these devices back to their controller. A common arrangement for the communications configuration into transaction terminals is the looped line configuration discussed in Chapter 2. Transaction terminals can be configured in large numbers on these loops and provided with very fast response times if the lines can operate at extremely high data rates (say at speeds faster than 1 million bits/sec). Many transaction terminals are in operation today, and the number is growing by leaps and bounds. An interesting network of transaction terminals is being developed by the Bell System for short inquiry/response applications in metropolitan areas. Reference [1] notes specific properties and typical network configurations for this new public Transaction Network Service. A majority of cash registers in the future will be designed as transaction terminals so that they can perform numerous traditional cash register functions off-line and also can communicate with other computers and data bases.

An important characteristic of transaction terminals is the necessity for being able to operate them idependently of higher level points of computational capability in the network. For example, in the typical network of Figure 5.3 transaction terminals connected on a loop feed a store controller, which in turn connects to a multipoint line into the regional concentrator. Regional concentrators in turn can connect to a central computer over point-to-point lines. Here is the complete hierarchy of facilities involving loops, multipoint, and point-to-point lines, as well as transaction terminals, loop controllers, remote concentrators, and central computers, all being used in integrated fashion to provide a complete network service. Failure of a system element at the loop controller level (or higher) must not prevent the transaction terminal itself from performing its basic functions, such as processing customers at a grocery store checkout stand or permitting a banking customer to make a deposit or cash a check. This requirement implies a certain distribution of functional capabilities traditionally unavailable in a totally centralized configuration. If there is a failure in a higher level system element, all lower elements must continue to operate until the failure is repaired. The typical method of using these hierarchical networks will require that the basic functions of the transaction terminal are capable of accomplishment without any dependence on the network. Higher level functions such as credit checking or collection and the summarizing of data for higher level management reports to regional and district centers are required. These functions can be superimposed and performed on a less frequent and less urgent basis.

Another compelling argument in favor of the distributed-function networking approach shown in Figure 5.3 is that fast response times of not more than 2 or 3 secs are usually required at the point-of-sale terminal for such functions as credit authorization. In large retailing or banking networks involving thousands of terminals, a hierarchical network, and a very high collective message rates during peak hours, it becomes virtually impossible to satisfy such response time requirements if all transactions must be funneled into a single, large, centralized data base. Here the loop controller or store controller can be equipped with a small data base of

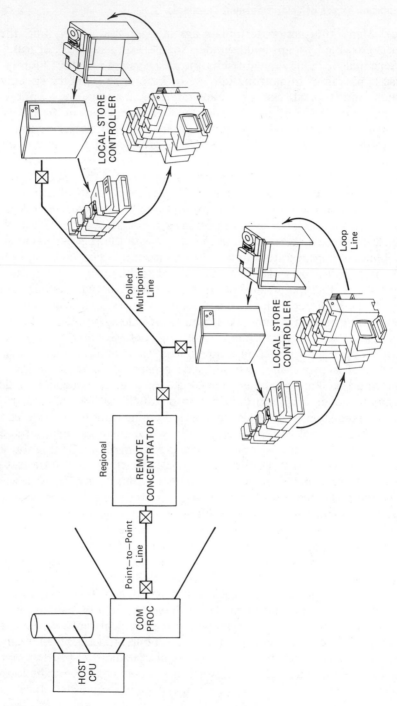

Figure 5.3. Hierarchical layers of function in network employing transaction terminals.

LOCAL STORE CONTROLLER

LOCAL STORE CONTROLLER

Loop Line

Polled Multipoint Line

Regional

REMOTE CONCENTRATOR

Point—to—Point Line

COM PROC

HOST CPU

234

credit information for customers typically using the store or bank in question. An out-of-town customer's transaction could be expected to take longer for credit clearance. This could either be done by switching the credit verification request message through the higher levels of the network to the appropriate data base or by obtaining the authorization via telephone.

Costs of transaction terminals again vary widely, but typically start in the $100/month level at a very minimum.[2] In making cost comparisons, it becomes essential that transaction terminals be compared strictly on a function-for-function basis with other kinds of input/output devices for teleprocessing networks. Transaction terminals may have a very low cost per input/output device, but by the time the necessary communication lines and controllers and concentrators are incorporated, the cost per workstation can be significantly higher. Anyone thinking of typical configurations using transaction terminals will be well advised to configure alternative arrangements in which the complete costs of all system elements are clearly laid out for evaluation and comparison.

Reponse time requirements at transaction terminals tend to be rather short, usually on the order of several seconds. The connection of transaction terminals onto looped communication lines and into other points of control must not slow down the basic operation of the transaction terminal itself. Transaction terminals for banking, supermarket, and retail store applications seldom use dial-up lines, primarily because of the fast response time requirements.

On the other hand, inexpensive terminals for completely different kinds of applications like lower priority credit verification and credit authorization can be operated quite effectively over the dial-up network for a very low cost, particularly if the data base being accessed is available on a local call basis. In fact, the Touchtone telephone itself is being increasingly used as a transaction terminal to provide at very low cost additional functions necessary to support some of the traditional applications of cash registers. See Reference [1] for additional discussion of this point.

5.1.5. Intelligent Workstation Terminal Systems for Distributed Processing

This category of terminal system is most difficult to distinguish clearly from the categories already discussed, primarily because the other functional types are increasingly being manufactured with substantial

---

[2]Extremely simple keyboard-only terminals for credit authorization and badge reading are currently available for $25 to $50/month in typical situations.

intelligence, using the modular workstation approach. However, in this category we place all workstation/controller-driven systems that (1) are vendor and/or user programmable, (2) are capable of supporting at least keyboard terminals, CRT display terminals, and printers, and (3) are capable of performing meaningful off-line functions for the local terminal operator without being connected to a central computer. The third criterion precludes many traditional host-dependent CRT display terminals from being included in the intelligent workstation terminal category. In addition to these functions, the workstation controller is often equipped to perform certain device and communications control functions for different types of locally attached peripherals like printers, readers, disks, diskettes, and cassettes, and possibly even for other nearby terminals attached to the workstation via communication lines. In general, however, few workstation controllers do an adequate job of combining the communication control functions of a contemporary concentrator with the required functions of an advanced terminal controller.

In describing distributed processing here, we refer to terminal systems that are capable of performing meaningful application processing like text editing, file retrieval, and mathematical calculations without being connected to a central computer. Obviously, a precise meaning of "distributed processing" is elusive, especially since one user's interpretation of application processing may be totally consistent with another user's view of mundane message preparation or data entry. Our key requirement, in summary, for this category of terminal is that the workstation be capable of performing a meaningful application function for the terminal users connected to it without being connected to another computer while performing this function.

To certain data entry users, the flexible key-to-tape, key-to-disk, key-to-cassette, key-to-diskette types of equipment with local file storage and text editing fit this definition. Other related examples can involve a remote branch office of a business performing its daily data entry, editing, and verification tasks without being connected to a central computer.

As shown in the generalized schematic of Figure 5.4, data base applications can be designed employing the strategy in which portions of a large data base are stored at remote stations, enabling frequently referenced records (which would otherwise be stored in a central file) to be positioned out at the intelligent workstation. This can provide for a much more responsive system and enable users to have substantially more work done independently of the central computer location.

Still another reason for using the distributed processing strategy employing intelligent terminals is the unique ability of the latter to cost-effectively prevent transactions with bad input data from ever entering

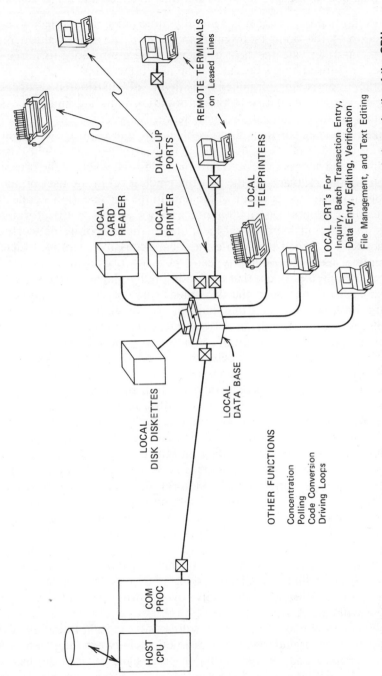

REMOTE TERMINALS
on Leased Lines

DIAL–UP
PORTS

LOCAL
CARD
READER

LOCAL
PRINTER

LOCAL
TELEPRINTERS

LOCAL CRT's For
Inquiry, Batch Transaction Entry,
Data Entry, Editing, Verification
File Management, and Text Editing

LOCAL
DATA BASE

LOCAL
DISK DISKETTES

OTHER FUNCTIONS

Concentration
Polling
Code Conversion
Driving Loops

COM
PROC

HOST
CPU

Figure 5.4. An intelligent terminal configuration capable of performing many local functions independently of the CPU.

the system for processing. It is generally more sensible to reject an error transaction at the point of origin than to let it in, send it through the network, and activate the host application program, only to purge the transaction subsequently because of invalid input data!

Another compelling argument in favor of distributed processing strategies is their similarity to the information handling and processing structures of the organizations they serve. Very few large or medium organizations keep all their filing cabinets in one central storage area, primarily because of the difficulties such an arrangement would pose in providing rapid access to desired information for all levels of the organization. Of similar relevance is the fact that each level in the user organization does not need to access all of the data in the organization's collective filing cabinet group. Distributed processing systems with information storage at different hierarchical locations in the corporate network can analogously be argued to provide the most accessible, storage-efficient, and minimal message volume types of network organizations.

Another related problem that has traditionally plagued large scale teleprocessing users has been the dependence of the entire teleprocessing network on certain things that happen in the central computer. For example, in highly centralized networks it is common for a failure of the operating system at the central computer to produce an outage of all teleprocessing terminals connected into that computer. Customers involved in using unintelligent data entry terminals or traditional CRTs are not in a position to utilize their devices until the main CPU is back in operation. Intelligent terminals of the type discussed here sever the strong dependence between the central computer and the remote workstations by enabling central node failures to be masked. Failures in communications lines and/or processors feeding into the central site can similarly be masked. When one of these elements fails, it is obviously not possible for the intelligent-type station to make inquiries of a central data base during the failure. However, much routine data entry work can continue to be performed. After all the data entry or data base update transactions for a given time period are entered, edited, and verified locally, they can be stored and sent to the central site subsequently. Hence the intelligent workstation terminal is having a significant positive effect in increasing the overall availability of teleprocessing networks by enabling its user terminals to be utilized productively, even during periods of outage at other network devices.

Intelligent terminals of the future will possess certain functions above and beyond those found today. The distinctions between intelligent workstation terminals and the remote batch processing devices discussed in Section 5.1.3 will gradually disappear, giving rise to a generalized workstation terminal in which all functions, including source data entry, input data verification, control of distributed data bases, off-line editing, remote polling, remote concentration, and local support for a broad variety of peripheral modules, can be accommodated from a single modular type of remote teleprocessing workstation. This type of terminal, by containing substantial amounts of bulk storage and support software, provides for remote data base accesses in addition to centralized data base accesses. This provision is an essential element in the implementation of the distributive data base networks expected to be so popular in the future.

5.2. TERMINAL REQUIREMENTS CHECKLIST

Table 5.2 summarizes the major items that should be considered in the selection and evaluation of terminals for teleprocessing. Many of the items in this table have already been discussed. Most terminals of the future will tend to be buffered and hence capable of providing error control over data links attached to the terminal location. However, substantial numbers of *low speed devices* such as teletypewriters will proba-

Table 5.2.   Summary of Major Terminal Requirements

1.   Buffered, unbuffered.
2.   Send only, receive only, send/receive.
3.   Human factor considerations.
4.   Operating speeds, switch selectability.
5.   Hard, soft copy.
6.   Portability.
7.   Modes of operation (HDX/FDX, lease/dial).
8.   Code format capabilities.
9.   Error control features.
10.   Security features.
11.   Peripheral attachments possible.
12.   Unattended operation.
13.   Off-line capabilities.
14.   Local message formatting capabilities.
15.   Automatic dial backup, reverse channel capabilities.
16.   Size and access speed of local storage for data base, applications processing.
17.   Support for efficient man/machine dialog.
18.   Compatibility.
19.   Level of user programmability.
20.   Built-in operator training functions.
21.   High-level language compilers available.

bly continue to be unbuffered for the next several years. In these systems, character-by-character error checking of input data can be accomplished by using echo checking approaches like those discussed in Chapter 6.

In selecting a CRT terminal it is essential to consider human factor aspects such as keyboard layout, screen adjustment, ease of operation, and ability to add and delete characters, to add and delete lines, to backspace easily, to overstrike, and to reposition readily the cursor on the screen. Most terminal user organizations are tremendously concerned with selecting terminals that can be used in a highly productive way by people with a minimum degree of training. Everything that can be done to employ devices which are easy for the layman to use will generally be well worth the investment in the sense that productivity enhancement will be maximized.

The operating speed of a terminal and its associated communication lines has traditionally been strongly influenced by the electromechanical characteristics of the peripherals attached to the terminal. For unbuffered terminal devices, the printing speed will dictate the line speed. On the other hand, in a buffered terminal it is possible to operate the communication line at a speed different from the printing speed of the terminal itself. For example, in a data collection application involving buffered teleprinters, a much higher speed line can be used than is possible with unbuffered terminals of the same type. This will have substantial implications in terms of possibly reduced transmission time requirements. Buffered terminals enable transmissions to take place at higher speeds for reduced periods of time over the dial-up network, so that substantially larger amounts of work can be done in a given time period.

The terminal user's ability to request hard copy selectively is important today and will become even more significant in the future. There are few applications where all character information returned to a terminal operator must be converted into hard copy. What is needed is the ability to have information displayed to the operator, with the operator deciding what portions should be converted into hard copy. This feature increases in significance as paper and other raw materials become scarcer because of the various shortages that have been plaguing users in recent years, and their costs rise.

Portability of terminals is important for the less costly kinds of devices, which are attractive to highly mobile users in applications such as law enforcement and construction management. For example, consider the terminal requirements of traveling salesmen, persons involved in monitoring construction projects, cruising law enforcement officials, doctors, and other individuals desirous of accessing a data base from a number of different locations throughout the day. In most of these cases the dial-up telephone network or mobile radios would be used by the terminal to access special data bases or computational routines. Acoustic couplers operating up to 300 bits/sec will continue to be a primary method for providing low cost access into the dial-up network in a highly portable environment where direct, permanent connections from a fixed terminal location are not practical.

Most terminals of the future will be designed flexibly enough to operate over both leased lines and dial-up lines in a variety of different modes, including half-duplex and full-duplex operation. It is important in selecting terminals to choose systems that have minimal impact on the kinds of lines, networks, and applications to which they may be connected. For example, recall the previously discussed requirement for the exclusive usage of point-to-point lines in remote batch stations employing typically available software. Obviously, such restrictions must be carefully evaluated in selecting terminals for the diverse application possibilities of the next decade.

Most terminals should be capable of accommodating a number of different code formats in order to enable them to communicate with as many different machines and centralized telecommunications control programs as possible. This would imply a minimum ability to support ASCII code, and possibly such other codes as BCD and EBCDIC (see Figures 5.5 and 5.6), in addition to any individual codes commonly used by the vendors with which these terminals must communicate. Other possible codes that may need to be supported are Baudot, IBM's 4-of-8 code, and variations of the standard BCD codes; these are discussed at length in Reference [2].

Bit positions 1,2,3,4

Bit positions 5,6,7,8	0000	0001	0010	0011	0100	0101	0110	0111	1000	1001	1010	1011	1100	1101	1110	1111
0000	NUL				Blank	B	−						>	<	t	0
0001							/		a	j			A	J		1
0010									b	k	s		B	K	S	2
0011									c	l	t		C	L	T	3
0100	PF	RES	BYP	PN					d	m	u		D	M	U	4
0101	HT	NL	LF	RS					e	n	v		E	N	V	5
0110	LC	BS	EOB	UC					f	o	w		F	O	W	6
0111	DEL	IDL	PRE	EOT					g	p	x		G	P	X	7
1000									h	q	y		H	Q	Y	8
1001							/	"	i	r	z		I	R	Z	9
1010					?	!		:								
1011						S	,	#								
1100					←	*	%	@								
1101					(	)	⌄	.								
1110					+	;	−	=								
1111					*	¢	±	✓								

Figure 5.5. Extended BCD code with plenty of unused bit groupings for graphic purposes.

		000	100	010	110	001	101	011	111
	0000	NUL	DLE	SPACE	0	@	P		p
	1000	SOH	DC1	!	1	A	Q	a	q
	0100	STX	DC2	"	2	B	R	b	r
	1100	ETX	DC3	#	3	C	S	c	s
	0010	EOT	DC4	$	4	D	T	d	t
	1010	ENQ	NAK	%	5	E	U	e	u
	0110	ACK	SYN	&	6	F	V	f	v
Bit Positions	1110	BEL	ETB	'	7	G	W	g	w
1,2,3,4	0001	BS	CAN	(	8	H	X	h	x
	1001	HT	EM	)	9	I	Y	i	y
	0101	LF	SUB	*	:	J	Z	j	z
	1101	VT	ESC	+	:	K	[	k	{
	0011	FF	FS	ʃ	<	L	\	l	l
	1011	CR	GS	−	=	M	]	m	}
	0111	SO	RS	··	>	N	^	n	~
	1111	SI	US	/	?	O	−	o	DEL

Bit positions 5,6,7

NUL	= All zeros	VT	= Vertical tabulation	SYN	= Synchronous/idle
SOH	= Start of heading	FF	= Form feed	ETB	= End of transmitted block
STX	= Start of text	CR	= Carriage return	CAN	= Cancel (error in data)
ETX	= End of text	SO	= Shift out	EM	= End of medium
EOT	= End of transmission	SI	= Shift in	SUB	= Start of special sequence
ENQ	= Enquiry	DLE	= Data link escape	ESC	= Escape
ACK	= Acknowledgement	DC 1	= Device control 1	FS	= Information file separator
BEL	= Bell or attention signal	DC 2	= Device control 2	GS	= Information group separator
BS	= Back space	DC 3	= Device control 3	RS	= Information record separator
HT	= Horizontal tabulation	DC 4	= Device control 4	US	= Information unit separator
LF	= Line feed	NAK	= Negative acknowledgement	DEL	= Delete

Figure 5.6.   ASCII Code.

Error control will become increasingly important in terminal systems of the future and must therefore be considered in the selection of devices for teleprocessing applications. Substantial numbers of terminals available today (particularly those that are not buffered) do not contain the capability for system-provided error control. In the future, increasing requirements for data accuracy and lower residual error rates, as well as a maturing LSI technology, will make possible the easy incorporation of a full range of detection and retransmission error control schemes in the terminals at reasonable costs. (Chapter 6 is devoted to a discussion of these alternative procedures for controlling errors.) Users selecting terminals today should make provisions for the incorporation of error control buffers and functions in their terminal devices.

Security of data and access restriction have received precious little attention in the design of most terminals presently available. Terminals must be designed to work in conjunction with teleprocessing software that permits the system to identify a particular terminal user who has signed on, to force him to supply certain passwords, and to prevent him from obtaining access to unauthorized information. In leased line systems it is much easier to identify, control, and restrict the physical terminals that can communicate with a particular computer than it is with dial-up systems. However, it is generally no easier in a leased line system to identify, control, and restrict the persons using such a terminal device. Many of today's dedicated line systems pay very little attention to access security, on the false premise that a terminal located within the confines of an organization's business premises will be utilized only by authorized individuals within that organization.

Terminals must be able to work in conjunction with higher level system functions that force both the *device* and the *user of the device* to satisfy certain access-permission criteria. This can be accomplished by using an operating-system-resident table of authorized device identification codes (IDS), valid user IDs and currently valid passwords for valid users. Terminals should be designed to "blindout" portions of the dialog process in which the user inputs IDs and passwords. This can be accomplished by overstrike approaches, whereby the user enters his password into a specified field that has been intentionally overstricken. The user-entered password will then be visible only to the system and not to any persons observing the sign-on process or to anyone subsequently obtaining a hard copy record of the sign-on dialogue. Another approach is to have a terminal feature that can be selectively activated to suppress local displays (either on CRTs or in hard-copy fashion) of password and ID types of information. Here it becomes the responsibility of the terminal user to judiciously employ such features and prevent others from obtaining access to passwords. This is sometimes referred to as a "print suppression" feature.

Once the access security precautions have been sufficiently considered, the other important dimension to the terminal security problem is data security. Data security procedures here refer to approaches that can be employed to prevent unwanted machines or persons, having somehow gained access to the system, from being able to interpret, copy, or monitor data flowing between a particular terminal device and an associated computer system. Perhaps the most feasible approach to providing this type of protection is to employ terminal encrypting procedures for all data transmission activity between authorized users and their destination processors. An excellent discussion of the myriad possible encryption approaches and their associated advantages and disadvantages may be found in Reference [3] and in Chapter 8.

Another crucial requirement for terminals to be employed in large volume data transfer applications is the ability to be operated in an unattended mode. Many organizations, for example, load large volumes of data into a terminal workstation at the end of a business day in a remote branch office. Using previously discussed dial-up polling techniques, the central computer will call each of these stations during the evening hours and collect data entered into storage at that terminal location during the preceding business day. Clearly, there should not be any requirement for operator involvement in these kinds of simple tasks. The central computer must be able to determine when a remote terminal is malfunctioning, when there are read checks on the magnetic tape, and so on, and to take appropriate remedial procedures. It will also be important for unattended terminals connected to dedicated lines to switch over automatically to dial-up lines for backup purposes. Very few devices currently available have this capability.

The desirability of being able to operate terminals independently of centralized computers and other devices in a teleprocessing system has already been discussed. It was pointed out that the substantially greater amounts of intelligence positioned in local terminals will have the effect of reducing the volumes of data that flow back and forth unnecessarily between remote terminals and their central computer partners. This means that local station message formatting capabilities enabling storage of the relatively invariant portions of input messages are highly desirable. They reduce transmission volumes and central processor machine overhead significantly. These economies in turn reduce communication costs and the amount of time an operator takes to compose a given message.

One final point that must be considered is the terminal's ability to use alternative types of facilities in case of failures of the basic communication paths into the central computer. Substantial dial-up backup capabilities are being designed into systems by users in today's networks. Unfortunately most of these schemes currently require human coordination. Users need terminals with the ability to be connected automatically to the dial-up network in the case of primary line failures of a dedicated variety. Clearly it is desirable to reduce the amount of dependence on human beings to an absolutely minimal level in the implementation of approaches to enhance network reliability and availability.

5.3. THE BUSINESS MACHINE/SIGNAL CONVERSION DEVICE INTERFACE

As mentioned earlier in this chapter, virtually all business machines that use telecommunication links employ a standard electrical interface whose specifications have been developed by the Electronics Industries Association (EIA) in the United States and by the CCITT in the other countries of the world. Generally speaking, the CCITT and EIA interfaces are functionally similar. The discussion here is primarily concerned with the EIA interface. Detailed information on either the CCITT or the EIA interface may be found in References [6], [7], and [8]. Scrutiny of these references quickly reveals that the CCITT and EIA interface specifications are not identical in all applications. Furthermore, each of these specifications permits a certain degree of applications engineering leeway. Great care must be taken in selecting stations (either stand-alone terminals or the clustered type) and signal converters whose options and functional requirements at the interface point are compatible. There is no implication that any modem with an EIA interface can be connected to an arbitrary station with an EIA interface. In fact, it will be seen that there are many variations of the standard interface (i.e., some functions are not always used) which become strongly application dependent.

The objective of this discussion is to explain the basic functions and typical implementation of the EIA interface, while avoiding the level of detail that becomes essential when two devices must actually be interfaced in a working system. Most vendors supply detailed timing diagrams and information about the interface requirements for specific products and application situations. In any given system, these sources of information should always be used for troubleshooting, installation, and routine diagnostic purposes.

An understanding of the EIA interface is vital to anyone concerned with the efficient planning, design, installation, operation, and maintenance of a teleprocessing network. Certain control signals can be readily monitored at the various EIA interface points in the network. Anomalous values can quickly enable the network operator to pinpoint the likely sources of failure or outage in any malfunctioning network.

The EIA and CCITT interfaces specify voltage levels whereby control and data signals are exchanged between an signal converter and a business machine in two-level digital form. All data signals are sent across the interface using a two-level, bit-by-bit serial signaling convention. The interface hardware consists of two 25-pin plugs (see Figure 5.7) from the business machine and the signal converter, which are physically connected together. Each pin on the interface (excepting the grounds) is activated by either the terminal or the signal converter; thus the pins may be regarded as directional. Each pin will, at any point in time, carry a voltage level corresponding to binary 1 or 0 (or, equivalently, marking or spacing, OFF or ON), as shown in Table 5.3. These binary signal levels are used to indicate the activation or deactivation of control functions on control pins and the values of bits in the data stream on data pins.

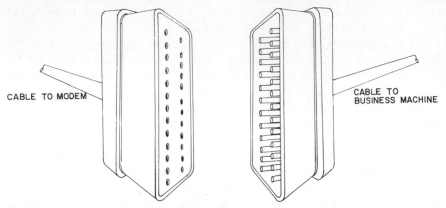

Figure 5.7. Twenty-five pin plugs for the EIA interface.

Each of the 25 interface pins can be placed in one of four categories on the basis of the dedicated function it performs:

1. Electrical ground.
2. Data exchange.
3. Control.
4. Timing or clock.

Table 5.4 summarizes the pin assignments, grouped according to functional categories. Figure 5.8 presents the interface pins in more detail, arranged in chronological order of the EIA pin numbers. A detailed presentation of these functions may be found in the appendix at the rear of the book.

As discussed in detail in Reference [8], the specific pins to be utilized in a given configuration will depend on the application and the type of line being used. For example, a minimum number of control pins are required

Table 5.3. Signal Level Conventions for the EIA Interface

	Interchange Voltage	
Notation	Negative	Positive
Binary state	1	0
Signal condition	Marking	Spacing
Function	OFF	ON

PIN NUMBER	CIRCUIT	DESCRIPTION
1	AA	PROTECTIVE GROUND
2	BA	TRANSMITTED DATA
3	BB	RECEIVED DATA
4	CA	REQUEST TO SEND
5	CB	CLEAR TO SEND
6	CC	DATA SET READY
7	AB	SIGNAL GROUND(COMMON RETURN)
8	CF	RECEIVED LINE SIGNAL DETECTOR
9	–	(RESERVED FOR DATA SET TESTING)
10	–	(RESERVED FOR DATA SET TESTING)
11		UNASSIGNED (SEE SECTION 3.2.3)
12	SCF	SEC. REC'D LINE SIG. DETECTOR
13	SCB	SEC. CLEAR TO SEND
14	SBA	SECONDARY TRANSMITTED DATA
15	DB	TRANSMISSION SIGNAL ELEMENT TIMING (DCE SOURCE)
16	SBB	SECONDARY RECEIVED DATA
17	DD	RECEIVER SIGNAL ELEMENT TIMING (DCE SOURCE)
18		UNASSIGNED
19	SCA	SECONDARY REQUEST TO SEND
20	CD	DATA TERMINAL READY
21	CG	SIGNAL QUALITY DETECTOR
22	CE	RING INDICATOR
23	CH/CI	DATA SIGNAL RATE SELECTOR (DTE/DCE SOURCE)
24	DA	TRANSMIT SIGNAL ELEMENT TIMING (DTE SOURCE)
25		UNASSIGNED

Figure 5.8.   EIA interface connector pin assignments summarized.

in dedicated point-to-point line applications. On conventional dial-up connections involving synchronous transmission, only one end may transmit at a time. There is thus a need to periodically reverse the direction of the transmission. This *line-turnaround* function is accomplished using the control signals on the interface. Figure 5.9 shows a typical interface timing diagram for the use of a dial-up line employing the Binary Synchronous Communication procedures (BSC is discussed at length in Chapter 8).

On multipoint lines a similar need for systematically activating and deactivating the remote modem transmit and receive subsystems necessitates the usage of the request-to-send and clear-to-send leads shown in the interface. Whenever a remote business machine wishes to send information over the data communications link, it activates request-to-send. The remote modem reacts by initiating procedures to establish bit synchronization with the central site modem's receiving subsystem. During this step, equalizers are set up, and any required test bit sequences are sent (only between the modems) before the transmission of actual data bits between business machines. At some point after the request-to-send has been issued by the remote station, the remote modem will respond to that station by raising clear-to-send. At the end of this request-to-send/

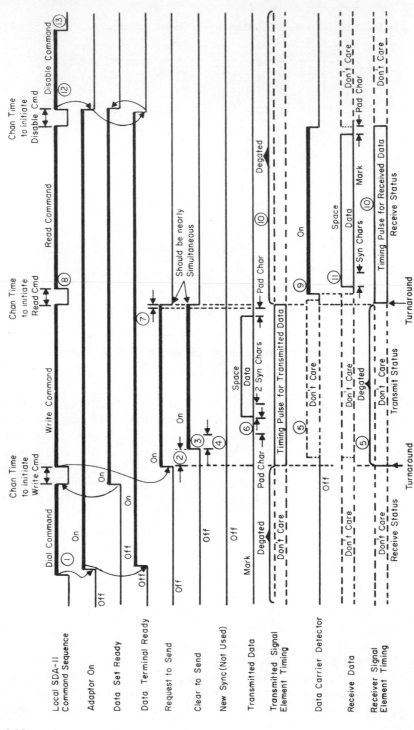

Figure 5.9. Typical interface timing diagram.

248

Table 5.4. EIA Interface Pins Grouped by Category of Function

EIA Pin Number	Interchange Circuit	C.C.I.T.T. Equivalent	Description (DCE: Data Communications Equipment, DTE: Data Terminal Equipment)	Ground	Data		Control		Timing	
					From DCE	To DCE	From DCE	To DCE	From DCE	To DCE
1	AA	101	Protective ground	X						
7	AB	102	Signal ground/common return	X						
2	BA	103	Transmitted data			X				
3	BB	104	Received data		X					
4	CA	105	Request to send					X		
5	CB	106	Clear to send				X			
6	CC	107	Data set ready				X			
20	CD	108	Data terminal ready					X		
22	CE	125	Ring indicator				X			
8	CF	109	Received line signal detector				X			
21	CG	110	Signal quality detector				X			
23	CH	111	Data signal rate selector (DTE—driver)					X		
23	CI	112	Data signal rate selector (DCE—driver)				X			
24	DA	113	Transmitter signal element timing (DTE)							X
15	DB	114	Transmitter signal element timing (DCE)						X	
17	DD	115	Receiver signal element timing (DCE)						X	
14	SBA	118	Secondary transmitted data			X				
16	SBB	119	Secondary received data		X					
19	SCA	120	Secondary request to send					X		
13	SCB	121	Secondary clear to send				X			
12	SCF	122	Secondary received line signal detector				X			

Table 5.5.   Data Transmission System Configuration Options for the EIA Interface

Data Transmission Configuration	Interface Type
Transmit only	A
Transmit only	B
Receive only	C
Half-duplex	D
Duplex	D
Duplex	E
Primary channel transmit only/secondary channel receive only	F
Primary channel transmit only/secondary channel receive only	H
Primary channel receive only/secondary channel transmit only	G
Primary channel receive only/secondary channel transmit only	I
Primary channel transmit only/half-duplex secondary channel	J
Primary channel receive only/half-duplex secondary channel	K
Half-duplex primary channel/half-duplex secondary channel	L
Duplex primary channel/duplex secondary channel	L
Duplex primary channel/duplex secondary channel	M

clear-to-send delay interval, data bits are submitted to the transmitted data pin and moved over the data link into the central computer. The RTS/CTS delay time is determined by specific hardware settings in the modem and is vitally important in determining the overall efficiency of data link use. Each time a remote station is polled, at least one RTS/CTS delay interval elapses before transmission can begin. In a system where 10 stations on a line are cyclically polled, for example, a reduction of 50 ms on each poll to a remote station can save a full ½ sec of overhead on a complete poll cycle (the action of polling all stations on the line). These overhead reductions can contribute substantially to improving response times and cost effectiveness. Most contemporary 9600 bits/sec modems cannot be used on multipoint, polled lines because the required RTS/CTS delays of not more than 50–100 msec necessitate very stringent line conditioning specifications which the carriers have not been able to provide up to the present time.

Tables 5.5 and 5.6 summarize the pins typically required for different types of applications. They should be used as a planning guide for configuring specific networks to assure that compatible terminal equipment and signal converters will be employed.

Note that many of the pins on the interface are unassigned. One very

Table 5.6. Interchange Circuit Requirements[a]

	Interchange Circuit	Interface Type												
		A	B	C	D	E	F	G	H	I	J	K	L	M
AA	Protective ground	—	—	—	—	—	—	—	—	—	—	—	—	—
AB	Signal ground	x	x	x	x	x	x	x	x	x	x	x	x	x
BA	Transmitted data	x	x		x	x	x	x	x	x	x	x	x	x
BB	Received data			x	x	x	x	x	x	x	x	x	x	x
CA	Request to send	x	x		x	x	x		x		x		x	
CB	Clear to send	x	x		x	x	x		x	x	x	x	x	x
CC	Data set ready	x	x	x	x	x	x	x	x	x	x	x	x	x
CD	Data terminal ready	s	s	s	s	s	s	s	s	s	s	s	s	s
CE	Ring indicator	s	s		s		s	s		s	s	s	s	s
CF	Received line signal detector			x	x	x	x	x	x	x	x	x	x	x
CG	Signal quality detector													
CH/CI	Data signaling rate selector (DTE)/(DCE)													
DA/DB	Transmitter signal element timing (DTE)/(DCE)	t	t		t	t	t	t	t		t	t	t	t
DD	Receiver signal element timing (DCE)			t	t	t	t	t	t	t	t	t	t	t
SBA	Secondary transmitted data							x		x		x	x	x
SBB	Secondary received data							x	x	x	x	x	x	x
SCA	Secondary request to send							x		x	x	x	x	x
SCB	Secondary clear to send							x		x	x	x	x	x
SCF	Secondary received line signal detector							x	x	x	x	x	x	x

[a]s: additional interchange circuits required for switched service; t: additional interchange circuits required for synchronous channel; x: basic interchange circuits, all systems; ——: optional.

common difficulty in data networks is resolving or keeping track of special uses that might possibly be made of these unassigned pins. It is common (although inadvisable) to utilize unassigned pins for specific purposes not spelled out in the interface standards. These situations cause substantial practical difficulties in fault isolation and system installation when interface leads are checked out by personnel not completely familiar with the application. Users and vendors should therefore avoid special uses of the unassigned pin functions whenever possible.

As a final note, many efforts are presently underway to define new interface standards for intelligent network services. These efforts, which will undoubtedly have an impact on present planning efforts, are discussed at length in Reference [9].

REFERENCES

1. L. R. Pamm, "Transaction Network: Data Communications for Metropolitan Areas," *Bell Laboratories Record,* Vol. 55, No. 1, January 1977.

2. J. T. Martin, *Teleprocessing Network Organization,* Prentice-Hall, Englewood Cliffs, N.J., 1970.

3. J. T. Martin, *Security, Accuracy, and Privacy in Computer Systems,* Prentice-Hall, Englewood Cliffs, N.J., 1974.

4. L. C. Hobbs, "Terminals," *Proceedings of IEEE,* November 1972, pp. 1273–1284.

5. Datapro Research Corporation, *Reports on Data Communications Terminals,* Report C20-100-101, Delran, N.J., 1976.

6. "International Specifications for Interface between Modems and Terminals," CCITT Interface Recommendation V24, (functionally similar to American Standard EIA RS-232, although not identical).

7. "Interface between Data Terminal Equipment and Data Communication Equipment Employing Serial Binary Data Interchange, EIA Standard RS-232-C," Engineering Department, Electronic Industries Association, Washington, D.C., August 1969.

8. "Application Notes for EIA Standard RS-232-C," Engineering Department, Electronic Industries Association, Washington, D.C., May 1971.

9. H. C. Folts and I. W. Cotton, "Interfaces: New Standards Catch Up with Technology," *Data Communications,* Vol. 6, No. 6, 1977, McGraw-Hill, New York.

SIX

CONTROLLING TRANSMISSION ERRORS

An unavoidable consequence of data transmission over any link exceeding a few hundred feet in length is the occurrence of errors. In preceding chapters it was noted that even the most sophisticated signal converters are not capable of always compensating for the numerous transmission limitations of telecommunication lines such as amplitude and delay distortion, random noise hits, and all other types of unpredictable anomalies that can cause a sink business machine to receive a different block of data bits than was actually transmitted. This chapter considers the possible approaches that can be implemented externally to the signal converter-circuit combination to provide a satisfactory degree of protection against transmission errors.

6.1. INTRODUCTION, APPROACHES TO ERROR CONTROL

The major approaches to be considered are summarized in Figure 6.1. The objectives of this chapter are to survey the functional requirements and distinguishing application aspects of each approach. The terminal hardware/software features, interface restrictions, and circuit properties required with each technique are discussed. Of equal concern are the overall transmission efficiency and the associated system parameters that determine how fast data may *actually* be transferred between two stations in light of overhead factors such as block retransmissions, line propagation delays, line turnarounds, and noninformation bits. Specific relationships are presented which may be used to quantitatively determine the net data transfer rate for the widely used family of detection and retransmission approaches to error control.

Ignoring transmission errors is a sensible approach in applications involving substantial amounts of English text or any type of message

1. Ignoring the Errors
2. Loop or Echo Checking
3. Detection and Retransmission (ARQ)
   - A. Stop-and-wait ARQ
   - B. Continuous ARQ
     - (i) Go-back-N schemes
     - (ii) Selective retransmission schemes
   - C. Adaptive ARQ
4. Forward Error Correction

Figure 6.1. Approaches to error control.

possessing inherent redundancy. In these situations, a human console operator can infer the true meaning of the message from its context and/or the natural redundancy of most languages. Other possible application areas that do not require any formal procedures for correcting transmission errors are those involving several data preparation and processing steps in which the data transmission errors are a negligible consideration in relation to those induced at other steps. For example, a well-trained keyboard operator will ordinarily make at least 10 times more typing errors than a typical communication link introduces in transmitting a block of data records.

When errors cannot be ignored, by far the most widely used protective scheme involves some type of detection and retransmission procedure, which may be implemented either manually or automatically. In manual systems the critical data fields of a message are entered more than once by the operator at the sending station. The operator or computer at the receiving station checks the content of the redundant fields. If they match, it is assumed that no errors occurred; otherwise an error is assumed, and the sending station is requested to retransmit the message. These manual approaches are widely used in lower speed applications involving teleprinters and other types of unbuffered terminals where automatic schemes cannot be readily implemented.

Another quasi-manual approach to error control is the *loop check* or *echo-back* scheme, in which each character entered from a low speed terminal is echoed back to the originating console from the distant computer site. Characters are thus verified one at a time, and the user may take appropriate correctionary measures whenever the locally typed and echoed characters do not match. Although this approach is not flawless (it may indicate an error when none actually occurred if the error was introduced coming back from the CPU), it has been used with considerable success for highly interactive applications like commercial time sharing in recent years. It has been employed mainly for terminal systems that do not contain the buffering capability required to implement more powerful schemes.

The remaining two approaches—*automatic detection–retransmission* and *forward error correction* (FEC)—both involve the transmission of redundant bits which are used by the receiving station to check for errors. With the detection and retransmission approach (also known as *automatic request for repeat* or ARQ) the redundant bits are used solely to *detect* errors. If an error is sensed, a request is made for the sending station to retransmit the message. With FEC, the redundant bits are used to *detect* and *correct* the errors in real time at the receiving station; there is no feedback signaling or retransmission of messages. Proportionately fewer noninformation bits are required for detection–retransmission techniques than to obtain the same degree of protection with FEC techniques. However, FEC permits the uninterrupted transmission of a continuous data stream and offsets other possibly undesirable requirements of the detect–retransmit methods. Regardless of which scheme is employed, *some* errors will usually evade or escape the detection process. The game plan is to reduce the residual bit or block error rate to an acceptably low level in the most economical way.

Choosing the most appropriate method of error control for a particular application is greatly simplified by an initial understanding of the conceptual fundamentals, without regard to the restrictions imposed by a particular terminal or common carrier facility. Toward this end, the subsequent sections first discuss the essential characteristics of automatic detection–retransmission and FEC; they conclude with a discussion of transmission efficiency and related application considerations.

6.2. DETECTION–RETRANSMISSION METHODS; BLOCK CODES

With detection–retransmission procedures, the sending station partitions or blocks the bits to be sent; the redundant bits in a given block relate only to the information bits of the same block. If an error in a received block is detected, a repeat request (RQ) is generated at the receiving station and transmitted back to the data source over a reverse channel. Figure 6.2 shows a schematic diagram of a simple detection–retransmission scheme.[1]

The simplest type of ARQ control involves sending encoded message blocks one at a time and making a repeat/no repeat decision, depending on whether any errors were detected, as shown in the timing diagram of Figure 6.3. The ARQ state of the art has evolved substantially in recent years to the point where many variations of the basic theme may be found in use. These are considered after the discussion of coding approaches.

Block codes used for ARQ procedures generally transform a group of k information bits from the data source into a larger group of n bits by

[1]An ARQ scheme of this type was originally proposed by Van Duuren for controlling errors on radio-telegraph circuits and is in widespread use throughout the world today. Reference [1] describes it more fully.

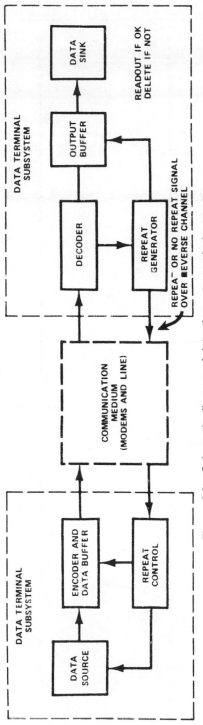

Figure 6.2. Schematic diagram of detection–retransmission system.

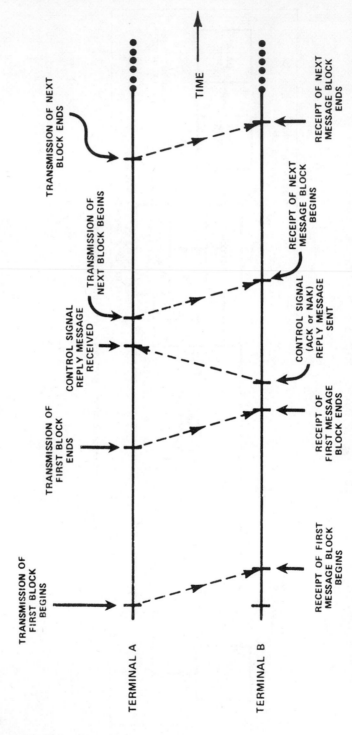

Figure 6.3. Timing diagram showing sequence of operations in a simple ARQ system. Terminal *A* is transmitting and terminal *B* is receiving so that data flow from *A* to *B* and control signals back from *B* to *A*.

computing and inserting $n - k$ redundant bits, which check only the k information bits in that block.

The rules for describing this transformation vary widely. Simplicity is a desirable characteristic of any code, since the inverse mapping must be performed in the decoder and the economics of a particular code depends critically on its implementational complexity.

Double-entry tables are frequently used with the more complex codes to compute redundant bits at the encoder and recovery of the information bit stream at the decoder. Since table lookups are readily suited for implementation using read-only memories (ROMs), ROMs have led to substantial breakthroughs in reducing decoding equipment costs and have made possible the practical implementation of many new block and nonblock codes for the first time.

As noted before, block codes operate on a sequence of k information bits to generate $n - k$ redundant bits. (If these $n - k$ redundant bits also check information bits in preceding blocks, the code is called a *convolutional* code; convolutional codes are used almost exclusively in forward error correction systems, which are considered subsequently.) The inherent efficiency of such a code is, of course, equal to k/n. It thus becomes apparent that any desired degree of protection against errors can be obtained by making n sufficiently larger than k. However, such protection results in reduced link efficiency, increased time delays, and greater hardware complexity, to mention a few factors. Larger buffers are required to generate and decode the n-bit blocks, the complexity of the decoding operation ordinarily increases, and the ratio of information bits sent to total bits sent decreases, reducing the net information throughput on a fixed-bit-rate channel. This is essentially the gist of one of Shannon's famous theorems, although it must not be used indiscriminately since certain restrictions and assumptions apply [2].

6.2.1. Parity Check Codes

Almost all the important block codes used for error detection and correction are parity check codes. These codes are formed by mathematically relating a sequence of k information bits to $n - k$ redundant bits, which are then combined and transmitted over the channel as an n-bit block. Usually the redundant bits are determined using modulo-2 arithmetic, in which only two results of an addition (or, equivalently, subtraction) are possible, regardless of the number of bits being added. Thus modulo-2 arithmetic obeys all the ordinary rules except that in mod-2 addition $1 \oplus 1 = 0$, and there are never any "carries." (The symbol $\oplus$ denotes addition without carries.) In general, for mod-2 additions an odd number of 1's sums to 1, while an even number of 1's sums to 0.

An (n, k) block code, $k < n$, is defined as the collection of 2^k n-tuples produced by encoding all possible k-tuples according to some predetermined set of parity checking rules. For example, Figure 6.4 shows a simple (5, 3) block code in which the leftmost two bit positions in a code word are parity positions and the rightmost three bit positions are for infomation bits. In this simple example, b_5 (the leftmost bit) of any code word is equal to $b_1 \oplus b_2$, while b_4 is equal to $b_1 \oplus b_2 \oplus b_3$.

Figure 6.5 illustrates a possible shift register implementation of the encoder for generating these parity bits. Since shift registers and mod-2 adders are generally available and relatively inexpensive in today's technology, this type of encoder is frequently used for parity check code implementation.

For every three information bits encoded, there are $2^5 = 32$ possible 5-tuples that could be received at the decoder. However, only the eight code words shown in Figure 6.4 are valid so that, if any one of the 24 possible invalid 5-tuples is received, an error is immediately detected. The manner in which check bits are assigned to information bits is strongly dependent on the types of errors that it is desired to correct, as will become even more evident shortly.

Systematic parity check codes are the class of codes in which the information bits are transmitted unchanged as part of the code word. In the example of Figure 6.4, the three bits (b_1, b_2, b_3) of a code word are identical to the information bits, so that the code of Figure 6.4 is systematic.

6.2.2. One- and Two-Dimensional Parity Check Codes

As seen in the preceding example, each parity bit in a code word is formed by taking the simple modulo-2 sum of various information bit positions in

Parity Bit Positions		Information Bit Positions		
b_5	b_4	b_3	b_2	b_1
0	0	0	0	0
1	1	0	0	1
1	1	0	1	0
0	0	0	1	1
0	1	1	0	0
1	0	1	0	1
1	0	1	1	0
0	1	1	1	1

Valid Code Words

Figure 6.4.   A simple (5, 3) block code.

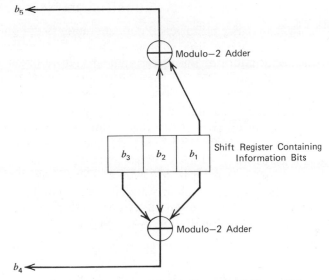

Figure 6.5. Encoder circuitry for code of Figure 6.4.

the code word. The simplest kind of parity check code makes use of a single parity bit to check all information bit positions of a code word (a one-dimensional parity check code). With this code, the encoder sets the parity bit so that the number of 1's in every code word must be even (an even parity convention) or must be odd (an odd parity convention). Then, if an odd number of bit errors occurs during transmission, the decoder can immediately detect the occurrence of the error and take appropriate measures. Figure 6.6 shows how a one-dimensional parity check is applied to the individual characters of a message block (also known as a row or horizontal parity check in this example). If the even parity convention is assumed, the row parity bit for the jth character (denoted RP_j) is determined by

$$RP_j = b_1^j \oplus b_2^j \oplus \cdot \cdot \cdot \oplus b_n^j$$

where b_i^j denotes the ith information bit of the jth data character.

One-dimensional parity check codes are in widespread use by business machines of all types to detect data transmission errors. In these instances, each data character usually is checked by its own parity bit. Since the one-bit parity check cannot detect an even number of bit errors, it is most effective in applications where a link is predominantly characterized by random (i.e., single-bit) errors. In such cases, the following inequality holds for each character:

Prob (single bit error) $>>$ Prob (two or more bit errors).

The use of a single parity bit for each data character is not particularly effective in most telephone line situations, however, because of the bursty or clustering nature of the errors that ordinarily occur. A burst error can be defined in several ways; the term generally includes all errors caused by a particular link disturbance (i.e., errors dependent on a particular event such as an amplitude hit or a dropout). Adding a second parity checking dimension gives a substantial improvement in the degree of error protection provided. For every M characters, an additional character composed entirely of parity bits is generated and inserted in the encoded data stream, as shown in Figure 6.6. The ith bit of this parity check character checks the ith information bit position in data characters 1 through M. Again, under the even parity convention, the ith bit of the parity check character, denoted as CP_i, is given by

$$CP_i = b_i^1 \oplus b_i^2 \oplus \cdots \oplus b_i^M, \qquad i = 1, \ldots, n$$

and

$$CP_0 = RP_1 \oplus RP_2 \oplus \cdots \oplus RP_M$$

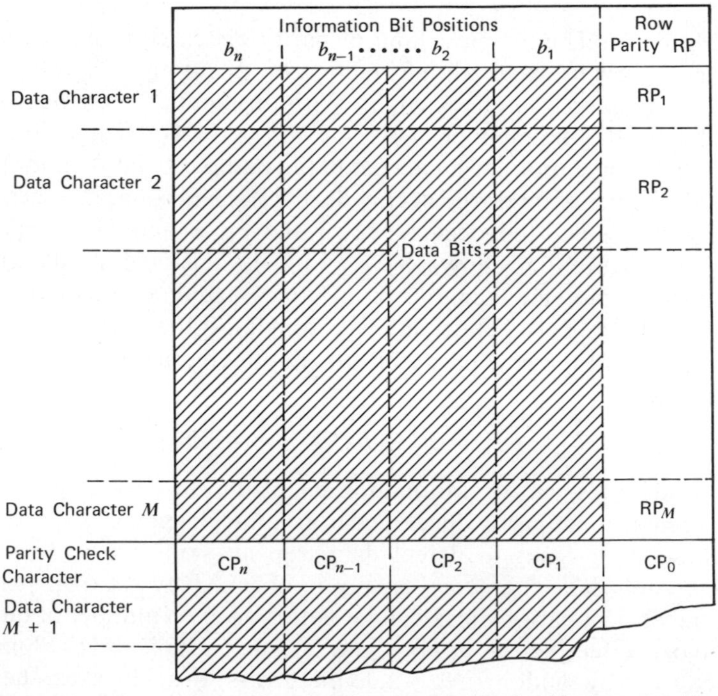

Figure 6.6. Use of two-dimensional parity checks for *M*-character block.

if b_i^k denotes the ith information bit in the kth character. The CP character of Figure 6.6 is also referred to as a logitudinal parity check, or longitudinal redundancy check (LRC). In such two-dimensional systems, the RP bit group is also often known as a vertical redundancy check (VRC). In typical teleprocessing systems a combined VRC–LRC approach is employed to have the VRC bits checking individual characters and the LRC bits checking fixed bit positions across all characters in a block.

It may be seen from Figure 6.7 that, for an undetectable error to occur, an even number of bits greater than 3 must be changed in offsetting positions in the two-dimensional grid.

In Reference [3], Martin notes that measurements of the effectiveness of this two-dimensional parity scheme indicate it lessens the number of undetected bit errors by a factor ranging from 100 to 10,000. Thus this type of coding could be used on a phone line having a raw error rate of 10^{-5} to obtain a residual or undetected bit error rate in the range between 10^{-7} and 10^{-9}.

6.2.3. The ASCII Code and Parity Checking

Although there is a proliferation of different codes used to encode characters into bit sequences for data transmission and computer storage, the American National Standards Institute has standardized the seven-bit code shown in Figure 6.8. Known as ASCII (American Standard Code for

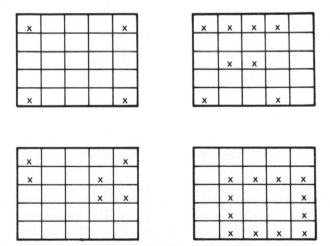

Figure 6.7. Example of some undetectable error patterns for two-dimensional parity check codes.

Bit Positions 1,2,3,4	Bit Positions 5,6,7							
	000	100	010	110	001	101	011	111
0 0 0 0	NUL	DLE	SPACE	0	@	P		p
1 0 0 0	SOH	DC1	!	1	A	Q	a	q
0 1 0 0	STX	DC2	"	2	B	R	b	r
1 1 0 0	ETX	DC3	#	3	C	S	c	s
0 0 1 0	EOT	DC4	$	4	D	T	d	t
1 0 1 0	ENQ	NAK	%	5	E	U	e	u
0 1 1 0	ACK	SYN	&	6	F	V	f	v
1 1 1 0	BEL	ETB	'	7	G	W	g	w
0 0 0 1	BS	CAN	(	8	H	X	h	x
1 0 0 1	HT	EM	)	9	I	Y	i	y
0 1 0 1	LF	SUB	*	:	J	Z	j	z
1 1 0 1	VT	ESC	+	;	K	[	k	{
0 0 1 1	FF	FS	⌐	<	L	\	l	|
1 0 1 1	CR	GS	–	=	M	]	m	}
0 1 1 1	SO	RS	.	>	N	^	n	~
1 1 1 1	SI	US	/	?	O	–	o	DEL

NUL = All zeroes	DC1 = Device control #1
SOH = Start of header	DC2 = Device control #2
STX = Start of text	DC3 = Device control #3
ETX = End of text	DC4 = Device control #4
EOT = End of transmission	NAK = Negative acknowledgement
ENQ = Inquiry	SYN = Synchronous idle
ACK = Acknowledgement	ETB = End transmitted block
BEL = Bell	CAN = Cancel
BS = Back space	EM = End of medium
HT = Horizontal tab	SUB = Start special sequence
LF = Line feed	ESC = Escape or break
VT = Vertical tab	FS = File separator
FF = Form feed	GS = Group separator
CR = Carriage return	RS = Record separator
SO = Shift out	US = Unit separator
SI = Shift in	DEL = Delete
DLE = Data link escape	

Figure 6.8. The ASCII code.

Information Interchange), the code permits $2^7 = 128$ different alphanumeric symbols to be represented, thus allowing upper and lower case and a full range of control characters to be accommodated.

The standards groups have also recommended a combined horizontal and vertical parity scheme for checking characters of the ASCII code. This procedure is identical to the one shown in Figure 6.6, where M is a variable depending on the application, and seven information bits are used in each row to represent an ASCII character. Thus, if M ASCII characters are checked by each longitudinal parity character, the efficiency of the code is given by

$$\frac{7M}{8M + 8}.$$

The inherent efficiency of this variable length block coding scheme ranges from 7/16 for $M = 1$ up to an asymptotic value of $7/8$ for very large values of M. Thus this code is substantially more powerful in detecting errors for small values of M than for large M, since there are fewer ways for compensating patterns like those of Figure 6.7 to happen. However, the level of redundancy used to obtain this protection is extremely high when M is small, since close to 50% of the transmitted bits are noninformation bits in these instances. As M increases, a smaller fraction of noninformation bits is sent, increasing throughput over a fixed-bit-rate link at the expense of higher undetected error probability.

6.2.4. Cyclic Codes

Another important category of parity check codes is the so-called cyclic or polynomial codes. The concept of cyclic codes is considered to be one of the major developments in coding theory history. The most noteworthy advantage claimed for cyclic codes is that simple feedback shift registers and modulo-2 adders can be used to perform the encoding and decoding operations. Even though the circuitry requirements are more complex than those for the two-dimensional parity check scheme of Section 6.2.3, they are still relatively simple. The key characteristic of a cyclic code is that any cyclic permutation or end-around shift of a code word results in another code word. Since the information bits to be transmitted always form part of the code block, cyclic codes are also systematic.

The basic idea underlying cyclic codes is to represent a data message of k bits in terms of a $k - 1$ degree polynomial in the variable x. Thus, if the data message is given by the binary number $a_{k-1}a_{k-2} \ldots a_1 a_0$, the corresponding polynomial is

$$M(x) = a_{k-1}x^{k-1} + a_{k-2}x^{k-2} + \cdots a_1 x^1 + a_0.$$

This polynomial is manipulated by selecting a generator polynomial $P(x)$ and performing various modulo-2 arithmetic operations on $M(x)$. The polynomial $P(x)$ must be of lower degree than $M(x)$, and usually will contain at least two terms. The selection of $P(x)$ is governed by the specific error patterns it is desired to detect; more will be said on this point shortly. Assume that the $P(x)$ polynomial has been specified. Then the encoding operation consists of the following steps:

1. Mulitply $M(x)$ by x^r, where r is the degree of $P(x)$. This operation effectively adds r 0's in the low order bit positions of the resulting n-bit word ($n = r + k$) without changing the high order k bits.

2. Divide $M(x)x^r$ by $P(x)$; this leads to a unique quotient $Q(x)$ and remainder $R(x)$, so that the result can be expressed as

$$Q(x) \oplus \frac{R(x)}{P(x)}$$

where $\oplus$ denotes mod-2 addition as before.

3. The message to be transmitted, denoted as $T(x)$, can be expressed as

$$T(x) = M(x)x^r \oplus R(x).$$

Since all of the above operations can be conveniently performed with feedback shift registers and mod-2 adders, the encoder looks as shown in the block diagram of Figure 6.9. Because the high order k bits of $T(x)$ are always equal to the bits of $M(x)$, a transmission always commences by sending these k bits first, followed by the bits of the remainder polynomial

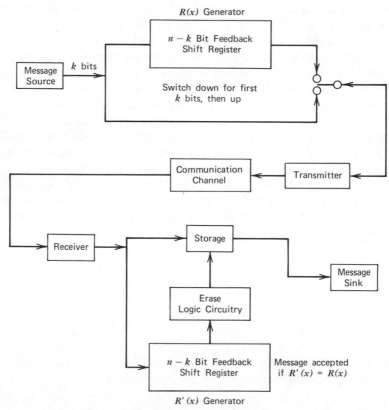

Figure 6.9.   Schematic implementation of cyclic codes.

$R(x)$ generated in step 3. It should be noted that cyclic codes may be implemented with either a k-bit or an $(n - k)$-bit shift register (the latter case has been illustrated). Since the shorter register is ordinarily less costly, it is often preferred. Decoding simply involves computation of a new remainder polynomial, denoted as $R'(x)$; the computation is performed on the first k bits of a received block and is identical to the computation performed in the encoder. If no errors occurred, $R'(x)$ will be equal to the $R(x)$ generated at the transmitting station. If errors do occur, the transmitted message $T(x)$ will be changed as though an error polynomial $E(x)$ were added to $T(x)$. Hence $T(x) \oplus E(x)$ will be received if an error took place; this error will be detected as long as $T(x) \oplus E(x)$ is not exactly divisible by $P(x)$.

Thus, in choosing the generator polynomial $P(x)$, the characteristics of the communication channel must be "known" so that the probability of $T(x) \oplus E(x)$ being exactly divisible by $P(x)$ can be kept as low as desired. The selection of the "best" $P(x)$ for a channel having a family of likely error patterns $\{E(x)\}$ involves a lengthy study of the algebraic characteristics of various polynomials and is certainly beyond the scope of this work. The interested reader is urged to examine References [3] through [9] for more detailed considerations of this topic. In actual practice, most of the recently announced line control procedures contain some jointly agreed-upon, standard generator polynomials for this so-called cyclic redundancy checking (CRC) operation.

The important advantages of cyclic codes may be summarized in the following manner. They are known to be relatively much more powerful than other types of codes in the detection capability afforded by a given level of redundancy. Cyclic codes are relatively easy to implement, since identical feedback shift registers are used in both the encoder and the decoder. In addition, the probability of undetected error decreases exponentially as a function of code redundancy. Finally, cyclic codes are generally more effective in detecting random errors than burst errors. However, if the burst characteristics (the set of error patterns $\{E(x)\}$) is well known, equally powerful degrees of protection can be provided with slightly more complex cyclic codes.

For example, the Bose–Chadhuri (BCH) class of cyclic codes was originally designed to correct random errors [4]. These codes are based on a complete mathematical theory furnishing an algorithm for constructing code words of length $2^m - 1$, in which k errors can be corrected by using no more than mk check bits. Smaller BCH block structures ($m \leq 6$) are almost always used to guard against random errors. Some burst protection is also provided by longer BCH codes. For example, when a (255, 223) BCH code is confronted with a burst of completely random noise (each bit is independent and has an equal probability of being a 1 or a 0), it will fail to detect an error with a probability of less than 1×10^{-9}. Other examples of cyclic codes are the Fire [5] and Melas [6] codes. These codes have extremely interesting properties, but their application utility is somewhat limited.

6.2.5. Constant Ratio Codes

Constant ratio codes (also known as M-out-of-N codes) derive their name from their unique characteristic of having a constant number of 1's (or 0's) in all code words. This important class of codes does not use parity checking, and its most significant features are simplicity and effectiveness in alphanumeric text applications. Errors are indicated in a received message whenever the number of 1's differs from the constant number of 1's known to be in all valid code words.

A 3-out-of-7 constant ratio code is used extensively in radio-telegraphy for ARQ applications. Each valid code word contains 7 bits, of which 3 are always 1's. The number of different characters that can be represented by this code is given by

$$\frac{7!}{3!4!} = 35$$

whereas, in general, 7 bits are capable of coding $2^7 = 128$ different characters. For this particular code, the required redundancy is fairly high, but this factor is offset by the ease of implementation. The code is completely secure against an odd number of single-bit errors. It also will detect an even number of single-bit errors as long as the number of 1's changed to 0's is different from the number of 0's changed to 1's by the channel disturbance.

IBM uses a 4-out-of-8 constant ratio code in some of its data transceivers. With the increase to 8 bits for each character, an alphabet of 70 characters can be accommodated. In Reference [3], Martin notes that this particular code has proved most effective when used in conjunction with some type of longitudinal redundancy check.

As a concluding point, it should be emphasized that constant ratio codes are best suited for transmitting alphanumeric text, in which the data consist of bit groups or characters generated within the terminal. The implementation of constant ratio codes has proved difficult in applications where the data source emits a random binary bit stream.

6.3. TYPES OF ARQ IMPLEMENTATION

Regardless of which type of block code is used to detect errors, a number of variations of the basic detection–retransmission (ARQ) scheme exist. The common requirements of these variants should first be noted. As shown in Figure 6.2, a reverse channel must always exist for control signaling. Also, sending stations must be provided with extra buffer or be capable of periodic interruption whenever a message block is received in error, so that the data source does not submit any new data blocks to the channel during such retransmission operations. Thus an additional embodiment of ARQ schemes is the requirement for some type of buffer storage to hold a copy of the in-transit messages. The size of this buffer storage is determined by the amount of information that must be reserved, which in turn depends on the type of ARQ scheme used. Other parameters that may vary from one type of ARQ to another are the number and type of control signals used and the nature of the ARQ—whether provided external or internal to the data link. Some variations of the basic ARQ technique are now discussed.

6.3.1. Stop-and-Wait ARQ (ACK–NAK after Each Block)

The simplest type of ARQ scheme involves transmission of one block at a time, with the receiver sending back either a positive acknowledgment (ACK) or a negative acknowledgment (NAK) over the reverse channel after the message block is decoded. If an ACK is received, the next data block from the source is encoded and transmitted over the channel, with a copy of the encoded block being preserved in the buffer at the transmitter (Figure 6.2).

If a NAK is received, the message block in the buffer is retransmitted over the channel, and the buffer contents are preserved, awaiting the receipt of the next control message. The size of the buffer required is determined by the length of the largest block that must be stored. This buffer can either be a subsystem within the transmitter or an integral portion of the terminal equipment. If the sending station is a tape unit, for example, the tape itself can act as the buffer, obviating any need for additional station buffering. As shown in Figure 6.10, the data channel must remain idle for the time taken to decode the received message block and to generate and transmit the return control signal. This overhead is particularly costly when block transmission times are approximately equal to the idle time. Generally, stop-and-wait ARQ is used most efficiently in applications where the message blocks are long enough to

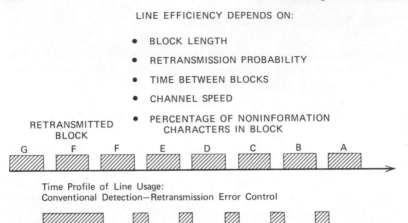

LINE EFFICIENCY DEPENDS ON:

- BLOCK LENGTH
- RETRANSMISSION PROBABILITY
- TIME BETWEEN BLOCKS
- CHANNEL SPEED
- PERCENTAGE OF NONINFORMATION CHARACTERS IN BLOCK

Figure 6.10.   Line efficiency factors for stop-and-wait ARQ.

minimize the effects of this interblock overhead time due to idling. A specific formula that can be used to quantitatively relate the effects of these overhead factors is presented in Section 6.5.

6.3.2.   Continuous ARQ (Overlapped Data and Control Signaling)

One means of reducing the interblock overhead is to overlap data and control signaling times by continuously transmitting message blocks over the forward channel while acknowledgment signals are in transit to the transmitter. As long as no block errors are detected, the overhead due to interblock times in stop-and-wait schemes is eliminated entirely.

Whenever a NAK is received at the sending station, two alternative actions are possible under continuous ARQ. These two options describe the major functional difference between *go-back-N* and *selective retransmission* implementations of continuous ARQ. With the go-back-*N* approach (shown in Figure 6.11), on receiving a NAK, the sending station must retransmit the block detected in error, the one being sent when the NAK is received, and all blocks in between these two. Hence the sending buffer size depends on the transmission delay between sender and receiver. It must be two blocks long in any event. The desire here is to simplify the continuous ARQ implementation by accepting error-free blocks at the receiving station in the same order in which they were generated at the data source.

Selective retransmission involves resending only the block detected in error. The number of retransmitted blocks is statistically lower than with

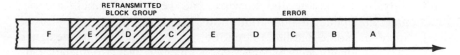

USER SENDS BLOCK A FIRST, THEN BLOCK
B,...ETC. BLOCK C IS DETECTED IN ERROR ON
FIRST TRANSMISSION ATTEMPT. NEXT TWO BLOCKS
ARE THEN IGNORED AND C, D, E ALL
RETRANSMITTED IN THAT ORDER. NO ERRORS
ARE DETECTED ON SECOND ATTEMPT.

Figure 6.11. Time profile of line usage for continuous ARQ using go-back-*N* version; *N* = 3 in this example.

the go-back-N approach, but more complex logic and larger buffers are required, because the receiving data station will have to collect arriving blocks and possibly reassemble them into the correct sequence before any local processing of the data can occur. With go-back-N, receive station buffers need not preserve any incoming block unless its cyclic check (CRC) indicates no bit errors *and* it has a sequence count value one larger than the last block accepted at the receiver. Additional detailed comparisons of these strategies may be found in References [10] to [13]. They are also considered in Section 6.5 and in Chapter 8.

The effectiveness of continuous ARQ procedures is greatest when the probability of detecting a block in error is low; the main disadvantage is the requirement for buffering all the blocks that are in transit when an error is detected. As will be seen shortly, continuous ARQ affords substantial potential advantages over stop-and-wait ARQ whenever the line propagation times and/or acknowledgment signaling times are substantial. It is often far more efficient than stop-and-wait, for example, in satellite channel applications likely to become increasingly popular over the next 10 years [10,11,33,34].

The reader will note that the sending station can learn of the occurrence of an error in either of two ways. Negative acknowledgments (NAKs) can be explicitly returned to the sending station or the sending station may periodically audit the number of blocks received correctly at the other end using sequence counts, with an error being indicated when the returned receive count does not equal the known send count. Such schemes can be used only when the reverse channel is functionally independent of the forward channel. Leased, four-wire telephone circuits often use two-wires for the forward channel and two for an independent reverse channel and are hence well suited for this type of ARQ scheme. Dial-up telephone circuits are ordinarily two-wire circuits capable of transmitting in only one direction at a time. If a dial-line channel must be turned around to send control information, the forward and reverse channels are not functionally independent and continuous ARQ technique may not be used. However, some dial-line telephone network modems are designed to provide functionally independent reverse channels using frequency multiplexing techniques. Business machines that use these modems may send control signals in the reverse direction independently of the forward channel. Hence they can be designed to implement continuous ARQ.

6.3.3. Adaptive ARQ

Adaptive ARQ involves using two or more different block lengths to send encoded messages in an attempt to keep the link efficiency as high as possible at all times. The receiver is equipped to monitor the RQ rate (fraction of retransmission requests) as well as the link noise characteristics. This information is fed back to a threshold decision device at the transmitter. When the RQ rate and noise level cause activation of the threshold decision device, a block length change is initiated in the transmitter. Whenever the threshold is crossed in either direction, the transmitter must also notify the receiver of the change. This decision feedback process forces short block lengths to be transmitted during noisy periods and long blocks to be sent when the RQ rate and noise characteristics indicate relatively good channel conditions.

The incremental advantages of adaptive ARQ over fixed ARQ appear to be limited, particularly in light of the increased control circuitry complexity associated with adaptive ARQ. Other disadvantages of adaptive ARQ stem from its inabiity to react rapidly and the link idle time necessitated by changeovers. The alert reader will note that adaptive ARQ can also be implemented with more than two block lengths and a multilevel threshold device. However, the literature suggests that little, if any, incremental advantage is gained by going to multiple (more than two) block lengths [12,13].

As a final point, it should be noted that a line using adaptive ARQ will present roughly the same intermittent operating characteristics as one with fixed ARQ from a systems standpoint, since adaptive ARQ does not eliminate the need for detection and retransmission circuitry. Its single advantage accrues from its potential ability to improve link efficiency on certain links.

6.3.4. Other ARQ Variations

Several other ARQ-oriented techniques have been proposed from time to time but have received relatively less attention than the variations of ARQ just discussed. If the user demands continuous data flow between source and sink, the basic ARQ system of Figure 6.2 can be modified by inserting an auxiliary buffer in front of the encoder to absorb all user data submitted to the channel during periods of retransmission. The buffer must be large enough to accommodate enough input data to preserve a given error rate. By introducing queuing for the channel, this variation causes an additional time delay proportional to the length of the auxiliary buffer. Furthermore, the channel must operate at a faster rate than the input data rate from the terminal to reduce the transmitter queue whenever the contents of the queue are nonzero. Clearly, these characteristics result in a reduction in channel efficiency, offsetting the advantages claimed for ARQ over other error control techniques such as forward error correction, as will be seen shortly.

In certain applications where ARQ communication channels are shared by many users, certain customers may demand much lower error rates than the common user links are able to provide. In these instances, a second level or user-provided ARQ can be introduced to gain the added protection. The major difficulty in this situation arises from the unpredictable behavior of the common user ARQ channel and the resulting effect on the user-provided buffer storage. Because the transmission delays for the forward and reverse common user channel are unknown, the best size for the user-provided buffer cannot be readily determined. Worst-case assumptions generally lead to substantial losses of channel efficiency; other alternatives give rise to serious control problems. This makes two-level ARQ a generally undesirable mode of operation, as was originally noted by Franco and Wall [12].

Another variation of stop-and-wait ARQ is widely used by IBM and other organizations in the Binary Synchronous Communications (BSC) line discipline. This set of control procedures is used to enable computers and remote peripheral equipments to automatically communicate over communication links. (An introduction to the philosophy of BSC and other contemporary protocols may be found in Chapter 8.)

Binary Synchronous Communications involves a detection–retransmission approach whereby NAKs are generated by the receiver whenever an error is detected in a received block. The receiver sends an ACK0 control signal for all even numbered blocks of a transmission that are not detected to be in error; a different control signal, ACK1, is used for all odd numbered blocks not detected to be in error. This odd–even record count scheme protects against complete loss of a block between source and sink, errors in the ACK control signals themselves, and other situations not covered by the basic ARQ methods. Even so, a number of important limitations of BSC have recently spawned interest in a more advanced generation of line protocols. The interested reader should consult References [14] and [15] and Chapter 8 of this book for detailed discussions of the BSC conventions and the major features of its next-generation successors. Still other ARQ variations are considered by Benice and Frey in References [19] and [20].

6.4. FORWARD ERROR CORRECTION

Forward error correction (FEC) techniques involve the continuous use of redundant information at the receiving end of a communication channel to detect *and correct* errors that may have occurred without any retransmission of the data bits in error. The basic idea is to use only as much redundancy as is required to achieve a desired error rate and throughput level.

Although nonblock codes often give rise to less complex decoders than block codes, either type may be used in FEC systems. For example, the two-dimensional block schemes discussed previously are capable of detecting *and correcting* errors within any row or column having only a single erroneous bit. In fact, there is a very close relationship between any code's ability to detect errors and its ability to correct them. It is basically the correction power that is of interest for FEC systems. Two advantages of FEC are that a continuous data stream may be readily accommodated and that no reverse channel is needed; the tradeoff disadvantages are closely related to the increased equipment and coding complexity necessary to achieve a given error rate with FEC as opposed to ARQ methods. Critics of FEC sometimes claim that the extra redundancy bits required over ARQ methods waste bandwidth of the channel which could be used for increasing the data throughput rate. Obviously such generalizations are dangerous, particularly in situations where reverse channels are not available or line propagation times are large. In these applications, FEC can be the only feasible alternative. More will be said about these matters in Section 6.5.

6.4.1. Block Codes for FEC: The Hamming Code

Many of the block codes discussed earlier afford substantial capabilities for FEC applications. The classic example of a forward error correcting block code is the Hamming code, which detects all single and double errors within a block of n binary bits [7]. Hamming observed that an (n, k) code can correct a single-bit error if the following relationship holds:

$$2^m \geq n + 1 = m + k + 1$$

where $m = n - k$, the number of redundant bits. This relationship is derived from the fact that the minimum number of bits necessary to locate a position in one of n places is $\log_2 n$. Adding an extra bit to detect the case where no errors occur, we obtain

$$m \geq \log_2(n + 1)$$

or

$$2^m \geq n + 1 = m + k + 1.$$

An example of the check bit pattern for a (7, 4) Hamming code is shown in Figure 6.12, where bits b_1, b_2, and b_4 are parity check bits used to protect information bits b_3, b_5, b_6, and b_7 in a seven-bit code word.

The Bose–Chadhuri block codes discussed in Section 6.2.4 may be regarded as a generalization of the Hamming code, since they always detect $2k$ errors and correct k errors and Hamming codes achieve the same result when $k = 1$. Other types of block codes may also be used for FEC purposes but are beyond the scope of this discussion. The interested reader should consult References [9] and [16] for a more detailed treatment of the subject. Since much recent interest has been focused on the use of convolutional codes for FEC applications, the remaining discussion of FEC will be confined to this type of nonblock code.

6.4.2. Convolutional Codes

Convolutional codes are generally preferred for FEC applications because their nonblock structure makes them easier to decode than block-

Bits in Error	Pattern of Check Bits in a Code Word		
	b_4	b_2	b_1
None	0	0	0
b_1	0	0	1
b_2	0	1	0
b_3	0	1	1
b_4	1	0	0
b_5	1	0	1
b_6	1	1	0
b_7	1	1	1

where b_1 checks b_3, b_5, and b_7
b_7 checks b_3, b_6, and b_7
b_4 checks b_5, b_6, and b_7

Figure 6.12. Check bit patterns in a (7, 4) Hamming code.

structured codes. Information bits and parity bits are continuously transmitted over the channel in an interleaved manner. The parity bits are computed by taking modulo-2 sums on various information bits for a period generally extending over more than one transmitter data block. The total number of bits in this sequence used as the basis for parity computations is also referred to as the *constraint length* of the code.

Consider the k-stage shift register shown in Figure 6.13. Each position in the register may be associated with a bit in the parity check network, although usually not all of the k stages are checked. The specific code determines how many and which connections are made to the parity check network. The encoding process may thus be regarded as a convolution of the information stream with the code-structure bit sequence through the parity check network.

The transmitted data are generated by alternating the two-position multiplexor switch so that an average of k information bits and $n - k$ redundant bits is contained in every n bits sent. A demultiplexing switch at the receiver sorts out received information bits and received parity bits by alternating in exactly the same manner as the multiplexing switch. The decoder contains an identical k-stage shift register and the same parity check network as is used in the transmitter.

Two basic types of decoding are most widely used for convolutional codes, sequential and threshold decoding. Threshold decoding is an extremely simple concept that works most effectively with short codes correcting a few errors [18]. Sequential decoding is more powerful but requires more complex circuitry, since relatively long constraint lengths are generally used and successive decoding decisions are highly dependent. In the 13 years of refinement since its invention by Wozencraft sequential decoding has been improved to the point where it is likely to become the bulwark of convolutional decoding techniques for future FEC applications [17,21,22,23].

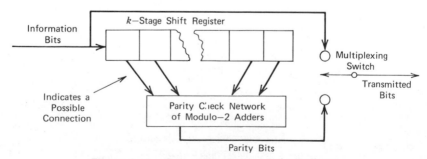

Figure 6.13. Convolutional encoder schematic.

6.4.2.1. Threshold Decoding

With the threshold approach, the decoder uses a majority count of the parity check bits associated with an information bit to make its decisions. An example serves best to illustrate the threshold decoding concept. Consider the convolutional encoder of Figure 6.14, where parity bits are generated as the modulo-2 sum ("exclusive-or") of information bit positions 6, 3, 2, and 1. A one-half rate code (code with efficiency of 50%) has been assumed so that $k = n/2$. In this example $n = 12$, since six information bits comprise the constraint length of the code. Each time a new information bit enters the leftmost stage of the shift register, a new parity bit is computed and transmitted over the channel, immediately following its associated information bit (the last one to enter the shift register).

The basic element of the decoding procedure involves the formation of *syndromes*, which identify the bits in error in a manner that is now explained. A *syndrome* is computed according to the following operation. Use the received information bits to compute a parity sequence in exactly the same fashion as at the encoder. Then compare these new parity bits to the corresponding parity bits actually received, using a mod-2 adder whose outputs form the syndrome (Figure 6.15).

It should be clear that, when no errors have occurred, the parity bits computed at the decoder will be equal to those actually received and all syndromes will be 0. Moreover, if a single error occurs, it will manifest itself by producing a 1 in the syndrome register at the time of the error. Thus it is known that a single error took place; whether the error is in an information bit or a parity bit will not be known when a 1 first appears in the syndrome register.

Looking at the syndrome register of Figure 6.15, however, it can be seen that an information bit error will cause the syndromes to equal 1 whenever the erroneous bit is stages 6, 3, 2, or 1 of the information bit

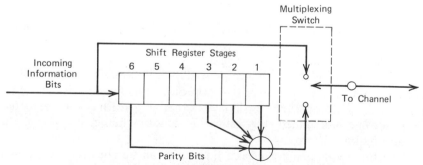

Figure 6.14. Example of convolutional encoder.

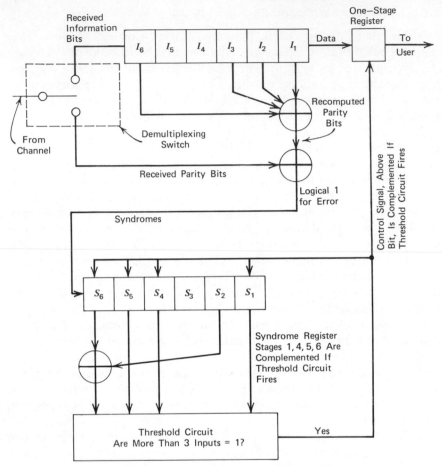

Figure 6.15. Example of double-error-correcting threshold decoder.

register. Thus for this particular decoder a single information bit error will produce a syndrome sequence of 1, 0, 0, 1, 1, 1, starting from the time the error first shows up. On the other hand, it can be seen that, if a parity bit was in error, the resultant syndrome pattern will look like 1, 0, 0, 0, 0, 0, starting from the time the error first appears. Thus the appearance of the first 1 in the syndrome register indicates that an error has been detected; the syndrome bits immediately following denote whether it is a parity or an information bit error.

Since the codes being used are linear, it can be shown that the syndrome pattern for double errors is simply the linear superposition (mod-2 sum) of the syndrome patterns for each of the individual errors. With this knowledge consider the operation of the decoder in Figure 6.15 at the instant shown, when six bits have already entered the upper shift register. The contents of the syndrome register can be described by the following logic equations:

$$S_1 = E(I_1) + E(P_1)$$
$$S_2 = E(I_2) + E(P_2)$$
$$S_3 = E(I_3) + E(P_3)$$
$$S_4 = E(I_4) + E(P_4) + E(I_1)$$
$$S_5 = E(I_5) + E(P_5) + E(I_1) + E(I_2)$$
$$S_6 = E(I_6) + E(P_6) + E(I_1) + E(I_2) + E(I_3)$$

where P_j denotes the parity bit actually received immediately after information bit I_j. $E(I_j)$ or $E(P_j)$ is equal to 1 only if I_j or P_j, respectively, is in error.

The above set of logic equations is then manipulated into a smaller set of equations each of which contains $E(I_1)$ once, while all other $E(I_j)$ and $E(P_j), j \neq 1$, terms appear no more than once in the entire set of equations. One such possible set of equations for the decoder of Figure 5.10 is given by

$$S_1 = E(I_1) + E(P_1)$$
$$S_4 = E(I_1) + E(I_4) + E(P_4)$$
$$S_5 = E(I_1) + E(I_2) + E(I_5) + E(P_5)$$
$$S_2 \oplus S_6 = E(I_1) + E(I_3) + E(I_6) + E(P_2) + E(P_6)$$

It can be shown that three or more of these equations can have the value 1 only if $E(I_1)$ is equal to 1, assuming that no more than two errors are present in the string of 12 bits under consideration (6 parity and 6 information bits). Thus, whenever the output of the threshold logic circuit is equal to 1, the erroneous bit I_1 can be corrected (complemented) before it is passed on to the user. Simultaneously the various stages of the syndrome register affected by $E(I_1)$ are also corrected (complemented).

It should be noted that the above decoder is capable of correcting certain error patterns containing more than two errors in the constraint length, and that any two errors within the constraint length can always be corrected. Protection against bursts can be afforded by using longer constraint lengths and codes that can correct larger numbers of errors in a constraint length. For example, one-half rate codes are known for which any six errors out of 52 consecutive information bits can always be corrected and for which any five errors out of 34 consecutive information bits can always be corrected.

An alternative technique for protecting against long bursts is called *diffuse convolutional coding.* The constraint length is extended over a long sequence of bits, only a few of which are checked by the parity logic. This technique is mathematically equivalent to an interleaving transformation, that is, sending consecutive bits departing from the encoder at delayed intervals and reassembling them before decoding. Diffuse coding and interleaving both make burst errors on the channel look like random errors to the decoder. The only requirements for such techniques are sufficiently long shift registers which necessitate certain delays between the time the last encoded bit of a message is actually received and the time when decoding is completed.

6.4.2.2. Sequential Decoding

The fundamental notion of sequential decoding involves the concept of maximum likelihood decoding. The game is as follows: Given that a particular encoded bit sequence has been received, which of the allowable bit sequences is most likely to have been transmitted? Maximum likelihood decoding depends on the (Hamming) distance between code words, where the (Hamming) distance between two k-bit binary sequences is defined as the number of bits that differ in the two sequences [7]. For example, if $x = 1001011$ and $y = 0011101$, the sequences differ in positions 1, 3, 5, and 6, moving from left to right, giving a distance between x and y of 4. In maximum likelihood decoding, the decoder examines a received bit sequence, compares it to a stored set of all possible code words called the *code book,* and chooses the one having the minimum distance from the received sequence. The major difficulty (not insurmountable, however) with sequential decoding lies in the rate at which storage for the code book increases as the constraint length of a particular code increases. Closely related is the difficulty of making the relatively large number of decisions fast enough to keep up with the incoming data.

Sequential decoding algorithms are very difficult to explain in the few paragraphs allotted here, but the basic underlying principle can be crudely sketched.[2] The decoder attempts to guess what sequence of bits was transmitted by hypotheses testing. When a sequence under test is acceptably close in distance to one of the valid code words, the low order bit of the test sequence is read out of the decoder and a new high order bit read in. (This shift register is assumed to shift in the direction from the high order to the low order position.) If none of the hypothetical sequences is initially close enough to the received sequence for another bit to be decoded, the lengths of these particular test sequences are successively changed until only one sequence satisfies the closeness criterion. These

[2]They are discussed at length in References [21], [22], and [23].

steps correspond to searching backward and forward along the branches of a decoding tree. Moving further out on a limb of the search tree corresponds to increasing the length of the hypothetical sequences. A step in this direction will have the desirable effect of reducing the expected number of remaining search decisions if the distance between the test sequence and the received bit sequence becomes smaller as the length of the test sequence is increased.

In the presence of excessive noise, it may happen that no hypothetical sequence tested satisfies the prescribed closeness criterion. Then the decoder must "give up" by declaring a decoding error and get started again to keep up with the data arriving at the receiver.

An important characteristic of sequential decoding is the variable length searches that occur as a consequence of the fluctuating channel noise levels. Clearly, when no errors are present in a received sequence, the length of the treelike search is minimal because the decoder will systematically move one step closer to the single acceptable match as the hypothetical sequences are successively made one bit longer at each search step. No backward steps or shortening of the test sequences will be required in the absence of errors. The search times will be substantially longer, however, in noisy situations. If the decoder cannot make a firm decision before another data bit arrives at the receiver, a buffer must be provided to preserve any arriving data until the decoder catches up.

Whenever this buffer overflows during long decoding searches, the decoder is obliged to jump ahead by skipping a block of data. These data go undecoded and produce a burst of errors at the decoder output. These bursts generally constitute by far the major contribution to the effective error rate of a sequentially decoded FEC channel, since the probability of the decoder accepting an incorrect hypothesis can be made negligible with very modest amounts of redundancy in the code.

It should be empasized that sequential decoding is extremely powerful but is primarily suited for the correction of random errors. Long bursts tend to either hang the decoder up or force it to make the wrong decisions. In actual application situations involving burst noise, this problem can be mitigated by using a scrambler/unscrambler mechanism between the encoder and decoder to randomize the effects of the burst. A device of this type is often referred to as an *interleaver* or *diffuser*.

As a final point one variation of the sequential decoding technique should be noted. Since the primary disadvantages of sequential decoding as described above relate to its relative equipment complexity and variable decoding time, any improvements in speeding up the comparison of the received bit sequence with possible messages are desirable. One promising approach to alleviating this problem involves the simultaneous correlation or comparison of a received sequence with all possible messages, instead of just with the possible code words in a single branch of the tree. Cleverly designed decoders that use fixed read-only memories and modified data sequences (as opposed to fixed data sequences and modifiable decoding trees) appear capable of producing substantial reductions in decoding time.

6.5. CALCULATING NET DATA TRANSFER RATE (LINE EFFICIENCY) FOR VARIOUS ERROR CONTROL STRATEGIES

In preceding discussion it has been suggested that the use of error control procedures will reduce the effective or net rate at which data may be transmitted between a data source and a sink because of various required overhead factors. Here we present the standard definition of net throughput and derive the special cases for stop-and-wait ARQ, go-back-N continuous ARQ, and the selective retransmission version of continuous ARQ. Throughput of a data link is a useful performance measure since there may be substantial differences between the line's bit rate and its net throughput, depending on whether two- or four-wire circuits are used, whether a slow speed reverse channel or line turnarounds are used for control signaling, whether terrestrial or satellite facilities are employed, and what basic strategy is employed for error control (see Figure 6.16).

If we define net throughput TRIB (transfer rate of information bits) as recommended by the American National Standards Institute (ANSI) in Reference [24], we have

$$\text{TRIB} = \frac{\text{number of information bits accepted by the sink}}{\text{total time required to get those bits accepted}}$$

Next, we can express the numerator as $K_1(M - C)$ and the denominator by

$$N_T\left(\frac{M}{R} + \Delta T\right)$$

where K_1 = information bits per character (bits/character)

M = message block length (characters)

R = line transmission rate (channel speed) (characters/sec)

C = average number of noninformation characters per block

N_T = average number of transmissions required to get a block accepted at the sink

ΔT = time between blocks (sec)

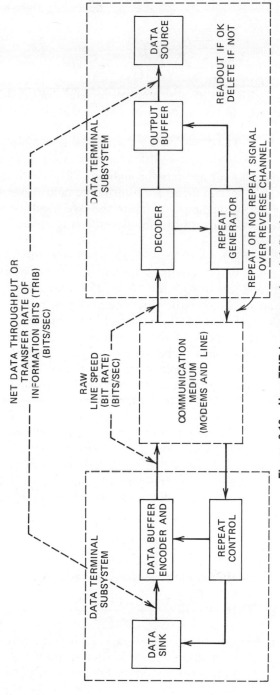

Figure 6.16. How TRIB is measured and defined.

283

so that

$$\text{TRIB} = \frac{K_1(M - C)}{N_T[(M/R) + \Delta T]}.$$

It can be shown without difficulty that $N_T = 1/(1 - P)$, where P is the probability of having to retransmit a block, so that we end up with

$$\text{TRIB} = \frac{K_1(M - C)(1 - P)}{(M/R) + \Delta T}.$$

as the final relationship for net data throughput. This is a general relationship with numerous special forms for alternative control strategies. This relationship for net throughput discounts the overhead associated with control characters, redundant bits, time spent waiting for control signals, and retransmissions.

It can be seen in Figure 6.10 that for conventional stop-and-wait ARQ the *two main controllable overhead factors* are those associated with *retransmissions* and the *interblock time*. For extremely short block lengths, M, retransmission overhead will be negligible but ΔT can become significant. On the other hand, for extremely long block lengths, ΔT can be a relatively smaller overhead component but retransmission probability P will become potentially more significant. This illustrates the important point that, for any given application, an optimum block length exists that will maximize throughput, other parameters being held constant. Of similar importance is the fact that there is no universally best block length.

It can be seen that E, the bit error rate of a channel, does not appear directly in the formula given above. This expression is, however, perfectly general and may be modified to include E by noting that block retransmission probability P depends on both the bit error rate E and the block length M. One possible relationship involving P, E, and M is

$$1 - P \cong (1 - K_2 K_3 E)^M.$$

This formula simply says that the probability of no block retransmission is the probability that all characters in a block are received without error. It also gives rise to an alternative form for the TRIB relationship:

$$\text{TRIB} \cong \frac{K_1(M - C)(1 - K_2 K_3 E)^M}{(M/R) + \Delta T}.$$

Here K_2 is the number of bits/character, and K_3 is some constant <1 that discounts the effects of multiple bit errors in a character and line errors that do not cause retransmissions (such as errors in parity bits themselves).

As a final point, it should be noted that the first TRIB relationship is an exact one, whereas the one immediately above is an approximation (since $1 - P$ was approximated). Obviously, the user should strive to eliminate any sources of computational error due to approximation whenever possible. Thus, if the approximate relationship for $1 - P$ is unrealistic, TRIB can alternatively be estimated using experimentally determined values of retransmission probability. Either way, the optimum block length should be determined and then implemented to maximize the net information transfer rate. If the analytic approximation for TRIB can be meaningfully used, the optimum block length, M^*, is given by

$$M^* = \frac{C - R\,\Delta T}{2} + \sqrt{\frac{R^2\,\Delta T^2}{4} + \frac{CR\,\Delta T}{2} + \frac{C^2}{4} - \frac{R\,\Delta T + C}{\log_e(1 - K_2 K_3 E)}}.$$

This relationship is obtained by using simple calculus techniques to differentiate the previous TRIB approximation with respect to M, then setting the result equal to 0, and finally solving for M. In concluding it must be emphasized that the buffer capacities of certain computers and buffered terminals may preclude use of the theoretically optimum block length. Nonetheless, every attempt should be made to implement systems that are as efficient as possible. The above techniques provide the means for accomplishing this objective.

In References [25] and [27] Doll also referred to TRIB as the net data throughput or NDT of a data link. Then, in Reference [26], Boustead and Mehta applied the general concept of TRIB (or, synonymously, NDT) for a wide range of different application configurations, including the following:

- Dial-up and leased lines.
- Terrestrial and satellite channels.
- Various modem synchronization (RTS/CTS) delays.
- Different transmission block lengths.
- Different line error rates.
- Modems with and without reverse channels.

An important assumption of the Boustead and Mehta application was the use of the TRIB relationship for the different conditions just listed, but always assuming the stop-and-wait ARQ technique. Since the widely used Binary Synchronous Communications (BSC) protocol [Reference 14] employs stop-and-wait ARQ and is restricted to a half-duplex mode of line usage, the analysis by Boustead and Mehta is applicable for BSC channels.

Recently there has been much interest by users in quantitatively evaluating the effects of new full-duplex protocols that make possible continuous ARQ control, such as IBM's Synchronous Data Link Control (SDLC) [28,29] and Digital Equipment's Digital's Data Communications Message Protocol (DDCMP) [30]. References [33, 34, 35] also provide additional discussion on how to compare the various error control strategies embodied in these protocols.

The purpose of this section is to present several simple, easy-to-use versions of the TRIB equation that are applicable in the case of most full-duplex line protocols such as SDLC and DDCMP. It should be emphasized that the concept discussed here is equally applicable for any other protocol in which blocks or frames of data may be continuously sent in the forward direction of a data link, while acknowledgments (or rejections) are being concurrently returned along a functionally independent path in the reverse direction. Both go-back-N schemes and selective retransmission schemes are considered.

The recent availability of satellite channels for domestic common carrier service, as well as an increased use of satellite channels on overseas links, has dramatized the adverse effect of longer propagation times on throughput (TRIB) if the parameters in systems using conventional stop-and-wait protocols like BSC are determined naively or cannot be varied widely enough to keep line overhead sufficiently low. Such considerations have prompted users to evaluate alternative control procedures embodied in full-duplex protocols like SDLC and DDCMP.

6.5.1. TRIB for Continuous ARQ Control

Here we develop a modified version of the TRIB relationship that is useful for both types of continuous ARQ procedures in which blocks continuously depart from the transmitter. Control messages confirming or rejecting these blocks are received later over an independent channel from the receive end. As shown in Figure 6.17, with continuous ARQ procedures the transmitting station will be sending block E at the time when the control message for block C is physically received back at the transmitter. At the transmitter, the number of blocks not confirmed or rejected at any instant is application dependent. In some situations it may be limited by the design of a particular protocol. For example, in SDLC's initial implementation, a maximum value of seven outstanding blocks is possible. In other protocols like DDCMP larger values can be used. However, this author has not yet seen any practical situations where end users employing typical block lengths of at least several hundred characters over single-

USER SENDS BLOCK A FIRST, THEN BLOCK B, . . ., ETC. BLOCK C
IS DETECTED IN ERROR ON FIRST TRANSMISSION ATTEMPT. IN
CURRENT SDLC, BLOCKS D AND E ARE REJECTED BECAUSE THEIR
SEND–COUNT VALUES ARE NOT ONE LARGER THAN THE SEND
COUNT FOR LAST BLOCK ACCEPTED (BLOCK B). C, D, E, ARE ALL
RETRANSMITTED IN THAT ORDER. NO ERRORS ARE DETECTED
ON SECOND ATTEMPT.

Figure 6.17. Time profile of line usage: go-back-*N* continuous ARQ with *N* = 3.
In the above system, a round trip from the sending station to receiver and back corresponds to the time for one and a fraction blocks. It is assumed that block transmissions will not be interrupted at the sender until a complete block has been transmitted.

hop satellite systems will be inconvenienced by the maximum value of seven outstanding blocks in initial implementations of SDLC.

As shown in Figure 6.17, if the maximum time for receipt of the control message back at the transmitting station is less than or equal to the time for seven SDLC frames, ΔT in the original TRIB equation goes to zero, and we have an SDLC throughput relationship:

$$\text{TRIB}_{\text{SDLC}} \cong \frac{K_1(M - C)(1 - NP)}{M/R}$$

where the only new parameter is N, the average number of blocks retransmitted whenever the sending station receives a negative acknowledgment (indicating a block error) from the receiving station. Note that line propagation delay and other components previously appearing in ΔT for the half-duplex protocols now disappear and no longer influence TRIB! The method for determining N is illustrated in the upcoming sample calculations.

The above special relationship for $\text{TRIB}_{\text{SDLC}}$ is a first order approximation which is easily contrasted on a factor-by-factor basis with the general TRIB equation developed earlier. Mr. W. C. McCain of the IBM Corporation, in reviewing the manuscript, pointed out that an alternative factor $(1-P)/(1-P + NP)$ can be used in the numerator, instead of $1-NP$, to yield an exact expression for $\text{TRIB}_{\text{SDLC}}$. Since most practical system design situations will involve small integer values of N, and P values less than 0.1, the difference between the exact and approximate forms will usually be negligible.

6.5.2. Two Possibilities for Handling Block Errors

Initial versions of SDLC implement a version of the continuous ARQ procedure known as "go-back-N" ARQ. The gambit here is for the transmitter to back up N blocks and resend all blocks starting with the one that contained the error, up through and including the one being sent when the NAK is received at the transmitting terminal. The objective is to assure that arriving blocks that satisfy the block parity check at the receiving SDLC station may be processed by the device in the same order in which they arrive. (A current SDLC rule prevents a receiving station from accepting any block unless it has a send sequence count value one larger than the send sequence count value for the last accepted block.)

Thus, this go-back-N strategy requires no block reordering or re-sequencing logic at the destination terminal, but generates N times as much line retransmission overhead as the stop-and-wait ARQ procedures, assuming equal block lengths. As a result, receive stations never need to store more than one block of incoming data. A block is rejected if it is out of sequence or contains bit errors, otherwise it is accepted.

It is possible to devise a continuous ARQ scheme employing "selective repeat" recovery procedures, which are more efficient than go-back-N schemes in the line overhead sense. Assume that the transmitter, while sending block E, receives a rejection (negative acknowledgment control message) for block C. With selective repeat ARQ systems, the sending station follows block E with a retransmission of block C and then block F, as shown in Figure 6.18.

Here the retransmission overhead per block error is a single block, so that TRIB_{SR} (TRIB for selective repeat continuous ARQ protocol) becomes

$$\text{TRIB}_{\text{SR}} \cong \frac{K_1(M - C)(1 - P)}{M/R} .$$

This is apparently the best of all worlds, since ΔT is gone from the

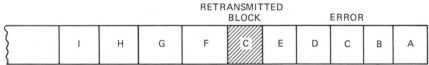

USER SENDS BLOCK A FIRST, THEN B, . . ., ETC. BLOCK C IS
DETECTED IN ERROR. C IS RESENT, FOLLOWED BY NEXT BLOCK
IN ORIGINAL SEQUENCE, NAMELY, F. NOTE HERE THAT THE
RECEIVING DATA LINK CONTROL MECHANISM MUST REASSEMBLE
INCOMING BLOCKS INTO ORIGINAL SEQUENTIAL ORDER BEFORE
DELIVERING THEM TO THE DATA SINK.

Figure 6.18.   Time profile of line usage for selective repeat continuous ARQ system.

general TRIB relationship and retransmission overhead is N times smaller than for the comparable go-back-N scheme. The key question that the user or system designer must ask is: How much more do these advanced protocols actually cost (in terms of increased equipment complexity) in relation to the old familiar standbys like BSC?

It has been this author's experience in working at DMW Telecommunications Corporation that the new full-duplex protocols are generally superior to their predecessors from a TRIB standpoint. Of course this assumes comparable application factors. The exact throughput benefits may be relatively small in good, well-designed stop-and-wait systems having several hundred or a few thousand character block lengths and four-wire lines (where ΔT is relatively small in comparison to M/R). In some cases, stop-and-wait procedures like BSC may even work reasonably well on satellite channels, especially when the user is free to dramatically increase the block lengths for the longer propagation delays.

One system encountered recently by DMW Telecommunications illustrates this point. A user experienced approximately a 10% throughput reduction when a BSC channel was converted from a terrestrial communications facility to a satellite-based channel. The user increased his average block length from 400 to 1200 characters in going to the satellite channel. The single-hop satellite system afforded slightly better bit error rates, but increased the time for receipt of a control message at the sending station by 450 to 500 msec. The added one-way propagation delay was between 225 and 250 msec. These values are typical of those experienced in other user situations.

In cases where the user is concerned with maximizing throughput and must employ longer propagation delay lines such as those in satellite channels, the one-way throughput benefits of full-duplex protocols like SDLC and DDCMP can become substantial, as the calculations below indicate, because these protocols make it possible to implement continuous ARQ procedures.

6.5.3. Examples of TRIB Calculations for Different Communication Line Environments and Line Protocols

Example 1

Typical terrestrial link, four-wire system operating in BSC mode (stop-and-wait ARQ) at 4800 bits/sec (600 characters/sec)

$$Assumed\ Parameters: K_1 = 7\ \text{bits/character}$$
$$M = 400\ \text{characters/block}$$
$$C = 40\ \text{overhead characters/block}$$
$$P = 0.01$$
$$\Delta T = 25\ \text{msec}$$

$$\text{TRIB} = \frac{(7)(400 - 40)(1 - 0.01)}{(400/600) + 0.025} = 3630 \text{ bits/sec}$$

Example 2

Same as Example 1 except that dial lines are used, necessitating two added modem synchronization (RTS/CTS) delays. Assume that one modem RTS/CTS delay = 100 msec, so that ΔT now goes to 100 + 100 + 25 = 225 msec.

$$\text{TRIB} = \frac{(7)(400 - 40)(1 - 0.01)}{(400/600) + 0.225} = = 2812 \text{ bits/sec}$$

Note that, even if, for example, the block error rate P increases by doubling to 0.02 because of dial-up lines, the resulting reduction in throughput is small for these application parameter values.

Example 3

Same as Example 1 except that a satellite channel is used, so that ΔT increases. Assume that ΔT now goes to 500 msec (arbitrary but typical).

$$\text{TRIB} = \frac{(7)(400 - 40)(1 - 0.01)}{(400/600) + 0.5} = 2138 \text{ bits/sec}$$

Example 4

Typical satellite link, four-wire system operating in SDLC mode at 4800 bits/sec, employing go-back-N ARQ

Assumed Parameters: K_1 = 7 bits/character
M = 400 characters/block
C = 40 characters/block
P = 0.01

To compute TRIB it is necessary to determine the average size of the time interval beginning when a block leaves the transmitting station and ending when the sending station has interpreted the control and readied itself for the next block transmission.[3] Call this time T^*. Then from Figure 6.19 for a four-wire satellite channel

$$T^* = t_{fp} + t_{rr} + t_{rp} + t_{cm} + t_{rs}$$

where t_{fp} = forward propagation delay
t_{rr} = reaction time at receiver

[3]Even though T^* is numerically equal to ΔT, it has a different physical interpretation; hence a different symbol is used.

t_{rp} = reverse propagation delay

t_{cm} = time for actual transmission of control message bits, excluding propagation

t_{rs} = reaction time at sender

Define N^* as the maximum number of blocks of length M characters that can be sent in T^* units of time at R characters/sec. Then

$$N^* = \left\lceil \frac{T^*}{M/R} \right\rceil$$

where $\lceil x \rceil$ means "x rounded upward if there is any fractional part." This reflects an assumption that the data link control mechanism will generally spew out an entire frame before being interruptable. Then the value of N for the go-back-N control strategy will be

$$N = N^* + 1$$

where N^* denotes all blocks that must be resent, excluding the error block. One more block is added to N^* to reflect the error block, which must also be resent.

In the above example, assume that $T^* = 500$ msec:

$$N^* = \left\lceil \frac{0.5 \text{ sec}}{400/600} \right\rceil = \left\lceil \frac{0.5}{0.667} \right\rceil = 1$$

Thus $N = 2$, and

$$\text{TRIB}_{\text{SDLC}} \cong \frac{(7)(400 - 40)(1 - 2 \times 0.01)}{400/600} = 3702 \text{ bits/sec}$$

Note here how the propagation delay effects are totally masked by using the go-back-N error control scheme. If selective repeat continuous ARQ was used instead,

$$\text{TRIB}_{\text{SR}} = \frac{(7)(400 - 40)(1 - 0.01)}{400/600} = 3740 \text{ bits/sec}$$

The improvement in throughput using selective repeat (instead of go-back-N) procedures will generally be nominal for these typical values of block retransmission probability.

In all the discussions of TRIB, it must be noted that we are computing only one-way transfer rates. In a true full-duplex data link usage where there are substantial requirements for information transfer in both directions, for example, an RJE station with simultaneous print and read workload, the full duplex protocols like SDLC can enhance the transfer rates in each direction, as noted above. However, they also permit the

1. Stop — and — Wait ARQ CONTROL

   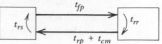

In the TRIB formula, ΔT is calculated as follows:

(A) FOUR-WIRE LINES: $\Delta T = t_{fp} + t_{rr} + t_{rp} + t_{cm} + t_{rs}$

t_{fp} = forward propagation delay
t_{rr} = reaction time at receiver
t_{rp} = reverse propagation delay
t_{cm} = time for control message transmission, excluding propagation
t_{rs} = reaction time at sender

(B) TWO-WIRE LINES— NO REVERSE CHANNEL:
$$\Delta T = t_{fp} + t_{rr} + t_{\text{modem}} + t_{rp} + t_{cm} + t_{\text{modem}} + t_{rs}$$

t_{modem} = request-to-send clear-to-send time for modem.

Assumes modem turnaround
and reaction time are
serial events.

(C) TWO-WIRE LINES— REVERSE CHANNEL: Same formula as (A)

Difference here is that control message time will usually be larger.

2. Continuous ARQ Control

$$\text{TRIB} \cong \frac{K_1(M - C)(1 - NP)}{M/R}$$

where N is number of blocks retransmitted per retransmission (may or may not be integer). In initial SDLC implementations this number is 7. The assumption here is that ΔT is completely eliminated. This is reasonable as long as the number of bits that can be sent in $t_{fp} + t_{rr} + t_{rp} + t_{cm} + t_{rs}$ does not exceed the total bit count for the maximum number of blocks the sender can hold.

Figure 6.19. Supplementary illustration for throughput computations: point-to-point lines.

send and receive activities to take place concurrently, providing parallel processing on the data link. This potential doubling of the overal bidirectional throughput capacity is an additional dividend of the full-duplex protocols that does not show up in any of the one-way throughput calculations.

One often overlooked caveat should be noted. As will be shown in

Chapter 8, the line control induced overhead in each SDLC frame is nominally six character equivalents since the block structure consists of the following:

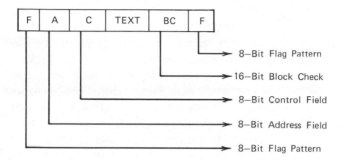

Other higher level control functions such as path control, network control, and device control require added control overhead, which is treated merely as text (or information bits) by the data link control mechanism. In comparing older networking approaches to newer teleprocessing network control architectures for comparable applications, it is essential that the required number of total noninformation characters (the variable C in the general TRIB formula) be used for each alternative available. In BSC, overhead would consist mainly of data link control and device control characters. By contrast, in advanced networking procedures, it is necessary to consider the overhead bits introduced by all functional control layers which must be involved between the data source and sink. Since there will usually be more overhead than just the FAC BCF bits associated with data link control, it is likely that the total number of overhead characters per block in BSC will be smaller than in advanced layered architectures with their rigid, formally defined separations of data link control, network control, and end-to-end control between devices.

In conclusion, it can be said that, generally, the newer full-duplex protocols give the user additional function. In some cases the added throughput is substantial; in other cases it is not so noticeable. The equations given above must be used to quantify the relative differences between different organizations and determine the relative cost effectiveness of each alternative.

It cannot be overemphasized, however, that there are numerous additional user benefits accruing from the new line protocols which have not been addressed here. These will be considered in Chapter 8.

6.6. APPLICATION CONSIDERATIONS

The relationships for TRIB given in Section 6.5 indicate clearly that the transmission efficiency of data links depends on numerous factors. Some can be controlled by the user, and some cannot. The user's primary goal is to select values for these variables that will result in the maximum efficiency at the lowest cost. Implicit in selecting the proper facilities for a specific application is a requirement that the user stipulate acceptable levels of transmission performance such as bit and/or block error rates, the level of burst protection required, tolerable propagation delays, and acceptable redundancy levels. These factors constitute his requirements and have nothing to do with any particular equipment or error control strategy. Achieving these objectives requires a joint consideration of equipment features, channel characteristics, and economics. For example, terminals affect error control decisions by determining whether data must be transmitted continuously or may be periodically interrupted, whether the data block size can be optimized, and whether parity checking calculations are done in hardware or firmware. Terminals also affect efficiency by influencing the capability to perform send- and receive-oriented tasks concurrently (e.g., card reading and line printing). They also influence error control decisions by requiring the control signaling procedure to be effected with a line turnaround in some dial-line applications.

The particular signal converter and circuit combination utilized will have a significant impact on the error patterns experienced, since errors naturally depend on the type of modulation used, the compensation circuitry in the modems, and the natural properties of the channel itself (e.g., signal-to-noise ratio). Of equal application importance are factors such as channel propagation delay and the nature of the channel, whether two- or four-wire. When being used in a half-duplex mode without reverse channel, a dial line operating at voice-grade speeds must be completely turned around just to send back a control signal. For the same application, use of a four-wire circuit with constant carrier in each direction can often reduce interblock times for control signaling dramatically.

Figures 6.20 and 6.21 summarize some of the main conclusions just cited and illustrate that the frequency with which the user reverses the primary direction of data transfer also influences overall line efficiency. The main objective of these figures is to show the multiplicity of ways in which overall efficiency can be improved by the following:

1. Reducing channel–modem synchronization delays (also known as RTS/CTS delays).

1. ACCEPTABLE BIT, BLOCK ERROR RATES

2. LEVEL OF BURST PROTECTION REQUIRED

3. ALLOWABLE EQUIPMENT COMPLEXITY AND COST

4. ACCEPTABLE REDUNDANCY LEVEL AND DECODING DELAYS

5. SYNCHRONOUS OR START-STOP TERMINALS

6. CAN TERMINALS USE REVERSE CHANNEL IF NECESSARY

7. ARE TERMINAL BUFFERS AVAILABLE

8. MESSAGE BLOCK SIZES

9. INTERBLOCK TIMES

10. BLOCK RETRANSMISSION PROBABILITY

11. CHANNEL NOISE AND PROPOGATION DELAY PARAMETERS

12. MODE OF OPERATION (HALF OR FULL DUPLEX) AND TYPE
    OF FACILITY (2-WIRE OR 4-WIRE)

Figure 6.20.   System parameters affecting error control decision.

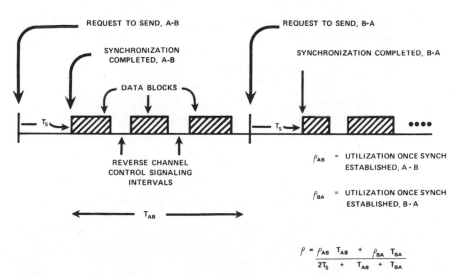

$$\rho = \frac{\rho_{AB}\ T_{AB}\ +\ \rho_{BA}\ T_{BA}}{2T_S\ +\ T_{AB}\ +\ T_{BA}}$$

Figure 6.21. Effects of line turnabounds and control signaling times on overall transmission efficiency when direction of transfer alternates between $A\!\rightarrow\!B$ and $B\!\rightarrow\!A$.

2. Eliminating the need for dial-line turnaround with techniques like reverse channels.

Although the user can consider changes in the basic error control procedures themselves to improve sluggishly performing systems, the two approaches just given will generally require few, if any, changes in software or hardware. This is so because most terminals and computers derive their clock signals from the signal converter and circuit combination; if the link can get synchronized and/or turned around faster, it notifies the business machine accordingly, the net result being reduced overhead without significant software and/or hardware modifications.

When FEC channels are being considered, performance evaluation will usually involve different parameters from those of interest for ARQ applications. For block-oriented FEC systems, the probability of an undetected block error will continue to be of major importance. Regardless of whether convolutional or block techniques are used, the general effect of FEC is similar to that of a transformation in which one channel having a certain error rate at a data transmission speed R is converted into another channel having a reduced error rate at a lower data transmission speed Rk/n where k/n is the efficiency of the particular code used. (See Figure 6.22.) The effective bit error rate for FEC channels corresponds to the probability of a decoder making a 1-bit decoding error. A knowledge of the correction power of the code and probability distributions of channel errors makes it possible to estimate the decoding or effective error rate using various analytic techniques.

6.6.1. Applications Favoring ARQ

Most data transmission applications fall naturally into one of two categories—those in which data are transmitted continuously from the source (e.g., time-division multiplexing) and those in which the source transmits in a periodically interruptable fashion. It was shown previously that ARQ techniques are generally restricted to the latter category.

Paper tape and magnetic tape units are inherently suited for ARQ since the tape storage can preserve copies of transmitted messages. Retransmissions can be readily accomplished by backing up the appropriate number of records or blocks and transmitting again. The notion of a satisfactory reverse channel is also important because the feedback channel is sometimes obtained by reversing the direction of transmission over a two-wire circuit. The circuit turnaround involves delays and must be accomplishable within milliseconds, or it can cause substantial overhead. Any application for which ARQ is being considered must satisfy these minimal requirements.

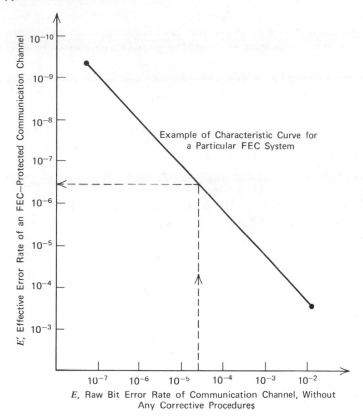

Figure 6.22.   **Effect of forward error correction.**

The application characteristics mentioned thus far are necessary for the satisfactory implementation of ARQ but are by no means sufficient to assure its superiority over FEC. Applications where ARQ is the preferred method can now be brought into better focus by recalling that the error detection power of any code is substantially greater than its correction power. Thus, whenever large amounts of redundancy cannot be afforded, ARQ techniques tend to be preferable to FEC. Another possible advantage of ARQ is that properly designed ARQ schemes are substantially more capable of protecting against burst errors than is FEC in most situations. This superiority is due partially to the fact that with ARQ a retransmission is requested whenever a block error is detected, regardless of how many bits are in error within the block. Although FEC channels can be modified to make burst errors on the channel look like random errors to the decoder, additional equipment and shift register delays result from this modification.

Most data transmission at speeds of up to 4800 bits/sec over the dial-up telephone network is well suited for ARQ since the average bit error rates at these speeds are usually moderate to good. Private or dedicated phone lines exhibit similar bit error rates at speeds up to 9600 bits/sec and are equally well suited for ARQ.

Another important application category for which ARQ methods are generally superior includes situations where communication between source and sink must take place very rapidly, as in real-time polling over multipoint telephone lines. Real-time polling often requires that a complete message transmission be completed in a matter of milliseconds. Simple parity check codes such as those previously discussed make possible the economic provision of error detection. The relatively long shift register delays associated with more powerful FEC codes and the comparative expense of FEC make it generally inferior to ARQ for such applications.

A final application where ARQ is definitely preferred is the situation shown in Figure 6.23, where a user having exceptional requirements for low bit error rates (e.g., less than 10^{-6}) must use a common carrier link whose intrinsic bit error rate is only moderately good (e.g., in the range between 5×10^{-5} and 5×10^{-6}). User-provided ARQ represents the only viable approach for the fraction of users not satisfied with the intrinsic channel error rate. User-provided FEC is not capable of economically furnishing the incremental protection required without excessive amounts of redundancy and long shift register delays.

6.6.2. Applications Favoring FEC

It has already been shown that FEC is particularly well suited for applications between terminals that must submit data to a channel in uninterrupted or continuous fashion. Since FEC does not interrupt the data flow from the source, it does not require any terminal buffers and is well suited for applications where such buffers are either not available or economically unjustifiable. Whenever a satisfactory return channel is not available for ARQ, FEC is the only possible error control technique. Lack of a return channel can arise either because one is not physically available or because reversing (turning around) a two-wire channel for conventional ARQ would introduce an excessive time delay. However, as mentioned previously, in applications involving long channel propagation delays where stop-and-wait ARQ would be highly inefficient, a possible alternative to FEC would be continuous ARQ. (The relative merits of continuous and stop-and-wait ARQ can be quantitatively estimated directly from the throughput expressions given in Section 6.5.)

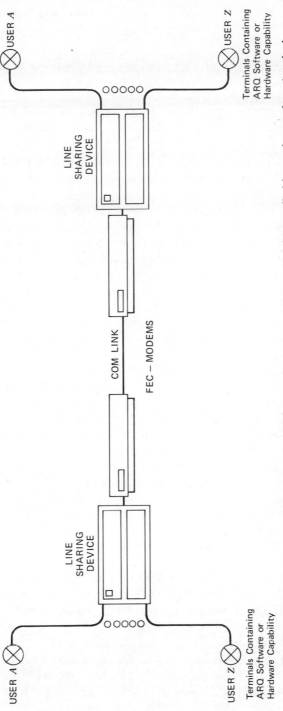

Figure 6.23. Hybrid error control arrangement; FEC is used on shared link, and ARQ is supplied by each user from terminal.

USER A

USER Z

Terminals Containing
ARQ Software or
Hardware Capability

LINE
SHARING
DEVICE

COM LINK

FEC — MODEMS

LINE
SHARING
DEVICE

USER A

USER Z

Terminals Containing
ARQ Software or
Hardware Capability

Full-duplex transmission (both directions simultaneously) between time-division multiplexers at speeds of 4800 bits/sec and higher is a possible application category well suited for FEC since data flow interruptions cannot normally be tolerated.

As shown in Figure 6.23, another example of an application particularly well suited to FEC involves shared user (common carrier) channels that must service a group of users having diverse error requirements. Shared-channel ARQ cannot simultaneously satisfy a broad range of user error rate objectives unless designed to provide all users with the same grade of service demanded by the user requiring the lowest error rate. Providing substantially more protection than many users require represents an inefficient use of redundancy. A common carrier-provided ARQ channel with intermediate protection capability will leave the users requiring extremely low error rates with no means to accomplish their grade of service, since user-provided ARQ in combination with channel ARQ is frequently an unacceptable alternative. A feasible solution in these situations is to use FEC on the shared channel to obtain an adequate bit error rate for most users (10^{-4} to 10^{-6}). A user with even more stringent requirements has the option of obtaining the incremental protection margin by adding a user-provided ARQ scheme. This situation illustrates an application where a hybrid arrangement or combination of ARQ and FEC techniques may represent the best approach.

It has been noted that convolutional codes used for FEC generally have limited ability to correct burst errors which appear at the decoder input. Thus, for telephone line applications the meaningful utilization of FEC necessitates some modification to the basic schemes since *errors on the channel* generally exhibit a pronounced sequential dependence. Interleaving or diffuse convolutional coding effectively transforms the bursty telephone channel into a predominately random error channel from the decoder's viewpoint. Interleaving is accomplished by transmitting adjacent bits that depart from the source at separated intervals in time. Thus adjacent bits on the channel do not correspond to adjacent bits from the source, and the channel errors are effectively spread out in time (randomized) before entering the decoder. The penalties associated with interleaving are increased equipment expense and propagation delays.

6.6.3. Applications Where Either ARQ or FEC Can Be Used

For either mode to be usable, an application must possess all the previously noted characteristics required for implementing ARQ and FEC. It is generally true that FEC requires few, if any, special channel or terminal equipment characteristics, mainly because this mode is generally provided within the modem equipment. The primary reasons for ruling out FEC are user objectives or requirements such as equipment cost and acceptable error rate. With ARQ just the opposite is generally true. The primary reasons for ruling out ARQ arise from channel or terminal equipment limitations and are not so likely to be caused by user objectives of economy and error protection required.

Thus, for either mode to be used, the application situation must involve a flexible user who has numerous options open to him as far as selecting terminal equipment, modems, and channels is concerned. His bit error rate objectives must fall somewhere between the extremes cited above since one of these two methods is generally preferred for applications in which the acceptable error rate is unusually high or low.

6.7. CONCLUDING REMARKS

Early interest in the more sophisticated error control procedures was prompted chiefly by space and governmental applications. Within the past 10 years, however, numerous commercial organizations in the data processing and data communications fields have developed successful products embodying many of the techniques considered in the preceding discussion. These error control devices are being used in diverse data transmission/processing applications in the various forms of sophisticated modems and stand-alone subsystems or as integral portions of terminal equipment.

Most of the major computer manufacturers use ARQ-oriented procedures in their computers and data communications terminals, primarily because of the wide variety of applications that must be economically accommodated with relatively simple equipment. Most data communications terminals have been designed around the stop-and-wait ARQ approach, so that a user typically has little or no possibility of modifying the specific technique chosen by the terminal vendor. However, he can and should make every effort to obtain efficient operation by selecting fast synchronizing, reliable modems, and optimum block lengths. In the future, as satellites become widely available for data transmission, it can be expected that other variations of ARQ (such as the previously discussed continuous ARQ method) will become more widely used, since the inherently longer propagation times will make stop-and-wait techniques increasingly inefficient.

On the other hand, FEC systems have historically been primarily the domain of the modem manufacturers and common carriers. Selection of a satisfactory channel–modem combination is generally not influenced substantially by the type of terminal equipment since standard electrical interfaces between business machines and modems are in widespread use. At the current time, FEC systems are generally marketed as optional equipment by some but not all modem manufacturers. This is evidence of the fact that numerous applications favor the use of alternate ARQ–oriented error control procedures for economic and various other reasons.

Future improvements in the degree of error protection provided to data communications users are contingent on the cooperative efforts of users, terminal equipment vendors, modem manufacturers, and the common carriers. It has been shown here that the efficiency of a data communications system depends jointly on the features of the terminal equipment and the statistics of the channel–modem combination. The best overall approach to error control for any application can therefore be obtained only with a system design in which the terminal equipment, modem, and communication channel are treated as interacting subsystems.

REFERENCES

1. H. C. A. van Duuren, "Error Probability and Transmission Speed on Circuits Using Detection and Automatic Repetition of Signals," *IRE Transactions on Communications Systems,* Vol. CS-9, March 1961, pp. 38–50.

2. C. E. Shannon, "A Mathematical Theory of Communication," *Bell System Technical Journal,* Vol. 27, July–October 1948, pp. 379–623.

3. J. T. Martin, *Teleprocessing Network Organization,* Prentice-Hall, Englewood Cliffs, N. J., 1970, Chapter 5.

4. R. Bose and D. Ray-Chadhuri, "A Class of Error-Correcting Binary Group Codes," *Information and Control,* Vol. 3, March 1960.

5. P. Fire, *A Class of Multiple-Error-Correcting Binary Codes for Non-independent Errors,* Technical Report 55, Stanford Electronics Laboratories, April 1959.

6. M. Melas, "A New Group of Codes for Correction of Dependent Errors in Data Transmission," *IBM Journal,* Vol. 4, 1960.

7. R. W. Hamming, "Error Detecting and Error Correcting Codes," *Bell System Technical Journal,* April 1950.

8. W. R. Bennett and J. R. Davey, *Data Transmission,* McGraw-Hill, New York, 1965, pp. 295–300.

9. R. W. Lucky, J. Saltz and E. J. Weldon, *Principles of Data Communication,* McGraw-Hill, New York, 1968, Chapters 10–12.

10. H. O. Burton and D. D. Sullivan, "Errors and Error Control," *Proceedings of IEEE,* Vol. 60, No. 11, November 1972.

11. A. G. Gatfield, "ARQ Error Control on the Satellite Channel," *Proceedings of IEEE International Communications Conference,* 1974.

12. A. G. Franco and M. E. Wall, *Communication User Constraints on Adaptive Error Control Procedures*, Report ICS-64-TM-72, ITT Communication Systems, August 1964.

13. M. Nesenbergs, "Comparison of the 3-out-of-7 ARQ with BCH Coding Systems," *IEEE Transactions on Communication Systems*, June 1963, pp. 202–212.

14. *General Information-Binary Synchronous Communications*, IBM Publication GA27-3004, IBM Corp., 1969.

15. J. L. Eisenbies, "Conventions for Digital Data Communication Link Design," *IBM Systems Journal*, Vol. 6, No. 4, 1967.

16. G. D. Forney, "Coding and Its Application in Space Communications," *IEEE Spectrum*, June 1970, pp. 47–58.

17. J. M. Wozencraft and B. Reiffen, *Sequential Decoding*, Technology Press of M.I.T., Cambridge, Mass., and John Wiley and Sons, New York, 1961.

18. J. L. Massey, *Threshold Decoding*, M.I.T. Press, Cambridge, Mass., 1961.

19. R. J. Benice and A. H. Frey, Jr., "An Analysis of Retransmission Systems," *IEEE Transactions on Communication Technology*, December 1964.

20. R. J. Benice and A. H. Frey, Jr., "Comparisons of Error Control Techniques," *IEEE Transactions on Communication Technology*, December 1964.

21. J. A. Heller and I. M. Jacobs, "Viterbi Decoding for Satellite and Space Communications," *IEEE Transactions on Communication Technology*, Vol. COM-19, No. 5, October 1971.

22. A. J. Viterbi, "Convolutional Codes and Their Performance in Communication Systems," *IEEE Transactions on Communication Technology*, Vol. COM-19, No. 5, October 1971.

23. I. M. Jacobs, "Sequential Decoding for Efficient Communication from Deep Space," *IEEE Transactions on Communication Technology*, Vol. COM-15, No. 4, August 1967.

24. *Communications of the ACM*, Vol. 8, No. 5, May 1965, pp. 280–286.

25. D. R. Doll, "Data Communications Systems: Basics of Network Design," *Data Communications Systems, Electronics Deskbook*, Vol. 1, No. 1, 1972. McGraw–Hill, New York.

26. Carl N. Boustead and Kirit Mehta, "Getting Peak Performance on a Data Channel," *Data Communications*, July–August 1974, McGraw-Hill, New York.

27. D. R. Doll, "Notes Prepared for ICC Institute Course 1010—Data Communications Fundamentals," ICC Institute Publication, Miami, Fla., 1974.

28. J. Ray Kersey, "Synchronous Data Link Control," *Data Communications*, May–June 1974, McGraw-Hill, New York.

29. *IBM Synchronous Data Link Control: General Information*, IBM Publication GA27-3093, IBM Corp., March 1974.

30. S. Wecker, "DEC's Advanced Link Control," *Data Communications*, September–October 1974, McGraw-Hill, New York.

31. A. G. Franco and L. J. Saporta, "Performance of Random Error Correcting Codes on the Switched Telephone Network," *IEEE Transactions on Communication Technology*, December 1967, pp. 861–864.

32. W. W. Peterson, *Error Correcting Codes*, M.I.T. Press, Cambridge, Mass., and John Wiley and Sons, New York, 1961.

33. M. A. Reed and T. D. Smetanka, "How to Determine Message Response Time for Satellites," *Data Communications,* Vol. 6, No. 6, 1977, McGraw-Hill, New York.

34. E. R. Cacciamani and K. S. Kim, "Circumventing the Problem of Propagation on Satellite Data Channels, *Data Communications,* July–August, 1975, McGraw-Hill. New York.

35. D. R. Doll, "Calculating Throughput on Full Duplex Data Link Controls, " *Data Communications,* January–February 1976, McGraw-Hill, New York.

SEVEN

MULTIPLEXING AND CONCENTRATION TECHNIQUES FOR LINE SHARING

Obtaining a cost-effective teleprocessing network is postulated on efficient utilization of the communication links and processing equipment. A variety of line sharing devices and procedures are commonly used for this purpose. In this chapter, various functional and economic aspects of frequency-division multiplexing (FDM), synchronous time-division multiplexing (STDM), statistical time-division multiplexing (STATDM), message switching concentration (MSC), and line (or circuit) switching techniques are discussed.[1,2] Also considered are recently developed sharing techniques known as packet switching and inverse multiplexing. The motivations for line sharing stem from economies of scale in the cost of bandwidth and from the traffic smoothing effect that such devices produce when serving a large terminal population characterized by unscheduled requests for service.

The discussion of these techniques includes a detailed distinction between *multiplexing* and *concentration,* two terms often (and unfortunately) used synonymously. It is shown that FDM and STDM are examples of conventional multiplexing, whereas message switching, packet switching, and line switching usually illustrate concentration. Statistical time-division multiplexing is shown to be a hybrid line sharing scheme embodying certain features of both concepts. Thus it is often referred to as statistical multiplexing.

The first part of the chapter is devoted to a functional explanation of the above-noted techniques. The rest is concerned with applications and systems design situations involving multiplexing and concentration techniques. The application section focuses on important economic factors pertaining to the selection and use of the various methods. The role of line sharing devices in contemporary common carrier and end-user networks is also considered. The economic and technical aspects of these contrasting application environments are emphasized to illustrate the multiplicity of uses for line sharing devices.

The concluding portion of the chapter introduces system design considerations by illustrating precisely how the decision to use multiplexers or concentrators in a typical computer–communication network is implemented. Various techniques for geographically positioning multiplexers and concentrators to minimize total costs are presented. The use of one of these procedures is demonstrated, using a typical design problem as a case study.

Although the theoretical basis for many of these approaches may be found in well-understood concepts of conventional voice telephony, the

[1]Line switching concentration is sometimes also referred to as space-division multiplexing.
[2]Some of the material in this chapter was originally discussed by Doll in Reference [31].

myriad regulatory and economic nuances of today's unsettled communications environment and the unique requirements of the computer industry account for the recent surge of interest in line sharing techniques by noncarrier users. Before the famous Carterfone decision of 1968, such concepts were of concern mainly to the common carriers. Then came permission for complete interconnection and a subsequent realization by end users that costs could be appreciably reduced by employing relatively simple multiplexing devices.

Of the line sharing methods already noted, FDM and STDM are by far the most prevalent in contemporary end-user networks. However, falling minicomputer prices, cost-conscious data users, and a continuing spirit of regulatory permissiveness regarding interconnection are prompting increased interest in the application of STATDM, packet, and line or circuit switching concentration techniques in all types of computer–communication applications. This chapter attempts to present a balanced perspective of how multiplexing and concentration relate both to the end user and to the common carrier. To be sure, this is a difficult objective, particularly in light of today's increasingly nebulous distinction between the once well-separated roles of carrier and user.

7.1. MULTIPLEXING AND CONCENTRATION TECHNIQUES CONTRASTED

The motivations for line sharing stem from economies of scale in the cost of bandwidth and from the increased channel utilizations such devices can produce when serving a large terminal population with predominantly unscheduled requests for service. For example, with today's domestic tariff structure, leased voice grade lines typically cost up to twice as much as low speed lines of the same length. However, such voice-grade facilities are generally capable of transmitting data at speeds at least 20 to 30 times higher than those of the typical low speed link. Thus, by using line sharing, the cost per unit of capacity (bits per second) in a fully utilized voice-grade line can often be reduced to less than one tenth of that of an equal-length low speed line. These economies of scale in the cost of bandwidth generally extend over to carrier-provided broadband links as well.

Before proceeding further, it is appropriate to distinguish between multiplexing and concentration. *Multiplexing* generally refers to static channel derivation schemes in which given frequency bands or time slots on a shared channel are assigned on a fixed, predetermined (a priori) basis. Thus a multiplexer has generally balaced input and output bit rate capacities. *Concentration,* by contrast, describes schemes in which some number of input ports dynamically share a smaller number of output subchannels on a demand basis. Concentration thus involves a traffic smoothing effect not characteristic of multiplexing. Since the aggregate input bit rate and output bit rate need not be matched in a concentrator, statistics and queuing play important roles. Of the techniques discussed in this chapter, FDM and STDM are examples of multiplexing. Message switching, packet switching, and line switching illustrate the concept of concentration, whereas STATDM is effectively a hybrid sharing scheme embodying salient features of both methods. For this reason, a statistical time-division multiplexer is sometimes called a dynamic multiplexer or a multiplexer-concentrator [1,2]. In such systems, subchannels have a statistically high probability of being available for a given input port, but this availability is not a certainty, as would be the case with STDM.

7.2. FREQUENCY-DIVISION MULTIPLEXING (FDM)

Frequency-division multiplexing partitions a limited-bandwidth communication channel into a group of independent lower speed channels, each of which utilizes its permanently assigned portion of the total frequency spectrum. As shown in Figure 7.1, each channel in the sharing group thus uses a frequency slot that contains the unique pair of frequencies needed for sending its binary data signals. When FDM is used on a voice-grade line, each subchannel may typically transmit data asynchronously at speeds up to 150 bits/sec, although in special cases at faster rates. One of the limitations of FDM arises from the need for guard bands or safety zones between adjacent subchannels to prevent the electrical over-

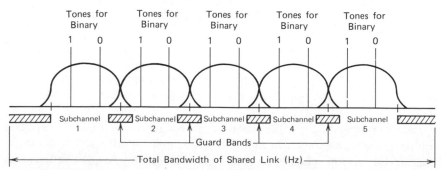

Figure 7.1. Spectrum partitioning and signaling frequency assignments in typical FDM System.

lapping of signals. These guard bands impose a practical limit on the efficiency of an FDM system. For example, with state-of-the-art FDM equipment operating on a leased voice-grade line, the maximum composite or aggregate low speed bit rate achievable will typically range from 1800 to 2000 bits/sec, although in some cases slightly higher. Generally speaking, other types of sharing must be used if a higher aggregate bit-rate requirement exists.

The primary advantage of FDM to end users is its relatively low cost in applications where its aggregate bit-rate limit is not constraining. Some of this economy is provided by eliminating the need for a separate modem or data set at each remote terminal site, since the FDM device is usually designed so that it also performs the modulation and demodulation functions. Also, FDMs are readily cascadable or, in other words, have features that facilitate dropping and inserting at intermediate points along a multiplexed channel. Thus FDM is particularly cost effective in multiplexing an unclustered terminal group (like the one shown in Figure 7.2) whose aggregate bit rate does not exceed the limit mentioned above.

As shown in Figure 7.2, each FDM subchannel is connected to the communications controller with a separate port. Viewed by the network control software, an FDM line containing the three subchannels and three terminals shown in Figure 7.2 cannot be distinguished from a configuration employing three separate leased lines. Thus a user may employ FDM to combine traffic of different terminals onto one communication line without using polling software.

In cases where a user is willing to control the remote terminals of a network with some type of polling software (or let multiple remote terminals share a port on the communications controller), a second level of

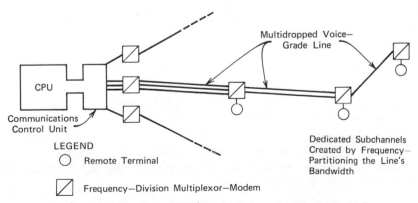

Figure 7.2. The Use of FDM to service unclustered terminals.

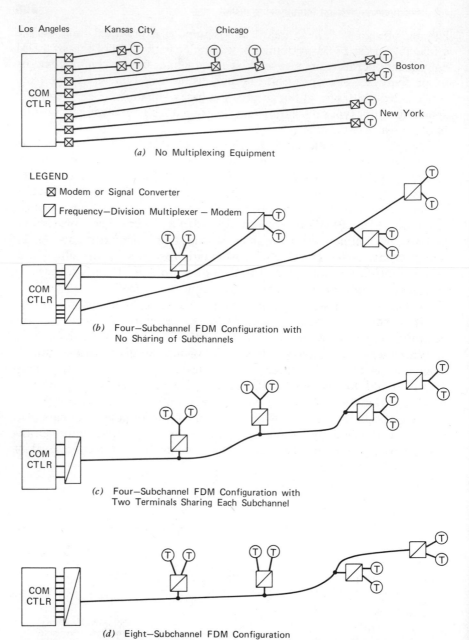

(a) No Multiplexing Equipment

LEGEND

⊠ Modem or Signal Converter

▨ Frequency—Division Multiplexer — Modem

(b) Four—Subchannel FDM Configuration with No Sharing of Subchannels

(c) Four—Subchannel FDM Configuration with Two Terminals Sharing Each Subchannel

(d) Eight—Subchannel FDM Configuration

Figure 7.3. Alternative FDM configurations for connecting eight terminals into CPU, using voice-grade lines.

sharing becomes possible. The capacity of the voice-grade line is shared by the FDM equipment, which creates multiple independent subchannels. Each subchannel in turn may be time shared, on either a contention or a polled basis, by multiple remote terminals.

For example, imagine that two asynchronous terminals in each of the following cities—Boston, New York, Chicago, and Kansas City—are to be tied to a central computer in Los Angeles. Figure 7.3 illustrates four possible configurations, the first of which uses individual leased lines to each remote terminal. The second approach utilizes FDM equipment with an assumed capacity of four subchannels per voice-grade line and no sharing of the subchannels. The third approach, which clearly has a still lower line cost, uses FDM equipment with an assumed capacity of four subchannels per voice-grade line and two terminals per FDM subchannel. The fourth approach has the same line costs as the third configuration. However, an FDM system with an assumed capacity of eight subchannels per voice-grade line (and no sharing of subchannels) is postulated. Note that all configurations (except the one in which sharing of the subchannels is permitted) require eight ports at the central site. Only four ports are required when each subchannel can be shared by two remote terminals.

Other popular examples of the application of frequency-division multiplexing techniques are their use in special modems to create a full-duplex channel over a two-wire circuit (discussed in Chapter 2) and to provide extra low-speed teletype-grade channels on voice-grade circuits, primarily in international applications. In such situations, the collective costs of separate voice-grade and teletype (sub-voice-grade) lines are often sufficiently large that it may be less expensive to operate one leased voice-grade line (for either voice communications or data transmission up to 9600 bits/sec) concurrently with one or more independent low speed side channels on the same physical line. The analog data modems can usually be switched out in favor of a telephone at each end, enabling either voice or data transmission to take place independently of slow speed subchannel activity.

7.3. SYNCHRONOUS TIME-DIVISION MULTIPLEXING (STDM)

Time-division multiplexing devices that create a permanently dedicated time slot or subchannel for each port in the sharing group are classified as STDMs. By contrast, statistical or asynchronous TDMs dynamically allocate the subchannels or time slots on a statistical basis to increase line efficiency by providing time slots only for ports actively transmitting data.[3]

As shown in Figure 7.4, STDMs share a synchronous communication line by cyclically scanning incoming data from input ports, peeling off bits or characters, and interleaving them into frames on a single high speed data stream. This effect is similar to that of a high speed conveyor belt picking up objects arriving at a common point from several lower speed belts. In utilizing a given channel, STDM is generally more efficient than FDM since it is capable of using the entire bandwidth available.

For example, STDMs can generally operate over dedicated voice-grade lines at speeds of 4800, 7200, and 9600 bits/sec, whereas FDMs' practical limit on the same line is probably in the 2000 bits/sec speed range. Generally speaking, the multiplexed data stream is transmitted serially, bit-by-bit, at a rate governed by the circuit-signal converter combination. The split-stream modems introduced in Chapter 2 are popoular devices that combine the modem and STDM functions into the modem device when the input port speeds are integer multiples of 2400 bits/sec and the total input rate does not exceed 9600 bits/sec.

Although voice-grade lines are shared in the majority of current STDM applications, a recent regulatory development now enables end users to multiplex broadband carrier links with customer-provided STDM equipment. Whereas STDMs can multiplex traffic from either asynchronous (start/stop) terminals, other synchronous devices, or combinations thereof, FDMs are generally used to multiplex only asynchronous terminals, although this is not an intrinsic limitation.

Contemporary STDMs may perform either bit or character interleaving on the shared line when serving start/stop terminals exclusively. In these applications, character interleaving is usually more efficient since a modest amount of bandwidth compression is possible. The start and stop bits of each character entering the STDM may be stripped off before the character's insertion into the frame of multiplexed data. (Figure 7.5 illustrates the technique of character-interleaved STDM, including data characters and the encodings of various end-to-end control signals.) Any bits stripped from incoming data characters are reinserted by the demultiplexing unit before distribution of the characters to their respective

---

[3]The reader should not confuse asynchronous time-division multiplexers, in the sense of their current interpretation, with STDMs that multiplex asynchronous (start/stop) terminal devices. Throughout this chapter, ''STDM'' describes the time-division technique in which dedicated subchannels are created for start/stop devices, synchronous devices, or a combination thereof. ''Statistical'' or ''asynchronous TDM,'' by contrast, describes all schemes where the multiplexer creates subchannels dynamically, regardless of the type of device being multiplexed.

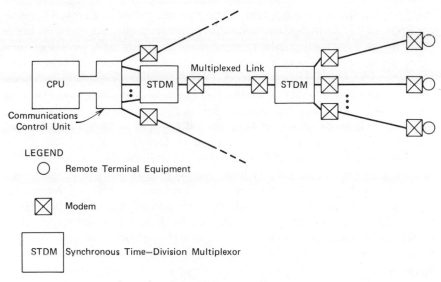

Figure 7.4. **Synchronous TDMs in a teleprocessing network.**

output ports. Thus the incoming characters are effectively encoded using fewer bits per character for transmission over the shared link, thereby enabling an aggregate low speed bit rate of 1.1 times the shared link's transmission rate to be accommodated in typical situations.

In newer applications involving the use of STDMs to multiplex synchronous data streams, the STDMs generally employ bit interleaving,

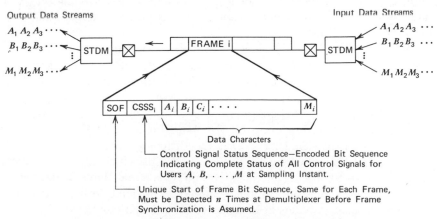

Figure 7.5. **Character-interleaved STDM and frame format.**

disregarding the textual content of the incoming data streams. This data transparency is an important requirement for multiplexers being incorporated in the long haul trunks of synchronous digital data networks now being implemented by certain users and common carriers. Whether bit or character interleaving is used, special predetermined code sequences are utilized between STDMs to define the beginning of each new frame of multiplexed data. Demultiplexing is thus accomplished by the assumption of an implicit relationship between the output line or buffer address and the relative position of the time slots in an arriving frame.

When all the multiplexed terminal devices are unbuffered, the problem of fixing the scanning rates within the STDM is straightforward—the subchannel scan rates are matched to the transmission rates of the respective input lines. Ordinarily this speed corresponds, in turn, to the operating speed of the remote terminal device being served. However, when messages and message segments are queued in remote terminal buffers, the solution to the scan rate assignment problem is not so obvious. In References [3] and [4], Doll has developed a queuing theoretic design technique for determining scan rates within the STDM so that the average queuing delay experienced at the remote terminals in the sharing group is minimized.

Noise disturbances on the shared channel can cause a variety of errors, depending on whether character or bit interleaving is used. With character interleaving, an individual data bit error will at worst cause a single output character to be received in error. With bit-interleaved STDM, a similar anomaly could cause the demultiplexing unit to deliver the outputs to the wrong addresses, unless the STDMs contain their own error control capability. As a consequence, character STDMs are less sensitive than bit multiplexers to channel disturbances, although resynchronization (reestablishing the start of a data frame) takes somewhat longer than with bit-interleaved STDMs.

Higher quality STDM devices have been designed on the philosophy that random and burst errors can be allowed to cause data errors, but must virtually never cause errors in the end-to-end control signals between user terminals or in the internal network control signals between STDMs themselves. This goal may be accomplished without substantial degradation of shared link capacity by using highly redundant encodings of all vital control signals. For example, frame synchronization is obviously critical and must be preserved in the presence of noise bursts. Elaborate time averaging and/or thresholding schemes have been devised whereby frame synchronization is assumed at the demultiplexer only after a unique bit sequence has been detected a specified number of times in a given time period. Similarly, frame synchronization is assumed to be lost only when this same condition cannot be detected. Typical noise disturbances may thus be smoothed over without catastrophic effect, even though some data bit errrors may occur during intervals when frame synchronization is being reestablished.

In comparison to FDMs, STDMs are expensive to cascade because a relatively complete STDM system must be used at any point where one or more subchannels are being inserted or removed. Also, when STDMs are used in cascade, the problem of coordinating the timing across multiple synchronous links must be addressed. Fundamentally, two choices exist here—to use one master clock from which all system elements derive their timing, or to use independent synchronous clocks on each link. The former alternative may be illustrated by the simple configuration shown in Figure 7.6. The modem at A provides the master clock signal, and the lefthand modem at B derives its clock from the incoming data on link AB. The righthand modem at B is slaved to its lefthand counterpart at B and, in turn, provides a master clock to link BC. With the alternative approach of independent synchronous clocks, some type of elastic buffer must be provided at node B to absorb data buildups caused by slight variations in the rates of the two independent clocks. Most STDM networks to date have been implemented using the single-master-clock scheme for various economic and reliability reasons.

As with FDM, an STDM configuration provides each port in the sharing group with its own dedicated appearance at the communications control unit. (See Figure 7.4.) Here it is assumed that STDMs are used in pairs, one for multiplexing and the other for demultiplexing. It is possible to eliminate the central site STDM if the communications control unit can perform the STDM function in hardware or software. (An early IBM Corporation STDM product combination known as the 2712 Multiplexor operated with a hard-wired transmission control known as the 2702, eliminating the need for two separate central site devices.)

Since most computer vendors have not emphasized time-division mul-

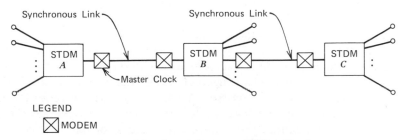

LEGEND

⊠ MODEM

Figure 7.6. A synchronous TDM network.

tiplexing equipment (and vice versa), users continue frequently to use the approach of paired STDMs for multiplexing and demultiplexing. It creates a well-defined hardware interface point between the communications controller and the network. It also enables conventional, vendor-supported teleprocessing control software to be utilized without modification or extension. The advantages arising from these two characteristics often outweigh the extra costs associated with the two-separate-box approach to time-division multiplexing.

Subsequent discussions of statistical multiplexing, packet switching, and intelligent communications networks based on minicomputers will reveal certain advantages of dynamic bandwidth sharing not available with conventional STDM. When such benefits can be coupled into networks with minimal requirements for modifications to the line control software, the user stands to achieve the best of both worlds—a flexible network and the full support of vendors supplying the teleprocessing control software.

7.3.1. Configuration Options in Cascaded STDM Networks

Consider a user with a Los Angeles CPU and numerous remote terminals in Chicago and New York. For illustration purposes, assume that the following terminal–speed combinations are required:

New York	Chicago
Two 2400 bits/sec terminals	One 2400 bits/sec terminal
One 4800 bits/sec terminal	Two 4800 bits/sec terminals
One 9600 bits/sec terminal	Two 9600 bits/sec terminals

Also assume that 19,200 and 56,000 bits/sec line speeds are available for use on the multiplexed STDM links; the problem is to connect all nine remote terminals into separate ports on the Los Angeles communications control unit. Figure 7.7 illustrates that the New York channels may be demultiplexed in either Chicago or Los Angeles. If demultiplexed in Chicago, the New York channels must be remultiplexed with the Chicago traffic onto the Chicago–Los Angeles link. This so-called drop-and-insert arrangement would provide convenient access to the New York channels in the Chicago site if such an arrangement is desirable. Also, extra STDM capacity could be used between New York and Chicago, if required. On the other hand, the Los Angeles demultiplex alternative would place more equipment in one location, providing easier access for maintenance and diagnostic functions from a centralized location.

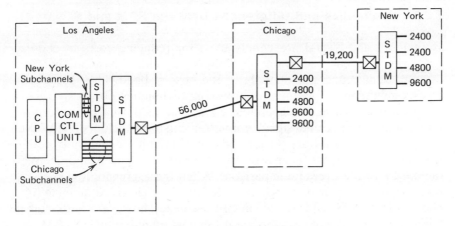

(a) Completely Centralized Demultiplex Approach

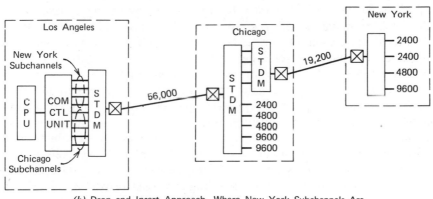

(b) Drop and Insert Approach, Where New York Subchannels Are
Available in Chicago

Figure 7.7. Configuration options in a cascaded STDM network.

The user planning a cascaded STDM network needs to consider carefully whether the flow patterns in his network are centralized or noncentralized, and how the initial STDM network layout could be affected by a need to add new channels at a future date. The strategy of performing as much demultiplexing of inbound data streams as possible at the central site appears to offer numerous advantages in centralized-flow situations. On the other hand, the drop-and-insert scheme of Figure 7.7(b) affords more flexibility in decentralized applications where the subchannels need to be directly accessible at intermediate locations in the STDM cascade.

7.3.2. Similarities and Differences between FDM and STDM

Both FDM and STDM are widely used for reducing costs in end-user networks, the cost-reduction possibilities in either case arising from often-present economies of scale in the cost of bandwidth. Meaningful cost comparisons of various multiplexing techniques obviously require that necessary mileage-independent costs such as those for line terminations, multiplexers, and signal converters also be included. However, many present tarriffs are structured so that multiplexing can produce substantial net savings, even after the costs of all required equipment are factored into the overall comparison. When the aggregate low speed bit rate for all terminals does not exceed 2000 bits/sec (give or take 10%), either FDM or STDM can probably be used; however, with current technology, FDM will probably be more cost effective than STDM, particularly when remote terminals are not clustered at a single site. Whenever a higher aggregate bit rate is required or any synchronous terminals are included in the sharing group, STDM will usually be dictated. However, in higher bit rate applications involving geographically dispersed terminal locations, an integrated blend of FDM and STDM will be the most sensible choice. Frequency-division multiplexing can span isolated terminal sites, creating traffic clusters that are then synchronously multiplexed into one or more computer sites.

Historically, the predominant usage of multiplexing has involved the derivation of low speed teletypewriter-grade channels on voice-grade lines. More recently, newer applications of STDM have appeared, particularly with the increased availability of higher speed synchronous modems, the initial availability of all digital data networks from conventional carriers, the entry of specialized carriers into the data network business, and recent provisions enabling customer-provided multiplexing equipment to be used over carrier-provided wideband links. If the costs of a multiplexed wideband link between two points can initially be justified, users may expect generally lower error rates on all derived voice-grade and low speed channels, substantially increased flexibility, and the opportunity to assign initially unused capacity at a later date without increased modem or line costs on the shared link.

These points are now illustrated in detail using specific examples. The reader is cautioned that the tariffs used in these examples are strictly for illustration purposes. Exact rates should always be obtained from the carrier. Tariffs used were in effect at the time when comparisons were made.

Example Problem 1: Comparison of FDM and TDM

Assume that a central computer located in downtown Chicago needs to provide 712 mile connections to 10 separate terminals in the same building in New York City. The terminals operate at 110 bits/sec. Determine whether individual leased lines, frequency-division multiplexed analog lines, or time-division multiplexed analog lines would be the most cost-effective networking strategy. The cost assumptions below are illustrative of typical industry prices for comparable equipment at publication time.

Cost Assumptions:

Cost of FDM equipment: $30 per month per channel end
Cost of TDM equipment: $250 per month (fixed) plus $20 per month per low speed port
Cost of modem equipment: $50 per month for 2400 bits/sec units
$100 per month for 4800 bits/sec units
$200 per month for 9600 bits/sec units
Cost of individual low speed lines—AT&T Series 1006 FDX
Cost of voice-grade lines—AT&T Series 3002 (MPL)

Option 1: Individual Low Speed Lines

Monthly Cost of Individual 110 bit/sec circuit, including signal conversion equipment

$$= \underbrace{2.023 \times 100 + 1.416 \times 150 + .811 \times 250 + .605 \times 212}$$

Mileage

$$+ \underbrace{2(36.15 + 14.45)}$$

Terminations

So the monthly cost of 10 circuits provided with individual lines = $8469.10.

Option 2: Frequency-Division Multiplexing Approach

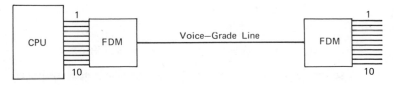

Since there are 10 FDM channel ends at each end of the voice-grade line, the FDM equipment cost is $20 \times 30 = \$600$/month. The monthly cost of the line (assuming no special conditioning) is

$$175.20 + 0.66(712 - 100) + 2 \times 25 = \$629.12$$

Hence the total cost of the FDM approach is $1229.12. This is clearly more attractive than Option 1.

Option 3: Time-Division Multiplexing Approach

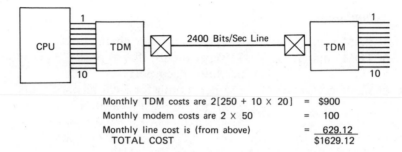

Monthly TDM costs are $2[250 + 10 \times 20]$ =   \$900
Monthly modem costs are 2×50 =   100
Monthly line cost is (from above)   =   <u>629.12</u>
      TOTAL COST   \$1629.12

Hence the FDM approach is the most attractive of the three considered.

The reader should also consider other types of approaches such as WATS, dial-up, or the packet switching networks of value-added carriers before choosing a specific configuration. However, these options would require some idea of traffic volumes and usage patterns.

Example Problem 2: Another Comparison of FDM and TDM

Assume the same problem as for Example 1 except that the number of terminals in New York is increased from 10 to 20. Assume that an individual FDM system can derive a maximum of 12 subchannels at 110 bits/sec over one voice-grade line and that the TDM system can provide 20 subchannels on a 2400 bits/sec line, 40 subchannels on a 4800 bits/sec line, and 80 subchannels of 110 bits/sec on a 9600 bits/sec line.

Option 1:

$$\text{Monthly cost} = 20 \times 840.50 = \$16,810$$

Option 2:

$$\text{Monthly cost} = 2 \times 1229.12 = \$2458.24$$

(since two separate lines and four FDM devices are now required).

Option 3:

$$\text{Monthly TDM cost} = 2[250 + (20 \times 20)] = 1300.00$$
$$\text{Monthly modem cost} = 2 \times 50 \qquad\quad = 100.00$$
$$\text{Monthly line cost} \qquad\qquad\qquad\quad = 629.12$$

$$\text{TOTAL COST} \qquad\qquad\qquad\qquad \$2029.12$$

Now the TDM approach is more favorable because of the required number of channels.

Example Problem 3: Synchronous TDM Possibilities

Assume that a Chicago computer center requires eight ports of 4800 bits/sec for connections of different synchronous terminals in a New York City regional office. Find the best way to provide the service, assuming that the following alternatives are available: (*a*) individual analog voice lines with modems, (*b*) wideband analog lines, and (*c*) digital service such as DDS (see Chapter 3 for service explanation and cost assmptions). Use the same equipment costs except that the cost of a synchronous TDM input port is assumed to be \$40/month.

Option 1: Individual Analog Lines

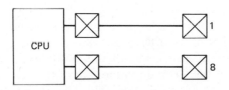

Monthly cost = 8 × (629.12 + 200) = \$6632.96

Option 2: TDM over Wideband Analog Lines

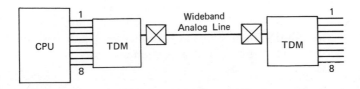

Monthly line cost of AT&T Series 8000 wideband analog lines, including signal conversion equipment,

$$= \underbrace{16.20 \times 250 + 11.40 \times 250 + 8.15 \times 212}_{\text{Mileage}} \times \underbrace{2 \times 460}_{\text{Terminations}} = \$9547.80$$

Monthly TDM cost $= 2[250 + (8 \times 40)] = \$1140$
TOTAL COST $= \$10,687.80$

Option 3: Individual Dataphone Digital Service (DDS)
          Lines at 4800 bits/sec

Monthly cost of individual 4800 bit/sec DDS line
$$= \underbrace{0.26 \times 71}_{\substack{\text{Mileage}}} + \underbrace{2 \times 20.60}_{\substack{\text{Intercity} \\ \text{link} \\ \text{termination}}} + \underbrace{2 \times 87.55}_{\substack{\text{Local} \\ \text{access} \\ \text{line}}} + \underbrace{2 \times 15.45}_{\substack{\text{Signal} \\ \text{conversion}}} = 688.64$$

Monthly cost of eight separate lines $= \$5509.12$

Option 4: Multiplexed 56,000 bits/sec Dataphone Digital Service

Monthly line cost, including signal conversion equipment,
$= 4.12 \times 712 + 2 \times 64.50 + 2 \times 206 + 2 \times 20.60 = \$3515.64$
Monthly TDM cost (from above) $= \$1140$
TOTAL COST $= \$4655.64$

Summary of Example

The best solution for this example appears to be multiplexed 56,000 bits/sec Dataphone Digital Service. However, the monthly cost savings over individual 4800 bits/sec DDS lines needs to be weighed against the fact that the reliability properties of the multiplexed network are much poorer. A failure of the TDM equipment or of the multiplexed line would cause all channels to become unavailable. The operational costs of such a catastrophic failure situation may mean that the multiplexed network is less desirable, in spite of the cost savings it offers.

The reader is also cautioned against generalizing about the relative merits of various networking approaches from this example. The conclusions here, and for other examples as well, are strongly dependent on all the cost assumptions, distances, and required numbers of channels. However, the solution techniques are quite general and are equally useful for alternative tariff structures and equipment costs.

7.4. STATISTICAL TIME-DIVISION MULTIPLEXING (STATDM)

Much of the theoretical work relating to STATDM has been done by Chu [2,5–8]. Related contributions have been made by Rudin [20], Birdsall et al. [9], Pan [10], Gordon et al. [11], and Chang [12]. Reference [30] also discusses STATDM in detail. Statistical time-division multiplexing differs from STDM in that a dedicated subchannel is not provided for each port in the sharing group. Since, under certain conditions of heavy loading, a STATDM may be incapable of accommodating all the terminals in its sharing group, statistics and queuing become important considerations. Thus it is a hybrid form of multiplexing and concentration.

The fundamental idea of STATDM is to exploit the property of STDM systems that many of the time slots in the fixed-format frames are wasted because a typical sending terminal will actually be transmitting data less than 10% of the time it is communicating with the CPU. A more detailed discussion of typical traffic arrival statistics is presented by Fuchs and Jackson [13]. As shown in Figure 7.8, STATDM dynamically allocates the time slots in a frame of data to the currently active users, reducing the fraction of wasted time slots and thereby increasing overall line utilization and throughput.

Although the diagram of Figure 7.8 illustrates addressing information being transmitted with data in each slot, it is of course not necessary to do so in cases where such a procedure could lead to excessive overhead. An alternative would be to send demultiplexing address information in a control frame only once at the beginning of each dynamic subchannel establishment. This demultiplexing rule can be dynamically updated only when subchannels are added or removed, without the need to include address information bits explicitly with the data in each slot. Another possibility is to vary the slot widths for the individual ports or to encode a control signal that tells the demultiplexer exactly which ports are idle in a given frame.

Most estimates of the exact performance improvements attainable with STATDM over STDM have to date been based on analytical studies described in certain of the references previously cited. From Chu's analytical studies, it would appear that from two to four times as many users could be accommodated on a voice-grade line as with STDM, assuming an application environment where either method could be used. In certain situations where low duty cycle terminals are serviced by a statistical multiplexer over a broadband link, the margin could be substantially greater.

The tradeoff disadvantages of statistical multiplexing are the costs of substantially more elaborate addressing and control circuitry, the need for data buffers to hold incoming messages, and the possibility of blocking and/or appreciable queuing delays under heavily loaded conditions. The references previously noted contain substantial traffic studies, investigating the relationships between such factors as traffic intensity, distribu-

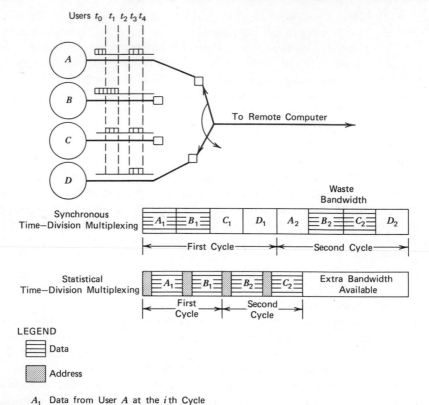

LEGEND

▤ Data

▨ Address

A_1 Data from User A at the ith Cycle

Figure 7.8. STDM contrasted with STATDM.

tions of message arrivals and lengths, queue sizes, queuing discipline, and blocking probability. To illustrate, several of the major results described in Chu [2,5–8] are now summarized.

Chu has analyzed a Markov model of a statistical multiplexer in which messages arrive at a finite-capacity multiplexer according to a batched Poisson process where the size of the batch corresponds to the length of the arriving message in characters. A unit service interval μ is the time to transmit a character on the shared line; for a synchronous line with a transmission speed of R characters/sec. $\mu = 1/R$. Message lengths are assumed to be geometrically distributed with mean $\overline{l}$, and the number of messages arriving during a unit service interval is Poisson distributed with a mean rate of λ messages every 1 sec. The buffer overflow probability is obtained from the steady-state solution to the state equations for an embedded Markov chain. The average queuing delay per message D is shown to be given by

$$D = \frac{\lambda(2 - \theta)}{2(\theta - \lambda)\theta} \quad \text{(character service times)}$$

where $\theta = 1/\bar{l}$. The buffer overflow probability is assumed to be sufficiently small that virtually all traffic arriving at the multiplexer is transmitted over the line.

At the demultiplexing end of the line, Chu has used a simulation model to estimate overflow probabilities and the following analytic relationship to describe average waiting time W_i for sending messages to the ith destination:

$$W_i = \frac{\rho_i(2\bar{l}_i - 1)}{2(1 - \rho_i)} \quad \text{(character service times)}$$

where $\bar{l}_i$ = average message length for the ith destination
λ_i = message arrival rate for the ith destination
μ_i = transmission rate for the ith destination
$\rho_i = \lambda_i \bar{l}_i / \mu$

Figure 7.9 indicates the parameters of a generalized model that may be used to evaluate design tradeoffs in configuring statistical multiplexers. It also suggests that a statistical multiplexer can perform two levels of concentration when the input terminals are not permanently connected to the input ports.

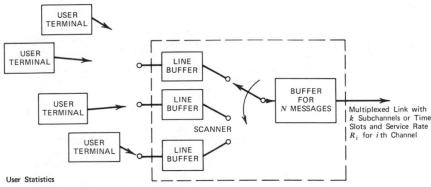

User Statistics

  Number of Terminals with Dial and Leased Line Connections
  *Calling Rate per Terminal
  *Holding Time per Terminal
  Message Arrival Distribution per Terminal
  Message Length Distribution per Terminal
  Acceptable Blocking Probability

*Not Applicable for Leased Line Ports, Since Connections are Permanent

Figure 7.9. Schematic diagram of STATDM for traffic studies.

It appears that STATDM has a promising future, particularly in applications where queuing delays are not of material concern or can be readily minimized. It is this author's conviction that statistical multiplexers will be of primary use, not in replacing STDM en masse, but in new

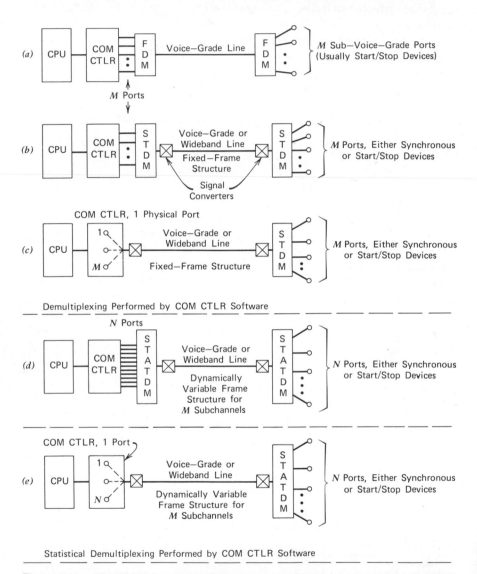

Figure 7.10.   FDM, STDM, and STATDM approaches to line sharing. In the STATDM approaches, the number of physical ports, N, connected to the sharing devices is usually larger than M, the number of subchannels created at any instant in time. M changes with time because of fluctuations in user traffic patterns.

applications involving store-and-forward message switching, loop transmission systems, system-provided error control, and so on. For example, CRT display controllers can be equipped to implement STATDM in conjunction with ARQ error control. A request for retransmission would be issued either when a data block error is detected at the receiving terminal or when the buffer area in the multiplexing control unit is full. One of the major problems is incorporating enough intelligence in STATDM to anticipate when an input line is about to become active so that proper steps may be taken to assign the next available time slots to the user in question. A related problem lies in accurately sensing when a terminal has completed its transmission so that time slots are not filled with "idle" characters. In certain applications this problem can be mitigated somewhat by having the STATDM unit track the input buffers for special end-of-message or end-of-block characters. However, this approach requires a knowledge of the terminal code format and would be of limited use in transparent text applications.

Figure 7.10 illustrates the relative equipment requirements for using FDM, STDM, and STATDM to service a remote cluster of terminals. Note that demultiplexing of inbound channels may take place either in a stand-alone box or in the communications control unit. Because the STATDM approach requires user traffic flows to be monitored anyway, the combined-function, single-box approach makes the most conceptual and economic sense. The only potential problem with the combined-function approach is the issue of communications control unit horsepower. Since STATDM requires virtually continuous tracking of the ports, an already heavily loaded communications control unit may not be able to accommodate the added STATDM function. Even with contemporary microprocessor technology, a separate STATDM unit may often be necessary at the central site.

Another substantial advantage of STATDM over STDM is its flexibility in providing different subchannel mixtures across the shared link at different times. This benefit is essentially independent of the increases in throughput resulting from statistical use of shared lines. For example, an STATDM system could easily function as an STATDM for a while and then convert automatically to operate as a conventional STDM system with different subchannel mixtures at other times.

7.5. MESSAGE AND PACKET SWITCHING CONCENTRATION

Message switching concentration (MSC) and packet switching concentration are functional extensions of statistical multiplexing involving the "multiplexing" of entire messages and fixed-length portions of long messages, respectively. They are more properly categorized as concentration techniques since a buffer queue stores entire blocks of data. Thus, to illustrate MSC, Figure 7.9 would be changed only to reflect the format of data frames transmitted over the shared link. The MSC accumulates message blocks in its buffer until one is completely assembled and the high speed line is available to transmit it. Thus the high speed line transmits variable-length frames of data with appropriate addressing and control information; all data characters in each frame are generally associated with the same source–sink terminal pair.

In most teleprocessing systems where remote concentration is suitable, messages from different users will fluctuate in length. Occasional long messages can occupy the line for prolonged periods, thereby causing other users to experience significant delays while their messages wait in the high speed line queue.

In these situations, predictable system behavior can be restored by having the concentrator chop up long user messages into shorter segments known as packets. As shown in Figure 7.11, packets are individually interleaved onto the shared link. At the receiving end of the link, the packets are sorted out and user messages reconstructed within the individual user buffer areas. As packet sizes become shorter and shorter, the performance of a packet switching concentrator begins to resemble that of the statistical multiplexer previously discussed.

Certain ancillary benefits accrue with MSC and packet switching, such as their inherent capability of performing remote line control, code conversion, error checking, and selective routine, and of implementing the most suitable type of error control on the multiplexed link. The primary disadvantages are economic in nature, and relate to the cost of the stored program computer and buffer storage usually required. A further disadvantage of MSC and packet switching relates to reliability characteristics. Since programmable computers are involved, most individual component failures will be catastrophic in the sense that the entire system becomes inoperative. The standard solution to this problem in most existing message switching networks involves the use of duplexed (paired) devices at the concentration nodes, with the redundant unit being automatically switched into operation whenever the primary fails. Although this approach provides the necessary redundancy, the attendant costs often make other line sharing schemes more cost effective in applications involving moderate traffic levels.

In large, multiuser networks, message and packet switching concentration afford certain flexibility and performance advantages over other line sharing schemes. A substantial amount of recent effort has been devoted to the development of models for predicting queuing delays and allocating channel capacity in MSC and packet networks. Some of the more sig-

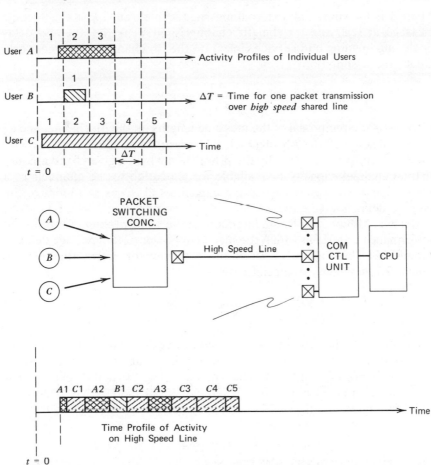

Figure 7.11. Schematic diagram of packet switching concentration.

nificant accomplishments have been made by Kleinrock [21,22]; Meister, Muller, and Rudin [23]; and Frank et al. [17]. For example, Kleinrock showed that the average message delay in a message switching network could be determined using a weighted average of the delays over all the channels of the network, given Poisson message arrivals, exponential message lengths, and other assumptions discussed in the references. Symbolically stated, the total average delay T is given by

$$T = \frac{1}{\gamma} \Sigma \lambda_i T_i \tag{7.1}$$

where γ is the sum of all external message arrival rates, λ_i is the average message arrival rate for the ith channel, and T_i is the average delay (including queuing and service times) on the ith channel of the network. Under the assumptions given,

$$T_i = \frac{1}{\mu_i C_i - \lambda_i} \qquad (7.2)$$

where μ_i is the reciprocal of the message lengths on the ith channel and C_i is the capacity of the ith channel. This result was ultimately used by Kleinrock to solve analytically the problem in which a given fixed amount of total channel capacity is available for allocation to the channels of a network and it is desired to assign capacities C_i so as to minimize the average delay T given above.

Meister, Muller, and Rudin later solved the same problem for different performance criteria in which the mean rth power of the average delay is minimized. Their approach used the following objective function, of which (7.1) is clearly a special case:

$$T^{(r)} = \sqrt[r]{\sum \frac{\lambda_i}{\gamma} T_i^{(r)}} \qquad (7.3)$$

The primary shortcoming of these and the other models developed to this point in time centers around the traffic assumptions that must be made to obtain convenient analytical results. Progress in the development of more generalized non-Poissonian/exponential models has been continual but slow.

7.6. LINE OR CIRCUIT SWITCHING

Circuit switching concentration involves a switching device that electrically bridges a group of n inputs to a group of m output links on a demand basis (n is typically from three to five times the value of m in commercial applications). Ordinarily, the input links and the output trunks to which they are switched have similar bandwidth and transmission properties. A communication channel is thus formed by the electrical concatenation of the input and output link segments within the switch. Thus no message queuing delays are introduced at the switch once a connection is established and held for the duration of a complete data transmission or voice call. When the connection is no longer needed, the corresponding trunk line is freed and made available for assignment to the next input link desiring a trunk connection. Private automatic branch exchanges

(PABXs) are examples of circuit switches. Although historically they have been used primarily in conventional voice telephony, such devices may function equally well as line switching concentrators for computer–communication applications. Devices of this type may be built inexpensively since special purpose computers and software are not required.

From a technology standpoint, the connections between inputs and outputs in a circuit switching concentrator may also be accomplished digitally, using a high speed time-division scanning mechanism. The time-division mechanism samples bits from the incoming lines at the correct scanning rate and moves them to the appropriate output trunks without delay in much the same manner as an STDM would perform. The multiple outbound channels can also be created by the formation of frames on one or more physical lines leaving the switch, indicating a further similarity with conventional STDMs. Clearly, however, this so-called TDM/circuit switch differs from a conventional STDM in the sense that the aggregate bit rate of incoming lines can generally be quite different from the aggregate bit rate of outgoing lines.

Figure 7.12 illustrates a typical use of a line switching concentrator. This illustration depicts all output trunks connected to the same device (the communications control unit), but line switching units may also function with a mixture of local terminals and remote circuits on both the input and output sides of the switch. Although not widely available at this time, future line switching units may be expected to accommodate a mixture of different (from a bandwidth standpoint) types of input and output links as well. These advanced switching units will still connect input and output links of the same type but will be able to concurrently accommodate different groups of link types, using common control hardware and software.

In the basic line switching unit illustrated in Figure 7.12, several possibilities exist for handling requests for connection to the output trunk lines. One possibility involves the servicing of incoming requests on a first-come/first-served (FCFS) basis. Connection requests arriving at the switch when all output trunks are occupied receive a busy signal and are permanently lost. The multiserver loss (blocking) model presented in References [14] and [26] may be used to relate blocking probabilities (percentage of calls rejected), the number of input and output links, holding times, and arrival rates, assuming that blocked requests are lost and incoming requests arrive at random(are Poisson). A more complex scheduling arrangement would involve incoming requests being queued when all trunks are occupied. In this situation, the no-loss queuing model discussed in References [14] , [26], and elsewhere is an appropriate vehicle for conducting detailed traffic studies.

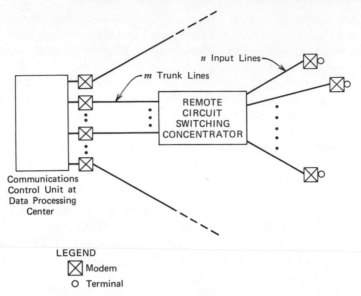

Figure 7.12. Use of circuit switching concentrator.

The application of this multiserver model to a line switching unit that holds incoming calls results in the queuing model shown in Figure 7.13. Here it is assumed that arrivals to the queuing system correspond to call requests which appear at the concentrator. Each call that arrives when one or more of the m identical trunk lines is unoccupied is serviced immediately. Calls arriving at the concentrator when all trunks are busy are queued and subsequently assigned to output trunk lines as the latter become available. Other assumptions for this particular model are that the holding time for all calls is an exponentially distributed random variable

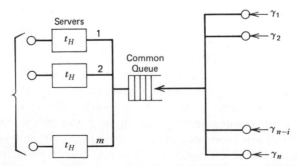

Figure 7.13. Queuing model for line switching concentrator.

with mean $\bar{t}_H$ and that calls arrive at the concentrator according to a Poisson process, where γ_i denotes the Poisson average rate of call requests from the ith terminal or source. For data communications applications, the exponential holding time assumption is satisfied by a constant-speed trunk line transmitting messages whose lengths are exponentially distributed. Calls correspond to message transmissions, each of which occupies an output trunk line for the duration of a single transmission. Finally, the model assumes that, when a trunk line becomes free after all have been busy, a call is selected from the list of those waiting on an FCFS basis.

The average traffic intensity per trunk line is given by

$$t_H \times \sum_{i=1}^{n} \frac{\gamma_i}{m}$$

and the probability P_N of there being exactly N calls in the system (either undergoing service or awaiting access to a trunk line) is given by

$$P_N = \begin{cases} \dfrac{(m\rho)^N P_0}{N!}, & \text{for } N < m \\[3ex] \dfrac{(m\rho)^N P_0}{m! \, m^{N-m}}, & \text{for } N \geq m \end{cases}$$

where

$$m\rho = \bar{t}_H \sum_{i=1}^{n} \gamma_i$$

and

$$P_0 = \frac{1}{\displaystyle\sum_{K=0}^{m-1} (m\rho)^K/K! + (m\rho)^m/(1-\rho)m!}$$

These relationships may then be used to obtain Q, the average time a call request spends both waiting for service and receiving it once a trunk is acquired:

$$Q = \bar{t}_H \left[1 - \frac{1}{m(1-\rho)} \times \sum_{k=m}^{\infty} P_k \right].$$

Curves for Q, normalized to the mean holding time t_H as a function of the

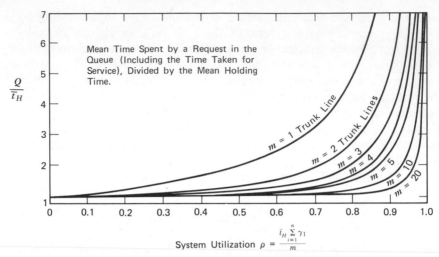

Figure 7.14. Queuing times for accessing and using a trunk line in the line switching concentrator.

number of trunk lines and average system utilization ρ, are plotted in Figure 7.14.

Problems related to the design of networks of circuit switching concentrators are considered in great detail by Benes [24] in his classic book. Similar subjects are also addressed by Rubin and Haller [25]. Since the existing voice telephone network is in effect a very large circuit switching network, the application of line concentrators in computer–communication networks is by no means a new concept. However, they have traditionally been used solely by means of PBXs already installed for voice telephone use. It would appear that special purpose line concentrators designed solely for data transmission applications are likely to become much more popular in end-user networks in the years ahead.

7.7. INVERSE MULTIPLEXING

Recently, substantial interest has developed in the application of multiplexing ideas to create wideband transmission paths using several lower speed lines in parallel.[4] Technically speaking, several independent lines are shared to create one logical path, as shown in Figure 7.15.

[4]Products employing this idea are currently offered by the Codex Corporation, Newton, Massachusetts, and by International Communications Corporation, of Miami, Florida. They are discussed in Reference [27].

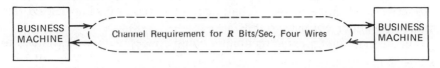

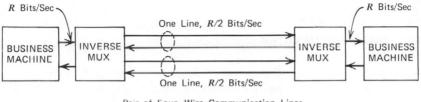

Pair of Four—Wire Communication Lines,
Each Operating at $R/2$ Bits/Sec

Figure 7.15. Inverse multiplexing example.

The economic justification for such configurations arise from peculiar pricing characteristics in common carrier tariffs, total lack of wideband service availability in some countries, lack of wideband service availability in a timely fashion, and some naturally attractive reliability properties of this inverse multiplexing scheme.

For example, assume that a user requires a 19,200 bits/sec channel between two points. In the United States, a Bell System user would probably be forced to lease a full Series 8000 channel with a maximum bit rate equivalent to 50,000 bits/sec.[5] Since he also must pay the full price of the 50,000 bits/sec link, the arrangement would hardly be economical unless the user could find application for the extra capacity.

An alternative to this wideband offering would be to use a pair of 9600 bits/sec lines connected to these inverse multiplexers at each end. Clearly, four signal converters would be required, two at each end of the individual 9600 bits/sec links. In many applications studied by this author, such a configuration has proved to be extremely economical and cost effective. An attractive reliability feature of the inverse multiplexing technique is the ease of cutting the normal operating speed in half should one of the leased lines fail. Another way of viewing this feature is that the user is able to employ the capacity of both a regular line and a backup line in normal circumstances. Only if one should fail must he cut back to single-line operation. This philosophy is a conceptually and practically

[5]Typical 1976 prices for AT&T Series 8000 channels may be found in Chapter 3.

attractive alternative to the archaic idea of letting a backup leased line stand idle under normal circumstances.

The inverse multiplexing technique could conceptually be extended to provide R bits/sec, using links individually operating at R/N bits/sec, although the application benefits of such a configuration may not be as significant or apparent as in the specific case of two parallel lines (where $N=2$).

7.8. TYPICAL NETWORK CONFIGURATIONS INVOLVING SHARING DEVICES

Having completed the discussion of individual line sharing devices, we now consider some typical network configuration problems involving sharing devices. No new devices are introduced here; rather, the objective is to tie previous material together, using several examples. The five examples presented here involve synchronous time-division multiplexing in four instances and a packet switching concentration situation in the other. For purposes of simplicity and clarity, the time-division multiplexer examples will be illustrated using split-stream modems which combine the STDM and signal conversion function. The concepts noted here are equally valid, however, in situations where stand-alone STDM systems are required instead of split-stream modems.

Case 1. Computer in Los Angeles, 2400 bits/sec terminal in Chicago for remote job entry (RJE), 2400 bits/sec terminal in Chicago for data collection, and 4800 bits/sec terminal in Chicago for inquiry response. Assume that all terminals are on same customer site and that software constraints will not permit different devices to be multipointed on a line.

Solution. For the solution see Figure 7.16. The split-stream modems operating at 9600 bits/sec provide three functionally independent subchannels to the remote terminals. An interesting feature of contemporary split-stream equipment is its ability to be operated in several modes should the multiplexer mixture need to be changed from one time of day to another. For example, the user's inquiry application may not require support after 5:00 P.M. local time in Chicago, whereas the other two terminals need continuing connections. By switching to another mode, either of the following multiplexing possibilities could be achieved: 7200 bits/sec +2400 bits/sec or 4800 bits/sec +4800 bits/sec. Such flexibility should be an important requirement for users planning networks with multiplexing equipment.

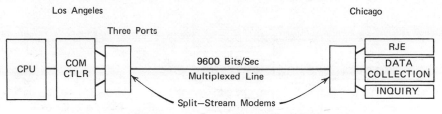

Figure 7.16. Example network for Case 1.

Case 2. Same problem as in Case 1, except that the RJE terminal is moved to New York.

Solution.

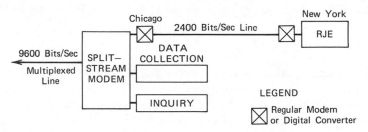

Case 3. Same problem as in Case 1, except that one more inquiry terminal in New York is to share the inquiry subchannel with the Chicago inquiry terminal.

Solution. In this configuration of Figure 7.17, it is assumed that the inquiry terminals are polled on a single port from the Los Angeles computer site. The computer views these inquiry terminals as remote drops on a multipoint line. Note that three 4800 bits/sec modems are required, even though the Chicago inquiry station is on the same customer location premises as the split-stream modem. Another alternative, the *channel remoting* arrangement employing the *digital bridge* discussed in Chapter 2, would eliminate the need for one of the remote 4800 bits/sec modems. It is shown in Figure 7.18. Some alternative names used for this digital bridge are *modem sharing unit, modem sharing device, modem contention unit, port contention unit, port sharing unit,* and *port sharing device.*

Case 4. Computer in Los Angeles, 2400 bits/sec RJE terminal in New York, 2400 bits/sec data collection terminal in Chicago, 4800 bits/sec inquiry terminal in Chicago, and 4800 bits/sec inquiry terminal in New

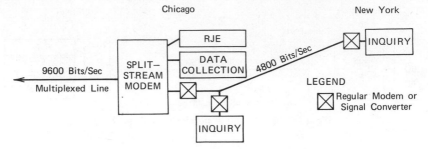

Figure 7.17. Example network for Case 3.

York. Assume that the RJE and data collection terminals cannot be multipointed on the same subchannel because of software restrictions in the main CPU. The inquiry stations may, however, be multipointed.

Solution. See Figure 7.19.

Case 5. Assume that a packet switching concentrator is to be used in Chicago to consolidate numerous kinds of traffic from other locations in the eastern United States. As before, the central computer is in Los Angeles. The example assumes a concentrator with polling capability, and the reduction of all traffic to packets before transmission over the high speed line to Los Angeles. The communications control unit in Los Angeles will collect the packets, sort them out, and deposit them in the correct buffer areas. The illustration of Figure 7.20 shows a broad mixture of line types feeding into the packet switching concentrator. It also illustrates two alternative strategies for handling the second-stage STDM lines. In one case a separate STDM at the concentrator site demultiplexes incoming data. In the other, demultiplexing is performed within the concentrator.

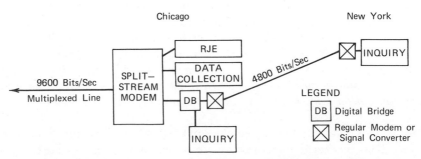

Figure 7.18. Solution for Case 3 employing digital bridge in Chicago.

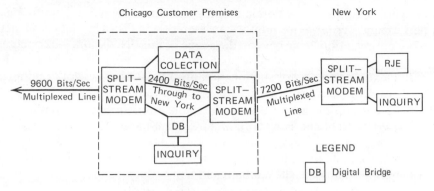

Figure 7.19. Solution for Case 4.

7.9. POSITIONING REMOTE MULTIPLEXERS AND CONCENTRATORS

It has previously been noted that the primary motivation for using multiplexing and concentration techniques is the reduction of total network costs. Obviously, the determination of the most suitable techniques and locations of remote devices to accomplish the sharing constitutes an important systems design problem that is closely related to the subject of

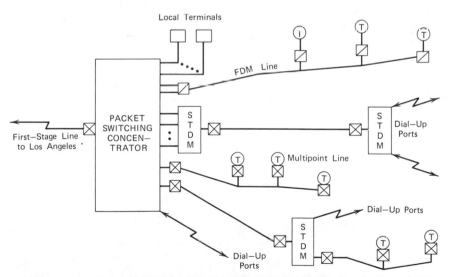

Figure 7.20. Example concentrator configuration illustrating termination of different types of second-stage lines.

network optimization, wherein topology, channel capacities, traffic, and performance criteria are jointly considered [15–17]. The details of network optimization being beyond the scope of this discussion, we conclude with a brief discussion of how such procedures may be applied to the multiplexer–concentrator site-location problem. Other network optimization problems are discussed in a paper by Frank and Chou [29].

Different approaches to the site-location problem have recently been proposed by Bahl and Tang [18], McGregor and Shen [28], and Doll et al. [19]. The Bahl and Tang paper describes a heuristic approach in which remote terminals are initially connected to many remote concentrators. All possible candidate sites initially contain concentrators. The algorithm removes a link between a concentrator and a remote terminal at each step until finally no more can be removed. It allows concentrators to die a graceful death instead of a violent one, as in alternative procedures. McGregor and Shen apply conventional operations research ideas for site-location positioning to the concentrator positioning problem. Doll et al. describe a heuristic interactive procedure that includes the topology between terminals and concentrators as a design variable. The essence of this procedure and the results of its application to a specific example are now summarized.

It is assumed that all remote terminal sites, central processing sites, and candidate sites for the multiplexers or concentrators to be positioned are given as inputs. The design procedure is based on the premise that remote line sharing devices will not be used unless they produce net cost savings in comparison to the best network without any multiplexers or concen-

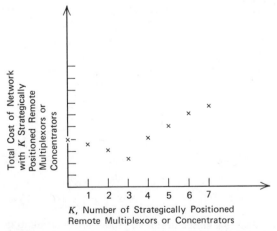

Figure 7.21. Typical cost curve of network with multiplexers of concentrators.

trators. Using an exhaustive search procedure, it effectively "finds" the best location for a first multiplexer. Then, assuming that a multiplexer exists at this site, it determines at which of the remaining candidate sites the second multiplexer should be positioned. The procedure is continued for as many iterations as desired, each subsequent iteration picking the best remaining site, on the assumption that any previously selected location will not be reconsidered. This restriction is currently imposed in the interest of computational feasibility and in order that topology can be considered as a variable. Research on other, possibly less restrictive variations of this theme is continuing.

Practical design experience to date has failed to produce any situations where manual improvements to the heuristically obtained solutions were possible, although no claim to true optimality is being made. Similarly, the use of this approach suggests that the cost of a network using multiplexers or concentrators tends to be a J-shaped function of the number of devices used, as shown in Figure 7.21. (In some networks, of course, it may cost more to use one multiplexer or concentrator than none.) The desired number of devices is given by the value of K in Figure 7.21 for which the total cost of the network is minimized. The geographic locations of these devices are also directly determined at consecutive steps in the iterations of the site selection routine.

Consider a nationwide network with terminal locations as shown in Figure 7.22 and a single computer center located in Chicago. It is assumed that the computer center in Chicago is to be fed by an unknown number (≤ 5) of remote STDMs and/or regionally positioned terminals with leased

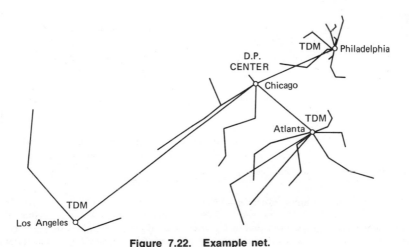

Figure 7.22. Example net.

Table 7.1. Results of Design Example for Varying Numbers of Remote STDMs

Number of STDMs K	Best Sites for Multiplexers	Monthly Cost of Network ($)
0		39,100
1	Los Angeles	35,200
2	Los Angeles, Philadelphia	32,400
3	Los Angeles, Philadelphia, Atlanta	31,700

point-to-point or multipoint lines.[6] We consider five possible sites for the placement of these remote STDMs—Atlanta, Los Angeles, Denver, New York, and Philadelphia.

Table 7.1 shows that Los Angeles is found to be the best site for the first STDM. Then, if Los Angeles is assumed as a fixed location for a multiplexer, Philadelphia is found to be the best of the remaining four sites for the second STDM. Finally, a third multiplexer is positioned at Atlanta, yielding total net savings of about 18%. The complete network configuration containing three STDMs is illustrated in Figure 7.22. Proportionately greater savings could reasonably be expected in applications involving relatively more terminals at substantial distances from the CPU site.

REFERENCES

1. H. Rudin, Jr., "Data Transmission: A Direction for Future Development," *IEEE Spectrum,* Vol. 7, February 1970, pp. 79–85.
2. W. W. Chu, "Design Considerations of Statistical Multiplexors," *Proceedings of First ACM Symposium Probl. Optimization Data Commun. Syst.* (Pine Mountain, Ga.), October 1969.
3. D. R. Doll, "The Optimal Assigmment of Subchannel Capacity in Multiplexed Data Communication Networks," *Proceedings of Third Hawaii International Conference on Systems Science,* Western Periodicals Co., January 1970.
4. D. R. Doll, "The Design of Optimal Synchronous Time Division Multiplexors," *Proceedings of 1971 International Communications Conference* (Montreal, Canada), June 1971.

[6]In the example, all links, excepting those from STDMs to the CPU, were costed using typical tariff rates for 150 bits/sec service. The multiplexed links were assumed to be conditioned voice-grade lines driven by commercially available modems. Commercially available STDMs having monthly rentals of $500 plus $30 for each low speed line termination were (arbitrarily) assumed in the cost calculations.

5. W. W. Chu, "Demultiplexing Considerations for Statistical Multiplexers," *Proceedings of Second ACM Symposium Probl. Optimization Data Commun. Syst.* (Palo Alto, Calif.), October 1971.

6. W. W. Chu, "Selection of Optimal Transmission Rate for Statistical Multiplexors," *Proceedings of IEEE International Conference on Communications* (San Francisco, Calif., June 8–10), 1971.

7. W. W. Chu, "Buffer Behavior for Batch Poisson Arrivals and Single Constant Output," *IEEE Transactions Communication Technology on* Vol. COM, 18, October 1970, pp. 613–618.

8. W. W. Chu, "Dynamic Buffer Management for Computer Communications," *Proceedings of Third ACM Data Communications Symposium* (Tampa, Fla., November 1973), pp. 68–72.

9. T. G. Birdsall et al., "Analysis of Asynchronous Time Multiplexing of Speech Sources," *IRE Transactions on Communication Systems,* Vol. CS-10, December 1962, pp. 390–397.

10. J. W. Pan, "An Approach to Asynchronous Time Division Communications Network Design," *Proceedings of IEEE International Conference on Communications* (San Francisco, Calif., June 8–10), 1971.

11. T. H. Gordon et al., "Design and Performance of a Statistical Multiplexer," *Proceedings of IEEE International Conference on Communications* (San Francisco, Calif., June 8–10), 1971.

12. J. H. Chang, "Comparison of Synchronous and Asynchronous Time Division Multiplexing Techniques," *Proceedings of IEEE International Conference on Communications* (San Francisco, Calif., June 8–10), 1971.

13. E. Fuchs and P. Jackson, "Estimates of Distributions of Random Variables for Certain Computer Communication Traffic Models," *Communications of the ACM,* Vol. 13, December 1970.

14. *Analysis of Some Queuing Models in Real Time Systems,* IBM Manual F20-0007-0, IDM Corp., Poughkeepsie, N.Y., 1965.

15. L. R. Esau and K. C. Williams, "On Teleprocessing Network Design—A Method for Approximating the Optimal Network," IBM Systems Journal, Vol. 5, 1966.

16. D. R. Doll, "Topology and Transmission Rate Considerations in the Design of Centralized Computer–Communication Networks," *IEEE Transactions on Communication Technology,* Vol. COM-19, June 1971, pp. 339–344.

17. H. Frank, I. T. Frisch, W. Chou, and R. Van Slyke, "Optimal Design of Centralized Computer Networks," *Proceedings of the 1970 IEEE International Conference on Communications* (San Francisco, Calif., June 8–10), Vol. 1, pp. 19–1 to 19–10.

18. L. R. Bahl and D. T. Tang, "Optimization of Concentrator Locations in Teleprocessing Networks," presented at P.I.B. International Symposium XXII on Computer–Communication Networks and Teletraffic, Brooklyn, N.Y., April 1972.

19. D. R. Doll, M. Frazier, G. Runner, and R. See, "The Communication Network Configurator," *Raytheon Data Systems Application Manual,* Norwood, Mass., January 1972.

20. H. Rudin, Jr., "Performance of Simple Multiplexer-Concentrator for Data Communication," *IEEE Transactions on Communication Technology,* Vol. COM-19, April 1971, pp. 178–187.

21. L. Kleinrock, *Communication Nets—Stochastic Message Flow and Delay,* McGraw-Hill, New York, 1964.

22. L. Kleinrock, "Analytic and Simulation Methods in Computer Network Design," *1970 Spring Joint Computer Conference,* AFIPS Conference Proceedings, Vol. 33, Spartan, Washington, D.C., 1970, pp. 569–579.

23. B. Meister, H. R. Muller, and H. R. Rudin, "Optimization of a New Model for Message Switchng Networks," *Proceedings of 1971 International Communications Conference* (Montreal, Canada), pp. 39–16 to 39–21.

24. V. Benes, *Mathematical Theory of Connecting Networks and Telephone Traffic,* Academic Press, New York, 1965.

25. M. Rubin and C. Haller, *Communication Switching Systems,* Reinhold, New York, 1966.

26. A. O. Allen, "Elements of Queuing Theory for Systems Design," *IBM Systems Journal,* Vol. 14, No. 2, 1975, pp. 161–187.

27. G. Held, "Wideband Substitutes Offer Flexibility and Backup at Lower Prices," *Data Communications,* Vol. 4, No. 5, 1975, McGraw-Hill, New York.

28. P. McGregor and D. Shen, "Locating Concentration Points in Data Communication Networking," *Proceedings of Fourth ACM Data Communications Symposium* (Quebec City, Canada), October 1975.

29. H. Frank and W. Chou, "Topological Optimization of Computer Networks," *Proceedings of the IEEE,* Vol. 60, No. 11, November 1972.

30. R. Sarch, "Special Report—What Intelligent Time-division Multiplexers Offer," *Data Communications,* Vol 6., No. 7, 1977, McGraw-Hill, New York.

31. D. R. Doll, "Multiplexing and Concentration," *Proceedings of the IEEE,* Vol. 60, No. 11, November 1972.

EIGHT

LINE CONTROL PROCEDURES, NETWORK PROTOCOLS, AND CONTROL SOFTWARE

Since the great majority of contemporary data communications applications involve electronic machines as the sources and/or sinks for the information being transmitted, it is necessary that standard procedures and conventions govern the following:

1. Call establishing or connection.

2. Terminal accesses to a line.

3. Message blocking and format organization.

4. Acknowledgment signaling for handshaking and error control.

5. Line turnaround procedures.

6. Character synchronization between terminals.

7. Escape, interrupt, and disconnect activities.

To speak of these functions is to include all the purposes of line control (see Figure 8.1). Such procedures are also referred to throughout the industry as *communication line formats, conventions, line protocols,* or *line disciplines.* Regardless of the descriptive term used, their objective is to provide for the *systematic, unambiguous, orderly, reliable, and generally automatic* use of communication lines by electronic data processing equipment of all types.

Note that control procedures cover all steps and actions that must be taken to effect an information transfer, including all preliminary steps before the actual data transfer as well as all final signaling steps that effectively sever a connection. In practical applications these functions

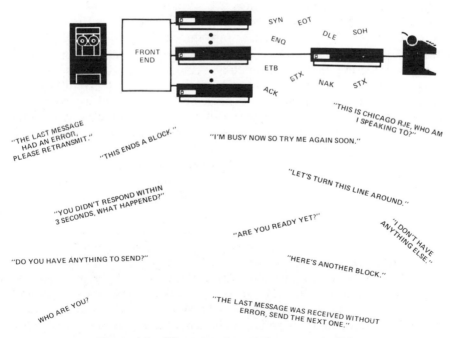

Figure 8.1. Why control procedures are needed.

are accomplished via an integrated blend of hardware, software, and sometimes human resources. This chapter first covers the functional aspects of the main approaches to line control for point-to-point, multipoint, and looped lines. Discussed next are the specific techniques whereby control procedures are used for message formatting, character synchronization, acknowledgment signaling, escape, disconnection, and turning links around. These points are first illustrated using a well-known half-duplex protocol, the Binary Synchronous Communications (BSC) protocol, as an example. Then some limitations of BSC-like protocols are cited and used to justify the need for the development of advanced data communications control procedures like IBM's Synchronous Data Link Control (SDLC), High Level Data Link Control (HDLC), and Digital's Data Communications Message Protocol (DDCMP).

After these discussions of approaches to *line control,* higher order concerns of *path control* and complete *network control* are introduced. Networks employing distributed intelligence for communications control require unified strategies for creating and managing logical paths or channels through multiple transmission stages. These ideas have been emerging recently as major worldwide suppliers of intelligent network products and services reveal their architectural philosophies for networking.

Investments in such architectures are so immense that such protocols can be expected to remain in the industry for many years to come. For example, IBM Corporation has introduced its unified networking strategy, known as *System Network Architecture* (SNA), whereas Digital Equipment Corporation has unveiled its standard approach, the *DECNET* protocol. Both philosophical approaches are examined to give the reader insight into the network control strategies being espoused by two of the world's major networking suppliers. Of course, it should be noted that most other vendors have also announced plans to develop similar such network architectures.

Other organizations offering intelligent network products and services, including the domestic value-added carriers (see Chapter 3) and certain common carrier organizations in other countries, have developed similar network control strategies. Most of the common carrier strategies are designed around some form of the packet switching technique introduced in Chapter 7. In this chapter, the extended application of packet switching to complete networks will be considered. To complete the discussion of networking approaches, the alternative strategies employing dynamic time-division multiplexing (TDM) are introduced. The advantages and disadvantages of packet switching and TDM approaches are cited to note the application situations in which each technique will be of greatest value and benefit for the network user and supplier.

Since security is a vital network control function to be considered in selecting a sensible networking strategy, major approaches to providing access security and security for in-transit data are briefly discussed. The chapter concludes with a presentation of the control software philosophy of current-generation computer systems. The roles of host-resident *tele-communications control software and network control software* outside the CPU are portrayed, along with their interface to *user-written applications programs* and *operating systems programs.* Sometimes known as *telecommunications access methods,* these communications control programs perform the bulk of line control and network control activity; they are intended to isolate the applications programmer and user from the need to know specific details about the network layout and its control.

8.1. APPROACHES TO CONTROLLING ACCESS TO A LINE

In teleprocessing networks involving multiple terminals and lines, efficient system operation requires some type of discipline or control for the access and utilization of shared network resources such as ports and lines. The most suitable approach will obviously depend on which type of communication line configuration (switched point-to-point, dedicated point-to-point, multipoint, or loop) is being utilized. Nonetheless, there are several general categories of control which can be adapted to each of these application environments, depending on traffic levels, response time requirements, and other factors. These alternatives range from virtually no control (contention-based systems) to strong centralized control methods such as polling by a master station on the line.

8.1.1. Contention

The simplest type of line control is known as *contention.* With contention control, the terminals effectively compete for access to the line. On multipoint lines the effect of contention is similar to that of sharing a party line telephone. If a terminal with a message to send requests an unoccupied line, transmission of the message proceeds. If the line is busy, the terminal must wait until the line becomes free. The communication control program in the main computer may build up a queue of output service requests by remote terminals and subsequently fill these either on a first-come/first-serve basis or according to a prescribed sequence. Contention is relatively uncontrolled because individual terminals can tie up a line for lengthy periods of time even if they are not actually transmitting data. Hence contention is not very effective for heavily loaded multipoint line networks like those typically used within commercial organizations (where polling or some other technique is more suitable).

A form of contention control is widely utilized, however, as shown in Figure 8.2, to govern access to remote ports of time sharing/computer service networks. Here, since the terminals usually correspond to customers who pay for their use of the network and the computer, there is no need to limit their usage or holding times. The simplicity of contention control in which customers contend or compete for the dial-up ports into a distant-city multiplexor, coupled with the impracticality of polling schemes in these applications, makes contention the preferred approach. Contention is also often used on point-to-point links (dial-up or leased) between two compatible business machines, either of which is capable of initiating a message transfer. The station desiring to transmit sends a special initialization or request sequence, which is received by the other. The receiving station replies that it is ready to receive or that it cannot receive or that it temporarily cannot receive. To avoid problems associated with simultaneous contention requests, one of the two stations is usually designated as the master. It ignores all contention request messages from the other end when it is attempting to seize the line.

Another application area where the contention approach has been successfully utilized involves a satellite channel, such as the one shown in Figure 8.3, which is in use at the University of Hawaii. Here the receiver portion of the satellite is contended for by any of the remote terminal consoles on a first-come/first-served basis. If two terminals happen to activate the receiver simultaneously, as shown in Figure 8.4, built-in detection and retransmission error control procedures will cause their retransmission after a certain time interval. A key requirement for the design of this system is that different terminals wait for different time intervals before attempting retransmission. Without this feature, an interlock could well develop that would cause a repetitive occurrence of the interference on successive attempts at retransmission. This contention scheme was developed because polling procedures would be very time consuming and inefficient on the long-propagation-delay satellite channel and because the capacity of the channel is sufficiently large (24,000 bits/sec) that no user terminal would be likely to occupy the channel for prolonged periods of time. Additional details about the Aloha system at Hawaii may be found in Reference [1].

Contention types of control can also be employed in loop transmission configurations if certain restrictions are imposed on the maximum length of time a station can seize the line. For example, in the configuration of Figure 8.5, the loop may be organized into groups of time slots (call them *frames*) which can be accessed on a demand basis by remote stations

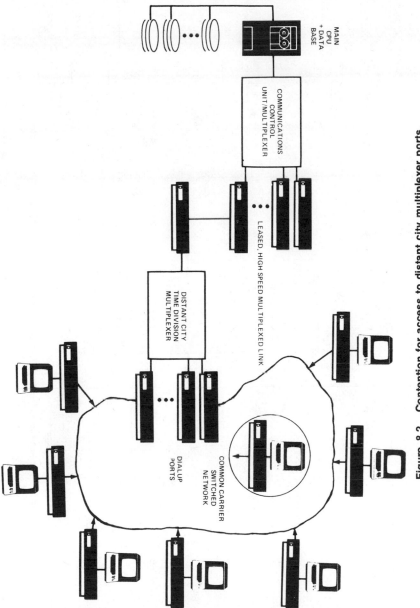

Figure 8.2. Contention for access to distant city multiplexer ports.

MAIN
CPU
+ DATA
BASE

COMMUNICATIONS
CONTROL
UNIT/MULTIPLEXER

LEASED, HIGH SPEED MULTIPLEXED LINK

DISTANT CITY
TIME DIVISION
MULTIPLEXER

DIALUP
PORTS

COMMON CARRIER
SWITCHED
NETWORK

351

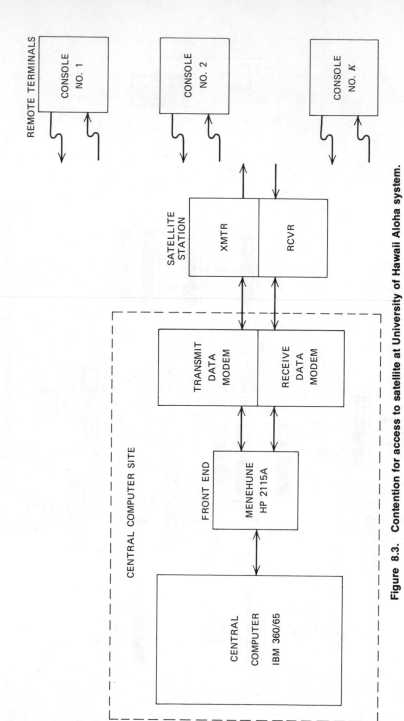

Figure 8.3. Contention for access to satellite at University of Hawaii Aloha system.

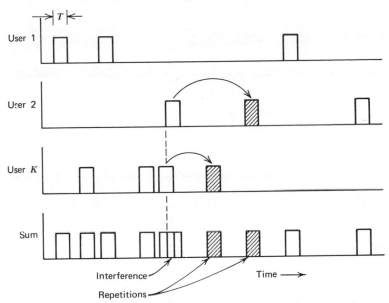

Figure 8.4. Time profile of satellite channel activity in Aloha system.

wishing to send messages back to the loop controller (or to other stations on the loop). Each frame contains an occupancy tag and the destination address of any message contained within that frame. As the frames circulate continuously around the loop, each station continuously monitors them in search of its own address. If an address matchup is found, the content of the frame is removed and the occupancy tag changed back to empty. Stations wishing to send data merely wait for the next available frame that is not occupied and load the message to be transmitted, along with the address of the destination location on the loop. An important requirement for the efficient operation of the loop is that no station be permitted to seize more than a certain number of consecutive frames; otherwise some stations further around the loop could be prevented from obtaining access to the line for prolonged periods of time.

In summary, contention procedures may be desirable because they impose minimal overhead requirements on the line control mechanism. They work quite well in situations where facility utilizations are low, and in some cases are the only viable control alternative. Line protocols traditionally used in commercial systems have generally not supported the operation of contention control. However, the advanced procedures like SDLC which are just now becoming available recognize the impor-

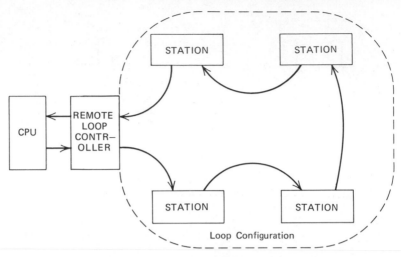

Figure 8.5. Loop communications configuration.

tance of contention control; they permit lines to be controlled in this fashion if the user desires.

8.1.2. Polling

Polling procedures are used mainly on multipoint lines, although some applications involving dial-up and loop lines also employ variations of polling techniques. There are two primary types of multipoint line polling: roll call polling and hub polling.

Roll call polling, which is far more prevalent, involves a central station on the line selectively querying each remote station, according to a predetermined sequence, to learn whether it has anything to send. If a station has nothing to send, it responds with a "nothing-to-send" reply code, as shown in Figure 8.6. Otherwise the pending message is transmitted back to the central station before the next station is polled; this activity is shown in the timing diagram of Figure 8.7. Polling is usually performed under the control of vendor-provided software, the list of station addresses being modifiable to suit the application. Each station on a multipoint line has a unique address and may respond only to polls preceded by this address code. (Group addresses are possible if it is desired to broadcast a common message to more than one station on the line.) The order and relative frequency of address entries in the polling list determine the sequence in which polls are made. With this approach the frequency of polling may be varied or changed via software modification

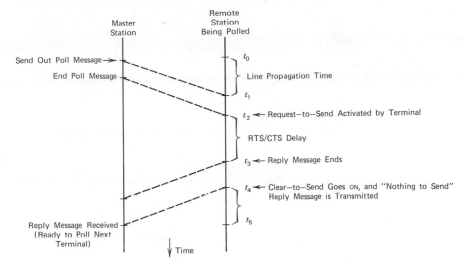

Total time to poll terminal with nothing to send: T_N

$T_N = t_1 - t_0 + t_{poll} + t_{rts\text{-}cts} + t_{reply} + t_5 - t_4$

where $t_1 - t_0$ = forward line propagation time

t_{poll} = transmission time for the poll message = $t_2 - t_1$

$t_{rts\text{-}cts}$ = remote modem synchronization time = $t_3 - t_2$

t_{reply} = transmission time for the reply message = $t_4 - t_3$

$t_5 - t_4$ = reverse line propagation time

Figure 8.6. Timing diagram for polling a terminal with nothing to send.

of the entries in the poll table. For example, to poll one station twice as frequently, its address is merely inserted twice as often in the poll list. In systems where the peak load traffic distribution varies with the time of day, the polling list entries may be changed dynamically, so that the heaviest volume stations can be polled more frequently throughout the day, even though the load distribution changes.

Specific poll refers to roll call polling activity in which both station addresses and device addresses are used in the solicitation. By contrast, *general poll* describes the solicitation of a station, without any specific designation of a particular device attached to it. A general poll issued to a station will invite *any* device with a pending message to access the line.

Hub polling is an alternative to roll call approaches that generates fewer control characters and less overhead time on the line, but requires special signal conversion devices and modifications to the station equipment. As shown in Figure 8.8, if used on a multipoint line, it involves a logical superposition of a regular multipoint line with a looped control channel which passes a single poll message from one station to the next. Each

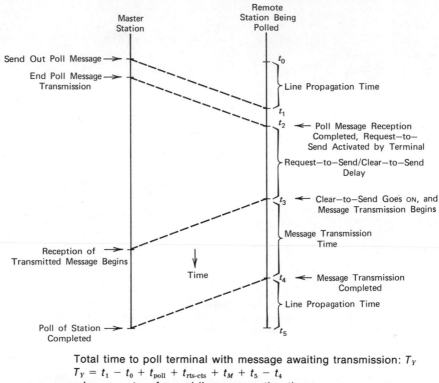

Total time to poll terminal with message awaiting transmission: T_Y

$T_Y = t_1 - t_0 + t_{poll} + t_{rts\text{-}cts} + t_M + t_5 - t_4$

where $t_1 - t_0$ = forward line propagation time

t_{poll} = transmission time for poll message = $t_2 - t_1$

$t_{rts\text{-}cts}$ = remote modem synchronization time = $t_3 - t_2$

t_M = message transmission time = $t_4 - t_3$

$t_5 - t_4$ = reverse line propagation time

Figure 8.7.   Timing diagram for polling a terminal with message to send.

remote station, upon receiving the poll, sends any pending data messages back to the central station over the return data channel and then passes the poll message to the next station down the line.

The key advantage of hub polling is the elimination of roll call polling's out-and-back transmission scenarios for each terminal solicitation. The disadvantages are related to the reliability properties of the control loop and the special hardware modifications required both inside the common carrier network and at the user's premises. With hub polling, response times can be improved noticeably and/or cost savings effected by allowing more stations to share a given line. Many airline reservations networks use hub polling for these reasons [2].

A variation of hub polling is also employed in controlling loops. In

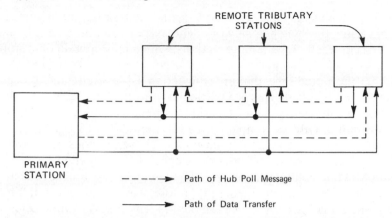

REMOTE TRIBUTARY
STATIONS

PRIMARY
STATION

– – – – ▸ Path of Hub Poll Message

──────▸ Path of Data Transfer

Figure 8.8. Schematic diagram of multipoint line, controlled by using hub polling.
In many hub polling systems the control signal path and message transfer path are
provided over the same wire pair, using special frequency splitting modems.

contrast with the multipoint layout of Figure 8.8, where there are separate
data and control paths, the loop system involves only a single path, over
which control signals and data messages are interleaved in time-division
fashion. One polling control message can be circulated from station to
station. A station having a message to send holds the poll message,
deposits the data characters to be transmitted onto the loop, and finally
reinserts the poll message onto the loop after all data characters have
been sent.

Still another variation of the hub polling approach would be to circulate
the poll message completely around the loop to find out which stations
have messages awaiting transmission. Then, on a second traversal, access
to the line would be given to each terminal that had placed a reservation
during the previous solicitation cycle. This approach would permit a
quasi-scheduled usage of the line with moderate amounts of control
overhead. A comprehensive discussion of alternative polling approaches
for loop control may be found in Reference [3].

As previously noted, polling is usually more suitable for multipoint line
control than is contention, mainly because tight control of line usage is
essential for efficient performance. Polling systems can easily incorporate
multilevel priority schemes, the higher priority terminals being polled
with greater regularity. One final disadvantage of polling is that terminals
cannot send messages at any time, but can do so only when queried. This
is the reason why polling is seldom used in applications where terminal
users (e.g., a computer service firm's customers) require an immediate
and continuing connection to the distant computer.

Polling schemes may also be used to gather data from multiple remote locations using the switched network. The master computer station selectively dials up each of the remote stations, which may contain data stored on magnetic tape, disc, paper tape, and other media. After the data have all been transmitted, the dial-up connection is severed, and the next remote station is called. This is a particularly useful technique for collecting sales and inventory data at periodic intervals throughout the day, week, or month. Often a company uses full-period WATS lines primarily for voice communications at certain hours. These facilities may be used for dial-up polling during off-hours at negligible incremental cost.

Multipoint line polling may be performed at any of several speeds up to and including 4800 bits/sec. Generally, a four-wire communication line is used, as shown in Figure 8.9.[1] All remote modem receiver subsystems are permanently synchronized to the master station modem transmitter. A remote station becomes an active transmitter only after its station address has been recognized on a poll message. Polling applications at speeds faster than 4800 bits/sec are infrequent because modem synchronization delays are so significant that user response times would be materially degraded.

Most real-time polling systems are designed so that each remote station is polled at regular intervals, often milliseconds or seconds in duration. The timing diagrams of Figures 8.6 and 8.7 illustrate how one would compute polling times for stations with and without messages to send, respectively. The total polling time to cycle completely through all stations on a line may be determined by adding the times taken for all stations, including those *with* messages awaiting transmission and those having *no* messages waiting to be sent. Properly designed polling systems must be capable of accepting all messages awaiting transmission during peak traffic periods without undue delays. It is clear from Figure 8.6 and 8.7 that line propagation time, message length, and modem synchronization times all directly influence poll cycle time, and hence the user response time.

8.1.3. Selection Procedures

Polling procedures, in summary, are used to solicit input from remote stations. A complementary function known as *selecting* is used to accomplish output transmission to remote stations over various types of lines. The selecting process may be accomplished in two basic ways. The first

---

[1]In some cases, two-wire lines are used. However, line efficiency and responsiveness are not as good as in four-wire systems.

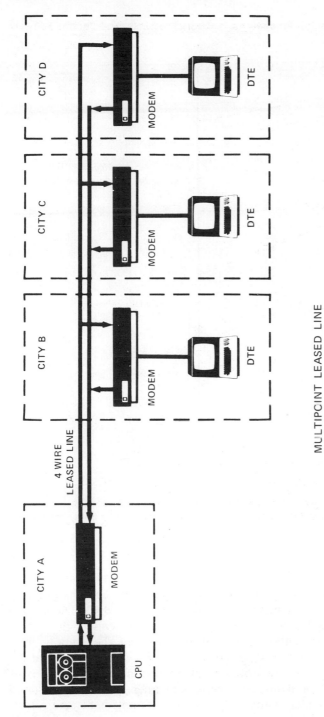

CITY D

CITY C

CITY B

MODEM

MODEM

MODEM

DTE

DTE

DTE

CITY A

MODEM

CPU

4 WIRE
LEASED LINE

A

B

C

D

MULTIPCINT LEASED LINE

Figure 8.9. Conventional polled multipoint line.

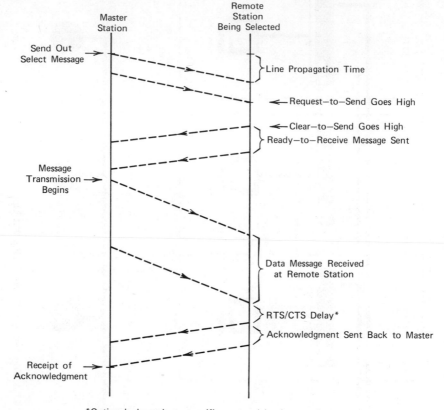

Send Out
Select Message →

Line Propagation Time

←— Request—to—Send Goes High

←— Clear—to—Send Goes High
Ready—to—Receive Message Sent

Message
Transmission →
Begins

Data Message Received
at Remote Station

RTS/CTS Delay*

Acknowledgment Sent Back to Master

Receipt of →
Acknowledgment

Master
Station

Remote
Station
Being Selected

*Optional; depends on specific protocol implementation.
Usually will not be required if master station transmits
outbound message immediately after receipt of the
Ready-to-Receive message

**Figure 8.10. Timing diagram for selecting a remote station to send it a message.
Note that four line propagations and one modem synchronization delay are usually
involved.**

and more traditional approach known as *select-hold* involves a two-step
process wherein a remote station is asked to verify its ability to receive
before any messages are sent to it, as shown in Figure 8.10. The second
approach, sometimes known as *fast-select,* involves sending the output
message immediately, without an a priori query of the station. This
fast-select approach is obviously more efficient in using the line, but the
error recovery procedures are more complicated. Reference [4] discusses
the various selecting approaches in a general manner. As an illustration of
these concepts, the widely known BSC protocol implements the *select-*

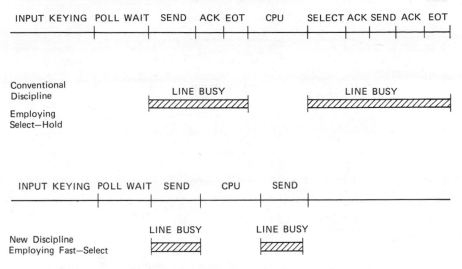

See Figure 8–14 for additional discussion of EOT character and its uses

Figure 8.11. Inquiry/response scenario, multipoint polled line.

hold approach of Figure 8.11, whereas newer protocols like SDLC enable the fast-select output procedure of Figure 8.11 to be used. References [5] through [12] discuss BSC and SDLC procedures in detail and should be consulted by the reader interested in additional background material on these protocols. These topics are also discussed in subsequent sections of this chapter.

8.2. GENERAL FUNCTIONS OF LINE CONTROL PROCEDURES

In this section, the general functions of line protocols are discussed without considering the specific code sequences used for their implementation in a specific protocol. (In the next sections, specific examples of BSC and SDLC implementations of these functions are presented.) Here we identify the main modes or phases of communication between machines and then discuss the control functions that must be performed in each mode.

As a point of departure, the contrasts between device control functions and data link control functions shown in Figure 8.12 are noted. (The discussion here is concerned only with data link control.) Regardless of the facilities used, data transfer may be broken down into the five phases summarized in Figure 8.13. *Circuit connection,* for example, refers to all

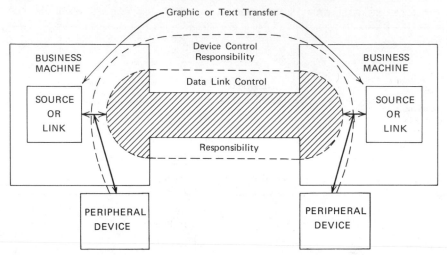

Figure 8.12. Hierarchical relationship of data link control and device control functions in code-sensitive protocol.

activities required to assure the existence of an electrical path between two points. The existence of a circuit is, however, by no means sufficient to guarantee existence of a usable data link. As an example, no usable link exists until the sending modem raises "clear-to-send" to notify a business machine that the entire link is properly synchronized. Once a *link* is *established, message transfer* activity may take place. On dial line systems, turnarounds may require *termination of a link* in one direction, followed immediately by a *link establishment* and *message transfer* in the other direction, all accomplished without severing the *circuit connection.* Thus *link termination* is a separate and distinct concept from *circuit termination* (although, of course, circuit termination will cause link termination).

Generally, line control procedures are not considered to include the circuit establishment and termination phases of Figure 8.13. However, they do encompass the *link establishment, message transfer,* and *link termination* phases of a data transfer. Our objective here is to identify and discuss the control procedures typically required in each of these three phases of data transfer. We also briefly consider the control sequence used to reverse the direction of communication on a dial line. Central to any protocol is the existence of a *code* for representing all the data characters that must be transmitted between the business machines; the code specifies unique bit sequences for all characters (an example was cited in Chapter 5 in the discussion of the ASCII character code).

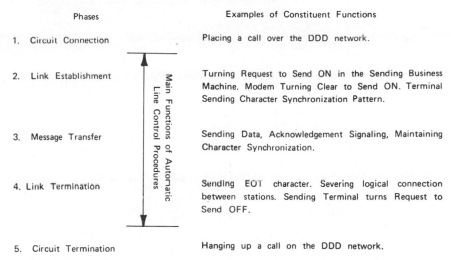

Phases		Examples of Constituent Functions
1. Circuit Connection		Placing a call over the DDD network.
2. Link Establishment		Turning Request to Send ON in the Sending Business Machine. Modem Turning Clear to Send ON. Terminal Sending Character Synchronization Pattern.
3. Message Transfer		Sending Data, Acknowledgement Signaling, Maintaining Character Synchronization.
4. Link Termination		Sending EOT character. Severing logical connection between stations. Sending Terminal turns Request to Send OFF.
5. Circuit Termination		Hanging up a call on the DDD network.

Figure 8.13. Five phases of data transfer.

Most codes contain *three types* or *categories* of characters—graphic, end-to-end (device) control, and data link control. *Graphic characters* consist of all letters, numbers, the comma, the period, and all device-independent symbols that generally have no special meaning unless viewed in the context of a user program, data file, and so on. *End-to-end control characters* are used by terminals for positioning carriages, line feed, tab, printer control, and other device-dependent functions. *Data link control characters* are used to regulate data transfer and constitute the special purpose alphabet of characters used for the line control functions of interest here. Since line control procedures must not be device dependent (i.e., the same protocol must be usable for many different types of devices), the control characters must be general purpose in nature.

Figure 8.14 portrays the 10 major data link or communication control characters used in the ASCII standard code. This code has formed the basis for virtually all efforts concerned with the standardization of line control procedures over the past 10 years. The uses of these control characters in the link establishment, message transfer, and link termination phases of a data transfer activity are now illustrated.

8.2.1. Link Establishment

The term *handshaking* is often used interchangeably with *link establishment*. It includes all functions that must be completed before the

SOH (Start of Heading): A communication control character used at the beginning of a sequence of characters which constitute a machine-sensible address or routing information. Such a sequence is referred to as the "heading." An STX character has the effect of terminating a heading.

STX (Start of Text): A communication control character which precedes a sequence of characters that is to be treated as an entity and entirely transmitted through to the ultimate destination. Such a sequence is referred to as "text." STX may be used to terminate a sequence of characters started by SOH.

ETX (End of Text): A communication control character used to terminate a sequence of characters started with STX and transmitted as an entity.

EOT (End of Transmission): A communication control character used to indicate the conclusion of a transmission, which may have contained one or more texts and any associated headings.

ENQ (Enquiry): A communication control character used in data communication systems as a request for a response from a remote station. It may be used as a "Who Are You" (WRU) to obtain identification, or may be used to obtain station status, or both.

ACK (Acknowledge). A communication control character transmitted by a receiver as an affirmative response to a sender.

NAK (Negative Acknowledge): A communication control character transmitted by a receiver as a negative response to the sender.

SYN (Synchronous Idle): A communication control character used by a synchronous transmission system in the absence of any other character to provide a signal from which synchronism may be achieved or retained.

ETB (End of Transmission Block): A communication control character used to indicate the end of a block of data for communication purposes. ETB is used for blocking data where the block structure is not necessarily related to the processing format.

DLE (Data Link Escape): A communication control character which will change the meaning of a limited number of contiguously following characters. It is used exclusively to provide supplementary controls in data communication networks.

Figure 8.14. ASCII control characters and meanings.

source and sink machines are both fully satisfied that they want to communicate with each other. Many switched network systems handshake by following a prearranged dialog wherein the calling station first raises its "request-to-send." On receipt of "clear-to-send" from the modem at the calling station, the calling station transmits its identification; the called station then responds with its identification. If for any reason either station does not want to converse with the other, nothing further is permitted to happen. Otherwise message transfer commences. On leased line point-to-point systems controlled with these data link control characters, a station typically bids to establish a link by sending an inquiry (ENQ). The other station responds with either a positive or a negative acknowledgment (ACK or NAK), depending on its status. If ACK is received at the bidding station, message transfer commences; if NAK is received, the link cannot be established.

Polled multipoint systems work similarly, the poll being used to solicit messages from remote stations. Some type of negative acknowledgment is returned from a polled station with no message awaiting transmission. If the polled station has a message ready for transmission, the *message transfer phase* commences immediately with the transmission of the message. In transmitting messages from a master station to remote stations on a multipoint line, a *selection* phase is used. The control message from the master station contains the address of the station being selected; the format of the select sequence is similar to that of the poll sequence. A positive acknowledgment (ACK) by the remote station indicates that *message transfer* can commence:

8.2.2. Message Transfer

Once link establishment is completed, message transfer commences. As shown in Figure 8.15, a message block generally consists of up to three parts: a header, the text, and a trailer or ending. The header is indicated by the *start of heading* (SOH) control character and ends with the *start of text* (STX) character. The information contained in the header always relates only to the message block in question. The specific content of message headings depends on the application; however, the header may contain information on *message priority, security classification, source ID, length, destination ID, date–time of origination,* and *code format,* to mention a few possibilities.

The message text consists of all the information that must be delivered unaltered to the sink business machine. The message trailer begins with the ending of the message text and is typically indicated by the ETB or ETX character in ASCII. The purposes of the trailer may be several: *to separate messages being transmitted over a link,* to cause *disconnection* or *line turnaround* in dial-up applications, to force *certain block lengths* that optimize transmission efficiency, *to store block parity check* information, and so on.

It should be noted that use of an established link to transfer several data blocks is perfectly permissible. This type of operation has come to be known as a *select–hold* mode of usage, since the link is selected and held for the duration of several blocks' worth of data transmission. ETB is used to end physical blocks when more will follow immediately; ETX is used after the final block in a sequence. When ETX is received, *message transfer* is completed.

Throughout the message transfer mode, several control functions like error control and character synchronization are being continuously implemented. *Error control,* as previously explained, involves sending redundant (noninformation) bits with the text. Control signals such as ACK and NAK are transmitted back to the sending station to positively and

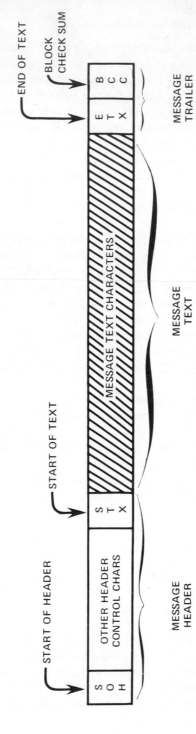

Figure 8.15. Typical message block organization.

negatively acknowledge, respectively, the receipt of a block at the other end. *Character synchronization* involves the continual and periodic insertion of SYN characters into the transmitted data stream; the receive station looks for predetermined sequences of SYN characters. The receiver is said to be in *character sync* when it detects the known pattern; it can then properly interpret the boundaries between subsequently received characters. Generally, all bits or characters received at a station not in character sync are ignored. The periodic transmission of these sync characters thus assures that the receiver is "tracking" with the transmitter, knowing where one character stops and the next begins. Note that *character and message synchronization* are the responsibility of data link control which is done in the business machines, whereas *bit synchronization* is the signal converter's responsibility.

8.2.3. Link Termination

Message transfer is always followed by *link termination*. This termination effectively *erases* or *clears* the previously established data link. It is initiated by an *end-of-transmission* (EOT) character. Once a station receives an EOT, it must go through link establishment again before it can communicate with other stations. Figure 8.16 shows how the EOT character is used to logically terminate a connection with one remote station on a multipoint line before the establishment of the next data link via polling or selecting in the BSC protocol.

8.2.4. Line Turnaround

On higher speed dial-up applications it is frequently necessary to reverse the direction of the transmission. Here the station that had been transmitting becomes the receiver, and vice versa. The original sending station, after sending its last characters, turns OFF its request-to-send lead, effectively terminating the link. The original receiving station knows that it must become a sending station when it receives the last character of a message (like ETX). It then turns its request-to-send ON. When its clear-to-send goes on, transmission may then proceed in the other direction. The business machines in this type of application are designed to turn their request-to-send OFF whenever the last character of a message expecting a reply has been sent. Similarly, they turn their request-to-send ON whenever they sense the last character of a received message for which a response must be generated. An example of this turnaround scenario was presented in Chapter 5 in discussion of the business machine–modem interface.

```
S1    EOT S2 ENQ        EOT s2 ENQ      STX–ETB BCC      STX–ETX BCC
S2            NAK             ACK0               ACK1
S3
time →                                                              → t₁

S1        EOT S3 ENQ        STX–ETB BCC      STX–ETX BCC        EOT
S2    ACK0                       ACK1              ACK0
S3
                                                                   → t₂

S1    EOT s3          STX–ETX BCC        EOT S2 ENQ
S2                                             NAK
S3            ACK0          ACK1
                                                                   →

S1 = PRIMARY STATION                SN ⇒ POLL STATION N
S2, S3 = SECONDARIES                sN ⇒ SELECT STATION N
BCC = BLOCK CHECK CHARS             STX-- denotes START OF TEXT followed by actual text
SYN, PAD CHARS NOT SHOWN
```

Figure 8.16. Example of multipoint scenarios under BSC.

8.3. BINARY SYNCHRONOUS COMMUNICATIONS (BSC) PROTOCOL OVERVIEW

Figures 8.16 and 8.17 contain several illustrations of the dialog followed by stations operating under the Binary Synchronous Communications (BSC) control procedure. No attempt is made to consider BSC in detail here; rather, the objective is to show a few examples of how some control functions cited in Section 8.2 are implemented in a widely used protocol. The reader interested in the details of this procedure should consult References [5] through [7].

Over the past decade since BSC was introduced, user requirements, available teleprocessing devices, and communication facilities have matured to the point where the BSC protocol architecture unnecessarily limits what can be accomplished. As discussed in References [5] through [13] and now summarized here, these limitations have spawned the development of a whole new generation of protocols such as the previously noted SDLC and DDCMP. Virtually all of these new protocols closely parallel the recommendations of the American National Standards Institute's Advanced Data Communications Control Procedure (ADCCP) [14].

The limiting features of BSC that gave rise to the development of new protocols may be summarized as follows:

- BSC uses the lines only in a half-duplex mode. This does not enable four-wire lines to be used to their full capacity.
- BSC was designed only for point-to-point and multipoint lines (not loops).
- BSC restricts all devices on a line to operate using an identical code format.
- BSC does not support operations such as hub polling and fast-select output scenarios.
- Under BSC, the initiation of an error recovery procedure at one station causes the line to become unavailable for other stations until the recovery is complete. (Section 8.6 discusses this problem in detail.)
- Transparent text operations, where the user wants to send arbitrary bit patterns as text, are cumbersome and inefficient.
- The BSC protocol is designed around, and therefore dependent on, a particular character code.
- Only the stop-and-wait ARQ method of error control is possible under BSC. It can therefore be inefficient on long-propogation-delay lines, as was noted in Chapter 6.
- Device control functions and data link control functions are not clearly separated under BSC. Specific control character sequences are some-

1. BATCH TRANSMISSION   (CONTENTION)

```
        BID          BLOCK #1        BLOCK #2
        →            →               →
S₁     ENQ          STX--ETB        STX--ETB        STX--ETB
S₂            ACK0           ACK0            ACK1
```

2. RECOVERY FROM BLOCK ERROR

```
        BLOCK N                  BLOCK N+1             N+1 REPEATED
S₁     STX--ETB                 STX--ETB              STX--ETB
S₂               ACK0                     NAK                    ACK1
```

3. RECOVERY FROM GARBLED BLOCK   (NO REPLY)

```
        BLOCK N       BLOCK N+1                                 N+1 REPEATED
S₁     STX--ETB      STX--ETB ----- TIME OUT | ENQ             STX--ETB
                                             |-----------
S₂               ACK0                                   ACK0              ACK1
```

4. RECOVERY FROM GARBLED RESPONSE

```
        BLOCK N         BLOCK N+1                        BLOCK N+2
S₁     STX--ETB        STX--ETB        | ----- ENQ      STX--ETB
                                       | GARBLED
                                       |   →
S₂               ACK0           ACK1   |   ACK1                     ACK0
```

5. INTERRUPTION TO REVERSE DIRECTION

```
        BLOCK N         BLOCK N+1           ANY VOLATILE DATA             BLOCK 1
S₁     STX--ETB        STX--ETB            STX . . EOT       ENQ         STX--ETB
S₂               ACK1            RVI                               ACK0
```

TRANSMITTER FOLLOWS BLOCK N+1 WITH SINGLE BLOCK CONTAINING ANY VOLATILE DATA.

6. CONVERSATIONAL EXCHANGE

S_1	ENQ		STX--ETX		ACK1	EOT
S_2		ACK0		STX--ETX		ACK1

7. TRANSMITTER-INITIATED DELAY

	BLOCK N				*BLOCK N+1*	
S_1	STX--ETB		DELAY	STX ENQ	STX--ETB	
S_2		ACK0	≤2SEC		NAK	ACK1

8. RECEIVER-INITIATED DELAY

	BLOCK N					*BLOCK N+1*			*BLOCK N+2*
S_1	STX--ETB		DELAY	WACK	ENQ	DELAY	ACK1		STX--ETB
S_2		ACK0	≤2SEC			≤2SEC		STX--ETB	

9. IGNORE BLOCK

	BLOCK N		*IGNORE*		*BLOCK N+1*		*BLOCK N+2*
S_1	STX--ETB		STX--ENQ		STX--ETB		STX--ETB
S_2		ACK0		NAK		ACK1	

Figure 8.17. Examples of BSC protocol scenarios for point-to-point lines.

times used for data link control, sometimes for error recovery procedures, and sometimes for the control of devices at the ends of the link. This gives rise to possible ambiguities in the implementation of the telecommunications control software routines.

- BSC does not efficiently support fully conversational exchanges except in limited application circumstances, that is to say, frequent reversals in the direction of transmission generate significant amounts of overhead (both in time and in control characters).
- BSC does not provide full error checking of all control and information transfer messages.
- BSC does not provide any system-assigned sequence numbering, except for positive acknowledgments (ACKs).

It must be pointed out that BSC was designed in the early 1960s and generally filled the needs of most applications at the time when it was designed. Most of these involved situations where a human being was situated at the remote station—hence the sufficiency of a half-duplex protocol. As transmission requirements and applications have become more demanding and sophisticated, a need for more advanced protocols that fully preserve the desirable attributes of older protocols has materialized. As noted in Reference [37], numerous standards organizations around the world, in response to the general need for improved data link control procedures, have evolved a common framework for now advanced line protocols. In the United States these procedures are referred to as the Advanced Data Communication Control Procedures (ADCCP) and internationally they are known as the High Level Data Link Control Procedures (HDLC). Each vendor organization designing equipment in accordance with these procedures generally introduces a specific name for its particular implementation, for example, IBM's Synchronous Data Link Control (SDLC) and Digital Equipment's DDCMP. In general, specific vendor implementations may be regarded as subsets of the broadly defined functions covered by ADCCP and HDLC. In the next section, the most widely known of these new protocols, IBM's Synchronous Data Link Control, is overviewed. A discussion of the evolution of SDLC may be found in References [9] and [11]; the details of its architecture are considered in References [8] through [12].

8.4. SYNCHRONOUS DATA LINK CONTROL (SDLC) OVERVIEW

This discussion is not intended to reconstruct all the background and history leading to the development of SDLC, nor is it intended to serve as a substitute for the details that may be found in the SDLC reference manuals. The purposes here are to briefly summarize the key architectural attributes of SDLC and to note the key consequences of these features to users and systems designers who must configure systems using protocols like SDLC.

Figures 8.18 through 8.26 portray the basic concepts embodied in SDLC. Some of these points are now considered in more detail.

As noted in Reference [12], SDLC has a structure that encompasses the following:

- Definitions of primary and secondary station functions.
- Definitions of possible transmission states.
- Specific positional groupings of control, checking, and information bits in a transmission.

- AN ARCHITECTURE FOR INFORMATION TRANSFER ON A LINK BASIS
- REPLACES BINARY SYNCHRONOUS (BSC) PROTOCOL (ULTIMATELY)
- SEPARATES DATA LINK CONTROL FROM DEVICE CONTROL FUNCTIONS
- BIT ORIENTED (INSTEAD OF CHARACTER)
- OPERATES INDEPENDENTLY OF DEVICE TYPES OR NETWORK
  CONFIGURATION
- SYSTEM-ASSIGNED SEQUENCE NUMBERING OF BLOCKS ENABLES
  CONTINUOUS ARQ
- TYPES OF LINKS SUPPORTED

     POINT-TO-POINT
     MULTIPOINT
     LOOP

- MODES OF OPERATION SUPPORTED OVER DATA LINK

     HALF-DUPLEX—ONE CHANNEL
     FULL-DUPLEX/MULTIMULTIPOINT
        FOR HDX SECONDARY STATIONS ⎱ TWO CHANNELS
     FULL-DUPLEX/REGULAR
        FOR FDX SECONDARY STATIONS ⎰
     SIMPLEX (IN LOOP)—ONE CHANNEL
- PRIMARY STATION RESPONSIBLE FOR EXERCISING CONTROL OF LINK
- SECONDARY STATIONS GENERALLY TRANSMIT ONLY AFTER BEING
     INVITED TO (SOMETIMES THEY MAY INITIATE TRANSMISSIONS IF
     DESIRED)
- ORGANIZED USING THREE TYPES OF COMMANDS/RESPONSES
     COMMANDS)

     INFORMATION TRANSFER   (I FRAMES)
     SUPERVISORY   (S FRAMES)
     NONSEQUENCED   (NS FRAMES)

Figure 8.18. SDLC: synchronous data link control.

Every SDLC data link has a *primary* station that is responsible for its control; every transmission either emanates from or is directed to a primary station. These designations of primary and secondary (or tributary) stations are made at the time when the system is defined to the control software.

It must be emphasized that SDLC governs only the operation of individual data links. These may be point-to-point, multipoint, or loop lines, as shown in Figure 8.19. Hence the communications conventions governing the movement of data between two stations separated by an intermediate station are beyond the scope of SDLC. These rules must be specified by higher level protocols for *path* and *complete network* control (which are discussed in the next sections). It is thus apparent that a physical station in a network may simultaneously function as a primary station for one data link and as a secondary station for another data link also connected to the same physical station (Figure 8.20).

Three basic *transmission states* provide a convenient way of describing the different possible conditions that exist on a data communications link. These are the *transient state*, the *idle state*, and the *active state*. The *transient state* describes the situation where a station is setting up for transmission, whereas the *idle state* denotes the condition where a link is neither being set up for nor actually involved in transmission. Whenever a station is transmitting or receiving control signals or information bits, the link being used is said to be in the *active state*. Since full-duplex data links can provide channels in both the forward and reverse directions, such a data link may be in different states in each direction.

Two levels of information grouping are found in SDLC. The lower or primitive level element is the *frame*, shown in Figure 8.21. All control and data messages moved over an SDLC data link employ this frame structure. The higher level grouping is a *frame sequence;* SDLC checks a sequence of frames for missing or out-of-sequence frames using the send and receive sequence counts shown in Figures 8.22, 8.25, and 8.26. In initial implementations of SDLC, the maximum number of send and receive sequence count values is eight, using the digits 0 through 7. The digit 7, upon being incremented by 1, will wrap around, that is, assume the value 0. This means that a sending station cannot transmit more than seven frames without receiving control information back from the receiving station. A copy of all outstanding (unacknowledged) frames is retained in the sending station in case retransmissions become necessary. Note the tradeoff implications of a large sequence counting value. More blocks can be sent without the need for a reply, but the buffer requirements of the station increase. As shown in Reference [13], Digital Equipment Corporation's Data Communications Message Protocol (DDCMP) permits up to

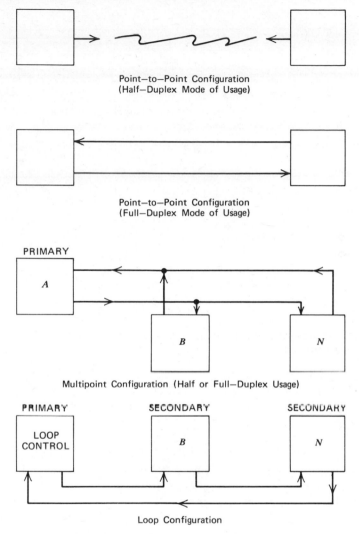

Point—to—Point Configuration
(Half—Duplex Mode of Usage)

Point—to—Point Configuration
(Full—Duplex Mode of Usage)

PRIMARY

A

B

N

Multipoint Configuration (Half or Full—Duplex Usage)

PRIMARY   SECONDARY   SECONDARY

LOOP CONTROL   B   N

Loop Configuration

Figure 8.19. Types of SDLC data links.

256 different send and receive sequence count values. On exceptionally long delay channels, SDLC's requirement to obtain an acknowledgment whenever seven frames are outstanding can result in periodic interruption of data transmission activity if the control message cannot be returned in time.

One significant characteristic of initial SDLC implementations is the

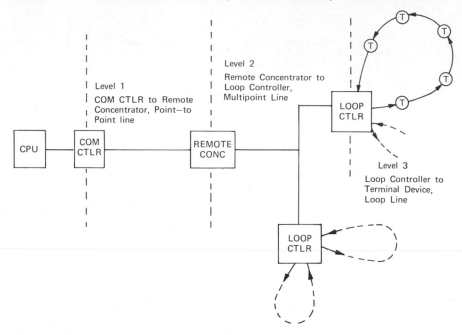

Figure 8.20. Levels of communication using different types of lines, all suported by common protocol under SDLC.

use of a go-back-N retransmission scheme whenever frame errors are detected. Since SDLC receiving stations will accept only successive frames with consecutive send count values, the sending station may have to periodically back up and retransmit several frames, because more than one may possibly be outstanding when the transmitter obtains the negative acknowledgment. In other words, SDLC does not currently permit the *selective retransmission* of frames that would cause a receiving station to be presented with out-of-sequence frames, even though they might individually contain no bit errors.

Figures 8.27 through 8.30 depict some possible SDLC scenarios for various line configurations and operating modes. References [10] and [12] give additional illustrations of typical command and response scenarios using SDLC.

8.5. SUMMARY AND IMPLICATIONS OF ADVANCED LINE PROTOCOLS FOR USERS

The main desirable features of advanced line protocols for users are varying degrees of improved efficiency, flexibility, network availability,

All Transcriptions of the Form

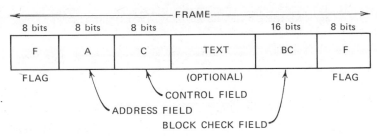

FLAG = {0 1 1 1 1 1 1 0}
- FLAG IS UNIQUE BIT SEQUENCE
  SENDING STATION MONITORS
    AC TEXT BC FOR FIVE CONSECUTIVE 1'S AND INSERTS 0 AFTER FIFTH 1
  RECEIVING STATION STRIPS OUT
    0 FOLLOWING 5 CONSECUTIVE 1'S
- ALL TRANSMISSIONS ARE CHECKED
- CONTROL FIELD USED FOR COMMANDS/RESPONSES AND (BLOCK) SEND AND
  RECEIVE SEQUENCE NUMBERS (NS AND NR)
- CAN FORCE RESPONSE USING POLL BIT = 1 FROM PRIMARY
- MINIMUM FRAME IS 16 BITS OF AC AND 16 BITS OF BC

Figure 8.21.   SDLC frame structure.

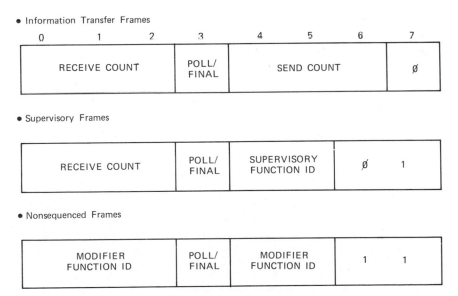

Figure 8.22.   SDLC commands (bits of C field).

POLL/FINAL BIT USAGE

POLL = 1 BY PRIMARY FORCES SECONDARY TO RESPOND
FINAL = 1 BY SECONDARY INDICATES FINAL FRAME
(NO MORE TRAFFIC)

SUPERVISORY FRAMES USED TO

ACKNOWLEDGE TRANSMISSIONS
PROHIBIT TRANSMISSIONS
REQUEST RETRANSMISSIONS

COMMANDS (BITS 4, 5 OF C FIELD)

0 0 RR ⇒ RECEIVE READY (ACKNOWLEDGMENT)
1 0 REJ ⇒ REJECT (NEGATIVE ACKNOWLEDGMENT)
0 1 RNR ⇒ RECEIVE NOT READY (WAIT)
1 1 RESERVED

RESPONSES ARE SAME

NS FRAMES USED FOR DATA LINK CONTROL FUNCTIONS AND TO SEND
INFORMATION WITHOUT USING SEQUENCE COUNTERS

Figure 8.23. Functions of control field in SDLC frame

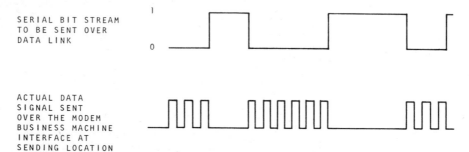

Figure 8.24. Nonreturn to zero inverted coding for asynchronous transmission.
Binary zero is encoded by sending the pulse train which generates the clock at the
receive station; binary one is denoted by absence of the pulse train. Since SDLC forces
periodic insertion of binary zeroes in the serial bit stream sent over the link, there can
never be prolonged periods where the receiver must operate without the ability to
easily generate clock from the incoming data stream.

378

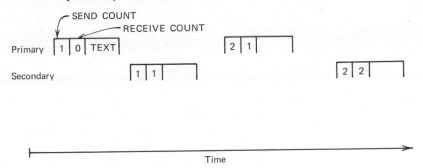

EACH STATION HAS 3 BIT SEND/RECEIVE COUNTERS (NS, NR).
PRIMARY STATION HAS RESPONSE BIT.

EVERY INFORMATION FRAME SENT CONTAINS:
  SEND COUNT AT TRANSMITTING STATION.
  NUMBER OF LAST BLOCK ACCEPTED AT TRANSMITTING STATION.

SEND COUNT VALUE IS SYSTEM-ASSIGNED SEQUENCE NUMBER FOR EACH
BLOCK ON LINE.

ERROR IF SEND COUNTS ON CONSECUTIVE INFORMATION FRAMES ARE NONAD-
JACENT INTEGER VALUES.

Figure 8.25. Simple SDLC block transfer scenario, normal half duplex exchange

and integrity of data. For users, the primary advantage of full duplex
protocols like SDLC over their predecessor half duplex protocols is the
former categories' ability to utilize four-wire communication lines simultaneously in both directions (to operate in the full-duplex mode). This
theoretically doubles the maximum amount of transmission activity that
can be performed in a given time period, since send and receive tasks can
be carried out concurrently. This capability is of prime significance for
such applications and devices as remote job entry and concentration.
Full-duplex usage of multipoint lines that service half-duplex devices or
control units is similarly beneficial. Known as *multimultipoint* operation,
it refers to simultaneous send and receive activity, with the requirement
that different remote stations be involved in the simultaneous sending and
receiving.

   A similar attribute of full-duplex data link usage enables continuous
ARQ error control to be employed. It was shown in Chapter 6 that this
approach is generally necessary for the most efficient use of long-
propagation-delay circuits like those provided using satellites. A related
feature that permits increased efficiency over longer delay multipoint

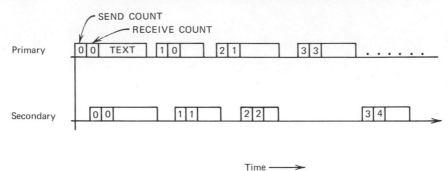

Figure 8.26. Send, receive sequence counts in normal operation of SDLC point-to-point link in full-duplex mode.

circuits is the ability of SDLC to support hub polling schemes, as discussed before.

Because of the bit-oriented characteristics of SDLC, different devices and/or different code formats can be mixed on the same multipoint or loop communication line. With previous protocols, such mixing and sharing was not possible, often resulting in a requirement for excess lines and transmission capacity. Completely flexible networks capable of supporting multiple applications require such a capability to be maximally efficient.

Another advantage for multipoint users of SDLC links (even when operating in the half-duplex mode) in contrast to BSC procedures, is the fast-select approach which SDLC can utilize for output activity. This decreases service time by reducing the number of modem synchronization delays, line propagation delays, and necessary overhead control characters for each transmission. Also in the flexibility enhancement area, protocols like SDLC enable transparent text to be accommodated more easily than before, because of the positional conventions used within the frame structure. It is thus not possible for certain bit patterns in the text to be mistakenly interpreted as control signals under normal circumstances. Related advantages are the SDLC support of three kinds of lines—point-to-point, multipoint, and loops, whereas BSC does not support loop structures.

The sequence counting and frame grouping provisions of the architecture provide enhanced data integrity, especially since all data and control messages are parity checked. In addition, SDLC makes conversational exchanges easier than before since control and data information can be piggybacked into the same frame. This characteristic (and the full-duplex feature) of SDLC also enable extended error recovery procedures to be

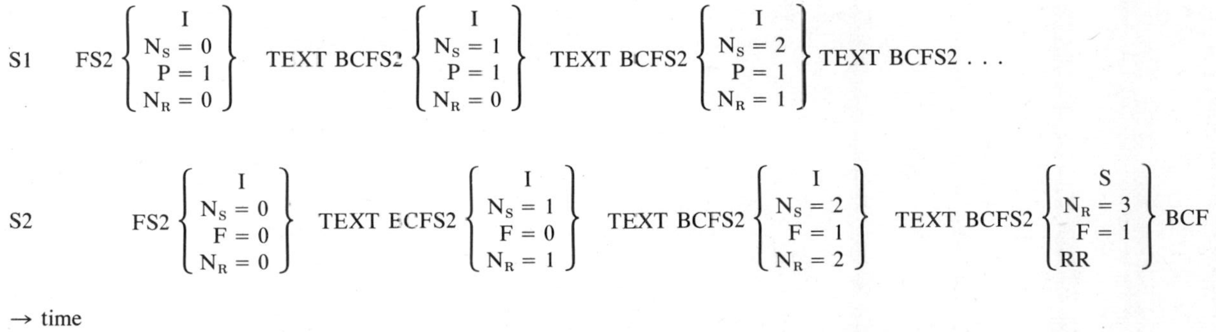

Figure 8.27. Normal exchange, full-duplex, point-to-point SDLC scenarios.

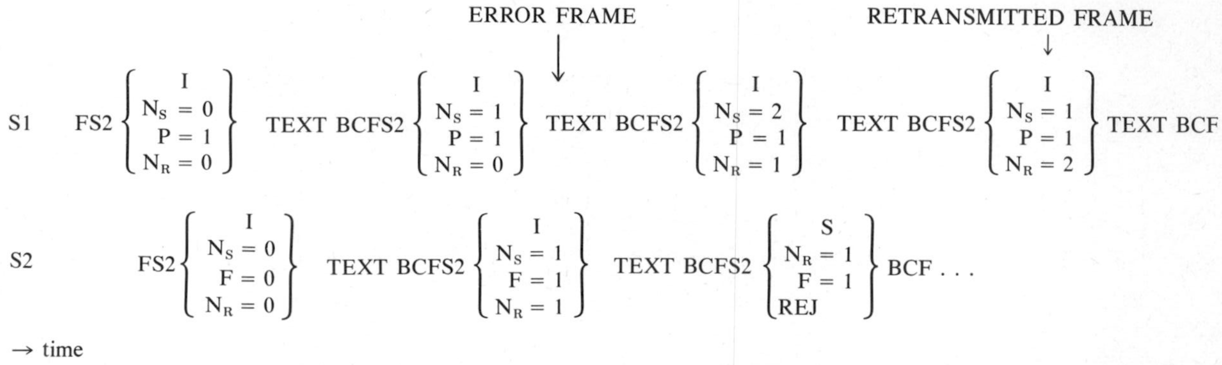

ERROR FRAME →

RETRANSMITTED FRAME →

S1 FS2 $\left\{\begin{array}{l} I \\ N_S=0 \\ P=1 \\ N_R=0 \end{array}\right.$ TEXT BCFS2 $\left\{\begin{array}{l} I \\ N_S=1 \\ P=1 \\ N_R=0 \end{array}\right.$ TEXT BCFS2 $\left\{\begin{array}{l} I \\ N_S=2 \\ P=1 \\ N_R=1 \end{array}\right.$ TEXT BCFS2 $\left\{\begin{array}{l} I \\ N_S=1 \\ P=1 \\ N_R=2 \end{array}\right.$ TEXT BCF

S2 FS2 $\left\{\begin{array}{l} I \\ N_S=0 \\ F=0 \\ N_R=0 \end{array}\right.$ TEXT BCFS2 $\left\{\begin{array}{l} I \\ N_S=1 \\ F=1 \\ N_R=1 \end{array}\right.$ TEXT BCFS2 $\left\{\begin{array}{l} S \\ N_R=1 \\ F=1 \\ REJ \end{array}\right.$ BCF $\ldots$

→ time

SECONDARY STATION AFTER ISSUING NEGATIVE ACKNOWLEDGMENT CANNOT ACCEPT ANY BLOCKS FROM PRIMARY UNTIL ONE WHICH HAS $N_S=1$ (SINCE LAST ONE ACCEPTED HAD $N_S=0$).

Figure 8.28. Full-duplex, point-to-point SDLC scenario. Error in 2nd frame S1→S2 is assumed.

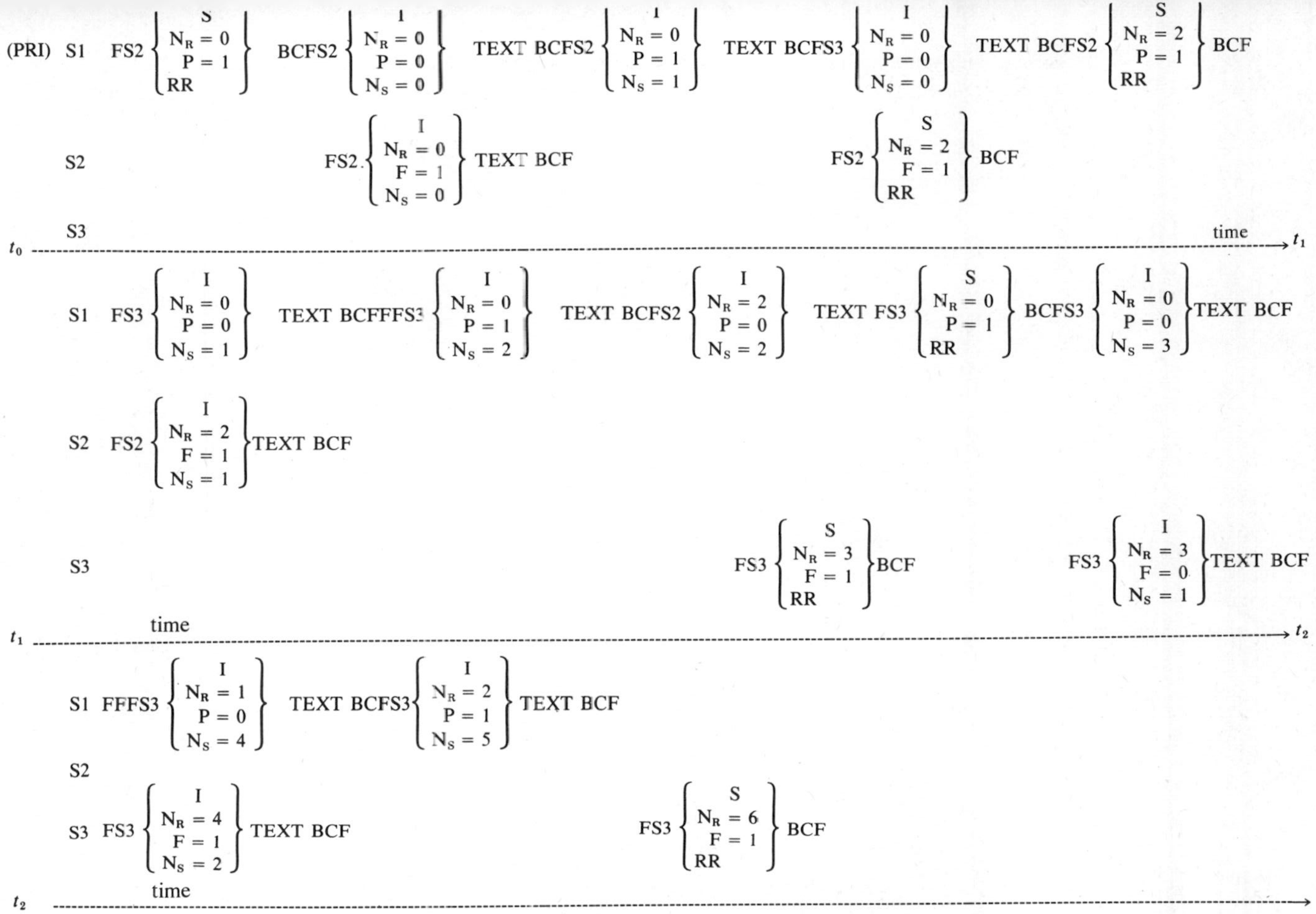

Figure 8.29. Example of SDLC Scenario: full-duplex, multipoint line usage.

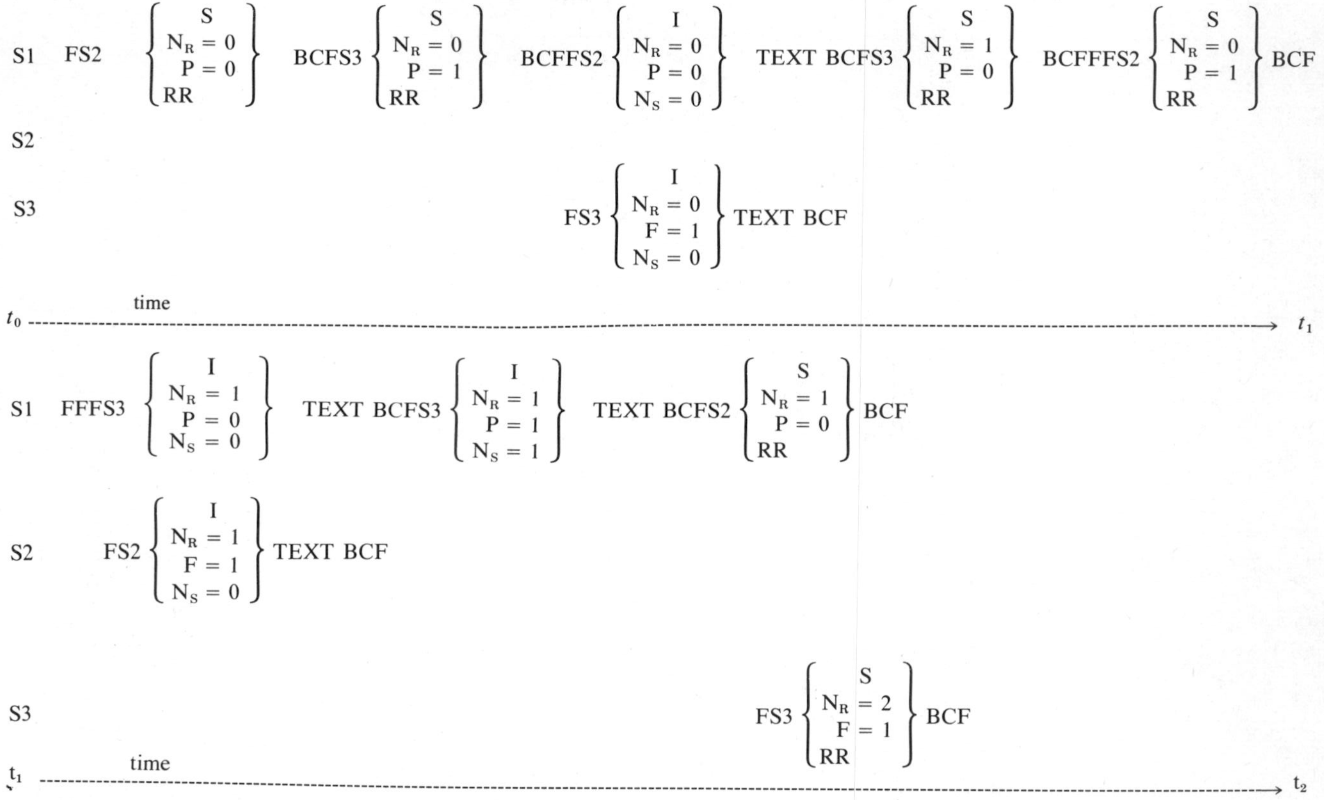

Figure 8.30. Examples of SDLC scenario: full-duplex multimultipoint line usage.

S1 = PRIMARY   S2, S3 = SECONDARIES
MMP = MULTIMULTIPOINT
NOTE CONCURRENCY OF SEND/RECEIVE ACTIVITY BUT NOT FOR SAME REMOTE STATION.

S1 FS2 BCFS3 $\left\{\begin{array}{l}N_R = 0 \\ P = 0 \\ RR\end{array}\right\}$ S   BCFS3 $\left\{\begin{array}{l}N_R = 0 \\ P = 1 \\ RR\end{array}\right\}$ S   BCFFS2 $\left\{\begin{array}{l}N_R = 0 \\ P = 0 \\ N_S = 0\end{array}\right\}$ I   TEXT BCFS3 $\left\{\begin{array}{l}N_R = 1 \\ P = 0 \\ RR\end{array}\right\}$ S   BCFFFS2 $\left\{\begin{array}{l}N_R = 0 \\ P = 1 \\ RR\end{array}\right\}$ S BCF

S2

S3   FS3 $\left\{\begin{array}{l}N_R = 0 \\ F = 1 \\ N_S = 0\end{array}\right\}$ I TEXT BCF

time t_0 ------- t_1

S1 FFFS3 $\left\{\begin{array}{l}N_R = 1 \\ P = 0 \\ N_S = 0\end{array}\right\}$ I   TEXT BCFS3 $\left\{\begin{array}{l}N_R = 1 \\ P = 1 \\ N_S = 1\end{array}\right\}$ I   TEXT BCFS2 $\left\{\begin{array}{l}N_R = 1 \\ P = 0 \\ RR\end{array}\right\}$ S BCF

S2   FS2 $\left\{\begin{array}{l}N_R = 1 \\ F = 1 \\ N_S = 0\end{array}\right\}$ I TEXT BCF

S3   FS3 $\left\{\begin{array}{l}N_R = 2 \\ F = 1 \\ RR\end{array}\right\}$ S BCF

time t_1 ------- t_2

FULL DUPLEX LINE USAGE VITAL FOR EFFICIENT USE OF

    REMOTE CONCENTRATORS

    REMOTE BATCH

    LONG PROPAGATION DELAY LINKS

    MULTIPOINT POLLED LINES

BIT ORIENTED CHARACTERISTIC

    CODE INSENSITIVITY

    DEVICE INSENSITIVITY

    MIX, MATCH TERMINALS ON SAME LINE

SYSTEM ASSIGNED SEQUENCE NUMBERING

    ALL STATIONS KEEP SEND, RECEIVE COUNT

    EVERY INFORMATION BLOCK SENT INCREMENTS SEND COUNT

    EVERY INFORMATION BLOCK RECEIVED INCREMENTS RECEIVE COUNT

    DISCREPANCIES CAUSE RETRY

    CONTINUOUS BLOCK TRANSMISSION POSSIBLE

Figure 8.31. Summary of key implications to users.

carried out with one station on a data link without preemption of other, normally functioning stations on the same link, thus tending to increase the availability of the stations throughout the network. Of related interest is the full removal of device control functions from the realm of the line control procedure's responsibility (see Figure 8.12). This makes error recovery less ambiguous and less time consuming, as well as increasing overall terminal availability.

Finally, both contention and polling types of procedures may be employed to control full duplex data links. It was previously shown that this flexibility of accommodating contention control may be of value in enabling satellite channels, loops, and in some cases even multipoint links to be used with greatest efficiency.

Not much experience presently exists in the actual operation of SDLC and other full duplex types of systems. However, some possible disadvantages and drawbacks of these new protocols may be worthy of consideration by potential users. An example of one possible disadvantage is the initial SDLC maximum value of send and receive counts. As noted before, this restricts the maximum number of frames that can be outstanding without acknowledgment to seven. With SDLC these seven frames have no restrictions on length. By contrast, Digital Equipment Corporation's recently announced DDCMP protocol permits as many as 255 unacknowledged messages of up to 16,000 characters/message to be outstanding. On long-propagation-delay channels, where seven SDLC frames correspond to less than a round-trip propagation delay, the sending station will have to stop and wait for the required acknowledgment before additional blocks can be sent. This will mean that the full advantages of continuous ARQ transmission cannot be realized, since interblock overhead time cannot be completely eliminated in such situations. Obviously, however, the ability to have 255 blocks outstanding requires a sufficiently large buffer to store all outstanding blocks. In CPU-to-CPU transmission applications such buffers will probably be readily available, but for terminal-to-CPU applications they may well be more difficult to provide. It is thus likely that the smaller sequence count values are quite satisfactory for stations like CRTs and CRT controllers, where smaller buffers are typically employed and user message lengths are generally shorter anyway.

An important distinction between SDLC and other full duplex protocols is that SDLC does not employ a character count. It indicates the end of a variable-length data block by using the unique flag bit sequence. Hardware is required at the sending and receiving stations to look for five consecutive 1's in the data stream, as noted in Figure 8.21. An alternative approach employed in DDCMP is to send a count value which indicates to the receiver how many multiples of eight bits are to be found in the data field. This approach requires the sending station to count characters and fill in 0's if the number of data bits to be sent in a block is not a multiple of 8. However, special bit insertion/stripping is not required.

Perhaps the only other possible disadvantage of SDLC and other advanced protocols is their inherent requirement for much more extensive equipment and logic capability at the ends of the data link. The wide range of line control approaches and devices that can be accommodated increases the requirement for hardware, software, and firmware to perform these functions. In certain applications where the line control options are not sufficiently explored and evaluated by the user, the overhead on the line may also turn out to be significantly larger than with more traditional, simpler approaches.

8.6. A COMMON PROBLEM IN POLLED SYSTEMS

A common problem in teleprocessing systems being polled on a roll call
basis is that certain terminals occasionally experience much worse response times than others on the same multipoint line. Under normal
circumstances, where the polling routine cycles continuously through the
terminal addresses on a polling list, each remote terminal (or clustered
control unit) will receive solicitations in proportion to its frequency of
appearance in the polling list. The problem should not show up under
normal circumstances, where each remote device is able to respond
(either positively or negatively) to each invitation.

Imagine, however, that in the five-station polling list of Figure 8.32 the
remote device with address DD is unable to respond to a poll. This can
happen because of an equipment malfunction, excessive line errors, or
such a routine circumstance as power being shut down when a station's
daily workload has been completed. Most half-duplex line protocols will
try anywhere from three to seven successive polls of the station that fails
to respond, before typing out an error message on the operator console. In
a half-duplex protocol, this error recovery procedure precludes any other
activity on the line while it is being executed. Since each poll failure may
typically take up to 3 sec (exact values depend on the time-out setting in
the line control software), the total time for this recovery activity for
station DD is $N \times t_R$, where N = total number of successive polling
attempts before control is transferred to a different recovery mechanism
(like the operator, for example), and t_R = maximum elapsed time for the

Addresses of Stations on Multipoint Line in Order in Which They Are Polled

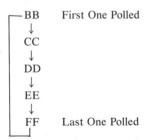

```
┌─ BB       First One Polled
│   ↓
│   CC
│   ↓
│   DD
│   ↓
│   EE
│   ↓
└── FF       Last One Polled
```

In many systems, failure of a particular station to respond to several successive polls will
cause the polling routine to return to the top of the list. This can cause stations near the
bottom of the list to experience significantly longer response times than those at the top
whenever such poll failures occur.

Figure 8.32. Hypothetical polling list.

polled terminal to respond. If no reply is received at the central control point within t_R time units, the time-out mechanism is activated, causing either another retry or termination of polling. When polling is terminated, the failing terminal may temporarily be removed from the list until the reason for its failure to respond is understood.

8.6.1. The Solution Alternatives

So far we have only discussed the problem in detail without commenting on why certain terminals receive degraded response times. The first observation is that all terminals on the poll list can expect to experience degraded response times whenever these error recovery procedures are invoked. However, if handled correctly, the degradation should be relatively uniform for each address on the polling list.

The problem of selectively severe degradations arises because of the action typically taken by the line control software after the failure of terminal *DD* to respond. Many control software packages examined by this author return to the *top of the polling list* to resume polling after such a failure as the one in question. Thus polling list addresses below the one causing the failure will be tried only when no time-outs or error recovery procedures are triggered by any terminals higher in the list.

One possible solution is to organize the line control software to continue on to the next address in the poll list for that line. For example, in Figure 8.32 when terminal *DD* times-out *N* times in succession, polling would resume with terminal *EE* rather than terminal *BB*.

Another strategy not requiring software modification per se is to organize the polling addresses in a sequence that places the terminals most likely to time-out nearest the bottom of the list. Here, even though the polling routine returns to the top of the list on a time-out failure, the number of terminals failing to be polled will be minimized. This approach is feasible only if certain terminals are known to have higher failure likelihoods than others.

Perhaps the best strategy from a response time standpoint is to use a full-duplex protocol in conjunction with line control software that will continue on to the next address on the list. While the remote terminal is being queried several times, output activity may still be taking place, leading to higher overall efficiency.

8.7. LINE CONTROL VERSUS PATH CONTROL AND NETWORK CONTROL

In Figure 1.2, it was shown that all of the functions associated with line control (or, equivalently, data link control) in one-stage networks have the collective purpose of enabling application programs and terminal devices to view their connections to the communications lines as virtually error-free paths over which data can be transmitted. Most teleprocessing systems constructed in the 1950s and 1960s did not contain remotely positioned intelligence for communications control. Consequently, remote terminals communicated with the central site (either the CPU or a front-end communications controller of some type), using a path composed of a single *data link*.

Note that even in the popular network structures utilizing one stage of conventional synchronous time-division multiplexing (see Figure 8.2) only one *data link* exists between the user terminal and the central communications control unit. Even though the bits flow over two separate communication lines, no message processing of any type takes place in the multiplexer. Error control procedures are implemented directly between the user terminal and the central communications control unit, and there is no intermediate buffering delay at the multiplexer (except for the one-bit or one-character delays intrinsic to the multiplexing action).

Recently, intelligent multiplexers, packet switching concentrators of the type discussed in Chapter 7, and other remotely positioned communications processing devices have become very popular in teleprocessing systems where users are concerned about increasing the efficiency and flexibility of their network structures. Often this will mean that remote terminal devices must communicate with an application program or data base over paths involving more than one data link and several intermediate points of nodal intelligence. In a generalized discussion of control alternatives for teleprocessing networks (including those with remote intelligence) it thus becomes necessary to extend previous thinking and consider the following concepts:

1. Sources and sinks.
2. Logical channels through the network.
3. Paths through the network.
4. Data links.
5. Intelligent nodes that perform multiplexing, concentration, or some combination thereof.

The purpose of the present discussion is not to present rigorous formal definitions of these concepts but rather to offer a brief discussion of how the problem of complete network control can be viewed in a simple hierarchical fashion.

Consider *sources* and *sinks* merely as any user application program, input/output device, or data file that interfaces to and communicates through the network's array of facilities. *Sources* supply information; *sinks* receive information from the network. Sources and sinks are connected to *logical channels*. Logical channels may be viewed simply as the collection of all physical communication lines, control routines, buffers, and nodal intelligence required to manage *paths* between the *sources* and *sinks*. The management of logical channels involves verifying that all network and source–sink facilities required for transmission are available before any data are accepted from the source. Another typical function is that of sequence-counting messages on an end-to-end basis to assure that all are delivered correctly. Specification of a logical channel thus involves selection of a *path*. Paths are, in turn, composed of data links and perhaps some intermediate intelligent nodes where physical communication lines are terminated. Intelligent nodes are capable of performing the data link control, path control, and network control functions required to manage the logical channels to which users connect.[2]

To illustrate these ideas in a complete system we consider Figure 8.33. Arbitrarily, we assume that all sources–sink entities are numbered 1 through 4; intelligent nodes are lettered *A, B, C,* and *D.* In this example, all nodes perform the store and forward function characteristic of concentration. Table 8.1 depicts the physical facilities that might be used to provide the logical channels required between the five source–sink pairs. In this example it is arbitrarily assumed that no logical connection is required between source–sink 1 and source–sink 2. This teleprocessing network may thus be viewed as a collection of four physical nodes and communications links that interconnect application programs and terminal devices.

As shown in Figure 8.33, it now becomes necesary for a network to provide virtually error-free *paths* (instead of *data links*) between the ultimate sources and sinks connected to the network. Overall network control embodies the establishment and management of logical channels between user sources and sinks which connect to the network. These logical channels are composed of network intelligence and control at each end of a *path*; paths are, in turn, composed of one or more data links. Whenever a path consists of more than one data link, it will be necessary

---

[2]Intelligent nodes that merely perform time-division multiplexing action on either a static or a dynamic basis do not perform data link control, since there is no processing of any information at the message or block level.

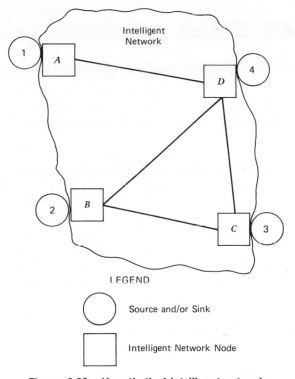

Figure 8.33. Hypothetical intelligent network.

for one or more intermediate communications nodes to logically connect the constituent data links.

Thus the overall network control problem can be viewed as one of providing the hierarchical layers of control shown in Table 8.2. Data link or line control is but one of the several functions necessary for orderly operation in intelligent networks.

Table 8.1.   Different Paths for Example Network of Figure 8.33

Source–Sink Connection Pair	Facilities Comprising Path through Network
1, 3	Node A, link AD, node D, link DC, node C
1, 4	Node A, link AD, node D
2, 3	Node B, link BC, node C
2, 4	Node B, link BD, node D
3, 4	Node C, link CD, node D

Table 8.2. Hierarchical Layers of Control in Intelligent Communications Networks

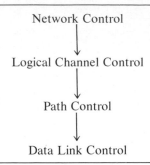

Network Control

↓

Logical Channel Control

↓

Path Control

↓

Data Link Control

In this hierarchical concept, rigidly structured roles or responsibilities are given to each layer in the hierarchy. The *path control* routines, assuming virtually error-free *data links,* address only issues associated with selecting and efficiently using the best sequence of data links and intermediate nodes. *Logical channel control* routines, assuming correctly functioning *path control logic,* address only such end-to-end issues as source–sink availability and assuring that messages are delivered in the correct sequence, without loss or duplication. Also, when input messages from the user source are decomposed into packets, an additional requirement exists for making certain that all packets of a user message are rearranged in the correct sequence at the intelligent node that interfaces directly to the user sink. Requirement for this added function is an intrinsic characteristic of packet switching networks, since each packet is processed as an independent entity by all data link and path control logic. It thus becomes possible for different packets of the same user message to traverse different paths in reaching their destination. Since different network paths may be used with this function known as *adaptive routing*, an end-to-end sequence counting function must be provided that ensures correct rearrangement of the packets into user messages before their departure from the network.

An understanding of these concepts is important because almost all major suppliers of networking products and services are basing their future product lines and network control strategies around such notions. As examples, IBM has introduced its System Network Architecture (SNA), and Digital Equipment Corporation its so-called DECNET protocol [15,16]. Both are unified, standardized approaches to organizing and controlling networks containing intelligent communications processing equipment. The general objective of each is to develop an efficient, reliable architectural framework in which users may view complex communications-based computer systems without concern for the physical details of how a specific network is organized.

The key to achieving such highly desirable goals is the ability to fully share all network resources, including lines, remote multiplexers and concentrators, terminals, and front-end processors, across all potential users in a highly demand-oriented time-variable environment. This flexibility can be achieved in a generalized way only if there is a clear-cut separation of functional responsibility in the distributed modules that control the network. In such an architectural view of networks, different functions can be clearly associated with different logic modules of the network. This makes possible, for example, the separation of all functions associated with data link control from the modules responsible for performing path control and managing the logical channels. Path control functions can, in turn, be cleanly separated from data link control and network control.

The desirability of such separation is deeply rooted in the advantages of being able to modify specific facilities and their associated control routines without affecting other functional control modules. For example, imagine that the user wants to change one physical communication line from a terrestrial facility to satellite in order to reduce costs. Because of satellite propagation delays, he may need to modify the error control method employed for that data link from stop-and-wait ARQ to continuous ARQ (as discussed in Chapter 6). Unless his overall network control strategy involves clean separation of data link control and higher order (e.g., path) control functions, such a low level change may have a monumental ripple effect on higher order control modules. By the same token, with the rigid separation philosophy, such a change at the data link control level need not affect any higher order functions.

8.8. TYPICAL NETWORK CONTROL PHILOSOPHIES OF COMPUTER VENDORS

The generalized, layered-networking approaches just discussed form the basis for the recently announced long range networking plans of most major computer organizations. To explain these concepts in more detail, approaches of the two presently most well-developed architectures—those of IBM Corporation and Digital Equipment Corporation—are considered, even though most other computer vendors are planning similar kinds of strategies. In this section the key ideas of IBM's plan, known as *System Network Architecture* (SNA), and Digital Equipment's, known as the *DECNET protocol*, are discussed. No attempt is made to consider the subjects at length; rather, the goal is to highlight how these networking architectures of major computer vendors approach the overall control problem.

Since many other non-computer-vendor organizations in the world have similarly strong interests in supplying intelligent networks, they have also developed approaches to network control. The key protocol approaches being proposed and employed by other intelligent networking suppliers such as the packet switching carriers and independent data communications companies are considered in Section 8.9. The goal of these discussions is to examine the major functional differences and similarities of the alternatives available for implementing intelligent networks.

8.8.1. System Network Architecture Example

The introductory page of IBM's SNA manual [15] states:

> SNA brings together multiple products in a unified communication system design upon which new teleprocessing applications can be planned and implemented; SNA defines both the functions and functional structure for IBM communications products . . . . SNA formally defines the functional responsibilities of communication system components. In an SNA structure, all nodes (linked elements) adhere to these definitions. The scope of SNA definitions ranges from bit-level message header formats to the protocol of message sequences and to the classification of network nodes according to functional capability.

Thus the intended purposes of SNA are to isolate the user and the application programmer from the details of the teleprocessing network and to stimulate increased use of teleprocessing by allowing all elements of a network to be fully shared. This is being accomplished via IBM's first formal sanctioning of distributed processing, making possible local transaction processing and removal to the network of many tasks previously performed at the central site.

From an architectural standpoint, our major interest here, SNA is based on several key concepts:

- Distribution of function across different points of intelligence (nodes).
- Separation of function into well-defined logical layers.
- Attachment independence based on the *logical channel* concept.
- Data link control standardization based on SDLC.

The following example of Figures 8.34 and 8.35 illustrates how such network control functions as *path control* and *data link control* are allotted to paired functional elements at the two ends of a communication path or logical channel. Figure 8.34 illustrates the physical structure for the example, whereas Figure 8.35 depicts the logical structure. Only one *logical channel* or *path* between the remote terminal user and the central application program is of interest.

In an SNA network, each such logical channel must be provided between a pair of *network-addressable units* which interface with the source and the sink, respectively. These units are the logical network ports that user programs and terminals refer to symbolically and the network refers to by *network address*. Any *network address* can be reached from any other in the communications system by specification of a *path*. The transmission control subsystem is responsible for selecting and controlling a physical path between the two network-addressable units or ports. In this example, the path involves two data links and one intermediate intelligent node. Integrity of transmission along each data link is assured by the data link control mechanism. Note, however, that path integrity from *A* to *C* is by no means assured just because of correctly functioning data link control mechanisms for links *AB* and *BC*. For example, the incoming path control routines at node *B* must route incoming messages or packets to the correct outgoing path control routine. From information passed through the network by the *transmission subsystem* for each message on each *logical channel*, intermediate nodes know the appropriate outgoing path control routine to which each incoming frame or block should be transferred.

The reader interested in further details of SNA should consult References [15], [17], and [38]. A detailed evaluation of SNA is beyond the scope of our discussion here. The only purpose is to illustrate conceptually how a particular advanced networking architecture embodies the concepts of data link path and network control. To contrast SNA with another computer vendor's advanced networking protocol we now consider Digital Equipment Corporation's DECNET protocol.

8.8.2. DECNET Protocol Overview and Philosophy

It is apparent from the statement of purposes in Reference [16] that the Digital Equipment DECNET protocol addresses certain issues that go beyond the control of an intelligent network. For example:

> "DECNET is the set of software tools added to operating systems to allow inter-system communication between DEC computer systems. These

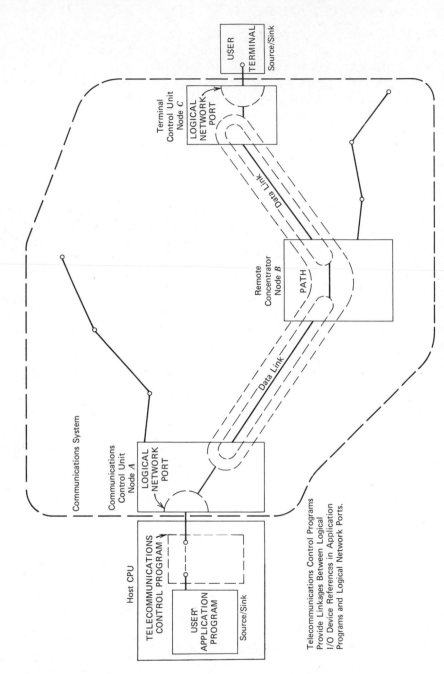

Figure 8.34. Schematic diagram for System Network Architecture example of Figure 8.35.

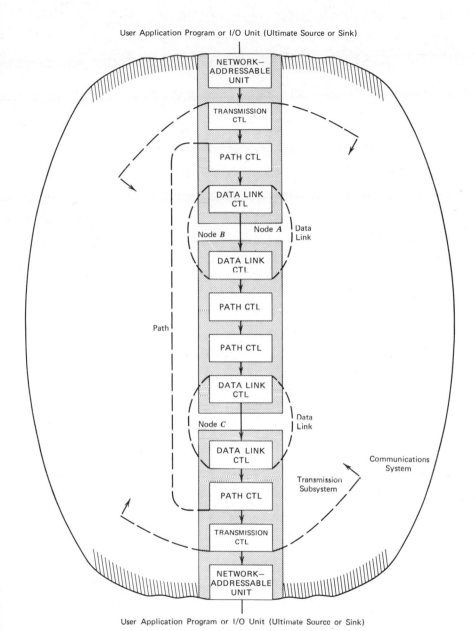

User Application Program or I/O Unit (Ultimate Source or Sink)

NETWORK—
ADDRESSABLE
UNIT

TRANSMISSION
CTL

PATH CTL

DATA LINK
CTL

Node B   Node A   } Data
                       Link

DATA LINK
CTL

PATH CTL

PATH CTL

Path

DATA LINK
CTL

Node C   } Data
            Link

DATA LINK
CTL

PATH CTL

Communications
System

Transmission
Subsystem

TRANSMISSION
CTL

NETWORK—
ADDRESSABLE
UNIT

User Application Program or I/O Unit (Ultimate Source or Sink)

Figure 0.35. Logical structure for example of Figure 8.34.

software tools . . . are invoked and controlled by simple commands that permit a user or program to
  - "establish contact with a remote computer(s), and
  - request or transmit data and/or commands."

Thus DECNET embodies additional features for programs on one node of the network to utilize input/output services available at other nodes. This is accomplished by use of a network standard method for file transfers between machines.

Since our main concern here is the network architecture, only the elements of DECNET pertinent to the communications system portions of networks are considered in detail.

It is of considerable interest to note that the key DECNET architectural philosophy is the use of a layered-structure approach, as was found also in SNA. As shown in Figure 8.36, four levels have been introduced.

In comparing SNA with DECNET, the following observations are relevant:

- DECNET's dialog level has no strictly equivalent functional counterpart in SNA. This is an important level of control in teleprocessing systems which IBM addresses in its so-called access method programs.[3] SNA does not concern itself with such functions.

- SNA's concept of the *data link control* layer corresponds to DEC's notion of the *physical link control* layer. DEC has standardized its control of physical links, using the previously discussed DDCMP protocol.

- SNA makes no specific mention of a control layer corresponding to DECNET's *hardware level* layer. It thus appears that the DECNET protocol may be somewhat more modular than SNA in applications where the user is desirous of modifying transmission techniques and other variables down at the actual bit level on physical links. For example, DECNET's DDCMP protocol enables either bit serial and parallel transmission to take place over physical links, whereas SNA's SDLC requires bit serial transmission.

- The *logical link* level in DECNET corresponds to the SNA *transmission subsystem* layer. As with SNA, DECNET control at the *logical link level* is accomplished using distributed logic routines that support the creation of logical links and the transfer of user data over these links. For example, the use of logical links in DECNET means that the

---

[3]See Section 8.11 on teleprocessing control software for a discussion of access method programs.

Application Program

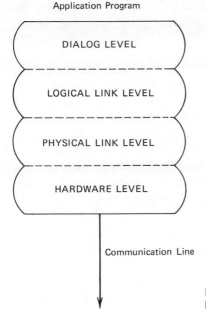

Communication Line

Figure 8.36. Four layers of function in the DECNET protocol.

New York user in Figure 8.37 could pass messages to the Paris computer, even though the two systems are not directly connected by a physical link. As noted in Reference [39], this level of control is concerned with acknowledgment, sequence counting, and routing of *user* messages on an end-to-end basis. Since packet switching is commonly employed in DECNET networks, packets from a single user input message may arrive out of sequence at the destination. The *logical link*

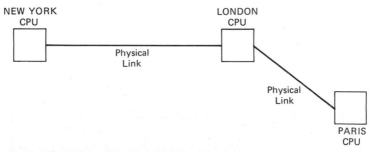

Figure 8.37. Example of DECNET configuration.
The CPUs may be either model PDP10 or PDP11. Possible logical links (transparent to user): New York–London, New York–Paris, London–Paris.

functional layer at the destination node must correctly resequence the packets, thereby reconstructing the individual user message before transferring control of it to the *dialog* layer of functional control at the destination.

A major architectural difference between DECNET and SNA is the peer-coupled structure of DECNET contrasted with the hierarchical, centrally controlled structure of SNA, as described in References [15], [39], and [40]. Since DECNET has been designed around the premise that each user nodal element will contain general purpose computational capability equivalent to at least that of contemporary minicomputers, each user node is capable of locally establishing logical channels to any other user node without involvement of other user nodes. Hence the notion of DECNET being a peer-coupled architecture. By contrast, SNA specifically defines a master control point denoted the *System Services Control Point (SSCP)* which is responsible for controlling all session establishment requests for a specific group of end user terminal nodes. Since these terminal nodes cannot establish sessions without involvement of their controlling SSCP, a hierarchy of different nodal types is implied. Originally SNA was defined to only accommodate a single SSCP in each network as noted in Reference [15], but subsequent enhancements to the architecture noted in References [40] and [41] introduce support for multiple processor nodes, each capable of performing SSCP functions for its own group of terminal nodes. Within this framework a peer-coupled capability also becomes evident among nodes equipped with SSCP functions. However, the decision about which physical nodes are given the ability to perform SSCP functions and hence participate in the peer-coupled activity is purely an economic one. Historically, the costs of processing power and storage required to implement full scale SSCP functions in a single centralized node have been significantly larger than costs for typical minicomputers and intelligent terminal controller units, making it difficult to cost-justify substantial peer-coupled capability. It should be noted that continuing reductions in the relative costs of processing power and storage could change this situation, however. Also, as SSCP functions are split up and spread across multiple control nodes in a network, the required functional capability at each node may be expected to decline in relation to that required for the centralized control approach.

In summary, both DECNET and SNA utilize strict separation of functional layers of responsibility in their network architectures. Both strategies enable users to directly pass messages between systems not physically connected by direct physical links. The key to accomplishing this is the use of store-and-forward transmission techniques (such as those employed in packet switching) over several contiguous data links which comprise a logical channel or path. In DECNET, adaptive, variable path routing may be employed whenever non-tree-structured networks are involved. By contrast, in SNA the paths comprising the logical channel are fixed at the time of network definition. In both SNA and DECNET, the actual management and control of the physical links and nodes in the network is transparent to the network user (it is done behind the scenes by the appropriate network control software).

8.9.　TYPICAL INTELLIGENT NETWORKS APPROACHES OF NONCOMPUTER VENDORS

To complete the discussion of network architectures, the key ideas es- poused by major organizations not involved in the sale of computer equip- ment are now presented. Two types of architectures are considered. First are the packet switching networks in various stages of development and operation by users and common carrier organizations around the world. Second are the less well known but equally important network structures designed around intelligent, dynamic time-division multiplex- ing equipment. The distinctions between these two network architectures are very significant indeed, as subsequent discussions will indicate.

8.9.1.　Packet Switching Network Architectures

Numerous organizations around the world are implementing intelligent networks based on the transmission technique known as packet switch- ing. For example, in the United States several organizations known as value-added carriers are in various stages of developing intelligent net- works that will employ transmission techniques based on packet switch- ing technology [18,19]. In other countries, various governmental and private business concerns are also developing packet-switched types of networks.[4] Even though certain of the previously discussed computer vendor architectures may utilize packet switching, there is an important difference between value-added carrier types and computer-vendor- provided nets. The key distinction is that value-added carriers must develop standardized software-dependent interfaces to their networks, which are as universal as possible. Computer vendors, on the other hand,

---

[4]For example, in Canada the Bell System has developed a packet switching system known as the Datapac network. It is described more fully in Reference [20] and subsequent portions of this chapter.

are free to distribute the different overall system control functions across a broader range of control points on both sides of the communication network interface so as to maximize their ability to supply complete systems. Fortunately, it appears that growing pressure from governmental regulatory agencies, user groups, and trade associations is likely to lead eventually to relatively standardized interfacing procedures for all intelligent networks, regardless of who supplies them. One highly significant effort is the so-called X-25 protocol described in Reference [20], designed to specify all interface standards for attaching terminals and computers (DTEs) to public data networks operating in packet mode.

In packet switching networks, special purpose communications switching minicomputers are typically used in conjunction with leased lines, as shown in Figure 8.38. These minicomputers provide logical channels between user terminals and computers or between computers. Messages from network users are accepted by the network minicomputers, which break them down into fixed-length segments called *packets*. Packets are transmitted through the network in store-and-forward fashion. (See Figure 8.39.) Each packet is individually handed forward along the best available path; it is completely error checked each time another wideband link is traversed. The minicomputers in the Advanced Research Projects Agency (ARPA) network mentioned in Chapter 1, for example, have sufficient intelligence to detect physical link or node outages and to dynamically reroute packets over alternative paths. Complete messages are then reassembled from their constituent packets at the minicomputer which interfaces with the destination user site. With packet switching, the relatively expensive wideband lines can be fully shared via the interleaving action that the packet switching achieves.

Flow or routing control can be provided in numerous ways in packet networks, but most of the systems employ variations of the basic decision rule shown in Figure 8.40. The minicomputers, which perform this function in real time, can readily adapt to changing network conditions merely by having their table entries updated. The key ideas behind this basic routing rule are to keep it simple to implement (to avoid large minicomputer overhead) and flexible enough to be easily and rapidly updated by changing network conditions, and to minimize end-to-end delay for the logical connection by minimizing the number of queuing stages.

Very fast response times can be achieved for most types of user messages since each packet is held only momentarily and then sent along each physical link at wideband speeds. For example, in the ARPA network, user messages of up to 8000 bits are typically sent through the network between destination sites in well under ½ sec (including the time for acknowledgment signaling back to the originating host computer).

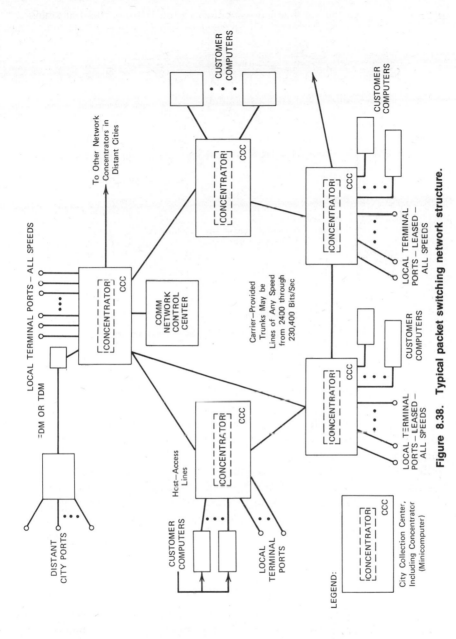

Figure 8.38. Typical packet switching network structure.

LOCAL TERMINAL PORTS – ALL SPEEDS

To Other Network Concentrators in Distant Cities

CUSTOMER COMPUTERS

CONCENTRATOR CCC

FDM OR TDM

DISTANT CITY PORTS

CONCENTRATOR CCC

COMM NETWORK CONTROL CENTER

Host–Access Lines

CUSTOMER COMPUTERS

LOCAL TERMINAL PORTS

Carrier–Provided Trunks May be Lines of Any Speed from 2400 through 230,400 Bits/Sec

CONCENTRATOR CCC

CONCENTRATOR CCC

CUSTOMER COMPUTERS

LOCAL TERMINAL PORTS – LEASED – ALL SPEEDS

CUSTOMER COMPUTERS

LOCAL TERMINAL PORTS – LEASED – ALL SPEEDS

LEGEND:

CONCENTRATOR CCC

City Collection Center, Including Concentrator (Minicomputer)

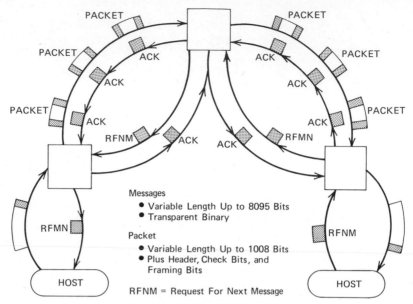

Figure 8.39. Packet switching between host computers.

Other advantages of the packet technology are that individual physical links may employ whatever physical speed is appropriate. These speeds may be increased or decreased with little or no impact on the rest of the network, assuring continuous provision of rapid response times on an end-to-end basis.

Reliability and availability, as seen by the user, are generally better than in conventional leased line systems, since the automatic rerouting feature masks heavy congestion or outages on physical links and intermediate nodes. (Note, however, that if the minicomputers directly connected to the user sources and/or sinks fail, the logical channels become unavailable.)

Bit and block error rates for the logical channels are noticeably enhanced because of the system-provided error checking of packets on a link-by-link basis.

One possible disadvantage of packet switching is the variability and unpredictability of network-induced delays during periods of heavy traffic loading. Another major disadvantage to the user of packet switching networks is the general requirement for extensions or modifications to network control software executing in his communications control units. The following section is intended to delineate the specific functions that

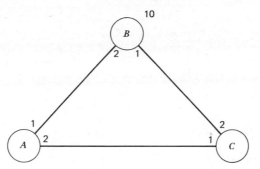

With multiple routes, each node maintains a route table. Each entry in the table is the number of links to other nodes in the network via the shortest path.

Desti-nation Node	Link 1	Link 2	Desti-nation Node	Link 1	Link 2	Desti-nation Node	Link 1	Link 2
A	0	0	A	2	1	A	1	2
B	1	2	B	0	0	B	2	1
C	2	1	C	1	2	C	0	0

| Node A Route Table | Node B Route Table | Node C Route Table |

Routing Rule: To send a message to node in row J of routing table, use link I^*, where $N(I^*)$ is smallest of table entries in row J.

Figure 8.40. Typical message routing approach in packet-switched network.

typically must be added to the user's network control software to interface with an intelligent network employing packet switching.

8.9.2. Interfacing to a Packet Switching Network

First consider the conventional user communications controller configuration with its leased line ports as shown in Figure 8.41. Messages trans-

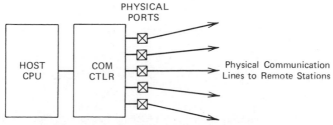

Figure 8.41. Conventional multiport network.

mitted over each of these lines merely contain station address information. The higher level network control software in the communications
controller must "route" or place messages going out to the network in the
correct buffer areas or physical regions of the communications controller.
Thus the higher level routine must assign outbound messages to the
different physical ports of the controller.

Now consider the alternative schematic diagram of Figure 8.42, utilizing an access line to a packet switching system. Only one physical line or
port interfaces to the communications controller. The need arises for
creating and managing "virtual ports" in the user communications controller. Each message destined for any terminal in the network now
requires address information to distinguish it from all other terminals in
the network.

In intelligent networks the user communications controller must supply
the intelligent network with a network address value for each message
transmitted over the host-access line. Figure 8.43 illustrates the typical
format of a physical message being sent over the host-access link. The
line protocol employed between the user communications controller and
the network typically conforms to an industry standard line discipline like
SDLC, BSC, or the International Standards Organization's High-Level
Data Link Control (HDLC). The previously noted X-25 protocol which is
rapidly gaining worldwide acceptance defines HDLC as its standard for
data link control on the host access line; it also defines rules for the
establishment of virtual calls and the positioning of network control
information shown in Figure 8.43.

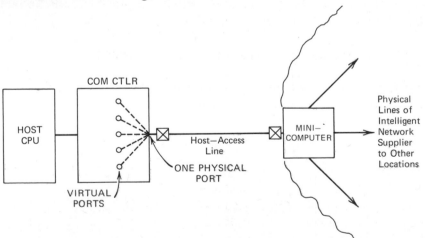

**Figure 8.42. Physical configuration for interfacing network of Figure 8.40 to packet
switching intelligent network.**

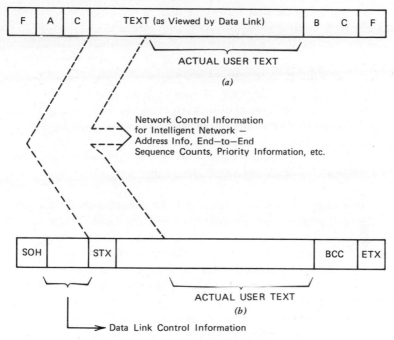

Figure 8.43. Typical message format on host-access line. (a) SDLC type of frame structure. (b) BSC type of frame structure.

Physical frames or blocks on the host access line must contain, in addition to data link control information:

1. Packet network control information such as network address, end-to-end sequence count values, virtual port reference numbers, type codes, and other header information.
2. User message data or bona fide information bits to be passed through the network to the ultimate sink.

The intelligent network minicomputer, which interfaces directly to the user, thus implements a physical line protocol with the user communications controller; it also implements the packet switching network control, employing information supplied in the network header field of incoming user messages. Very importantly, the *network control header* information is indistinguishable from actual user message information when handled by the host access line's *data link control* procedure.

In summary, the main requirements for software extensions to the user communications controller are for the following:

- Creating virtual ports that look just like physical ones to the higher level network control software operating in the user controller. With this approach, existing *user* network control software that drives the conventional network can be maintained. It need only be *extended* to interface with the packet type of network.

- Formatting physical frames or blocks of data sent to the intelligent network in a manner compatible with both *(a)* the data link control procedure, and *(b)* the network control procedure used by the intelligent network. This function means supplying correct network addresses and other control information in the network control header field of frames or blocks transmitted to the network.

8.9.3. Alternative Intelligent Network Architectures Employing Time-Division Multiplexed Circuit-Switched Connections

Packet switching networks of the ARPA network type were originally designed for computer-to-computer traffic, characterized by bursty, highly variable requirements for virtual channel bandwidth. Most successful packet networks to date have required the use of wideband physical lines (50,000 bits/sec or more) between the minicomputers in order to provide sufficiently low response times of less than 0.5 sec. Such networks obviously can also provide excellent response times for terminal–computer types of traffic but can be inefficient and relatively costly, unless user message sizes cause network packets to be fully loaded with characters. In addition, the user must modify his network control software to implement terminal-to-computer connections to packet types of networks.

An attractive, economical intelligent networking alternative to packet switching has been under continual refinement by various independent time-division multiplexer vendors and certain common carriers. The basic idea is to use networks of intelligent statistical time-division multiplexers to dynamically manage the subchannel allocations on the wideband lines that interconnect the time-division multiplexers (see Figure 8.44). Codex Corporation recently introduced such a system, which was "designed to offer a superior alternative to packet switching for terminal-oriented networks." Described in References [21] and [36], a network of these intelligent multiplexers can provide predictable delays of less than 50 msec for terminal users when shared link data rates are as low as 2400 bits/sec. End-to-end network error control for user connections can be provided with sophisticated ARQ procedures between the interface processors. Additional similar intelligent multiplexing schemes have been developed by other vendors like Computer Transmission Corporation,

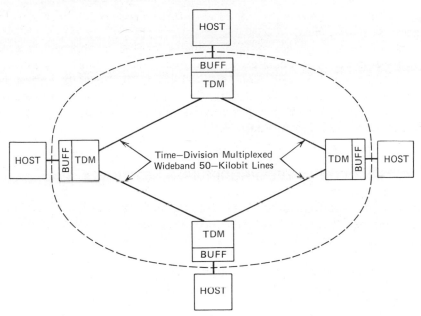

HYBRID PACKET-SWITCHED/CIRCUIT-SWITCHED CONFIGURATION
- ERROR CONTROL ON STORE/FORWARD BASIS ONLY BETWEEN SOURCE AND SINK HOSTS
- NO DELAY AT INTERMEDIATE NODES
- DEMAND ASSIGNED CONNECTIONS

Figure 8.44.   Intelligent TDM network.

which supplied multiplexing equipment for the Canadian Dataroute network. This networking strategy is described in Reference [22].

In the intelligent TDM network, there are no intermediate network queuing points between the user source and sink devices (except for those in user processors, which interface directly to the source and the sink). User connections are thus dynamically created by the real-time management of the time-division multiplexing hierarchy. As with packet switching systems, bypass connections can be established by using alternative TDM routes, should certain shared links or intermediate TDM's fail. Also, user data channels can be optionally equipped with encryption features on an end-to-end basis, providing enhanced *data security*. The net result is that the flexibility and error protection of packet switching networks can be provided with faster and more predictable response times. No modification of user network control software is required. Also, lower shared line costs usually result, since comparable user response times are typically provided with slower line speeds than those in packet switching nets.

The main disadvantages of this intelligent networking approach are the control complexity associated with real-time allocation and management of line slots in the frames of multiplexed links. Also, usually some time delay is associated with the allocation of time slots to user virtual channels, although this delay can typically be kept to millisecond values with well-chosen control algorithms.

8.10. SECURITY IN TELEPROCESSING NETWORKS

Another all-important control function that must be considered in selecting a network structure is security. Providing security involves two basically separate notions:

1. Controlling access to the system.
2. Assuring security of the data in their movements through the various subsystems.

In this section, commonly employed approaches to solving each of these problems are briefly summarized. The reader interested in more details of implementing the various techniques suggested herein may find them in References [23] through [35].

8.10.1. Access Security

Almost every communications-based system contains some features for selectively restricting access to it. The issue of how much access security should be provided can be resolved only by thoroughly evaluating costs, risks, and benefits that may accrue. Not every system should contain all the elaborate security mechanisms outlined herein. Every system planner should, however, be aware of the alternatives so that they may be evaluated for timeliness, suitability, and cost effectiveness in a given situation.

Access security is typically provided by a combination of software and hardware locks distributed across the terminals, communication network, and processing complexes. Both human beings and hardware devices must be considered in devising a sensible scheme of access security checks. Also, the system designer should realize that much can be done *outside the system* to facilitate successful implementation of access security procedures *within the system*. For example, strategic placement of terminals within building areas not accessible to the general public (or to all employees, for that matter) may substantially minimize the number of individuals physically capable of using the system.

Within the system, checks may be provided at any of the following levels in the typical usage procedure:

1. Physical locking of the terminal. Some type of hardware key, badge, or software key based on a physical characteristic of an individual may be used to "unlock" the terminal. These physical characteristics may range from knowledge of a code word to such exotic attributes as voice prints, hand geometry, and handwriting characteristics. Martin discusses the relative merits of these alternatives in greater length in Reference [23].

2. Checking of users of physical terminals. In systems with certain types of physical locks on terminals, a second layer of protection is possible via procedures that selectively enable persons to unlock them. (We are still talking about approaches for controlling the unlocking of the terminals.)

3. Once the terminal is physically unlocked, checking the establishment of a physical communication line. In dedicated line systems, one usually exists permanently. However, in dial-up systems, the number of individuals able to form physical communication links may be restricted and controlled by limiting the number of persons who know the correct telephone numbers to call to access a system. Furthermore, such numbers should be changed frequently, if security is important. In the time sharing business, most companies are very secretive about disseminating local dial-up numbers for their computer ports. Such information could be of value to competitors wanting to monitor grade of service. The unethical competitor who knows the right telephone numbers could even flood these lines with calls during the busy periods of the day to tie up the lines and cause an increased number of busy signals.

4. Physical terminal identification by system. For many early teleprocessing systems connected over dedicated lines it was naively assumed that any physical terminal connected to a leased line should be permitted to establish communications. More sophisticated networking procedures can be employed to screen all physical terminals, whether connected over leased or dial-up lines. In dial-up systems, access is often restricted to terminals capable of supplying the correct answerback code at the time when the physical link is established. This level of lock checking is often provided automatically without any opportunity for user intervention.

5. Identification of user by system. In contrast with level 2 above, the user now must pass an access check by the operating system of the computer with which he is attempting to communicate. Usually, there are two levels of checking here. Valid users are given specific identification codes that will be recognized by the system; they also are required to enter passwords or special code words which can be changed as often as desired. However, if users are careless about guarding identification codes and passwords, these schemes provide little or no protection against unauthorized system usage. A more elaborate scheme designed to prevent transferability of access involves the use of a security card containing some physical-attribute identifier of the authorized cardholder. This attribute is checked dynamically against the measured value of the comparable attribute value for the person presenting the security card.

6. Control over the establishment of logical links by the system. As intelligent network structures become more prevalent, mere control over the establishment of physical communication links will not suffice. Selective schemes for controlling shared-user packet-type networks will have to prevent unauthorized users and devices from establishing logical connections. Organization A may have numerous users and/or devices authorized to establish connections with other users and/or devices controlled by Organization A. Organization B users and/or devices may share the same physical facilities but must not be permitted to establish logical connections to other users unless *both* organizations agree in advance to do so. Network control software must contain elaborate security checks to prevent one user's data from being transmitted to an unauthorized user destination. Authorization tables of the type shown in Figure 8.45 and discussed in Reference [23] will need to be designed into the network control software. All pairwise cross combinations of sources and sinks can be checked for validity during the logical link establishment phase of control activity between two ports. The link will be established only if it is shown to be valid in the authorization table of the master network control program.

7. Control over access to specific programs and data files by specific users and devices. These capabilities are typically provided in the operating system of the computer being accessed. They are discussed at length in the references noted below.

The general ideas of improving security by (a) minimizing the number of persons who must be trustworthy, (b) frequently changing the code words that authorized users must enter, and (c) tying authorization pro-

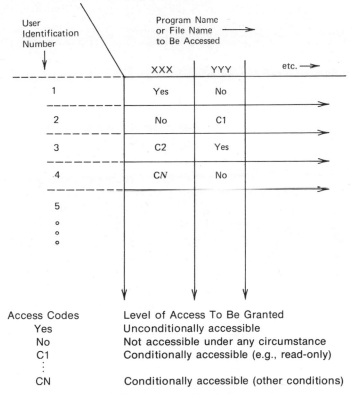

	XXX	YYY	etc. →
1	Yes	No	
2	No	C1	
3	C2	Yes	
4	CN	No	
5			

User Identification Number

Program Name or File Name → to Be Accessed

Access Codes	Level of Access To Be Granted
Yes	Unconditionally accessible
No	Not accessible under any circumstance
C1	Conditionally accessible (e.g., read-only)
⋮	
CN	Conditionally accessible (other conditions)

Figure 8.45. Authorization table structure.

cedures to specific physical attributes of the human beings authorized to access the system are all pointed out by Martin [23]. Other significant contributions to the access security problem, for both teleprocessing systems and computer systems in general, have been made by Hoffman [24], Farber and Larson [25], Winkler and Danner [26], and Lipner [27]. Other relevant works are the six volume series entitled *Data Security and Data Processing* by IBM, noted as References [28] through [34], and a group of papers presented at an IBM data security symposium [35].

8.10.2. Approaches to Assuring the Security of Data in Their Movements through the Network

The approaches available for providing data security in the network subsystems are now considered briefly. Focus is placed on terminal-oriented techniques, features usable in the transmission network, and alternatives available in the processing complexes. Obviously there will be interaction between the various stages, but the basic decision to enhance security will usually translate into requirements for added functions in the terminals, in the networking devices, and at the processing complexes where the data files are located.

8.10.2.1. Terminal Subsystem Approaches

All terminals in a system will generally not require the same level of security. The following options are available to enhance security at the terminal level:

1. Features for selective print suppression, keyboard locking, overstriking, and blinding of confidential information. Equipment that enables the user to guard the privacy of his identification codes, passwords, and other confidential data may be employed. Hard copy terminals should have features to suppress printing of these characters to avoid unauthorized or unnecessary dissemination of the information. Similarly, CRT types of terminals should provide options for suppressing the local display of identification characters and confidential data values entered by the user.

2. Source–sink encryption procedures. Most terminals of the future will contain optional functions for performing data transformation operations known as encryption procedures. Reference [27] discusses several approaches to encryption and presents the details of a proposed U.S. federal information processing standard algorithm. Other options for source–sink encryption are discussed in References [23] and [26]. The general idea behind successful encryption operations is illustrated in Figure 8.46.

   The key is a sequence of bits known at both the source (encoding) end of a logical link and the sink (decoding) end. To provide maximum security on an end-to-end basis, the key must be long enough so that all possible combinations cannot be exhausted in reasonable amounts of time by trial and error. It also must be changed frequently enough to minimize the likelihood of unauthorized users obtaining the key values in other ways.

   Martin [23] illustrates these points by citing a simple example of a key employing 12 alphabetic characters. Even if the enciphering algorithm is known by an intruder, who can test alternative keys at the rate of 1 every 10^{-6} sec using a computer, it will take him an average time of $26^{12}/2$ μsec or approximately 1500 years to discover the correct key!

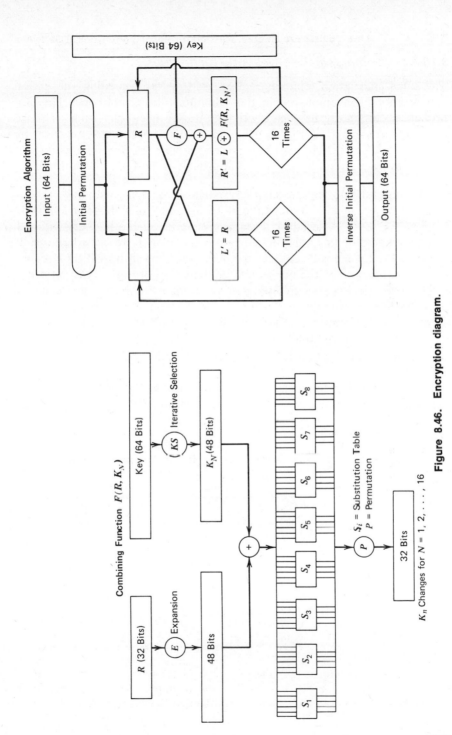

Figure 8.46. Encryption diagram.

415

8.10.2.2. Communication Network Techniques

The same encryption techniques discussed in the preceding subsection can of course be employed in the communications network. This approach is commonly used in shared multiuser networks such as those being operated by the domestic value-added carriers and in some cases by the satellite carriers. These organizations propose to offer enhanced security for in-transit data by a twofold approach embodying the following:

1. The natural interleaving characteristics of packet switching, which make physical lines more difficult to monitor than those in conventional systems. A serial bit stream passing through a packet-switched communication line contains many packets from different source–sink pairs. Predetermined schemes for decoding such in-transit bit streams are complicated by the unpredictable dynamics of traffic flow patterns. However, *access lines* to intelligent network switching centers can still be monitored just as easily as those in conventional systems. For users with extreme security requirements, a second level of protection is provided on an optional basis.
2. End-to-end encryption between user terminals and computers.

Table 8.3, taken from Telenet Communications Corporation's filing to the Federal Communications Commission, summarizes its basic strategy

Table 8-3.   Data Communications Security in the Telenet System[a]

Protection Provided against	Protection Provided by	
	Customer	Telenet
Unauthorized access to resources	Password protection	Limited address capability
	Terminal identification check	Password translation service
Unauthorized monitoring of data in transit	User encryption of data	End-to-end encryption service

[a]Excerpted from Reference [18], the FCC filing of Telenet Communications Corporation to obtain authority to establish and operate a packet-switched data communications network in the continental United States, Oct. 9, 1973.

both for providing access security and for preventing unauthorized monitoring of data in transit.

Other security approaches being employed in both dedicated intraorganizational networks and shared-usage interorganization networks involve the use of end-to-end coding procedures to achieve *data compression*, thereby reducing the number of bits that have to be sent over the network.

Reference [36] describes a data compression technique employed by the Codex Corporation of Newton, Massachusetts, to reduce network transmission volume requirements significantly, in some cases by as much as 30 to 40%, in comparison to the bits used in conventional code representations of the user's data. These situations are most appropriate in applications involving lengthy transfers of bulk data. The computation overhead and added delays associated with the compression algorithms make such procedures less attractive in interactive applications.

8.10.2.3. Data Security in the Processing Complexes

Files and programs may be stored in encrypted form once they reach the computer processing locations. However, the added overhead requirement of decryption before processing can take place makes such approaches cumbersome, time consuming, and costly. Other popular possibilities are the use of authorization tables and elaborate user password recognition schemes such as those discussed in References [23] through [35].

Most intelligent communication network architectures proposed and implemented to date have opted for the service philosophy of delivering data bits as quickly as possible to the destination. This minimizes the need for in-transit storage facilities of large data files, thereby minimizing, in turn, the need for additional encryption functions at intermediate store-and-forward nodes. In intelligent networks such as the one proposed to the FCC by IT&T's Domestic Transmission Systems in Reference [19], intermediate bulk storage facilities will be required for the accumulation of messages not requesting intermediate delivery. In these cases, security can be enhanced by storing such messages in their network-encrypted form. No decryption would take place until messages were deposited at the ultimate destination. The other option, involving decryption of incoming messages at each intermediate node of the network, would require a new encryption operation for storage of the messages in secure form at the intermediate nodes. Clearly the processing overhead would be greater in the latter case; it is not obvious that the additional protection afforded would be proportionately significant.

8.11. CONTROL PROGRAMS AND SOFTWARE IN TELEPROCESSING SYSTEMS

In contemporary data processing systems, all the control functions discussed previously are accomplished via an integrated blend of hardware and software techniques, with some functions like circuit establishment even being performed manually in certain applications. Much has already been said about the hardware aspects of the terminals, modems, lines, multiplexers, and front-end processors that comprise most contemporary networks. Here our objective is to briefly describe the characteristics of and the interrelationships between the different types of programs used in typical systems. Of particular interest are the communications control programs that perform the line control functions in third- and fourth-generation data processing systems.

Non-communications-based data processing systems involve *two main categories* of programs, *operating system* or *supervisory programs* and user-oriented *applications programs*, which perform the actual data processing tasks such as inventory control, payroll, and accounts receivable. Operating system programs control the flow of jobs through the data processing system by allocating all the *hardware* and *software* resources to the various users to achieve maximum job throughput. Operating systems are thus responsible for scheduling and controlling the applications programs; they perform such tasks as user program loading, coordinating the input/output requests of user programs, selecting and loading compilers, composing main program and subroutine linkages, interrupt processing, and the handling of all abnormal or emergency conditions.

In *communications-based systems,* numerous additional software tasks must be repetitively performed at the point where all the lines interface with the main processing complex. As shown in Figure 8.47, the *communications control program* effectively interfaces the *users'* application programs with their remotely located input/output units. These types of programs are completely responsible for performing all the data-transmission-related control functions required for applications programs to read and write data at remote terminals (see Figure 8.48). As the previous discussion in this chapter suggests, these functions are uniquely related to the data transmission environment, enabling us to discuss four main categories of programs in communications-based computer systems:

1. Operating system programs.
2. Communications control programs.
3. Applications programs involving communications.
4. Noncommunications applications programs (e.g., standard batch).

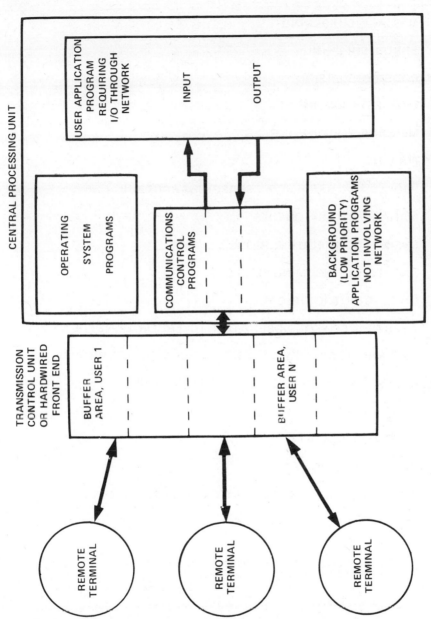

Figure 8.47. Relationship of user programs and communications control programs.

419

- MESSAGE BUFFERING

- ERROR CHECKING

- CODE CONVERSION

- LINK ESTABLISHMENT

- MESSAGE FORMATTING

- POLLING

- PROCESSING BREAK OR ESCAPE CHARACTERS

- MANAGING TASK QUEUES

- CHECKING TIMEOUT PERIODS

- ANSWERING INCOMING CALLS

- DIALING OUTGOING CALLS

- ALERTING CONSOLE OPERATOR TO ERROR CONDITIONS

- ASSIGNING PRIORITY CLASSIFICATIONS TO TERMINALS

- COLLECTING MESSAGE TRAFFIC STATISTICS

- MESSAGE EDITING

- LINK TERMINATION

- CIRCUIT TERMINATION

- CHECKING FOR CHARACTER SYNCHRONIZATION

- PROCESS INPUT-OUTPUT REQUEST FROM USER APPLICATIONS PROGRAMS

Figure 8.48. Typical functions of sophisticated communications control programs.

420

Figure 8.49 illustrates the hierarchy of these types of programs in most installations.

The *operating system*, since it controls all aspects of how the machine is assigned to job and task processing, must necessarily be *top priority*. Since much of the activity in a communications-based system is characterized by completely random requests for service at remote terminals, the *second-priority programs* must handle all communications-related functions as they occur, that is, processing for these types of functions

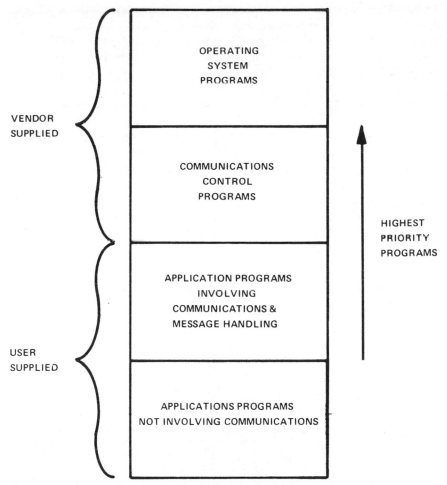

Figure 8.49. Hierarchy of programs in traditional communications-based computer system.

cannot be scheduled at convenient times in the way applications processing tasks usually are. Another important function of these *communications control programs* is to allow the applications programmer to write *high level* input/output statements. The communications control programs automatically translate these high level I/O requests into complex sequences of low level machine language instructions, thereby eliminating any need for the applications programmer to worry about generating his own machine language instructions for the myriad line control functions discussed in preceding sections of this chapter. Examples of familiar communications control programs are IBM's Basic Telecommunications Access Method (BTAM), IBM's Virtual Telecommunications Access Method (VTAM), IBM's Telecommunications Access Method (TCAM), Univac's Exec VIII, Burroughs' Master Control Program (MCP), and Digital Equipment's Communications Oriented Multiple Terminal Executive (COMTEX) packages. Although these programs have been designed by vendors aimed at penetrating broadly varying application markets with a wide spectrum of processing hardware, they generally enable applications programmers to use high level input/output instructions. These control programs inplement varying percentages of the line control operations, thereby performing the highly desirable function of removing very complex programming tasks from the duties of the applications programmer.

The communications control programs may be executed by the main computer itself or by a programmable, special purpose front-end computer. Until recently, the approach used in most systems involved special

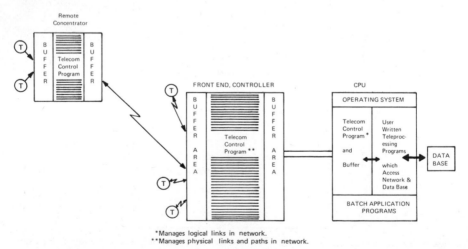

*Manages logical links in network.
**Manages physical links and paths in network.

Figure 8.50.   Layers of telecommunications control in CPU and remote concentrator.

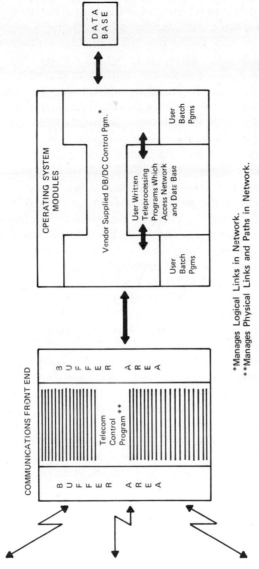

Figure 8.51. Vendor-supplied canned programs for data base/data communications (DB/DC) access control and buffering.

*Manages Logical Links in Network.
**Manages Physical Links and Paths in Network.

hardware-oriented front-end control units that were generally not programmable, so that the communications control programs had to be executed by the same device that processes applications programs. Performing all the software tasks associated with communications line control thereby reduced the main processing unit's overall ability to handle user programs, in many cases by a significant amount. Recently, however, stored program front ends have been receiving increased attention by users. Devices of this type effectively perform all the communications handling software tasks in a separate computer, freeing the main computer to perform applications processing tasks exclusively. Other major advantages of these contemporary front ends will center around their ability to implement the newer, more efficient line disciplines, like SDLC and DDCMP. Such techniques will make possible true full-duplex link operation, thereby achieving efficient use of satellite channels, reduced overhead on multipoint lines, and more efficient RJE network usage. In conjunction with the advanced access methods, they also provide the means whereby several different applications like CRT, data entry, and remote job entry may share the same lines. Since the control functions are then performed in numerous places outside the CPU, more complicated multiple layers of telecommunications control software are required, one module in the host CPU, one in each adjacent communications front end, and one in each remote controller or concentrator (Figure 8.50). In such systems it becomes increasingly difficult for users to maintain responsibility for the network control programs, so that standard data communications monitors are frequently supplied by the CPU vendor. Other independent vendors also offer similar canned network control programs, which automatically permit the user to write real-time application programs that access remote stations with the same simplicity as is inherent in accessing local peripherals from a batch program (Figure 8.51). Examples of both types of host-resident, network and data base access programs are IBM's well-known CICS and Cincom System's Environ-1 packages.

An additional advantage of these canned teleprocessing driver programs is their ability to readily collect, tabulate, and display numerous statistics about message lengths, arrival rates, retransmissions, and so on and to provide checkpoint restart on a transaction basis in most instances. Such features are essential for most users.

REFERENCES

1. N. Abramson, "The Aloha System," Chapter 14 in *Computer Communication Networks*, Prentice-Hall, Englewood Cliffs, N. J., 1972.

2. J. R. Knight, "A Case Study: Airline Reservations Systems," *IEEE Proceeding— Special Issue on Computer Communications*, November 1972.

3. L. West, "Loop-Transmission Control Structures," *IEEE Transactions on Communications*, Vol. COM-20, June 1972.

4. B. Stutzman, "Data Communication Control Procedures," *ACM Computing Surveys*, Vol. 4, No. 4, December 1972.

5. J. L. Eisenbies, "Conventions for Digital Data Communication Link Design," *IBM Systems Journal*, Vol. 6, 1967, pp 267–302.

6. *General Information: Binary Synchronous Communications*, IBM Publication GA27-3004, IBM Corp., 1969.

7. J. W. Cullen, "Binary Synchronous Communications," *Computer Design*, October 1968.

8. James P. Gray, "Line Control Procedures," *IEEE Proceedings—Special Issue on Computer Communications*, November 1973.

9. R. A. Donnan and J. R. Kersey, "Synchronous Data Link Control: A perspective," *IBM Systems Journal*, No. 2, 1974.

10. J. R. Kersey, "Synchronous Data Link Control," *Data Communications*, May–June 1974, McGraw-Hill, New York.

11. J. R. Kersey, "Taking a Fresh Look at Data Link Controls," *Data Communications Systems*, Vol. 2, No. 1, September 1973, McGraw-Hill, New York.

12. *Synchronous Data Link Control: General Information Manual*, IBM SRL GA27-3093, IBM Corp., 1974.

13. S. Wecker, "Dialog-Digital Data Communications Message Protocol," *Data Communications*, September–October 1974, McGraw-Hill, New York.

14. "Proposed American National Standard for Advanced Data Communication Control Procedures," ANSI X3S3, 7th Draft, December 1973.

15. *System Network Architecture—General Information*, IBM Publication GA27-3102, IBM Corp., January 1975.

16. *DECNET*, Digital Equipment Corporation Brochure, Maynard, Mass., 1975.

17. *IBM System Network Architecture and SDLC*, Auerbach Computer Technology Special Report, Auerbach Publishers, Philadelphia, Pa., 1975.

18. Telenet Communications Corp. filing before the FCC, Application for Authority to Establish and Operate a Packet-Switched Data Communications Network in the Continental United States, Oct. 9, 1973.

19. ITT Domestic Transmission Systems, Inc., filing before the FCC, Application for Authority to Lease Circuit Facilities and to Establish and Operate a Packet-Switched, Digital Data Communications Network Providing Store-and-Forward Capability in the Contiguous U. S. Which Allows Communications between Technically Incompatible Data Terminals, Dec. 5, 1975.

20. "Datapac, Standard Network Access Protocol (SNAP)," the Computer Communications Group, Trans-Canada Telephone System, March 1976.

21. "Binary Synchronous Communication and Statistical Multiplexing," Codex Corporation 6000 Application Note 1, Newton, Mass., December 1975.

22. D. R. Doll, "The Real World of Digital Communications—the User's Current Needs," WESCON conference paper, Los Angeles, Calif., September 1974.

23. J. T. Martin, *Security, Accuracy and Privacy in Computer Systems*, Prentice-Hall, Englewood Cliffs, N. J., 1973.

24. Lance J. Hoffman (Ed.), *Security and Privacy in Computer Systems*, Melville Publishing Co., Los Angeles, 1973.

25. D. Farber and K. Larson, "Network Security via Dynamic Process Renaming," *Proceedings of Fourth Data Communications Symposium* (Quebec City, Canada), October 1975.

26. S. Winkler and L. Danner, "Data Security in the Computer Communication Environment," *IEEE Computer*, February 1974.

27. S. B. Lipner, "Secure Computer Systems for Network Applications," *Proceedings of ACM Fourth Data Communications Symposium* (Quebec City, Canada), October 1975.

28. *Data Security and DP: Introduction and Overview*, IBM Publication G320-1370, Vol. 1, IBM Corp., June 1974.

29. *Data Security and Data Processing: Study Summary*, IBM Publication G320-1371, Vol. 2, IBM Corp., June 1974.

30. *Data Security and Data Processing*, Part 1. *State of Illinois: Executive Overview*, IBM Publication G320-1371, Vol. 3, IBM Corp., June 1974.

31. *Data Security and Data Processing*, Part 2. *Study Results: State of Illinois*, IBM Publication G320-1373, Vol. 3, IBM Corp., June 1974.

32. *Data Security and Data Processing: Study Results—Massachusetts Institute of Technology*, IBM Publication G320-1374, Vol. 4, IBM Corp., June 1974.

33. *Data Security and Data Processing: Study Results—TRW Systems, Inc.*, IBM Publication G320-1375, Vol. 5, IBM Corp., June 1974.

34. *Data Security and Data Processing: Evaluations and Study Experiences—Resource Security System*, IBM Publication G320-1376, Vol. 6, IBM Corp., June 1974.

35. *Proceedings of IBM Data Security Symposium* (Boston, Mass.), April 1973.

36. "Data Compression," Codex Corporation 6000 Application Note 2, Newton, Mass., December 1975.

37. D. C. Zatyko and J. W. Conard, "Bit Oriented Data Link Control Protocols," *Auerbach Data Communication Management Reports*, Auerbach Publishers, Philadelphia, Pa., 1977.

38. J. H. McFadyen, "Systems Network Architecture: An Overview," *IBM System's Journal*, Vol. 15, No. 1, 1976.

39. "DECNET Specification for Network Services Protocol (NSP) Version 2," Digital Equipment Corp. Publication, Maynard, Mass., November 1976.

40. *ACF/VTAM Design Objectives*, IBM Publication GC38-0253, IBM Corp., 1977.

41. *Network Operation Support Program—General Information Manual*, IBM Publication GC38-0251, IBM Corp., 1977.

NINE

SYSTEMS DESIGN CONSIDERATIONS— AN OVERVIEW

The ultimate justification for any business data communications system is an expectation that the network will provide more timely management information, reduce costs, decrease delays in filling customer orders, increase corporate productivity, or favorably affect some combination of these and related factors. Such fundamental business considerations should be an overriding influence on the systems design effort at the time when all the previously discussed subsystem components (terminals, lines, signal converters, line sharing devices, software, etc.) are interconnected into a cost-effective network configuration. The key element of the design philosophy espoused here is that the first step in network design must be concerned solely with establishing the user's requirements. These application-dependent objectives, once sufficiently well defined, can form the basis for subsequent efforts concerned with determining the most suitable line routings, transmission speeds, terminal types, and other characteristics of the ultimate network layout.

The user requirements should be stipulated solely in terms of the application objectives and should not be influenced by particular hardware, software, or available communications services. For example, such factors as terminal locations, transaction frequencies, growth parameters, computer locations, and urgencies are characteristics of the application. On the other hand, a factor like the decision to use leased or dial-up lines is not directly related to the primary application requirements of a system.

To summarize, our design philosophy is that the *user's business application requirements should dictate the ultimate technical specifications for the network*, and not vice versa. Planning steps must be concerned primarily with quantifying the so-called *constants* of the application environment. Once these factors are determined, the specific characteristics of the data communications network can be established by considering the design *variables* outlined in Figure 9.1. The objective of network configuration procedures is to determine the specific option for each of these variables that results in the least costly layout capable of satisfying the user's application requirements.

This chapter considers the constants, variables, and tradeoffs as-

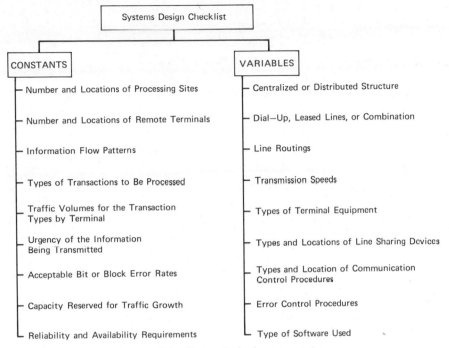

Figure 9.1. Network design parameters.

sociated with network design. Alternative approaches to the stipulation of *user requirements* in *leased line* and *dial-up* networks are considered, as are the factors that influence whether the network is *centralized* or *distributed*. The final portion summarizes the main types of network organization most commonly employed in contemporary communications-based computer systems. Approaches to configuring minimum-cost layouts for each of these network forms are presented. The design techniques emphasize the use of loopback and fault isolation devices throughout a network to enable rapid troubleshooting, identification, and replacement of malfunctioning components with minimal involvement by maintenance/operations personnel.

9.1. PRELIMINARY DATA NEEDED—THE DESIGN CONSTANTS

Before any of the numerous possible network arrangements are considered, the constants of the design problem must be properly gauged.[1] This

¹For further discussion of this subject, see References [1] and [22].

initial step requires obtaining estimates of the following application parameters:

- Number and location of the processing sites.
- Number and location of the remote terminals.
- Information flow patterns between the remote and central sites.
- Types of transactions to be processed.
- Traffic volumes for the transaction types, by terminal.
- Urgency of the information to be transmitted (when must a response be supplied to the remote station?).
- Acceptable undetected error rate (bit or block).
- Capacity reserved for traffic growth.
- Reliability and availability requirements.

These factors, which essentially define the geography and performance requirements of the network, must be thoroughly assessed before any major equipment decisions are made. There will inevitably be some interplay between the above parameters and the equipment in a network, but these items are essentially implementation-free. Their importance cannot be overemphasized, since the need to obtain timely access to data bases and computational resources from geographically diverse locations is the primary justification for using a data communications network.

9.2. DESIGN VARIABLES AND TRADEOFFS

Once the general nature of the design constants has been established, the variables to be considered must be assessed. The primary intent here is to itemize the factors that may have a major impact on the design effort. Obviously there will be many specific applications in which one or more of these parameters is fixed a priori for some reason or other. In general, any or all of the following variables may have an influence on the cost/performance characteristics of a network:

- Type of network organization (centralized or distributed).
- Type of lines (dial-up, leased, or combination).
- Line routings.
- Transmission speeds or capacities.
- Types of terminal equipment used at remote sites.
- Locations and types of line sharing techniques and devices.

- Locations and types of communications control procedures.
- Error control procedures and software.

An optimal network design procedure attempts to determine the most suitable combinations of these parameters that satisfy the user's stated objectives of performance and reliability. Tradeoffs associated with centralized and distributed architectures were discussed in Chapter 1. The topology or link routings of a network constitute one of the most critical variables; with an ill-chosen line layout little can be done with all other factors combined to produce an efficient, cost-effective network. The options here involve considerations as to whether the links are switched or leased, and multipoint or point-to-point, in addition to the multitude of different routing possibilities. Another basic option is whether an intelligent public data network service like those offered by the value-added carriers would be more cost-effective than the above-noted privately supplied network alternatives which utilize conventional common carrier offerings. In fact, the combinatorial complexity associated with these topology options is one of the major reasons for developing computer programs that perform certain network design functions. To illustrate, for a network having exactly n remote nodes to be interconnected to a central site using leased lines of a single speed, there are $(n + 1)^{n-1}$ different possible tree layouts. If redundant links must also be considered, the number of possible layouts is increased.

The transmission speed used on the links of the network is an equally important consideration, since the basic throughput capacity and responsiveness of the entire communication subsystem are determined by this parameter. However, unless some type of buffered terminal is used at the remote sites, the choice of line speeds may be dictated exclusively by the terminal operating characteristics. The basic tradeoff here involves whether an inexpensive, unbuffered terminal operating over low speed (teletype grade) lines at rates less than 300 bits/sec is more cost effective than a buffered terminal operating over higher speed lines. The buffered terminal is capable of transmitting its data traffic more rapidly over the higher speed line, thereby reducing line holding times and possibly providing net economies over the lower speed alternative. Further complicating the design process is the lengthy array of tariffs and services available from the carriers and other telecommunications suppliers, as was seen in Chapter 3.

The basic motivation for considering line sharing devices stems from the economies of scale in the cost of bandwidth for any particular link. For example, voice-grade lines have historically cost from 1.5 to 2 times as much as lower speed lines of the same length. However, voice-grade lines are capable of transmitting data at speeds at least 20 to 30 times greater than the typical low speed facility. Thus the cost per unit of throughput in a fully utilized voice-grade line can be forced down to less than one tenth of that of the low speed line by using suitably chosen techniques such as multiplexing and concentration. Sharing also provides economies at faster speeds. In addition, the intelligence of contemporary sharing devices enables users to dynamically allocate transmission capacity to the applications and remote terminals in greatest need at any point in time.

Design options for communications control in teleprocessing networks involve the way in which the control is distributed across various stages and the specific approach utilized for line, path, and network control (see Chapter 8). Several possibilities for location of the control function generally exist. It may be performed in the CPU on a cycle stealing basis, in a separate preprocessor unit at the CPU site, or at various intelligent nodes in the network. The actual location used will be strongly influenced by the characteristics of the main CPU, since mainframes seldom afford the complete latitude most users desire.

Using a simple line buffer or adapter in the CPU as the communications interface forces the CPU to be regularly interrupted, using cycle stealing, so that bits and/or characters may be accumulated as fast as they arrive. This communications-generated overhead can consume as much as 30 to 40% of the available main processor cycles and limits the capability of the CPU to perform standard processing tasks. Nevertheless this approach may be the most economical one in lightly loaded systems, in those with relatively few lines, or in applications where sophistication of the preprocessor and/or remote communications control units cannot be justified.

The second location option for communications control—a separate preprocessor or communications control unit standing adjacent to the main CPU—represents the next level of increasing sophistication. The control device may be hardwired or programmable; it may perform such functions as terminal identification and speed sensing, message/character assembly, polling, code conversion, error control, and possibly automatic dialing/answering functions in certain applications. The preprocessor interacts with the main CPU, using compatible speeds and message formats to minimize unnecessary communications overhead in the main processor. This approach (as opposed to cycle stealing) is used in most medium and large current generation mainframes. Its primary disadvantages stem from the relative expense (purchase prices of typical preprocessors, including software, currently range upward from $50,000 to $100,000) and from a lack of flexibility inherent in some of the more widely used hardwired devices. Other features of communications processors are discussed in References [2] and [3].

Even though many of these same network control functions can often be performed equally well at remote sites, equipment costs and capabilities have historically not provided substantial incentives for this approach in most applications. The primary reason is that a fairly elaborate processor will still be required at the central site when a sophisticated remote communications control unit is used. Such schemes tend to be economical only in networks with large clusters of remote terminals in various remote geographic regions. However, as hardware costs continue to decline, the number of networks that can economically afford remotely positioned controllers will increase dramatically. Determining the optimum location for these remote controllers is a complex question involving many of the same tradeoffs previously cited. Of course, the lower level functions of data link and path control are often found distributed across one or more stages of remote intelligence in the network.

The design issue of how best to provide line control is generally not a major concern in leased line networks that exclusively use frequency-division multiplexing (FDM), synchronous time-division multiplexing (STDM), and point-to-point links, or some combination thereof, because these types of static sharing techniques provide each remote terminal with its own dedicated or private communication path to a CPU. However, in networks with multipoint lines, switched lines, concentrators, or multiple CPUs the scheduling procedure for accessing shared lines and concentrators usually has a critical effect on response times and system efficiency.

As previously noted, the two most widely used methods for line control are contention and polling. With full contention control, lines or dial-up ports on a communications device are assigned on a first-come first-served or free-for-all basis. Once a user has established a connection or acquired a line, he retains control and prevents other users from access to his particular line or port until he actively relinquishes control. The simple contention queuing model of Figure 9.2 indicates how congestion and response times rapidly become excessive even if only a few terminals share a line. Contention is widely used in switched networks, particularly when user requests for access to the CPU are unpredictable in both the geographic and the temporal senses. Contention requires little or no extra equipment but is generally inefficient or unacceptable on a line whose throughput requirements exceed 30 to 40% of its maximum transmission capacity. Also, it is difficult to accommodate different classes of user or terminal priorities with contention control, or to conveniently limit the maximum (worst-case) response times in contention systems.

It was seen previously that polling is more suitable than contention in large networks where tight control of line usage is essential for efficient

N = Number of remote terminals on the line, regardless of actual line routings

t_q = Average time spent by a transaction, including waiting and servicing after the line has been obtained

λ = Average arrival-rate of requests for the line (transactions) from a given terminal, assuming a Poisson arrival process at each terminal

$\bar{s}$ = Average time spent on the line for a given terminal once the line has been acquired, assuming holding times are distributed according to a negative exponential distribution

$$t_q = \frac{\bar{s}}{1 - N\lambda\bar{s}}$$

Model assumes that service time for one transaction consists of all transmission and processing activity. Only one transaction may be in service at a time.

Number of Terminals N	$\lambda = \frac{1}{30}$ $\bar{s} = 10^b$	$\lambda = \frac{1}{30}$ $\bar{s} = 5$	$\lambda = \frac{1}{45}$ $\bar{s} = 5$	$\lambda = \frac{1}{60}$ $\bar{s} = 5$	$\lambda = \frac{1}{60}$ $\bar{s} = 10$
1	15	6	5.5	20	12
2	30	7.5	6.5	30	15
3		10	7.5	60	20
4		15	9		30
5		30	11.25		60
6			15		
7	∞	∞	22.5	∞	∞

Table entries are t_q values in minutes

[a]Units for λ are transactions/sec.
[b]Units for $\bar{s}$ are sec/transaction.

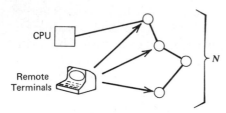

CPU

Remote Terminals

Figure 9.2. Multipoint line queuing model, contention control.

performance. Polling is better than contention when transmitted messages have different levels of priority. If a particular terminal tends to submit many high priority messages, the polling procedure may be designed to query it more frequently than the other terminals. The query sequence can be readily modified under program control. On the other hand, although polling generally yields better performance than contention, it requires costlier hardware and software. Another disadvantage of polling is that remote terminals cannot send data at any time, but can do so only when queried. This is one reason why polled networks are seldom used in applications where all users are not affiliated with the same company or organization. In most networks, some combination of polling and contention is probably best, with polling used for heavily loaded lines and contention for lightly loaded ones. References [7] and [23] contain comprehensive mathematical models of polling strategies which may be used in estimating response time and throughput for various line control options.

9.3. PERFORMANCE MEASURES, USER REQUIREMENTS

Since the objective of most networks is to provide an adequate level of performance at minimum cost, it is immediately apparent that a host of alternative definitions of performance is possible. The most suitable one is usually determined strictly on the basis of user preference. Thus the numerous possible configurations and applications of teleprocessing networks make completely general definitions of performance measures such as throughput and response time elusive and unnecessary. Probably the most significant feature in determining the appropriate performance definition is whether the network uses switched communication connections or is composed of leased lines. Since most networks (or logical subnetworks in large distributed networks) seem to fall naturally into one of these two categories, this distinction is convenient. The classical models used for switched networks have been under continuing refinement for the past 50 years as essential tools in designing existing telephone plants; hence the emphasis here is placed on leased line networks. However, several specialized design problems, such as determining an optimum mixture of WATS and Direct Distance Dial service, are becoming increasingly important to large data users of the switched network.[2]

In leased line networks, the remote terminal users are connected to a processing site by dedicated, full-time communication links. The first step in reducing the seeming complexity of a large network design problem is to individually consider the performance of each functionally independent group of dedicated links in the network. Individual segments and multipoint lines are examples of such independent groups. Only the most heavily loaded lines will have a substantial effect on the overall performance of the network, so that the more lightly loaded portions may be given less consideration in the early stages of design.

[2]See Chapter 3 for details of WATS and Direct Distance Dial services.

The different line sharing techniques employed will have a substantial effect on the particular performance levels obtained. In multiplexed networks, for example, performance is usually characterized in terms of the number of available subchannels in a remote city or region. However, with multipoint lines, the performance measure is usually tied to the time delay between submission of an input message at a remote terminal and receipt of a response back at that terminal, as shown in Figure 9.3. Numerous factors such as the type of terminal, operator characteristics, types of transactions, line speed, line loading, message lengths, line control disciplines, and CPU processing delays will determine the actual delays for a given application.

Each design application usually starts with a statement of a performance constraint such as one of those shown in Figure 9.4.[3] The appropriate type of constraint to use will be determined by the level of detail desired and the advance knowledge of traffic submitted by each remote terminal. As more terminals are multipointed on the same line, the congestion increases up to some maximum acceptable level. Since most response time delay measures increase continually as congestion builds up, the design strategy is to reduce line costs by increasing traffic on shared links to the maximum level of congestion that results in acceptable delays.

Type 1 constraints are generally used when little is known about terminal traffic patterns. It is often assumed that response times will be satisfactory if line loading (utilization) is kept below 60 to 75%, more or less independently of the exact nature of the traffic distributions. These assumptions about acceptable utilization levels are usually based on elementary queuing models, such as those discussed in References [5] to [7]. This approach has been used with substantial success in designing numerous contemporary networks.

A Type 2 performance constraint represents the next level in increasing sophistication. Simple queuing studies, operating experiences, or simulation studies can be used to estimate (in advance of actual design) the maximum number of remote terminals that can satisfactorily share a line. Figure 9.2 shows a tabulation of queuing delays as a function of congestion for a fairly crude model of a multipoint line. More elaborate queuing models and even simulation can be used to estimate N_{max} if the model of Figure 9.2 is not appropriate. This type of constraint is particularly useful in applications where the transmission properties of multipoint lines dictate a practical limit to the number of remote stations that can share the line.

---

[3]These constraints and other related issues are discussed at length in References [4] to [8].

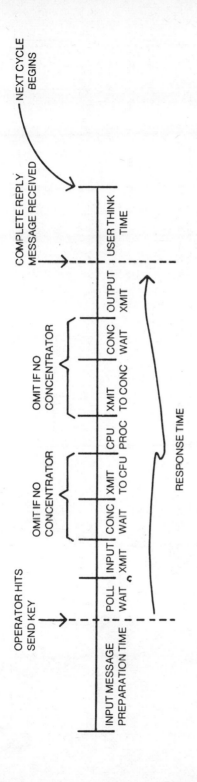

Figure 9.3. Time profile of response time components and operator activities in polled multipoint network, assuming polling in remote concentrator, and buffered terminals (so that entire output message must be sent before reply is displayed on screen).

Notes: If unbuffered terminals are used then response time will only include time for first character of output. If output message is several screens or pages long, response time only includes time for first transmission message, even tho output xmit will take a longer time.

437

TYPE OF CONSTRAINT	TRAFFIC PARAMETERS REQUIRED BY THE DESIGN ALGORITHM	APPLICATION INTERPRETATION
1. Maximum utilization	Enough traffic data to calculate or estimate the utilization of each channel or link in the communication network. This data typically consists of a peak period message volume in characters or words. ρ_{MAX}: the maximum acceptable utilization for any channel or link.	$\rho_i \leq \rho_{MAX}$ is the utilization of the ith channel or link in the network. ρ_i is calculated in the design algorithm, and ρ_{MAX} is an input parameter.
2. Maximum number of terminals	N_{MAX}: the maximum number of terminals that may share any multipoint line. NOTE The designer estimates the most suitable value of N_{MAX} prior to execution of the design algorithm. Traffic data is considered in this manner only; it is not directly used by the design algorithm.	The maximum number of terminals that share a multidropped line or other network segment may not exceed N_{MAX}. This constraint is used primarily in the design of multidropped, leased line networks.

438

3. Flow	α_i: the peak period (or average) message volume originating at the ith remote terminal. Units are bits, characters, or words. β_i: the peak period (or average) message volume originating at the central facility destined for the ith remote terminal. Units are bits, characters or words. α_{MAX}: the maximum peak period (or average) total message volume that can be transmitted to the central facility by a single line or channel. β_{MAX}: the maximum peak period (or average) total message volume that can be transmitted to the remote terminals by a single line or channel.	$$\sum_{i \in S} \alpha_i \leq \alpha_{MAX} \text{ and/or } \sum_{i \in S} \beta_i \leq \beta_{MAX}$$ where S is the set of all terminals sharing a line or channel in the network. This constraint is also used primarily in the design of multipoint, leased line networks.
4. Performance measure	Probability descriptions of the message arrivals, message lengths, or holding times at each terminal, plus any other statistical parameters required by the queuing or simulation models being used in the design algorithm. Maximum acceptable value(s) of performance measure.	Performance of the networks as given by some closed form expression or simulation model, may not exceed the input constraint value(s). For example, X% of messages must be processed within Y seconds, where X and Y values are constants of the application.

Figure 9.4. Summary of performance constraint formulations.

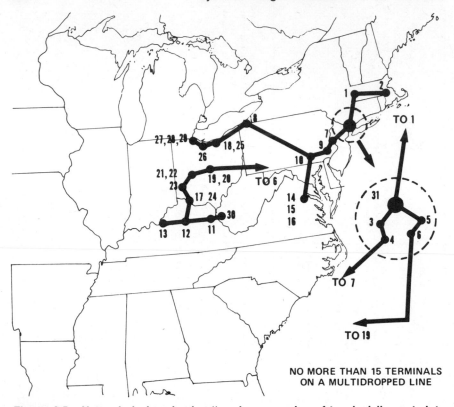

NO MORE THAN 15 TERMINALS
ON A MULTIDROPPED LINE

Figure 9.5. Network designed using "maximum number of terminals" constraint.

Figure 9.5 illustrates the results of a network designed using a Type 2 constraint, where not more than 15 terminals are permitted to share the same line. The rationale for this type of constraint may be related to either the terminal traffics or the electrical properties of the transmission link. It is thus a particularly flexible type of constraint. Response time goals can be converted into line loading criteria using this constraint, as shown in Figure 9.6.

Type 3 constraints are similar to Type 2, except that substantially more specific traffic data and operating experiences are available. For example, forward and reverse network traffic during the busy period may be provided in units of characters, words, or messages. These volumes are used to assure that a required level of data throughput can always be obtained, even on the most heavily loaded links.

A Type 4 constraint differs from other constraints in that a more detailed knowledge of terminal traffic patterns is available (e.g., probabil-

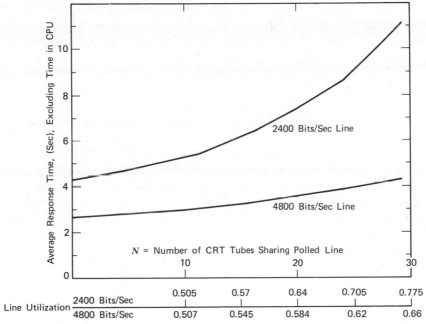

Three Polls/sec, Inquiry/Response: M_{in} = 100 Characters, M_{out} = 640 Characters.

Figure 9.6. Teleprocessing network delay for CRT user on multipoint polled line.

ity distributions and transaction types). Hence more sophisticated queuing and/or simulation models can be used to predict performance in the various topological configurations considered. This approach is required when multiple line speeds and the use of multiplexers and/or store-and-forward concentrators are jointly being considered.

9.4. FAULT ISOLATION CONSIDERATIONS IN DATA COMMUNICATIONS NETWORK DESIGN

One crucial design consideration is the incorporation of features and functions for isolating malfunctioning terminals, modems, lines, and other network elements. Several different approaches that have recently come into common usage are now discussed. The motivation for incorporating fault isolation capabilities into network subsystems stems from the desire of most users to lower maintenance costs and increase system uptime by reducing the duration of a typical system outage.[4] The objective here is to

---

[4]Also see References [9] and [10].

show how automatic loopback features in terminals, modems, multiplexers, and concentrators can be used to rapidly pinpoint malfunctioning elements in typical data communications systems. These loopback features may be operated either manually or, in many instances, via remote control, enabling unattended remote sites to be examined by the test procedures.

Consider the polled multipoint line configuration shown in Figure 9.7. Assume that some type of trouble is being experienced on the line, but it is not known whether the difficulty lies in the line itself, the remote modems, the local modem, or the remote terminals. Often, in such a system, the first indication of difficulty is that one or more remote terminals fail to respond to polls. This situation usually causes a message to be displayed at the operator console in the central complex. Frequently the difficulty can be isolated to a particular link or node without activating any loopback switches at all. For example, assume that only terminal C is not responding to polls. Here the difficulty is very likely to be in either the link between B and C, the modem at C, or the terminal at C. Loopback procedures can then be invoked to determine exactly which of these subsystems is responsible. If terminal B alone is not responding to polls, it is very unlikely that the interexchange link is the problem (or terminal C would also be failing to respond). Hence in this case the difficulty is probably in either the modem, the terminal equipment at B, or the local loop serving terminal B. Similar approaches can be used to focus on the most likely faulty components for other combinations of poll response failures.

Once loopback features need to be activated, the following approach (or variations thereof) can readily be used to precisely identify the faulty network element. Analog loopback switches cause the modulated line signal to be reversed without undergoing signal conversion. Digital loopback switches involve demodulation and remodulation at the loopback point. In Figure 9.7, switch 1 is an analog loopback switch used to check out the local modem at the main site; switch 2, an analog loopback used to check out the first leg of the multipoint circuit to city A; and switch 3, a digital loopback switch used to probe the modem at city A.

The entire circuit can be checked by systematically moving out from the center, with each step in the fault isolation procedure examining an additional element in the remote subsystem. At some step, the activation of the next loopback switch will cause the test signal transmitted out from the center not to be returned. The remote subsystem last added to the test loop is probably the malfunctioning component. Caution must be exercised in making certain that loopback features do not come to be regarded as a panacea for the designer. There are inevitably going to be certain

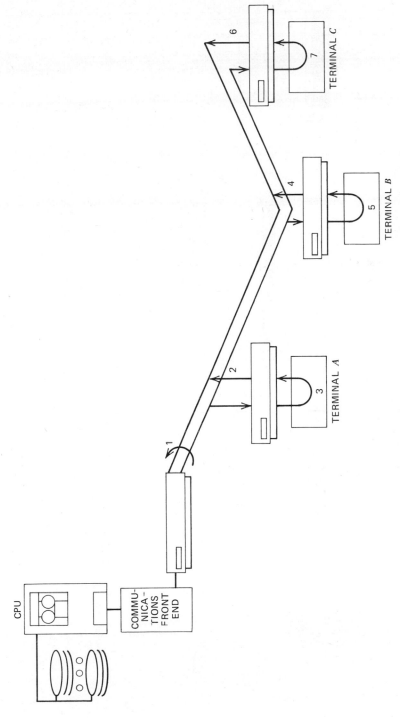

Figure 9.7. Use of loopback switches for fault isolation on multipoint circuit.

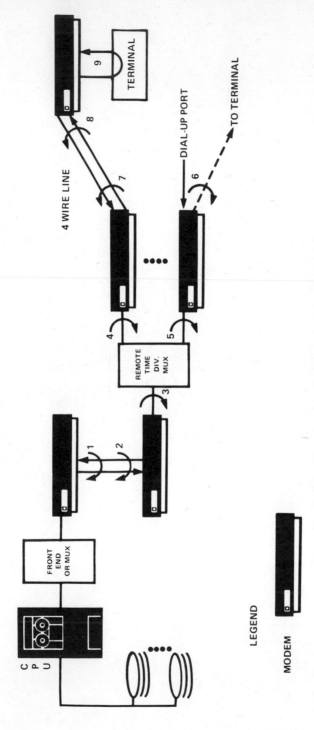

Figure 9.8. Use of loopback switches in multiplexer network.

types of situations where loopbacks will not isolate the problem. For example, in Figure 9.7, loopbacks would be of little use in diagnosing a failure such as a remote modem transmitter being locked in the active state. This might be caused by a malfunctioning modem or a malfunctioning business machine that permanently turns on the "request-to-send" interface lead.

Obviously these types of system level procedures are concerned with rapidly obtaining very crude "yes or no" answers to questions about whether a given subsystem is functioning. They do not address the detailed issues of which electrical subsystems within a modem or terminal may be malfunctioning. Nonetheless, they do enable faulty units to be identified and replaced with spare or backup units while detailed maintenance is performed on an individual modem or terminal. They also have the desirable effect of helping the user obtain prompt responses from a supplier in cases where its equipment is identified as the source of trouble. Still another benefit is the reduction of common carrier charges to the user for repair calls in which carrier facilities subsequently turn out *not* to be responsible for the difficulty.

Extensions to the procedures cited above may be employed in more complex networks involving multiplexers and concentrators. Figure 9.8 shows how the various loopback switches might be positioned in a typical network involving a remote TDM. In multiplexed networks additional diagnostic features are often employed to automatically activate alarms at the instant a network element ceases to function properly. One commonly used diagnostic approach involves the "threading" of a continuously operating control loop or channel through all subsystems to be monitored. This control channel circulates a special test pattern that can be tracked by the individual modems and multiplexers through which it passes. Should the closed control loop be "opened up" because of any type of equipment or communication link malfunction, all receivers tracking the test pattern downstream from the faulty element will lose synchronization and immediately activate whatever alarm mechanisms are built into the system.

9.5. COMPLETE NETWORK CONFIGURATION CONSIDERATIONS

In this section, various techniques for configuring the overall network are briefly outlined. No attempt is made to duplicate the extensive related material found in References [7] and [8]. Rather, our goals here are to highlight the major configuration issues and to cite appropriate references. In most applications, the following six basic types of network organization should be considered:

I.   Centralized organizations

- Switched network, no multiplexers or concentrators.
- Switched network, with multiplexers and/or concentrators.
- Leased line network, single line speed.
- Leased line network with multiplexers and/or concentrators.

II.   Distributed organizations

- Hierarchical distributed network, regional subnetworks.
- Nonhierarchial distributed network.

Each of these approaches is now discussed, and a methodology for obtaining an optimum network in each instance is presented. The most suitable network for any application can be obtained by comparing the cost/performance characteristics of the best design configuration from each of these six categories. For various reasons, all six options will not be of interest in every application. However, it should be noted that a more cost-effective network will usually be obtained when all possibilities are considered.

9.5.1. Networks Using Switched Common Carrier Links

Most of the major design decisions here are concerned with the line speeds used, the terminal traffic volumes, the number of computer-access ports provided, and the tariffs, which dictate the costs of using the respective carrier networks. Switched networks are often the only choice for regional and local network connections to a geographically fluctuating terminal population, as is the case in commercial computer service time sharing systems, for example.

This design problem has two main aspects: first, determining the level of service required (number of simultaneously active access ports needed and line speeds to be used), and, second, determining the particular carrier offerings that provide these levels of service in the least costly way. Figure 9.9 depicts the use of switched lines in accessing a distant computer or regional concentrator. As shown, the number of access ports on the communications control unit determines the maximum number of simultaneous users that can be accommodated. Ordinarily, the number of ports will be smaller than the total number of remote terminals that use the system, since not all of the remote terminals need to use the computer

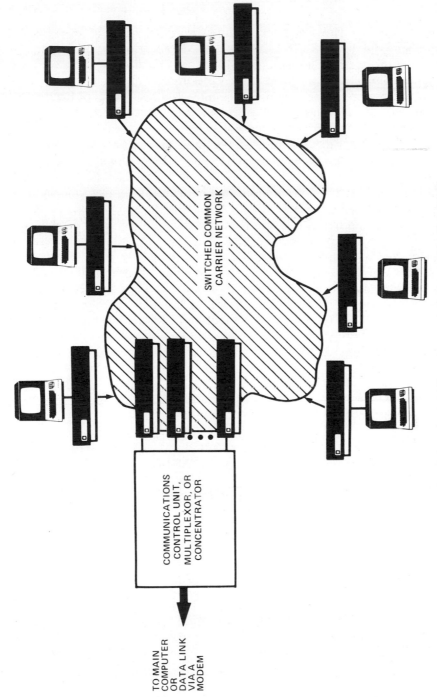

SWITCHED COMMON CARRIER NETWORK

COMMUNICATIONS CONTROL UNIT, MULTIPLEXOR, OR CONCENTRATOR

TO MAIN COMPUTER OR DATA LINK VIA A MODEM

Figure 9.9. Using switched lines to access a communications device.

simultaneously. However, using too few ports may lead to an excessive number of busy signals for incoming calls. Most systems are designed so that, on the average, no more than 1 to 3 calls/hundred will receive busy signals. Simple queuing models may be used to determine how many ports are required. For example, the multiserver loss model of Figure 9.10 is appropriate in applications where incoming access requests for the communications device are given a busy signal and are not held or queued in any way. Other models are available for estimating how many ports are needed to provide acceptable service times when incoming message requests are held in a waiting line to be serviced by the next free port. The various line speed options are reflected in the mean service time parameter used in these models.

Once the approximate level of service required has been established, the remaining decision involves choosing the particular carrier offering that will provide the needed service in the least costly way. As was seen in Chapter 3, by far the most common approaches are to pay for calls as they are made (regular long distance service) and to use special blanket tariffs such as ATT's WATS service in the U.S. In either instance, modems will be required to connect the remote terminals into the switched network. Either acoustic couplers or conventional modems provide connections to the carrier network. Acoustic couplers generally

ASSUMPTIONS

- NO WAITING LINE
- INPUT ARRIVALS ARE RANDOM WITH MEAN RATE λ
- THERE ARE n IDENTICAL, INDEPENDENT SERVERS
- SERVICE TIME DISTRIBUTION IS NEGATIVE EXPONENTIAL, WITH MEAN $\bar{s}$ SEC
- PROBABILITY INCOMING REQUEST IS LOST IS P_L

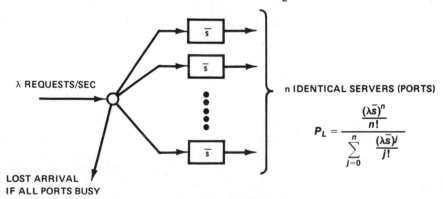

$$P_L = \frac{\dfrac{(\lambda \bar{s})^n}{n!}}{\displaystyle\sum_{j=0}^{n} \frac{(\lambda \bar{s})^j}{j!}}$$

Figure 9.10. Multiserver loss queuing model.

cannot operate at speeds in excess of 1200 bits/sec. With proper modems, transmission speeds of between 3600 and 4800 bits/sec can be attained over the regular analog telephone network in most countries. Faster speeds usually require leased lines with special conditioning and sophisticated modems with powerful equalizers.

The cost of using regular long distance service can be estimated in a straightforward manner, using the known geography of an application, the terminal traffic volumes, and the long distance tariff information (see Chapter 3). This estimated cost can then be compared with other blanket tariffs such as WATS.

In cases where a number of WATS lines are needed, the optimum combination may be too difficult to determine manually. In these situations, linear programming packages are offered by the carriers and various consultants to determine the least costly combination of such blanket-tariff plans that provides the desired level of service.[5] The optimum overall plan is then obtained by comparing the costs of the best pay-as-used and blanket-tariff plans.

Although most dial-up or switched networks today employ conventional circuit-switched analog lines of the Bell System (or the appropriate carrier organization in countries outside the United States), other service options are rapidly becoming available. For example, it was noted in Chapter 3 that the Southern Pacific Communications Company (originally Datran) provides switched *digital transmission* services in certain major U.S. cities. Also, the domestic value-added carriers provide usage-sensitive pricing structures and services which must be evaluated in the category of switched alternatives. The user of a packet switching network estimates his costs in virtually the same manner as he does for conventional dial-up connections. However, he must carefully include all software modification costs and costs for accessing the public intelligent network via required access lines.

At the current time, the large user has only a limited range of switched carrier offerings from which to choose. Except for regular dial-up service, there are significant geographic areas where the switched digital and value-added types of services cannot be obtained. However, with the prospect of increased competition arising both from new services and from new carriers for data transmission, the range of future options is certain to increase. Although the complexity of the design problem will likewise increase, the prospects for a concomitant reduction in end-user communications costs will be significantly enhanced.

[5]Examples of such design tools are described at length in References [7] and [8].

9.5.2. Leased Line Networks, One Line Speed

We now consider the design of leased line networks that do not contain any remote multiplexers or concentrators. In the next section it is proposed that such line sharing devices be used only when the incremental costs of doing so are more than offset by resulting reductions in total line costs. However, the key parameter in making this determination is the cost of the least expensive network layout that does not contain any concentrators or multiplexers. In this section the problem of configuring minimum-cost, leased line networks without such special line sharing devices is considered.

Over the past decade, common carriers, large computer manufacturers, and selected systems engineering firms have developed algorithms and software packages of varying size and complexity for designing minimum-cost leased line communication networks. Since most typical end-user networks have begun to use sophisticated multiplexing and/or concentration equipment only in the last few years, the costs of the circuits themselves were historically the sole target of the algorithms used for these cost-minimization software packages. Recent emphasis on increasing the utilization of communication links has prompted a shift toward greater concern for the costs of other network components such as remote multiplexers and concentrators, terminals, and the communications interfaces used at the primary computer center locations.

Although some of the currently used design algorithms are based on simulation, the most successful incorporate a blend of multivariate mathematical programming and specialized analytic techniques suited directly for network design. Analytic techniques are used to isolate a relatively small number of more cost-effective network configurations, which may then be analyzed in detail using specialized simulation models. Purely simulation-based design approaches tend to be of limited value, primarily because network design generally involves too many different topological and equipment combinations.

Since multipoint lines reduce total circuit mileage costs by enabling multiple users to share circuits, early design algorithms were geared to find a treelike network of multipoint lines having a minimum total leased line cost. In cases where the traffic loadings of such lines are not a factor, an algorithm originally developed by J. B. Kruskal at Bell Telephone Laboratories can be used.[6] The method assumes knowledge of the geographic location of n terminals and their point-to-point connection costs. As shown in the flowchart of Figure 9.11, it develops a *minimum spanning*

[6]See Reference [11].

NOTATION:

e_i :   the i th link of the network
$d(e_i)$:   The cost of using link e_i in the solution net
S :   The set of links included in the solution net
n :   The total number of nodes in the network
$|S|$:   The number of links in the partially formed tree

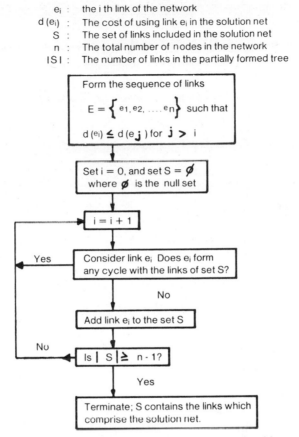

Figure 9.11. Flow chart for minimum spanning tree algorithm.

tree by adding a link at a time. Initially, all possible links are classified according to increasing cost. Then, starting with the least costly one, each successive link is considered. It is added to the partially formed tree if no loops are formed; otherwise it is permanently discarded, and the next more expensive link is tried. The solution network is obtained when a tree containing $n - 1$ links is formed. An example illustrating the results of applying this procedure is shown in Figure 9.12.

This algorithm does not incorporate provisions for treating line transmission speed as a variable, for positioning remote concentrators, or for considering link traffic and response time, nor does the routine consider the use of redundant links for increased reliability. Such restrictions

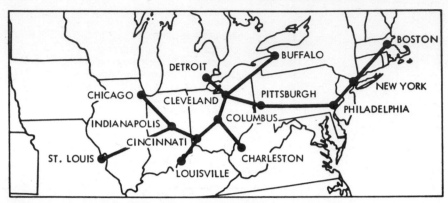

Figure 9.12. A minimum spanning tree network interconnecting selected eastern and midwestern cities.

motivated the development of more sophisticated routines in the middle 1960s, as the importance of limiting peak-period message traffic on the more heavily loaded links became universally realized. Esau and Williams developed a design technique that has formed the basis for many well-known proprietary leased line design packages, including IBM's Teleprocessing Network (TPNET) and Network Design Tool (NDT) configurators.[7]

The Esau–Williams technique assumes that a star network of point-to-point links from every remote terminal to the closest central complex is the most costly (worst-case) layout. In successive iterations it removes a link that attaches to one of the centers, and replaces it with some other, shorter link to reduce line costs by the formation of multipoint lines. At each iteration the method selects a particular pair of links (one to be removed and another to be added) to produce the greatest net reduction in link cost without violating line traffic constraints. Although this method takes care of traffic overloads, it assumes the placement of multiplexers and/or concentrators and disregards the use of mixed grades of service in the same network. Figure 9.13 illustrates the type of input data typically required for computerized leased line network design using procedures similar to those developed by Esau and Williams.

Numerous tariff changes and new service alternatives have recently created a need for substantial modifications of software packages implementing the Esau–Williams algorithm. For example, the domestic MPL tariff discussed in Chapter 3 complicates implementation of the algorithm

---

[7]See Reference [12] for the original discussion of the Esau–Williams algorithm. It is also presented in Chapter 40 of Reference [7].

TELECOMMUNICATION NETWORK DESIGN MODEL D R DOLL

BELOW ARE TERMINAL INDICES AND LOCATIONS FOR THE TC'S IN THE NETWORK

5986	3426	CHGOM, CHGOA	164787.	131100.	
5986	3426	CENTM, CENTA	12540.	10431.	
5986	3426	CENTO, CHGOB	147420.	449415.	
5986	3426	CHGOX,	7011.	0.	
6020	3440	CLMTM, CLMTA	8094.	7524.	
6020	3440	CLMTO,	130545.	0.	
6023	3461	HNDLM, HNDLA	6726.	5472.	
6272	2992	IMPSM, INPSA	17328.	16815.	
6272	2992	INPSO, IPLSB	3510.	97200.	
6272	2992	IPLSM, IPLSA	46797.	27246.	
8084	3476	MGNLM, MGNLA	6099.	6099.	
8084	3476	MGNLO,	15312.	0.	
8476	2874	BTRGM, BTRGA, B	45714	108546.	
8513	2867	PLAQO, PLAQA	157815.	107535.	
8513	2867	PLAQM,	76266.	0.	Total monthly terminal-to-computer message volume
8436	4034	DLLSM, DLLSA, B	135270.	159576.	
8938	3536	HSTNM, HSTNC	80655.	91785.	
8938	3536	HSTNO, HSTNB	13635.	100980.	
8938	3536	HUSTO,	2295.	0.	
8938	3536	HSTNX,	798.	0.	
6891	3477	PVLYM, PVLYA	10545.	13929.	Total monthly computer-to-terminal message volume
6891	3477	PVLYO,	62100.	0.	
6807	3482	STLSM, STLSB	238950.	176040.	
6807	3482	STLSO, STLSA	17010.	75660.	
6789	3483	MADNM, MADNA	70737.	81111.	
6789	3483	MADNO,	138780.	0.	Both volumes are in chars.
7707	4173	TLSAM, TLSAA	31750.	30900.	
7707	4173	TLSAO, TLSAB	24000.	1178.	
7707	4173	TULSM, TULSA	15260.	17040.	
7707	4173	TLSAP,	7870.	0.	
7707	4173	TULSO.	17580.	0.	
7027	4203	KCTYO, KCTYB	32040.	70740.	
7027	4203	KCTYM, KCTYA, C	103113.	158910.	
9096	3466	FEPTO, FEPTA	126225.	90468.	
9096	3466	FRPTO, FRPTA	630180	405156.	
9096	3466	FRPTM, FRPTB	314013.	122670.	
9096	3466	FPBDM, FPBDA	14991.	14556.	
9096	3466	FEPTM,	42750.	0.	
9096	3466	FRPIO,	155790.	0.	
9096	3466	FPBDO,	41040.	0.	
9096	3466	OCDVO,	2835.	0.	
5394	3136		0.	0.	V.H coordinates for terminal locations

MAX ALLOWABLE BUSY PERIOD TRAFFIC ON A LINE
IN THE FORWARD NET IS.... 5200.00000 WORDS Design constraints
MAX ALLOWABLE BUSY PERIOD TRAFFIC ON A LINE
IN THE REVERSE NET IS.... 5200.00000 WORDS

Figure 9.13. Input data for typical computerized network design program.

by introducing different line cost functions for connections between different locations. Specifically, one mileage rate applies for links between major (high density) cities, another between major and minor cities, and a third rate between minor locations. DMW Telecommunications Corporation has modified the Esau–Williams algorithm for the MPL tariff in its proprietary Network Design and Management System, as discussed in Reference [13]. Other organizations have employed similar approaches, some of which are surveyed in References [14–17] and [23].

9.5.3.   Leased Line Networks with Multiplexers and Concentrators; Distributed Networks

It has been seen that remote line sharing devices can lead to substantial reductions in total system cost, so the primary subject of this section involves the design questions of where, what types, and how many. The fundamental reason for using such devices is to reduce communications costs and/or improve line efficiencies. Thus, from a cost argument, none should be used unless the total cost of a multiplexed network, including lines, signal converters, and sharing devices, is less than the cost of some previously considered type of network.

With these line sharing techniques, a remote device serves terminals in some region via high speed lines connected to the main CPU. Centralized design procedures may be employed to connect terminals in a region to their respective multiplexers or concentrators. Thus the cost of using a remote line sharing device is the sum of costs for the high speed shared line, the sharing devices, and the regional network. Techniques from the preceding section can be used to optimize the centralized regional subnetwork and the total costs of numerous possible design decisions tabulated.

Most teleprocessing users want to position remote line sharing equipment at sites where other terminal equipment exists for various administrative, maintenance, and security reasons. Furthermore, it is easy to show that the greatest cost benefits accrue when such devices are positioned near the centers of a remote terminal or traffic cluster. Thus, in many instances, a list of possible locations for concentrators and/or multiplexers can be developed by eliminating numerous unsuitable locations from the list of remote terminal sites. Then, using the procedures suggested above, the cost benefits of iteratively positioning line sharing devices at the various locations that remain can be itemized. The combination of locations and devices producing the minimum total network cost is then selected for comparison with the solution networks obtained from the other types of basic design alternatives. Networks containing cascaded multiplexer stages and remote concentrators are becoming widely utilized as the traffic of many users exceeds the volume that can efficiently be handled by conventional multipoint networks. This trend, which is expected to accelerate in the next 5 years, is primarily a consequence of the need for increased throughput in so many contemporary teleprocessing networks.

In Reference [22], Doll describes network structures in which *all* application processing and data base processing is performed at a single network node as centralized nets, even though distributed intelligence may be utilized to spread control functions across multiple network nodes. *Distributed processing networks,* by contrast, involve application and/or data base processing activities at two or more network nodes.

A brief comment on distributed networks concludes the discussion of basic design alternatives. Since this option is the most complex considered, it is very difficult to generalize about specific design techniques. Much understanding of how these types of networks operate has been obtained from the pioneering ARPA network. Many key ideas for designing such networks may be found in the Chapter 8 section on intelligent networks and in References [18] to [22].

The state of the art in distributed networks is indicated by the effort (5 calendar years and hundreds of man-years) involved in getting the ARPA network to its recent status of serving approximately 50 nodes. One of the biggest deterrents to the widespread implementation of similar nets is the cost of wideband communication lines (in the ARPA net 50,000 bits/sec links are used to interconnect host processor sites). At this point in time very few organizations can economically justify this type of communications for a nationwide or worldwide network of interconnected computers. In addition, all of the other factors cited in Chapter 1 which favor the development of centralized systems continue to impede any mass movements to the distributed, hierarchical type of network.

Some organizations today, however, are implementing distributed networks on a much smaller scale than the ARPA network. Instead of interconnecting the numerous processor sites with leased broadband links, slower speed switched network alternatives, plus starlike point-to-point layouts, are being used between a central headquarters location and several dozen regional computers. Also, packet switching networks using lines of intermediate speed (4800, 9600, and occasionally 19,200 bits/sec) are often utilized to interconnect the regional computers at a lower cost than if wideband 50 kilobits/sec lines were used.[8] Then regional

---

[8]Packet switching alternatives were discussed in Chapters 7 and 8.

subnetworks are superimposed on the higher level network, rendering a hierarchical type of structure.

One of the big problems in such systems has been the limitations of the current switched telephone network for interconnecting the regional centers. Since most processor-to-processor traffic is bursty (much information needs to be transmitted at broadband speeds but only on a rather infrequent basis), economic justification of leased lines is often difficult. Unfortunately, the current switched telephone network does not enable transmission to take place at speeds much in excess of 4800 bits/sec, which is well below the speeds at which I/O channels in most current-generation computers can operate. As the commercial services of the value-added carriers become more widely available, more organizations of all types will begin to interconnect their CPUs residing in different locations.

In hierarchical nets involving multiple CPUs and/or data bases, the design problem can be viewed as having two fundamentally independent aspects. One aspect is the design of the regional subnetworks, which can generally be approached using the techniques suggested in the preceding portions of Section 9.5. These regional subnetworks handle the terminal-to-computer traffic. The second aspect involves the backbone or processor-to-processor portion of the network. This backbone network may use either switched or leased lines. If switched links are used, line speeds in excess of 4800 bits/sec will be difficult to obtain. On the other hand, if leased lines are used, faster transmission rates can be obtained, but the costs of lines and minicomputers can grow rapidly to the point where such configurations may be difficult to justify economically. Leased line backbone networks composed of voice-grade lines can be warranted if the urgency of the transactions is great enough. Applications for which the interconnection of more than a few host processors or the use of faster transmission speeds is essential will require an intensive assessment of the transaction urgencies and the true value of introducing this level of system complexity and its associated costs.

9.6. EXAMPLES OF SPECIFIC DESIGN PROBLEM FORMULATIONS

The basic types of network organizations, both centralized and distributed, are summarized in Figure 9.14. To obtain minimum-cost networks, it is necessary to establish realistic performance criteria that enable the different types of structures to be compared. Although it is not the intent of this book to elaborate further on the details of these models, we

I. CENTRALIZED

    A.   Switched Links, No Multiplexers or Concentrators (DDD or WATS)

        Flexible, Cost Effective
        Popular, Widely Available
        Limitations on Response Time, Availability, Error Rate

    B.   Switched Links With Multiplexers and/or Concentrators

        Possibly More Cost Effective
        Can be More Responsive

    C.   Leased Lines, Single Line Speed

        Fast Response Times
        Better Transmission Environment
        Poorer Reliability/Availability Than Switched Nets

    D.   Leased Lines With Multiplexers and/or Concentrators

        More Equip to Fail
        Can be (10–25%) Less Expensive

II. DISTRIBUTED PROCESSING MULTICENTER NETWORKS

    A.   Hierarchical

        Favorite Organizational of 70's — Intracompany

    B.   Non Hierarchical (E.G. Arpa)

        Each Node Has Comparable Processing and Data Base Capability
        Good for Interorganizational Linkages

Figure 9.14. Types of network organization.

conclude with a summary of the typical kinds of problem statements involved.

9.6.1. WATS Optimization Problem

Given traffic intensities, measured in CCS[9] or erlangs,[10] for the unique geographic zones associated with Band 1, Band 2, Band 3, Band 4, and Band 5 WATS lines, determine the optimum mixture of each line type that will minimize total costs. Calls may come into or go out from a computer center, and arrive on either a scheduled or a random basis. The level of service criterion is stipulated as either the busy signal probability, maximum acceptable response time delay, or a time interval in which all data transfer must be accomplished.

[9]CCS refers to "hundreds of call seconds."
[10]Erlangs are defined in Reference [7].

9.6.2. Calculation of Number of Dial-Up Ports Needed to Satisfy Given Blocking Criteria

During the busy hour, each of a specified number of dial-up terminals is connected to the system for a given length of time. Determine how many ports are required on the communications controller if no more than $X\%$ of the incoming calls are to receive busy signals. Assume random call arrivals and a negative exponential distribution of call holding times.

Example Calculation

Given: 30 terminals, each connected for 20 minutes during the busy hour. No more than 3% of the calls should receive busy signals.

Solution: Total traffic $= \dfrac{30 \text{ terminals/hour} \times 20 \text{ min/terminal}}{60 \text{ min/hour}}$

$= 10 \text{ erlangs}$

From Table 11 in Martin [7] or Figure 9.10:

Blocking probability for $M = 15$ ports is 0.0365
Blocking probability for $M = 16$ ports is 0.0223

Hence 16 ports are required.

9.6.3. Response Time as Function of Line Loading

Determine how many CRT stations can share a multipoint line operating at R characters/sec if the average response time is not to exceed x seconds. The solution is obtained by relating such variables as operator keystroke time, response time, modem delays, line speed, polling procedures, line propagation delays, delays, number of stations on line (N), CPU processing delays, message lengths, and operator think times.[11] Once the maximum value of N has been determined, a multipoint line layout can be developed which will maximize line sharing and minimize costs. Figure 9.6 shows an example curve for an existing nationwide network; it was developed using models discussed in Reference [24].

9.6.4. Determining the Optimum Multipoint Network Layout

Given all terminal locations, traffic volumes, response time goals, and data processing center sites, determine the minimum-cost network that

---

[11]The implicit relationships between these variables are shown in Figure 9.3. Reference [24] also discusses widely used solution techniques in more detail.

GIVEN: LOCATIONS   DETERMINE: MINIMUM COST
         TRAFFIC DATA   NETWORK
         RESPONSE CRITERIA

Figure 9.15. Network design problem formulation.

does not exceed the stipulated response time criteria. Approaches discussed in Section 9.5.3 may be employed to solve this type of problem,
illustrated in Figure 9.15.

9.6.5. Determining Optimum Concentrator or Multiplexer Types and Locations

This problem involves determining where to position remote line sharing
devices to maximize line cost reductions and improve performance. The
statement usually involves known terminal locations, traffic volumes,
computer center sites, and a list of candidate sites for the concentrators or
multiplexers. Techniques for determining the optimum type of and location for these devices were discussed in Chapter 7. It was shown that the
most successful approaches involve techniques that rank the locations on
the basis of cost savings produced. Depending on the application character-

istics and costs of possible sharing devices, multiplexers are either iteratively added or dropped from an initial reference configuration to produce the lowest cost network.

9.6.6. Estimating Network Availability and Reliability; MTBF and MTTR

Every teleprocessing network will experience failures. It is important to quantitatively relate the impact of various subsystem failures on users and on the cost of maintenance in the network. Models for using and determining mean time between failures (MTBF) and mean time to repair (MTTR) are developed in References [9] and [10]. These models can be employed to objectively determine the most sensible sharing strategy for investing in redundancy enhancement to maximize system availability and reliability.

REFERENCES

1. D. R. Doll, "Data Communications Systems: Basics of Network Design," *Data Communications Systems, Electronics Deskbook,* McGraw-Hill, Vol. 1, No. 1, 1972, New York.
2. D. L. Mills, "Communication Software," *Proc. of IEEE—Special Issue on Computer Communications,* November 1972.
3. C. B. Newport and J. Ryzlak, "Communication Processors," *Proc. of IEEE—Special Issue on Computer Communications,* November 1972.
4. D. R. Doll, "Topology and Transmission Rate Considerations in the Design of Centralized Computer–Communication Networks," *IEEE Transactions on Communications Technology,* Vol. COM-19, pp. 339–344, June 1971.
5. *Analysis of Some Queuing Models in Real Time Systems,* IBM Publication GF 20–0007, IBM Corp., White Plains, N. Y., 1969.
6. J. T. Martin, *Design of Real-Time Computer Systems,* Prentice-Hall, Englewood Cliffs, N. J., 1967.
7. J. T. Martin, *Systems Analysis for Data Transmission,* Prentice-Hall, Englewood Cliffs, N. J., 1972.
8. D. R. Doll, "Notes Prepared for ICC Institute Course 1020—Advanced Teleprocessing Systems Design and Management," ICC Institute Publication, Miami, Fla., July 1975.
9. D. R. Doll, "Where to Spend Money to Improve System Availability," *Data Communications,* Vol. 3, No. 4, November–December 1974, McGraw-Hill, New York.
10. D. R. Doll, "How to Calculate Network Reliability," *Data Communications,* Vol. 4, No. 1, January–February 1975, McGraw-Hill, New York.
11. J. B. Kruskal, "On the Shortest Spanning Subtree of a Graph and the Traveling Salesman Problem," *Proceedings of American Mathematical Society,* Vol. 7, 1956.
12. L. R. Esau and K. C. Williams, "On Teleprocessing Network Design—a Method for Approximating the Optimal Network," *IBM Systems Journal,* Vol. 5, No. 3, 1966.

13. DMW Telecommunications Corporation, *Network Design and Management System User Manual,* Release 2, Ann Arbor, Mich., January 1976.

14. M. Gerla, "Approximations and Bounds for the Topological Design of Distributed Computer Networks," *Proceedings of Fourth ACM Data Communications Symposium* (Quebec City, Canada), October 1975.

15. D. R. Doll, "New Pricing Structures Upset Data Network Strategies," *Data Communications,* July–August 1974, McGraw-Hill, New York.

16. H. Frank and W. Chou, "Topological Optimization of Computer Networks," *Proceedings of IEEE—Special Issue on Computer Communication,* November 1972.

17. C. D. Pack, "Configuring a Private Line Circuit According to the HiLo Tariff—A Minimal Steiner Tree Problem," *Proceedings of Fourth ACM Data Communications Symposium* (Quebec City, Canada), October 1975.

18. *Spring Joint Computer Conference Proceedings,* Vol. 40, AFIPS Press, Montvale, N. J., May 1972.

19. L. G. Roberts and B. D. Wessler, "Computer Network Development to Achieve Resource Sharing," *Proceedings of 1970 Spring Joint Computer Conference,* Vol. 36, AFIPS Press, Montvale, N. J., 1970.

20. R. E. Kahn, "Resource Sharing Computer Communications Networks," *Proceedings of IEEE—Special Issue on Computer Communications,* Vol. 60, November 1972.

21. L. G. Roberts and B. D. Wessler, "The ARPA Network," Chapter 13 in *Computer Communication Networks,* edited by F. K. Kuo, Prentice-Hall, Englewood Cliffs, N. J., 1973.

22. D. R. Doll, "Relating Networks to Three Kinds of Distributed Function," *Data Communications,* March 1977, McGraw-Hill, New York.

23. M. Schwartz, *Computer Communication Network Design and Analysis,* Prentice-Hall, Englewood Cliffs, N. J., 1977.

24. DMW Telecommunications Corporation, *Response 1 and 2 User Manuals,* Release 2, Ann Arbor Mich., 1977.

APPENDIX

DETAILED DESCRIPTION OF EIA INTERFACE PINS AND ASSOCIATED FUNCTIONS

Pin Number 1
Circuit AA—Protective Ground (C.C.I.T.T. 101)
Direction: Not applicable

This conductor shall be electrically bonded to the machine or equipment frame. It may be further connected to external grounds as required by applicable regulations.

Pin Number 7
Circuit AB—Signal Ground or Common Return (C.C.I.T.T. 102)
Direction: Not applicable

This conductor establishes the common ground reference potential for all interchange circuits except Circuit AA (Protective Ground). Within the data communication equipment, this circuit shall be brought to one point, and it shall be possible to connect this point to Circuit AA by means of a wire strap inside the equipment. This wire strap can be connected or removed at installation, as may be required to meet applicable regulations or to minimize the introduction of noise into electronic circuitry.

Pin Number 2
Circuit BA—Transmitted Data (C.C.I.T.T. 103)
Direction: TO data communication equipment

Signals on this circuit are generated by the data terminal equipment and are transferred to the local transmitting signal converter for transmission of data to remote data terminal equipment.

The data terminal equipment shall hold Circuit BA (Transmitted Data) in marking condition during intervals between characters or words, and at all times when no data are being transmitted.

In all systems, the data terminal equipment shall not transmit data unless an ON condition is present on all of the following four circuits, where implemented:

1. Circuit CA (Request to Send).
2. Circuit CB (Clear to Send).
3. Circuit CC (Data Set Ready).
4. Circuit CD (Data Terminal Ready).

All data signals that are transmitted across the interface on interchange Circuit BA (Transmitted Data) during the time an ON condition is maintained on all of the above four circuits, where implemented, shall be transmitted to the communication channel.

Pin Number 3
Circuit BB—Received Data (C.C.I.T.T. 104)
Direction: FROM data communication equipment

Signals on this circuit are generated by the receiving signal converter in response to data signals received from remote data terminal equipment via the remote transmitting signal converter. Circuit BB (Received Data) shall be held in the Binary One (Marking) condition at all times when Circuit CF (Received Line Signal Detector) is in the OFF condition.

On a half-duplex channel, Circuit BB shall be held in the Binary One (Marking) condition when Circuit CA (Request to Send) is in the ON condition and for a brief interval following the ON to OFF transition of Circuit CA to allow for the completion of transmission (See Circuit BA—Transmitted Data) and the decay of line reflections.

Pin Number 4
Circuit CA—Request to Send (C.C.I.T.T. 105)
Direction: TO data communication equipment

This circuit is used to condition the local data communication equipment for data transmission and, on a half-duplex channel, to control the direction of data transmission of the local data communication equipment.

On one-way-only channels or duplex channels, the ON condition maintains the data communication equipment in the transmit mode. The OFF condition maintains the data communication equipment in a nontransmit mode.

On a half-duplex channel, the ON condition maintains the data communication equipment in the transmit mode and inhibits the receive mode. The OFF condition maintains the data communication equipment in the receive mode.

A transition from OFF to ON instructs the data communication equipment to enter the transmit mode. The data communication equipment responds by taking such action as may be necessary and indicates completion of such actions by turning ON Circuit CB (Clear to Send), thereby indicating to the data terminal equipment that data may be transferred across the interface point on interchange Circuit BA (Transmitted Data).

A transition from ON to OFF instructs the data communication equipment to complete the transmission of all data which were previously transferred across the interface point on interchange Circuit BA and then assume a nontransmit mode or a receive mode as appropriate. The data communication equipment responds to this instruction by turning OFF Circuit CB (Clear to Send) when it is prepared to again respond to a subsequent ON condition of Circuit CA.

Note: A nontransmit mode does not imply that all line signals have been removed from the communication channel.

When Circuit CA is turned OFF, it shall not be turned ON again until Circuit CB has been turned OFF by the data communication equipment.

An ON condition is required on Circuit CA as well as on Circuit CB, Circuit CC (Data Set Ready), and, where implemented, Circuit CD (Data Terminal Ready) whenever the data terminal equipment transfers data across the interface on interchange Circuit BA.

It is permissible to turn Circuit CA ON at any time when Circuit CB is OFF regardless of the condition of any other interchange circuit.

Pin Number 5
Circuit CB—Clear to Send (C.C.I.T.T. 106)
Direction: FROM data communication equipment

Signals on this circuit are generated by the data communication equipment to indicate whether or not the data set is ready to transmit data.

The ON condition, together with the ON condition on interchange circuits CA, CC, and, where implemented, CD, is an indication to the data terminal equipment that signals presented on Circuit BA (Transmitted Data) will be transmitted to the communication channel.

The OFF condition is an indication to the data terminal equipment that it should not transfer data across the interface on interchange Circuit BA.

The ON condition of Circuit CB is a response to the occurrence of a simultaneous ON condition on Circuits CC (Data Set Ready) and CA (Request to Send), delayed as may be appropriate to the data communication equipment for establishing a data communication channel (including the removal of the MARK HOLD clamp from the Received Data interchange circuit of the remote data set) to a remote data terminal equipment.

Where Circuit CA (Request to Send) is not implemented in the data communication equipment with transmitting capability, Circuit CA shall be assumed to be in the ON condition at all times, and Circuit CB shall respond accordingly.

Pin Number 6
Circuit CC—Data Set Ready (C.C.I.T.T. 107)
Direction: FROM data communication equipment

Signals on this circuit are used to indicate the status of the local data set.

The ON condition on this circuit is presented to indicate that—

    a.   The local data communication equipment is connected to a communication channel ("OFF HOOK" in switched), and

    b.   the local data communication equipment is not in test (local or remote), talk (alternate voice), or dial* mode, and

---

*The data communication equipment is considered to be in the dial mode when circuitry directly associated with the call origination function is connected to the communication channel. These functions include signaling to the central office (dialing) and monitoring the communication channel for call progress or answer back signals.

   c. the local data communication equipment has completed, where applicable,

      1. any timing functions required by the switching system to complete call establishment, and

      2. the transmission of any discrete answer tone, the duration of which is controlled solely by the local data set.

Where the local data communication equipment does not transmit an answer tone, or where the duration of the answer tone is controlled by some action of the remote data set, the ON condition is presented as soon as all the other above conditions (a, b, and c-1) are satisfied.

This circuit shall be used only to indicate the status of the local data set. The ON condition shall not be interpreted as either an indication that a communication channel has been established to a remote data station or the status of any remote station equipment.

The OFF condition shall appear at all other times and shall be an indication that the data terminal equipment is to disregard signals appearing on any other interchange circuit with the exception of Circuit CE (Ring Indicator). The OFF condition shall not impair the operation of Circuit CE or Circuit CD (Data Terminal Ready).

When the OFF condition occurs during the progress of a call before Circuit CD is turned OFF, the data terminal equipment shall interpret this as a lost (aborted) connection and take action to terminate the call. Any subsequent ON condition on Circuit CC is to be considered a new call.

When the data set is used in conjunction with Automatic Calling Equipment (ACE), the OFF to ON transition of Circuit CC shall not be interpreted as an indication that the ACE has relinquished control of the communication channel to the data set. Indication of this is given on the appropriate lead in the ACE interface.

Attention is called to the fact that if a data call is interrupted by alternate voice communication, Circuit CC will be in the OFF condition during the time that voice communication is in progress. The transmission or reception of the signals required to condition the communication channel or data communication equipment in response to the ON condition of interchange Circuit CA (Request to Send) of the transmitting data terminal equipment will take place after Circuit CC comes ON, but prior to the ON condition on Circuit CB (Clear to Send) or Circuit CF (Received Line Signal Detector).

Pin Number 20
Circuit CD—Data Terminal Ready (C.C.I.T.T. 108.2)
Direction: TO data communication equipment

Signals on this circuit are used to control switching of the data communication equipment to the communication channel. The ON condition prepares the data communication equipment to be connected to the communication channel and maintains the connection established by external means (e.g., manual call origination, manual answering, or automatic call origination).

When the station is equipped for automatic answering of received calls and is in the automatic answering mode, connection to the line occurs only in response to a combination of a ringing signal and the ON condition of Circuit CD (Data Terminal Ready); however, the data terminal equipment is normally permitted to present the ON condition on Circuit CD whenever it is ready to transmit or receive data, except as indicated below.

The OFF condition causes the data communication equipment to be removed from the communication channel following the completion of any "in process" transmission. See Circuit BA (Transmitted Data). The OFF condition shall not disable the operation of Circuit CE (Ring Indicator).

In switched network applications, when circuit CD is turned OFF, it shall not be turned ON again until Circuit CC (Data Set Ready) is turned OFF by the data communication equipment.

Pin Number 22
Circuit CE—Ring Indicator (C.C.I.T.T. 125)
Direction: FROM data communication equipment

The ON condition of this circuit indicates that a ringing signal is being received on the communication channel.

The ON condition shall appear approximately coincident with the ON segment of the ringing cycle (during rings) on the communication channel.

The OFF condition shall be maintained during the OFF segment of the ringing cycle (between "rings") and at all other times when ringing is not being received. The operation of this circuit shall not be disabled by the OFF condition on Circuit CD (Data Terminal Ready).

Pin Number 8
Circuit CF—Received Line Signal Detector (C.C.I.T.T. 109)
Direction: FROM data communication equipment

The ON condition on this circuit is presented when the data communication equipment is receiving a signal which meets its suitability criteria. These criteria are established by the data communication equipment manufacturer.

The OFF condition indicates that no signal is being received or that the received signal is unsuitable for demodulation.

The OFF condition of Circuit CF (Received Line Signal Detector) shall cause Circuit BB (Received Data) to be clamped to the Binary One (Marking) condition.

The indications on this circuit shall follow the actual onset or loss of signal by appropriate guard delays.

On half-duplex channels, Circuit CF is held in the OFF condition whenever Circuit CA (Request to Send) is in the ON condition and for a brief interval of time following the ON to OFF transition of Circuit CA. (See Circuit BB.)

Pin Number 21
Circuit CG—Signal Quality Detector (C.C.I.T.T. 110)
Direction: FROM data communication equipment

Signals on this circuit are used to indicate whether or not there is a high probability of an error in the received data.

An ON condition is maintained whenever there is no reason to believe that an error has occurred.

An OFF condition indicates that there is a high probability of an error. It may, in some instances, be used to call automatically for the retransmission of the previously transmitted data signal. Preferably the response of this circuit shall be such as to permit identification of individual questionable signal elements on Circuit BB (Received Data).

Pin Number 23
Circuit CH—Data Signal Rate Selector (DTE Source) (C.C.I.T.T. 111)
Direction: TO data communication equipment

Signals on this circuit are used to select between the two data signaling rates in the case of dual rate synchronous data sets or the two ranges of data signaling rates in the case of dual range nonsynchronous data sets.

An ON condition shall select the higher data signaling rate or range of rates.

The rate of timing signals, if included in the interface, shall be controlled by this circuit as may be appropriate.

Pin Number 23
Circuit CI—Data Signal Rate Selector (DCE Source) (C.C.I.T.T. 112)
Direction: FROM data communication equipment

Signals on this circuit are used to select between the two data signaling rates in the case of dual rate synchronous data sets or the two ranges of data signaling rates in the case of dual range nonsynchronous data sets.

An ON condition shall select the higher data signaling rate or range of rates.

The rate of timing signals, if included in the interface, shall be controlled by this circuit as may be appropriate.

Pin Number 24
Circuit DA—Transmitter Signal Element Timing (DTE Source) (C.C.I.T.T. 113)
Direction: TO data communication equipment

Signals on this circuit are used to provide the transmitting signal converter with signal element timing information.

The ON to OFF transition shall nominally indicate the center of each signal element on Circuit BA (Transmitted Data). When Circuit DA is implemented in the DTE, the DTE shall normally provide timing information on this circuit whenever the DTE is in a POWER ON condition. It is permissible for the DTE to withhold timing information on this circuit for short periods provided Circuit CA (Request to Send) is in the OFF condition. (For example, the temporary withholding of timing information may be necessary in performing maintenance tests within the DTE.)

Pin Number 15
Circuit DB—Transmitter Signal Element Timing (DCE Source) (C.C.I.T.T. 114)
Direction: FROM data communication equipment

Signals on this circuit are used to provide the data terminal equipment with signal element timing information. The data terminal equipment shall provide a data signal on Circuit BA (Transmitted Data) in which the transitions between signal elements nominally occur at the time of the transitions from OFF to ON condition of the signal on Circuit DB. When Circuit DB is implemented in the DCE, the DCE shall normally provide timing information on this circuit whenever the DCE is in a POWER ON condition. It is permissible for the DCE to withhold timing information on this circuit for short periods provided Circuit CC (Data Set Ready) is in the OFF condition. (For example, the withholding of timing information may be necessary in performing maintenance tests within the DCE.)

Pin Number 17
Circuit DD—Receiver Signal Element Timing (DCE Source) (C.C.I.T.T. 115)
Direction: FROM data communication equipment.

Signals on this circuit are used to provide the data terminal equipment with received signal element timing information. The transition from ON to OFF condition shall nominally indicate the center of each signal element on Circuit BB (Received Data). Timing information on Circuit DD shall be provided at all times when Circuit CF (Received Line Signal Detector) is in the ON condition. It may, but need not, be present following the ON to OFF transition of Circuit CF.

Pin Number 14
Circuit SBA—Secondary Transmitted Data (C.C.I.T.T. 118)
Direction: TO data communication equipment

This circuit is equivalent to Circuit BA (Transmitted Data) except that it is used to transmit data via the secondary channel.

Signals on this circuit are generated by the data terminal equipment and are connected to the local secondary channel transmitting signal converter for transmission of data to remote data terminal equipment. The data terminal equipment shall hold Circuit SBA (Secondary Transmitted Data) in marking condition during intervals between characters or words and at all times when no data are being transmitted.

In all systems, the data terminal equipment shall not transmit data on the secondary channel unless an ON condition is present on all of the following four circuits, where implemented:

1. Circuit SCA (Secondary Request to Send).
2. Circuit SCB (Secondary Clear to Send).
3. Circuit CC (Data Set Ready).
4. Circuit CD (Data Terminal Ready).

All data signals that are transmitted across the interface on interchange Circuit SBA during the time when the above conditions are satisfied shall be transmitted to the communication channel.

When the secondary channel is usable only for circuit assurance or to interrupt the flow of data in the primary channel (less than 10 baud capability), Circuit SBA (Secondary Transmitted Data) is normally not provided, and the channel carrier is turned ON or OFF by means of Circuit SCA (Secondary Request to Send). Carrier OFF is interpreted as an "Interrupt" condition.

Pin Number 16
Circuit SBB—Secondary Received Data (C.C.I.T.T. 119)
Direction: FROM data communication equipment

This circuit is equivalent to Circuit BB (Received Data) except that it is used to receive data on the secondary channel.

When the secondary channel is usable only for circuit assurance or to interrupt the flow of data in the primary channel, Circuit SBB is normally not provided. See interchange Circuit SCF (Secondary Received Line Signal Detector).

Pin Number 19
Circuit SCA—Secondary Request to Send (C.C.I.T.T. 120)
Direction: TO data communication equipment

This circuit is equivalent to Circuit CA (Request to Send) except that it requests the establishment of the secondary channel instead of requesting the establishment of the primary data channel.

Where the secondary channel is used as a backward channel, the ON condition of Circuit CA (Request to Send) shall disable Circuit SCA and it shall not be possible to condition the secondary channel transmitting signal converter to transmit during any time interval when the primary channel transmitting signal converter is so conditioned. Where system considerations dictate that one or the other of the two channels be in transmit mode at all times but never both simultaneously, this can be accomplished by permanently applying an ON condition to Circuit SCA (Secondary Request to Send) and controlling both the primary and secondary channels, in complementary fashion, by means of Circuit CA (Request to Send). Alternatively, in this case, Circuit SCB need not be implemented in the interface.

When the secondary channel is usable only for circuit assurance or to interrupt the flow of data in the primary data channel, Circuit SCA shall serve to turn on the secondary channel unmodulated carrier. The OFF condition of Circuit SCA shall turn OFF the secondary channel carrier and thereby signal an interrupt condition at the remote end of the communication channel.

Pin Number 13
Circuit SCB—Secondary Clear to Send (C.C.I.T.T. 121)
Direction: FROM data communication equipment

This circuit is equivalent to Circuit CB (Clear to Send), except that it indicates the availability of the secondary channel instead of indicating the availability of the primary channel. This circuit is not provided where the secondary channel is usable only as a circuit assurance or an interrupt channel.

Pin Number 12
Circuit SCF—Secondary Received Line Signal Detector (C.C.I.T.T. 122)
Direction: FROM data communication equipment

This circuit is equivalent to Circuit CF (Received Line Signal Detector) except that it indicates the proper reception of the secondary channel line signal instead of indicating the proper reception of a primary channel received line signal.

Where the secondary channel is usable only as a circuit assurance or an interrupt channel (see Circuit SCA—Secondary Request to Send), Circuit SCF shall be used to indicate the circuit assurance status or to signal the interrupt. The ON condition shall indicate assurance or a noninterrupt condition. The OFF condition shall indicate circuit failure (no assurance) or the interrupt condition.

QUESTIONS

ON INTRODUCTORY MATERIAL

1. Define the basic terminological primitives: circuit, channel, line, signal converter, DTE, data link, and station.
2. What are the differences between 2-wire and 4-wire circuits? Which type of circuit is most commonly found on dial-up lines? on leased lines?
3. Discuss the advantages and disadvantages of point-to-point, multipoint, and looped lines.
4. Contrast half duplex terminals with half duplex lines. Contrast full duplex terminals with full duplex lines.
5. What is the difference between "bauds" and "bits per second"?
6. When and why would you use full duplex lines for half duplex terminals? What types of terminals are best suited for full duplex lines?
7. Discuss the uses and operational characteristics of analog and digital bridges.
8. Can a full duplex terminal ever use half duplex lines? vice versa?
9. What are the differences between synchronous and asynchronous transmission? Which modes are most widely used today? What about the future and why?
10. Why do certain half duplex terminals not require two dial-up connections at each end of a point-to-point line when using dial backup?
11. Computer vendors do not make split stream modems but Bell and most major modem independents (Milgo, Codex, etc.) offer various units at speeds of 4800, 7200, 9600 bps. Discuss the merits and demerits of this fact from the computer vendors' standpoint. From the user's standpoint.
12. What factors favor the use of decentralized teleprocessing systems? The use of centralized systems?

475

13. What is meant by "line turnaround"? When does it take place in teleprocessing system operation.

14. Discuss the leased line and dial-up options available for the user of full duplex terminals on leased lines when backup protection is required.

15. If two business machines need to exchange data, discuss the circumstances under which they would require a data communications connection and under which they could instead be directly attached.

ON COMMUNICATIONS SERVICES AND TARIFFS

1. For each of the following point to point distances, estimate the number of hours per day of DDD connect time which would be equivalent in cost to a leased voice grade line.
   (*a*) 100 miles
   (*b*) 500 miles
   (*c*) 1000 miles
   (*d*) 2000 miles

2. Satellite circuits afford significant potential price reductions for leased lines. Assuming satellite rates of $0.50/mile plus termination charges of $75/circuit end, what is the breakeven distance with MPL circuits (Schedules I, II, III)?

3. Explain the purposes and uses of the *V, H* coordinate system used by the common carriers. How do common carriers relate particular customer locations to specific *V, H* coordinates (discuss the relationship between a telephone number, its telephone exchange and the coordinate system)?

4. Discuss when you would recommend using a foreign exchange (FX) circuit for data transmission (instead of DDD).

5. Under what circumstances would WATS lines be preferable to FX lines (qualitatively)?

6. What is the cost per hour of usage time between locations in the WATS Band 5 Unique Service Area (with respect to New York City) for each of the following situations:
   (*a*) Full Business Day WATS line used 2, 4, 8 hours per day, respectively
   (*b*) Measured Time WATS line used 2, 4, 8 hours per day, respectively
   (*c*) Direct Distance Dial lines used 2, 4, 8 hours per day, respectively

7. Outline as many restrictions and limitations of existing services as

you can (including market voids), indicating how such shortcomings adversely impact the development of new TP applications.

8. Assume that your job is to provide data transmission capability for your company between a Chicago terminal and New York CPU. Outline all different services and their company affiliation that you might want to consider. Itemize relative advantages and disadvantages of each.

9. Repeat Problem 8 between New York and London.

10. Price out the minimum cost multipoint line (under MPL) to interconnect stations in the following cities:
Wayne, N. J.
Atlanta
New York City
Kansas City, Mo.
Columbia, Mo.
Erie, Pa.
Denver
Princeton, N. J.

11. Could multipoint service be provided for a user with a computer in New York and remote stations in Rome, London, Paris and Frankfurt? If so, sketch the service components and note which organization might provide each.

12. What service offerings and mechanisms would you consider for the nine cases indicated below?
    (*a*) For Teletype machines
    (*b*) For interactive CRT's

Number of different places called or from which traffic originates	Number of calls per day		
	Few	Many	Very many
Few			
Many			
Very many			

   (*c*) What other factors should be considered?

13. If you were the marketing vice president of the United States' largest specialized common carrier on the day Bell announced MPL, what

would you consider in the way of price changes/innovations to compete?

14. How do you think the widespread availability of new services like DDS, satellite offerings, specialized carrier, and value-added networks will influence the demand and pricing structures for conventional domestic services like DDD, WATS, leased lines and Telpak.

15. What will be the effect of competition in the international services market place?

16. What application requirements of the end user will be specifically addressed by the domestic and international value-added carrier offerings like Telenet and Tymnet? Identify as many possible advantages and disadvantages of such services as you can for the end user. What types of applications are not well-suited for such networks?

ON CARRIER FACILITIES AND MODEMS

1. Why does digital transmission provide better service than analog transmission for data transmission users?

2. Which analog transmission parameter gives rise to the need for equalization equipment in modems?

3. Of the analog transmission parameters discussed, which are most likely to adversely affect 4800 bps data transmission using 8-phase modems like the Bell 208 series? The least likely to affect a 208 series modem?

4. What is the maximum baud rate practically achievable over the most highly conditioned voice-grade lines? What is the maximum number of different signal levels practically detectable in modems which operate over voice-grade lines? What then is the maximum bit rate which can be achieved in practice by voice grade modems?

5. Trace through all conversions between analog and digital signal formats on a conventional point-to-point voice-grade line which employs digital transmission between one pair of ATT offices and uses analog transmission everywhere else.

6. In employing digital facilities for data transmission and digitized voice, the Bell System requires approximately 56 KBPS for every voice channel. This is obtained by sampling a voice channel input 8000 times per second and sending 8 bits (7 data + 1 control) over the line for each sample. How many regular analog channels operating at 4800 bps would equate to one digited voice channel in raw bit rate? If the Bell System would charge end users $2/mile per month for a 56

KBPS service what would be the cost per 4800 bps subchannel? How do these rates compare with 4800 bps DDS service?

7. Define the terms analog and digital loopback as applied to modems. Discuss their usefulness as features in data transmission systems. When would you recommend using automatic, remote controlled loopback switches? What would be some possible disadvantages of these modem options?

8. Discuss the terms short haul modem, line driver and limited distance adapter. What types of transmission facilities are required for these devices? How widely available are such facilities? What data rates can be achieved over what distances with such facilities and such signal conversion devices?

9. Discuss the similarities and differences between point-to-point and multipoint lines provided via satellite. Contrast the complexity of the carrier providing multipoint lines with terrestial facilities versus providing multipoint lines with satellite channels.

10. What strategies could be utilized by designers of digital voice encoders to reduce the digital bit rate required for the transmission of intelligible speech.

11. Outline as many user disadvantages of the DDS network service as you can.

12. What will be the bit error rate of a point to point DDS service with analog extension service on each end? (Assume analog channel error rates of 10^{-5} and digital channel error rates of 10^{-7} errors per bit). How many analog modems are required?

13. Why don't the business machine suppliers of terminals and computers generally provide features in their equipment for performing the important network diagnostic and fault isolation functions?

ON TERMINALS, CODING, AND INTERFACES

1. Identify and contrast the price-performance characteristics of the following terminal types: teleprinter, CRT, batch, transaction, intelligent, and distributed processing.

2. Which of the above terminal types use dial lines? leased point-to-point lines? multipoint lines? loops?

3. What is meant by the term "generalized workstation terminal"? Identify all functions which could be performed by such a device. Break these out into communications-related and terminal-related functions.

4. What approaches would you consider to provide enhanced data security for terminals connected by serial loops?

5. What are the major codes used to represent characters in TP systems? How many bits does each code use for each data character represented? How many different characters can each represent?

6. Contrast the meanings and uses of graphic (or text) characters, device control characters, and data link control characters in a code set.

7. Discuss some possible uses of the unassigned pins on the RS232-C interface between terminals and modems.

8. In synchronous dial-up applications, how does the sending terminal know when bit synchronization has been established at the other end?

9. Which interface pins does the terminal control? which does the modem control?

10. Discuss the application significance of being able to cluster CRTs on the same controller. Could the modem fan-out feature accomplish the same effect?

11. Explain how terminals employing conventional code-sensitive control accomplish the transmission of arbitrary bit patterns as graphic or text information?

12. What terminal control and communications-related functions could be incorporated into an intelligent terminal without making it a distributed *processing* terminal? (Itemize intelligence functions which do not provide local data base management or application processing capability).

ON ERROR CONTROL PROCEDURES

1. Identify all sources of inefficiency and overhead in conventional half duplex error control procedures based on the use of Stop and Wait ARQ.

2. In all the following problems, calculate TRIB using the standard relationship developed in the chapter:
   Stop & Wait ARQ; 4 wire constant carrier; 4800 bps modem; total block length of 600 chars (of which 100 are noninformation) Forward line propagation time=reverse line propagation time=20 millisec (ms); Control message length=8 chars; compute time for block check sum at receiver=20 ms; Reaction time at sending station is negligible; P = .05; 8 bits/character.

3. Same as Problem 2, except that now we have 2 wire lines requiring turnarounds. Assume modem RTS-CTS delay of 3 sec.

4. Same as Modem Problem 3, except for a RTS-CTS delay of 300 ms.
5. Same as Problem 2, except that now use reverse channel for control signaling @ 150 bits/sec.
6. Same as Problem 2, except that propogation time goes to 2 sec in each direction and P = 0.01.
7. Go-back-N ARQ; block length = 1000 characters (of which 100 are noninformation); line propagation time = 1/3 sec in each direction; 4 wire constant carrier; other parameters same as in Problem 2.
8. Same as Problem 7, except that line propagation time = 1 sec each way and P = 0.1 (in both Problem 7 and 8 assume integer values of N).
9. Rework Problems 7 and 8 under the premise that the sending station can interrupt its current block transmission and immediately commence retransmission activity on receiving a NAK.
10. Can you think up any realistic combinations of application parameters for which Go-back-N ARQ would be *inferior* to Stop and Wait ARQ, from a TRIB standpoint?
11. Under what circumstances will the effect of line propagation delay on TRIB *not* be completely masked by the use of Continuous ARQ procedures?

ON MULTIPLEXING AND CONCENTRATION

1. Identify *all* possible techniques and devices which can be used to share communication lines.
2. What types of terminal characteristics and network application requirements favor the use of:

   (*a*) Frequency division multiplexing
   (*b*) Conventional time-division multiplexing
   (*c*) Statistical time-division multiplexing
   (*d*) Packet switching concentration
   (*e*) Message switching concentration
   (*f*) Line switching concentration
3. How can FDM be employed to enable two degrees of sharing to be accomplished on a multipoint line?
4. Sketch a comprehensively detailed network schematic diagram for the following network requirements-CPU located in Boston, RJE terminals in New York, Chicago, Denver, and San Francisco. The RJE terminals all must have their own 2400 bit/sec dedicated access

paths to the computer. Show all modems, lines and port connections at the central site.

5. How would the additional requirement of low speed asynchronous terminals in the remote locations affect your answer to Problem 4?

6. Repeat Problem 4 assuming the speed requirement is increased to 4800 bits/sec at each remote location.

7. What strategies are available for providing network diagnostics and fault isolation capabilities in a generalized two-stage network involving multiplexer or concentrator nodes at the first level? Discuss the options and which vendor could provide each required function.

8. What is the maximum aggregate bit rate for all terminals sharing voice-grade line using
   (a) FDM
   (b) Conventional TDM
   (c) Statistical TDM
   (d) Concentration schemes

9. Discuss the different response time impact for a fixed number of remote CRT terminals
   (a) All connected to a CPU on the same multipoint line
   (b) Each connected to a CPU over its own line
   (c) All connected to a CPU over one time-division multiplexed line with each CRT having its own dedicated subchannel
   (d) All connected to a CPU through a common concentrator and high speed line

10. Use the line concentrator model with held calls to estimate the average time each call spends waiting, assuming 5 data trunk lines and an average holding (service) time of 2 seconds per call. Also assume an arrival rate of 1.5 calls per second to the concentrator in the peak period.

11. Use the multiserver blocking (no-queue) model to determine the number of ports required on a timesharing system to provide a level of service where no more than 5 calls out of 100 will receive busies. Assume the peak period calling rate is 20 calls per hour and that the average call connect time is 12 minutes per call. What assumptions are required for the valid use of this model?

ON LINE AND NETWORK CONTROL PROCEDURES

1. Distinguish between bit, character, and message or block synchronization. How is each accomplished in typical TP systems?

2. What types of telecommunications devices and facilities require a true full duplex protocol for efficient usage? Explain why this is so for each.

3. BSC is exclusively a half duplex line discipline which utilizes special characters in the code set for data link control. Since SDLC is a bit-oriented protocol, how will it perform comparable functions?

4. Identify all possible reasons why SDLC can possibly utilize a multipoint line more efficiently than BSC.

5. Draw a pair of timing diagrams illustrating how BSC and SDLC respectively would recover from a transmission block error detected by CRC failure. (Assume that SDLC is being deployed in the full duplex, continuous block transmission mode.)

6. What are the differences between polling and select activity? The differences between select-hold and fast-select activity?

7. List all changes a user would have to make to his network to convert from a conventional private network to an intelligent network service provided by a public carrier.

8. What are the general limitations of traditional teleprocessing network control approaches which have spawned the intelligent network architectures like DECNET and SNA? Discuss how these network architectures will achieve their goals of eliminating these restrictions.

9. What are the possible disadvantages of networks using these advanced architectures?

10. What are the differences between data link control, path control, and network control? Identify several specific functions in each category which would be performed by an intelligent, functionally layered network control strategy.

11. Identify the major data network security strategies and discuss which organization (user, common carrier, etc.) will be responsible for their implementation and enforcement.

12. What types of data network traffic are well-suited for packet switching nets? For TDM circuit switching nets? For neither?

INDEX